CULTURAL STUDIES AND CULTURAL
IN NORTHEAST ASIA

C000089474

Hong Kong University Press thanks Xu Bing for writing the Press's name in his Square Word Calligraphy for the covers of its books. For further information, see p. iv.

TransAsia: Screen Cultures

Edited by Koichi IWABUCHI and Chris BERRY

What is Asia? What does it mean to be Asian? Who thinks they are Asian? How is "Asian-ness" produced? In Asia's transnational public space, many kinds of cross-border connections proliferate, from corporate activities to citizen-to-citizen linkages, all shaped by media — from television series to action films, video piracy, and a variety of subcultures facilitated by internet sites and other computer-based cultures. Films are packaged at international film festivals and marketed by DVD companies as "Asian," while the descendents of migrants increasingly identify themselves as "Asian," then turn to "Asian" screen cultures to find themselves and their roots. As reliance on national frameworks becomes obsolete in many traditional disciplines, this series spotlights groundbreaking research on trans-border, screen-based cultures in Asia.

Other titles in the series:

The Chinese Exotic: Modern Diasporic Femininity, by Olivia Khoo

East Asian Pop Culture: Analysing the Korean Wave, edited by Chua Beng Huat and Koichi Iwabuchi

TV Drama in China, edited by Ying Zhu, Michael Keane, and Ruoyun Bai

Horror to the Extreme: Changing Boundaries in Asian Cinema, edited by Jinhee Choi and Mitsuyo Wada-Marciano

Series International Advisory Board

CULTURAL STUDIES AND CULTURAL INDUSTRIES IN NORTHEAST ASIA
What a Difference a Region Makes

Edited by

Chris Berry, Nicola Liscutin, and
Jonathan D. Mackintosh

香港大學出版社
HONG KONG UNIVERSITY PRESS

Hong Kong University Press
14/F Hing Wai Centre
7 Tin Wan Praya Road
Aberdeen
Hong Kong

© Hong Kong University Press 2009

Hardback   ISBN 978-962-209-974-6
Paperback   ISBN 978-962-209-975-3

British Library Cataloguing-in-Publication Data
A catalogue record for this book is available from the British Library.

Secure On-line Ordering
http://www.hkupress.org

Printed and bound by Liang Yu Printing Factory Ltd., Hong Kong, China.

Hong Kong University Press is honoured that Xu Bing, whose art
explores the complex themes of language across cultures, has written
the Press's name in his Square Word Calligraphy. This
signals our commitment to cross-cultural thinking and the distinctive
nature of our English-language books published in China.

"At first glance, Square Word Calligraphy appears to be nothing more
unusual than Chinese characters, but in fact it is a new way of rendering
English words in the format of a square so they resemble Chinese
characters. Chinese viewers expect to be able to read Square Word
Calligraphy but cannot. Western viewers, however are surprised to find
they can read it. Delight erupts when meaning is unexpectedly
revealed."

— Britta Erickson, *The Art of Xu Bing*

Contents

Acknowledgements

We are grateful to the editors at Hong Kong University Press, Colin Day and Michael Duckworth, for their support and encouragement throughout the development of this volume. Funding from Birkbeck and Goldsmiths Colleges of the University of London helped to support the initial conference this anthology grew out of. We are grateful to all the speakers at the conference — whether or not their essays are included here — as well as to the audience. Their work, questions, and comments helped to shape the final volume. Thank you to the authors here for their hard work and their co-operation throughout, and to the two reviewers appointed by the Press for their incisive and helpful suggestions. Finally, we are especially grateful to Rowan Pease for her help with standardizing Korean romanization throughout the volume.

Notes on Contributors

SooJeong AHN worked for the Pusan International Film Festival between 1998 and 2002. She is author of the chapter "Bibliography of Works on Korean Cinema" in *New Korean Cinema* (2005) and has completed a Ph.D. on film festivals at the University of Nottingham. Her recent publications include "Re-imagining the Past: Programming South Korean Retrospectives at the Pusan International Film Festival," in *Film International*, Vol. 6. (2008), a special issue on film festivals edited by Dina Iordanova (forthcoming); and "Re-mapping Asian Cinema: The Tenth Anniversary of PIFF in 2005," in *Cinemas, Identities and Beyond*, edited by Ruby Cheung and David Fleming (forthcoming).

Chris BERRY is Professor of Film and Television Studies in the Department of Media and Communication at Goldsmiths, University of London. His publications include (with Mary Farquhar) *Cinema and the National: China on Screen* (2006); *Postsocialist Cinema in Post-Mao China: The Cultural Revolution after the Cultural Revolution* (2004); (edited with Feii Lu) *Island on the Edge: Taiwan New Cinema and After* (2005); (editor) *Chinese Films in Focus: 25 New Takes* (2003); (edited with Fran Martin and Audrey Yue) *Mobile Cultures: New Media and Queer Asia* (2003); and (translator and editor) *Ni Zhen, Memoirs from the Beijing Film Academy: The Origins of China's Fifth Generation Filmmakers* (2002).

Michael DUTTON is currently Research Professor in Political Cultures at the Griffith Asia Institute and Professor of Politics at Goldsmiths, University of London. His books include *Beijing Time* (2008), *Streetlife China* (1999) and *Policing and Punishment in China* (1992). In 2007, he was awarded the Joseph Levenson Prize for the best book on contemporary China for his work, *Policing Chinese Politics* (2005). In addition to these major works, Dutton has also published a wide range of articles on popular culture, postcolonialism and China in journals such as *positions, Public Culture, Social Text,* and *Boundary Two.* He is the founding co-editor of the journal *Postcolonial Studies* and co-editor of the Routledge book series, Postcolonial Politics.

Mark HARRISON is Senior Lecturer in Chinese Studies at the University of Tasmania. He completed his Ph.D. at Monash University in Melbourne and was Research Fellow and Senior Lecturer at the University of Westminster in London. He is the author of *Legitimacy, Meaning and Knowledge in the Making of Taiwanese Identity* (2006).

Kōichi IWABUCHI is Professor of Media and Cultural Studies at Waseda University in Tokyo. He is the author of *Recentering Globalization: Popular Culture and Japanese Transnationalism* (2002) and the editor of *Feeling Asian Modernities: Transnational Consumption of Japanese TV Dramas* (2004), *Rogue Flows: Trans-Asian Cultural Traffic* (2004) and *East Asian Pop Culture: Analysing the Korean Wave* (2008).

Nicola LISCUTIN is Programme Director of and Lecturer in Japanese Cultural Studies at Birkbeck College, University of London. She is co-editor of *Between Burger and Sushi: Modern Japanese Food Culture* (2000) and editor of *Making History: Feminist Interventions in the Historiography of World War II, Japan and Germany* (forthcoming). She is currently preparing a volume on the discourses on "comfort women" and the recent history textbook controversy in East Asia.

Jonathan D. MACKINTOSH is Lecturer in Japanese Cultural Studies at Birkbeck College, University of London. He is author of *Homosexuality and Manliness in Postwar Japan* (forthcoming). Recent publications include "Embodied Masculinities of Male-Male Desire in Japan in the Early 1970s" in *Rethinking Gender and Sexuality in the Asia-Pacific* (2008) and "A Japanese Homo 'Moving' — Ito Bungaku and the Solidarity of the Rose Tribes," *Intersections* 13 (2006).

Mark MORRIS is University Lecturer in East Asian Cultural History at the University of Cambridge. He has taught Japanese literature and film, and organized Japanese and Korean film events in both Australia and the UK. Recent publications include "Magical Realism and Ideology: Narrative evasions in the work of Nakagami Kenji," in *A Companion to Magical Realism* (2005); "Passing: Paradoxes of alterity in *The Broken Commandment*," in *Representing the Other in Modern Japanese Literature* (2006).

Yoshitaka MŌRI is Associate Professor of Sociology and Cultural Studies at Tokyo National University of Fine Arts and Music. His publications in English include "Intellectual Discourses on the World Cup in Japan and the Unspoken Consensus of Japaneseness" in *Inter-Asia Cultural Studies* Vol. 5 no. 1, April 2004; "Culture=Politics: The Emergence of New Cultural Forms of Protest in the Age of Freeter" in *Inter-Asia Cultural Studies*, vol. 6 no. 1, 2005; and "Subcultural Unconsciousness in Japan: The War and Japanese Contemporary Artists" in *Popular Culture, Globalization and Japan* (2005).

Shinji OYAMA is Research and Teaching Associate in Japanese Creative Industries Studies at Birkbeck College, University of London, and a Ph.D. candidate at the Centre for Cultural Studies and Department of Media and Communications at Goldsmiths, University of London. Previously he was in advertising and banking, working with some of the world's biggest brands. He holds a master's degree from Columbia University, New York.

Laikwan PANG is Professor of Cultural Studies in the Department of Cultural and Religious Studies at the Chinese University of Hong Kong. She is the author of *Building a New China in Cinema: The Chinese Left-wing Cinema Movement, 1932–37* (2002), *Cultural Control and Globalization in Asia: Copyright, Piracy, and Cinema* (2006) and *The Distorting Mirror: Visual Modernity in China* (2007).

Rowan PEASE completed her Ph.D. on music of the Korean nationality while living in China in 2001. She lectures part-time in the Music Department of the School of Oriental and African Studies, University of London, and is editorial manager of *The China Quarterly*. She contributed two chapters to the volume *Korean Pop Music: Riding the Wave* (edited by Keith Howard, 2006).

Yoshi TEZUKA worked as a cinematographer in Japan. He moved to the United Kingdom in the 1980s and produced and directed award-winning documentary films for television. Recently, he has produced TV commercials for the Japanese market in Europe as the managing director of Chimera Films. Since April 2008, he has been Associate Professor of Media and Cultural Studies at Komazawa University in Tokyo.

Ae-Ri YOON recently completed her Ph.D. on the Korean animation industry at Goldsmiths, University of London. She has presented papers at numerous conferences, including the International Conference on Asian Comics, Animation and Gaming (2006) and the London Screen Studies Symposium (2005).

Note on Romanization

Where names have an established conventional spelling in English, we have retained the spelling. Otherwise, we have adopted standardized forms of romanization for all Asian languages that do not normally use Roman script.

Introduction

Jonathan D. Mackintosh, Chris Berry, and Nicola Liscutin

Cultural Studies and Cultural Industries in Northeast Asia: What a Difference a Region Makes is a collection of essays about the discipline of Cultural Studies and its use to analyze the cultural industries in Northeast Asia. It opens with a section considering the discipline itself — perhaps even treating it as a kind of cultural industry in its own right. It considers the challenges and possibilities that arise from its use in the context of Northeast Asia and when studying it from outside the region, and then follows with essays that use Cultural Studies approaches to analyze cultural industries and their products in Northeast Asia. The overarching unifying and original element of the book is the use of Cultural Studies to consider cultural industries in Northeast Asia.

The volume emerges from an international symposium of the same title, organized by the Japanese Department of Birkbeck, University of London, and the Pacific-Asia Cultural Studies Forum of Goldsmiths, University of London, in 2006. We conceived of the event as highly specialized and planned it initially as a roundtable discussion. However, when registration hit 120 we had to change to a bigger venue. Furthermore, the symposium itself generated unexpected creative energy through the intersection of Cultural Studies and Cultural Industries research. With the exception of some recent scholarship (see, for example, McGuigan and his call for a critical and reflexive cultural policy analysis, 2004),[1] these two approaches are rarely practiced in tandem. This volume not only seeks to record this productive energy. Culture and the cultural industries of Northeast Asia are gaining a global profile and both influencing and helping to constitute a new sense of the region as "New

Asia." Asian Cultural Studies is rapidly developing as a regionally distinct branch of the larger field. In these circumstances, we are also eager to amplify and extend this energy so that culture and its production are recognized as integral to an understanding and appreciation of the region, and vice versa.

The turn of the millennium has been accompanied by a massive shift in the cultural makeup of Northeast Asia. At the close of the first decade of the twenty-first century, popular culture, media and communications, as well as the creative, intellectual, and consumer product industries of the region are moving beyond national boundaries with ever-increasing strength. They enjoy unprecedented regional and global success and, according to some, are laying the foundations for future Asian co-operation.[2] Yet, just a decade before, the Northeast Asian region and its culture, in general, were characterized more by division and uncertainty exacerbated by unresolved histories, and in turn, often strident, defensive, and parochial nationalisms: Korea still maintained a ban on Japanese popular culture and media; Taiwanese democratization in the 1990s was expressed as political and cultural independence from the mainland; and Japan and China gazed inward, the former at the apparent failure of its samurai-cum-salaryman culture and the latter at the reunification of greater China with the return of Hong Kong.

Has the region changed so dramatically? What is the place of culture — in particular, popular and media culture, the industries that produce it, the policies that promote it, and the disciplines that study it — in the definition, construction, imagination, and interrogation of Northeast Asia? This collection of essays presents research that considers, within the context of regional change and continuity, a wide variety of cultural discourses, politics, products, practices, representations, and identities. Employing diverse methodological approaches and informed by an array of intellectual and vocational backgrounds, this collection seeks to analyze and challenge, in particular, an equation that is increasingly deployed by governmental, non-governmental, and economic elites. According to that equation, the region is discursively and normatively understood as an equitably balanced triangulation of power among three key actors: the nation, the market, and the individual. At the very least, exchange and dialogue is enhanced, so it is assumed. At its most ideal, culture is assumed to assuage historical grievance and to effect national reconciliation, regional peace, and global harmony.

Cultural Studies and Cultural Industries in Northeast Asia brings together scholars and experts from a diverse range of disciplines and fields: communications, advertising, and media; film and visual culture; anthropology and ethnomusicology; cultural policy, regulations, and industry; cultural studies and gender studies. This combination of academic and professional expertise introduces an important innovation to the multidisciplinarity that characterizes this volume's methodology. It brings into direct conversation two approaches that are usually seen as incompatible: Cultural Studies with its emphasis on intellectual criticism, text, meaning, power, and individual emancipation; and Cultural or Creative Industries, focused on economics, the market, policy, and personal freedom.

Ultimately, the goals of this volume are twofold. First, taken together, the individual essays composing it interrogate the very nature of the region by engaging with Northeast Asia at the points where the individual, nation, market, and region intersect. Second, they seek to understand how culture is constituted in complex, powerful, and — not always obvious — political ways that may do as much to undermine as stimulate lasting regional stability, prosperity, understanding, and peace. It is these tensions that come into focus by bringing Cultural Studies and Cultural Industries together in the work presented here.

With this in mind, this Introduction first describes the context within which culture and especially the cultural or creative industries have risen apparently to a place of primacy in the construction and mobilization of Northeast Asia as a regional identity and affiliation. In order to provide the reader with a wider context within which to situate each of the essays in this collection, it also discusses how we might understand globalization and the relationship of the market, cultural industries, and nation. Last, there follows a short guide to the chapters and how they relate to the overall themes of the anthology.

Context

In a speech entitled "Creative Industry: A Key to Solidify Bases for Regional Cooperation in Asia," Japanese Parliamentary Secretary for Foreign Affairs Itsunori Onodera declared to a gathering in Hong Kong of the Asia Cultural Cooperation Forum in November 2004, "In this age of globalization, culture is increasingly being shared, transcending national boundaries." Referring specifically to the "wealth of cultural exchange between Japan and other Asian countries" he went on to emphasize:

> culture as a matter of course nurtures a soundness and wealth of spirit, but given that it also encourages creative industry and supports economic vitality, it is an area that is the key for the future prosperity of Asia and also in terms of making a contribution to the world.[3]

Onodera's speech is significant. Although its emphasis on culture and the creative industries was neither unique in content or tone at the time, it articulated a certain mood characterizing the region and its relations in the first decade of the twenty-first century. In proclamation after proclamation across the region, culture was recognized, lauded, and made official. "Creativity matters" asserts the Hong Kong Trade Development Council's official 2002 statement calling for the promotion of creative industries.[4] In its *Challenge 2008* six-year plan to overhaul its cultural industries, the Taiwanese government aims at doubling employment and tripling production value through "building Taiwan's cultural creativity in the Chinese world."[5] China's 2006 launch of its international Confucius Institute and governmental Cultural Industries website herald an official embrace of culture,[6] while in Korea, the Culture Industry and Cultural Policy Bureaus seek to enhance the "national competitiveness of [the] culture industries" and the "globalization of Korean culture."[7] Finally, in Japan, 2002 is marked by the legislation of culture as a legal entity in the 2002 Fundamental Law for the Promotion of the Arts and Culture.

The apparent centrality of culture and the creative industries in Northeast Asia is, at first glance, easily explained by the profit-driven logic of the market. For example, it was estimated that, in 2006, the cultural industries of Japan and South Korea together accounted for thirteen percent of the international culture market; China and the other countries of Asia made up a further six percent.[8] To be certain, in contrast to a country like the United Kingdom, whose creative and cultural industries accounted for 7.3 percent of the national economy in 2007,[9] this sector still formed a small part in emerging economies like China (two percent in 2004,[10] though in major centres like Beijing, the total value-added output might be as high as ten percent).[11] And although the production value of cultural and creative industries was higher in small economies such as Hong Kong at four percent in 2007 (and near three percent in Taiwan in 2000),[12] its massive potential cannot be ignored. Figures put out by the Japan External Trade Organization (JETRO) suggested that the entertainment industry alone in Japan was worth up to ten percent of the GNP in 2004. Marubeni Research Institute, moreover, estimated that Japanese cultural exports have grown by 300 percent since 1992. In the same period, exports as a whole increased by only twenty percent in Japan.[13]

Crucially, as much as culture is a matter of sound business sense, the economic role of culture in the construction of Northeast Asia translates into ideational and normative goals. "The process of promoting mutual exchange, discovering what values are common to Asia," writes Onodera, "would contribute to an increased understanding among the people of Asia of the cultures of the different countries of Asia, and further promote the appeal of Asian culture and the culture of each country. In so doing, Asian values, which embrace peace and harmony, would, if transmitted more dynamically to the world, be able to make a significant contribution in the future of human civilization in the 21st century."[14]

The reference to Asian values may sound suspiciously like the traditionalistic, anti-Western ideologies of Singapore's Lee Kuan Yew, Malaysia's Mahathir bin Mohamad, and Japan's Ishihara Shintarō in the late 1980s and 1990s. But there is an important difference. Whereas the leaders of the so-called Asian Renaissance made nationalistic appeals to an assumed shared Neo-Confucian tradition,[15] the current focus on culture is the product of a neoliberal ideology espousing a global free-market — what Fu-Kuo Liu dubs "Asian Pragmatism"[16] — and the linking of post-industrial globalized consumerism to individual freedom, hence, individual and social well-being. Moreover, it is contemporary, open, transnational, and, in the lingo of twenty-first century Japanese foreign policy, "cool." Onodera, for instance, cites a variety of examples of the new Asian culture ranging from the recent Japanese love affair with all things Korean — the so-called "Korean Wave" — to the news that three global Chinese stars — Zhang Ziyi, Gong Li, and Michelle Yeoh — would portray Japanese geishas in a Hollywood production (Rob Marshall's *Memoirs of a Geisha*, 2005). To Onodera's list one could add Korean mobile phones and video games, Japanese *otaku* "geek" style from stylish Shibuya, hard- and software made in Taiwan, new waves of Chinese cinema and tourists, and Hong Kong Cantopop. In a novel development, national brands and images such as these are often reconfigured as regional ones, for instance, Taiwanese-Japanese star-actor Takeshi Kaneshiro and pan-Asian advertising campaigns of the kind discussed here in Shinji Oyama's essay. Thanks to burgeoning new information technologies, trends emerge regionally, such as queer Asian cinema and trans-Asian manga cults. At the beginning of the 2000s, then, culture and the creative industries, it seems, have the capacity to effect historical reconciliation and shrink spatio-temporal distance to create a cosmopole of consumers who identify themselves as Asian.

Or do they? Do flows of popular culture and media only promote transnational regional culture? As is well known, the casting of the three Chinese stars in *Memoirs of a Geisha* provoked outrage. Not only did Chinese men object vigorously to seeing Chinese actresses portraying "prostitutes" who sold themselves to Japanese men and condemn Zhang Ziyi, in particular, as a traitor. Japanese men were equally indignant that Hollywood could not find Japanese stars to incarnate something as allegedly quintessentially Japanese as geishas.[17] This is not an isolated misfire. For example, how do nationalist backlashes like the Japanese *Kenkanryū* ("Anti-Korean Wave") analyzed here in Nicola Liscutin's essay, and anti-Japanese demonstrations in the People's Republic of China and South Korea throughout the early 2000s fit into Onodera's vision? Do these transborder cultural flows result from reduced trade barriers and reflect a lessening of nation-state power or are they not, on the contrary, driven by national policy and interest? To what extent does twenty-first century Northeast Asian cultural regionalization displace twentieth-century asymmetrical power relations and social marginalization? What effect might an emergent regional consciousness have on individuals' ability to negotiate culture and their representation? As the final section — a kind of case study bringing together studies highlighting the contentious Korean-Japanese relationship — demonstrates, the answers are neither simple nor definitive.

Finally, how are such questions to be approached and considered? Critical Cultural Studies certainly aspires to address these issues. But what is the relation of Cultural Studies to Cultural Industries in Northeast Asia? First, is there a role for a Cultural Studies of Asia conducted outside Asia, in English-language academia for example, and what are the potential benefits and pitfalls it brings, both to Asia and to the academic world outside Asia? Michael Dutton attends to these questions in his critical piece here. His essay adds to a growing body of critical literature by a variety of scholars. This includes Chris Burgess's 2004 article on the "crisis" in Asian Studies in which he asks if Cultural Studies can provide a way out.[18] In 2005, Mingbao Yue and Jon Goss edited a special issue of *Comparative American Studies* on the role that Cultural Studies from Asia can play in "De-Americanizing the Global."[19]

The important questions that Yue and Goss's special issue of *Comparative American Studies* open up about the discipline of Cultural Studies in general extend far beyond the parameters of this book.[20] But a fundamental condition for their project is also central to *Cultural Studies and Cultural Industries in Northeast Asia*. This is the rapid growth of Cultural Studies within the region itself. The first Cultural Studies conferences held outside the English-speaking world took place in Taiwan. These were the first and second Trajectories conferences, held in Taipei in 1992 and 1995.[21] They were hosted at the Center for Asia-Pacific/Cultural Studies, established in 1992 at National Tsing Hua University, where Chen Kuan-hsing is Professor of Cultural Studies, and where a B.A. program in Cultural Studies is taught. Since then, a number of other courses, centers, and organizations have appeared in various parts of the region. For example, Lingnan University in Hong Kong launched its B.A. program in 1999.[22] In addition, Yonsei University in Seoul has a graduate program in Gender and Cultural Studies; there is the KUNCI Cultural Studies Center in Yogyakarta, Indonesia, and other centers exist in Taiwan at National Chiao-tung University and National Taiwan University.

As well as these various nationally based initiatives, Cultural Studies has emerged as a regional phenomenon through journals such as *Traces* and *Inter-Asia Cultural Studies*, whose success has also led to the formation of an *Inter-Asia Cultural Studies* society that holds biennial conferences. Although the editorial office of the former is based at Cornell University in the United States, the journal is published through Hong Kong University Press. Furthermore, its commitment to simultaneous English, Chinese, Korean, and Japanese editions demonstrates its strong commitment to the Northeast Asian region. *Inter-Asia Cultural Studies* is an avowedly regional phenomenon, based at National Tsing Hua University in Taiwan, but with an editorial collective drawn largely from across the region.

The editorial statement of *Inter-Asia Cultural Studies*, published in its 2000 inaugural issue and now also on its website, makes a clear distinction between the progressive political project of the journal and the forces of global capitalism driving the rhetoric and reality of the "rise of Asia."[23] Nonetheless, the decision to publish in English speaks to the complex entanglement of regionalism with global capitalism, even within the avowedly resistant domains of Asian Cultural Studies. Have the contemporaneous rise of Cultural Studies and the cultural industries in East Asia been parallel and separate, or is Cultural Studies in some way part of the cultural industries. These issues and more are discussed by Mark Harrison in his essay for this volume. But in this introduction, we hope that underlining this complexity helps to explain why bringing Cultural Studies and Cultural Industries into dialogue and debate is a useful move.

All the essays in this volume address the questions raised in this introduction, though in very different ways and with highly varying results. Nevertheless, when considered as a whole, some distinctive shared concerns about the Northeast Asian region appear across *Cultural Studies and Cultural Industries in Northeast Asia*. These concern globalization and the relationship of cultural industries to national power. They also consider Cultural Studies as a tool to deconstruct and demonstrate Northeast Asia as a region, and in particular, they alert us to how the region might shape the way individuals negotiate gender, class, community, and history, or in other words, their identities.

Globalization

James H. Mittelman has posited that "Regionalism today is emerging as a potent force in the globalization process." He explains that,

> If *globalization* is understood to mean the compression of time and space aspects of social relations then *regionalism* may be regarded as but one component of globalization. In this sense, regionalism is a chapter of globalization. But regionalism may also be a response or a challenge to globalization (emphasis in original).[24]

In this definition, the region is not simply reified as an intermediate socioeconomic or political position between the structure of the nation-state and globalizing forces of capital and/or ideology. Nor does its emergence in history as a more widely encompassing but not universal affiliation mark a middle point on a timeline that represents globalization as a teleology. Rather, the push/pull dynamic characterizing the region that Mittelman describes suggests that globalization is a complex, conflicting, and indeterminate process. This understanding is paramount in its importance, if subtle in its implications.

First, the region helps us to approach the key concepts of the "global" and the "local" not in dichotomous opposition but as an ongoing cultural negotiation. Crucially, then, the "global" from the Northeast Asian perspective does not derive geographically from "over there," since the "global" is always/already "local." This approach may bring to mind the concept of "glocalization" according to which products are tailored to meet local tastes and demands,[25] but this is not quite accurate. Notwithstanding its construction as a market strategy, "glocalization" starts from a normative premise derived from imperialism whereby globalization is homogenization driven from the (Euro-American) center to the (Third World) local. Many of the essays in this volume demonstrate that this is not the case, and that the global, far from being hegemonic, is a contested site where resistance and subversion generate cultural diversity and complexity. Laikwan Pang, for example, discusses copyright infringement and laws as a result of pirating practices in China which affect and are contested throughout the region. She alerts us to questions of how traditional social concepts like class are complicated and even undermined by new affiliations and communities borne of technological innovation in communications. In her study of Korean pop music fans in China, Rowan Pease's essay highlights a site of conflict in the music industry: its domination by a politically conservative elite of male producers and executives, on the one hand, and their female — sometimes highly subversive — fans, on the other. It is beyond the scope of *Cultural Studies and Cultural Industries in Northeast Asia* to provide definitive answers to these complex and contradictory questions, but the essays presented here serve to open a debate on how the region influences identity as individuals negotiate culture and cultural production.

Second, the lens of the region intervenes in postcolonial approaches to globalization. The twentieth-century colonial legacy of Northeast Asia is hugely complex, obliging us to interrogate basic concepts even as they may be deployed for their explanatory utility. Consider, for example, "hybridity." Developed to counter essentialist understandings of culture and nation and Orientalist conceptions of "us" and "them," its uncritical application can easily slide into the "presumption of the existence of once pure cultures that may have existed before the age of international capital compressed the globe:"[26] The "global" is rendered as modern — one homogenous modernity — and inauthentic; the "local" is traditional — one originary tradition, hence essential and pristine. Yet, through the regional perspective of Northeast Asia, the historical experiences of each of the countries treated in this volume belie such an easy schematic, as both Yoshitaka Mōri in his study of Japanese/ Korean pop music and Yoshi Tezuka in his case studies of film production argue. All are shaped by multiple, conflicting modernities brought into being through interlocking, mutually effecting histories of internal and external colonialisms, decolonization, and in the case of Japan, South Korea, and Taiwan, American Cold War and post-Cold War neo-colonialism. Put another way, Northeast Asian identity is inaccurately understood as a bifurcated history of tradition and transformation whose globalization originates from an imperialistic West to be followed by a colonized hybridized rest. Rather, the national and regional cultural identities of Northeast Asia are themselves articulations of globalization whose politics and ideologies, subversions and interrogations, subjectivities and representational practices, hierarchies and subjugations, and violations and marginalizations can be nothing other than hybrid. The contemporary Northeast Asian postcolonial experience is shaped by regionally informed proliferations of national cultural identity and national configurations of institutional modernity.[27] Just as the "global" is always/already Northeast Asian, so too is Northeast Asia always/ already modern. Shinji Oyama's challenging study of regional brands and branding requires us to consider this conception of globalization as modernity, and both Michael Dutton and Kōichi Iwabuchi's interrogations of Asian Cultural Studies and Cultural Studies of Asia point to the ways in which this history provides both fruitful territory for the field at the same time as it complicates its development.

The Market, Cultural Industries, and the Nation

To what extent is the nation displaced through trade, the market, and culture? This is a perennial question for the study of regionalization and globalization and is one of the central fault lines dividing theorists and experts. Answers fall across a wide spectrum whose end poles are aptly identified by Held and McGrew as "globalist" — "contemporary globalization is a real and significant historical development" — and "sceptic" — globalization "is primarily an ideological or social construction which has marginal explanatory value."[28] The general contours of this debate are productive when analyzing regionalism in Northeast Asia, but because of the specific configuration of global and regional politics, the market, and, crucially, of culture, it is worth reviewing this debate in more detail. In the process, it will become clear once again that the assumption of an either/or opposition between the nation and globalization is not the only way to think about these questions. Under conditions of globalizing market forces both the nation and the region can be reified as brands at the same time as they operate — often at cross-purposes — as political and ideological forces.

The Macro-economic Background of Northeast Asian Regionalism

Some, like Onodera as cited above, directly link the regional emergence and potential of Northeast Asia — and Asia more generally — to economic globalization. To be certain, the past decade has seen an expansion and deepening of links at the intergovernmental level. For example, Yeo Lay Hwee, executive director of the Singapore Institute of International Affairs, argues that the basis for a Northeast Asian rapprochement to decades of historical animosity and cultural suspicion is made possible through a strategically informed escalation of bilateral contacts, as a first step towards the development of a more far-reaching multilateralism.[29] Robert Scollay, director of the New Zealand APEC Study Centre, concurs. Examining the case of formal preferential trade agreements (PTAs) prior to 1998, he likens East Asia to an "'empty box' in the regional and global maps of PTAs: . . . Japan and Korea maintained a policy of avoiding involvement in PTAs, preferring to rely on the GATT's non-discrimination principle, while China was preoccupied with its transition to a market economy." A major sea-change was effected in 1998 by the decision of Japan and Korea to discuss a bilateral free trade area (FTA), which, according to Scollay, represents a "policy watershed." (Significantly, it was in 1998 that Korea formally lifted its ban on Japanese popular and media culture.) Henceforward, PTAs became the central trade-policy pillar in a wider strategy of bilateralism within the region and externally not just for Japan and Korea but also China and Taiwan: "The way was thus cleared," Scollay concludes, "for PTAs to become a central part of the trade architecture of East Asia, and possibly of the entire Asia-Pacific region."[30]

Despite the driving force behind region-building that economic factors appear to constitute, geopolitical policymakers and academics are guarded in their optimism. Yeo, for example, acknowledges that the future of East Asian regionalism is "fuzzy." Lacking a blueprint to deepen co-operation and advance communitarian integration, intergovernmental trade developments are largely reactive responses to global market forces, which nevertheless may ostensibly confirm a national commitment to openness and co-operation.[31] Dent is more challenging in his assessment. He describes Northeast Asian regionalism as "stunted."[32] Richard Baldwin, in his comparison of East Asian regionalism with Europe, is even more pessimistic: "Real regionalism has not yet started in East Asia."[33]

Caution about the prospects of Northeast Asian regionalism is well founded. Compared to the European and North American regional groupings, Northeast Asia is the least advanced, its organization characterized more by an array of intergovernmental, semi-formal, and informal consensus-building arrangements, and more reactive in nature, an effect of geopolitical circumstance, as opposed to formalized long-term visions and plans.[34] EU-style institutional supranationalism, NAFTA-like "big-bang" originating treaties,[35] and ASEAN communitarian aspirations[36] are responses, in part, to the vicissitudes of economic globalization. However, they also differ significantly, undercutting their ability to stand as models and measures for Northeast Asian regionalism and pointing to the importance of regionally specific histories and characteristics in each case.[37] This is where culture and the culture industries of Northeast Asia may play a distinctive and particularly crucial role, topping up, as it were, the necessary but not sufficient momentum of economic regionalization.

The Role of Culture and Cultural Policy in Northeast Asian Regionalism: Globalist Aspirations

Returning to Onodera's appeal to "develop creative industry," we find an attempt to construct a particularly Asian response to the question of how the individual, nation, and region relate. Commenting on twenty-first century conflict borne of terror and environmental degradation, he writes,

> It is only too easy for policymakers and citizens alike to turn their attention almost exclusively to security and economic considerations. True human happiness however, is to be found in spiritual wealth . . . the creative industries, will be the key for humankind, and above all Asia.[38]

Onodera's prescription for an Asia united through culture may read like an impractical flight of fancy, but a closer inspection reveals that his ideas, while cloaked by a rhetoric of aspiration, give evidence of a grounded familiarity with Cultural and Cultural Policy Studies. Consider the following when Onodera posits:

> the more material wealth people achieve, the more spiritual contentment they seek . . . [and] . . . people, including the elderly, who are no longer involved in the process of manufacturing goods in their jobs, will be able to focus their energies on a second phase of life in cultural and artistic creative activities.[39]

What he really is trying to describe, in the lingo of Cultural Studies and policy analysts, is the shift to a "post-industrial" or "post-Fordist" social and political economy in which membership in a "cultural public sphere" confers a particular kind of post-modern democratic "social and cultural citizenship" whose *modus operandi* is the market and culture; that is, "the individualization of cultural consumption" translates to "the commercialization of culture," hence the "commercialization of experience" so that the "individual is free to make himself or herself."[40]

Such a statement may be overly complex for official and popular consumption, but the same basic ideas are found in all their various national translations into government policy statement by bureaucrats. Consider two examples from Taiwan and Japan. A document published in May 2002 by the Taiwanese government, *Challenge 2008: The Six-Year National Development Plan*, gives emphasis to "Developing the Cultural Creative Industry" for a "new phase of industrialization" including "artistic and esthetic creation which has been ignored in the past" and which will "enhance the quality of life and the environment." More specifically, this will be achieved by a doubling of employment in and a tripling of production value of these industries, positioning Taiwan as the regional headquarters for domestic businesses and multinational corporations, and a center of creativity in the Chinese world.[41]

In Japan's Fundamental Law for the Promotion of Arts and Culture passed by the Diet in December 2001, the creation and enjoyment of culture and the arts are legislated as a civic right (Articles 2.2 and 2.3).[42] Framed within the context of the "Realization of an Emotionally Enriched Society through Culture," the law is a central pillar in the Ministry of Education, Culture, Sports, Science and Technology's (MEXT) overall vision for culture in twenty-first century Japan:

> Culture serves a range of purposes and roles in today's society and is significant in a variety of ways. Among other things, culture (1) is nourishment that allows people to live a human life, (2) forms the basis of a society in which we live together, (3) creates high quality economic activity, (4) contributes to the development of human truths, and (5) is the foundation for world peace.[43]

A comprehensive textual analysis of cultural policy documents throughout Asia is beyond the scope of this Introduction. Nevertheless, all of these excerpts demonstrate the central role that culture has been elevated to in the official shaping of twenty-first century conceptions of society, the economy, and by implication, politics. But, that is not all, since the uses of culture and the promotion of cultural industries and the creative economy are not solely explained by the logic of market functionalism. "Globalists" also aim at the ideational level, and it is through the region that culture becomes particularly potent.

According to Kevin Robins, who writes on globalization in relation to culture and identity,

> It is surely clear that the global shift — associated with the creation of world markets, with international communication and media flows, and with international travel — has profound implications for the way we make sense of our lives and of the changing world we live in.[44]

Robins's observation underscores a basic premise of economic-cum-cultural regionalization in Northeast Asia as spelled out in the various excerpts above. Culture — particularly popular, media, and consumer culture — transcends borders with such frequency and intensity as to constitute an irrevocable and irresistible force that regionalizes identity. It is this power that "globalists" celebrate. It is also this power that governments seek to promote through the articulation and legislation of cultural policy.

The Role of Cultural Policy and Cultural Industries in Northeast Asian Nationalism: The "Skeptics" Retort

Writing on the contemporary Japanese manga and anime industry, Roland Kelts writes, "Younger Japanese had grown up amid the wealth of the postwar Japan Inc. machine just as its cogs were starting to falter. But instead of stymieing them, the resulting slump actually cultivated their creativity."[45] Kelts's application of Horacian logic (which posits that adversity reveals genius and prosperity hides it) importantly highlights how the success of 1990s Japanese popular culture worldwide — Douglas McGray brands this "Japan's Gross National Cool" — is directly correlated with the failure of the dominant model of the Japanese politico-economic state.[46]

Here, culture is seen to empower individuals by releasing them from ideological and discursive strategies of the modern nation-state and market-driven representational practices. That is not all, for in also "discrediting Japan's rigid social hierarchy"[47] while relegating traditional culture like the tea ceremony and *bushidō* samurai ethics to a backseat position,[48] creativity radically acts as a leveling mechanism. It restores a kind of equalitarian and even democratic balance at a time when power seems to lie primarily in the hands of the state and the market — an understanding that places culture also in tension with rather than simply as a support for the state and the market. Cultural unpredictability and chaos are, in fact, key defining features of creativity, hence the marketability of creative industries. So, in a rather counterintuitive manner, it is this productive friction between the individual subject emerging through culture and the nation, that, on closer inspection, animates cultural policy thinking and that governments and business seek to harness. It is something that "Cool Japan," a potential cultural superpower, has reinvented and mastered. According to McGray, "Japan's growing cultural presence has created a mighty engine of national cool." In so doing, it has come to wield "soft power." McGray continues, "National cool is an idea, a reminder that commercial trends and products, and a country's knack for spawning them, can serve political and economic ends."[49]

It is from this economically realist perspective that a "globalist" reading of cultural policy statements and cultural industrial objectives given above can be challenged. In its opening statement, *Challenge 2008* states that it is formulated by the government of the Republic of China for the express purpose of "fostering the creativity and talent Taiwan needs." Japan's MEXT summary statement on culture directly links the Fundamental Law's objective to promote national culture and arts with the enhancement of "the presence of Japan and its people within the global community."[50] In other words, postures on internationalization, cultural exchange, and globalization may not only be about the promotion of a harmonious world order. They are also about projecting one's own national prestige, presence, and influence through a jockeying for position in a regional and global market structured by relative strength of economic — now linked to culture — and/or political power. Take, for example, Japan's proposal in September 2006 to create an East Asian Economic Partnership with ASEAN, China, India, New Zealand, and Australia. While impressive in scale and inclusive of such key cultural areas as intellectual property rights, this apparently regionalizing strategy has been interpreted by some as a cynical maneuver on the part of Japan to secure its own power. Outflanked by China and South Korea which have agreed FTAs with ASEAN, and stalled in its own attempts to secure a similar arrangement with ASEAN, Japan fears that it will be left behind in what may be a fundamental shift from bilateralism to multilateral regional trade agreements.[51]

In addition to the realpolitik that the culture-focused rhetoric concerning regionalization and globalization appears to mask, two factors need to be mentioned that are further examined in some of the essays here. First, while it is undeniable that, "with mobility, comes encounter"[52] in the emerging regional and global order, this experience may be highly circumscribed for certain segments of the population. Regional identity and affiliation comes only to those "who can afford a cosmopolitan identity," like certain sectors of the urban middle class and the business and media elite.[53] Yeo may be correct when he argues that a lack of popular support and public indifference in East Asia are not insuperable obstacles to regionalism, but he does acknowledge that "constituencies promoting these trends are narrowly based and therefore vulnerable to pressures from those with wider nationalist identifications and loyalties, including the desire to protect fragile national sovereignties."[54] Regionalism may marginalize individuals by alienating their loyalties, even as its supporters argue for its properties to soothe historical pain and ease national animosities, a point which Nicola Liscutin stresses in her study of the Japanese manga *Kenkanryū* ("Anti-Korean Wave") and which Mark Morris complicates in his textual reading of the representation of Japan in Korean film.

This raises a second point. Regionalism is far from minimizing or eradicating marginalizations and oppressions that emerged as a result of capitalism and development as structured in the bipolar world. As part of globalization in the twenty-first century, it replicates, reproduces, and regenerates them, if in slightly different form. So, although it was predicted that the region would take the form of a Japanese "core" surrounded by a developing "periphery," what has in fact evolved is a "complex division of labor involving symmetric as well as asymmetric power relationships between and within economies, industries and firms."[55] The case of the Korean animation industry's struggles to respond to the challenge of globalization by transitioning from outsourcing to original creations of its own is analyzed by Ae-Ri Yoon through the experiences of those who work in the industry. She powerfully demonstrates how the twentieth-century hierarchy that saw Korea in the shadows of Japan is in danger of being reproduced by the new regionalism.

Guide to Chapters

Reflections on Cultural Studies in/on Northeast Asia

Constructing a theoretical context for all the chapters that follow, this section presents essays by three leading theorists of Cultural Studies and Cultural Industries in Northeast Asia. As Cultural Studies has been established in one part of Asia after another, it has inspired ambitious programs of critical and political intervention. Wang Xiaoming, professor of Cultural Studies at Shanghai University, has written a "Manifesto for Cultural Studies." In it, he not only provides a devastating critique of Chinese intellectuals in the 1980s, asking, "Why did we fail to foresee that an arbitrary and corrupt power could create a completely different kind of market economy and use it to perpetuate even greater deceit and more ramified sorts of exploitation?"[56] He also assigns a special role for Cultural Studies in countering the consequences of the current crisis, writing that, "it seems urgent that contemporary cultural studies be expanded. For . . . each great change in society . . . has been not only an economic, political, or ecological phenomenon, but also a cultural one."[57] In Taipei, Chen Kuan-Hsing has consistently interrogated the work of the various organizations he is involved with, prodding and pushing them to remain engaged and resist complacency. For example, his epic two-part essay on the lasting consequences of the Cold War in producing political blockage in the Northeast Asian region also calls for Cultural Studies to play a special role in attempting the deconstruction of that situation.[58]

The essays included here have been produced specifically for this volume, to interrogate how Northeast Asia may be approached from within and without and to put into critical conversation Cultural Studies and Cultural Industries as theory, method, epistemology, approach, and practice. Like Chen Kuan-Hsing, Kōichi Iwabuchi is one of the pioneers of Cultural Studies in the Northeast Asian region. Here, offering personal reflections after a number of years of work and not shying away from the difficulties of the current situation, he intervenes in debates over Media and Cultural Studies. He asks how they may be made "useful," that is critical *and* practical, tools of intervention at a time when popular culture has become a convenient resource for expanding national interest. He argues that the propensity to narrowly apply the concept of culture overlooks the political implications of market fundamentalism and brand nationalism that drives and animates much popular cultural traffic in Northeast Asia under the guise of advancing social democratization.

The next two chapters shift our perspective, the essay by Michael Dutton drawing the reader out of the region to question what it means to practice Asian Cultural Studies in an English-language context. In a particularly novel look at Adorno and other theorists, he suggests what role Western-derived theories like those of the Frankfurt School may play in the effort to force open a space for critical thought in a territory dominated by the legacies of Orientalism and Area Studies. His open-ended conclusion leaves the reader to ponder the state and very nature of Cultural Studies itself and to query whether Western-based Cultural Studies of Asia can avoid the risk of resuscitating colonial/Orientalist positions of subject and object, and knowledge and power.

In some ways, Mark Harrison's critical survey of identity politics in Taiwan from the period of Japanese colonial rule to the democratization era seems to directly respond to both Dutton and Iwabuchi's work, extending the pointed questions they raise about the discipline to interrogate its role in Taiwan, a project he has traced in his monograph on the topic of intellectual disciplines and their role in the formation of Taiwan's identity.[59] Developed out of both a strong admiration of the pioneering work in Cultural Studies carried on in Taiwan and a very close reading of key cultural identity theorists, particularly those of the past decade, Harrison's research presents a situation in which Cultural Studies is neither indigenous nor long-standing, its ideas and questions instead often being appropriated all too easily for a national industry of cultural identity. Here, he seems to be saying, Cultural Studies runs the risk of becoming a cultural industry.

Cultural Industries in Northeast Asia

The distinctive feature of this set of chapters is that the authors combine personal and/or professional experience in specific cultural industries with Cultural Studies academic insight. Focusing on visual and film culture, the essays present the reader with intimate views from the inside, views that enhance the critical edge that each work brings to bear on questions of cultural production, marketing, and the impact of multinational employment practices, global markets, and the globalization of the creative industries.

SooJeong Ahn worked for one of the most influential film festivals in the region, the Pusan International Film Festival, before beginning to research it. Developing a detailed examination of the selection of specific films for particular sections of the festival, in particular the opening film, she hones directly in on the tensions between national objectives to promote Korean cinema and individual Korean filmmakers' strategies to enter the global film market, and the festival's deployment of regional ambitions as a site to negotiate those tensions. Her research records how those important few years when Korean cinema burst forth onto the world stage at the turn of the millennium were experienced by individuals, negotiated by institutions, and influenced the Korean construction of the region. Her conclusions are often surprising, since the relationship of the festival to the industry, its practitioners, its products, and the market is anything but straightforward.

Yoshi Tezuka, in contrast, takes a longer historical perspective. He combines his knowledge as a filmmaker in Japan and detailed interviews with film crew members to develop a comparative examination of two Japan-US film co-productions, *Shogun* (1980) and *Lost in Translation* (2003). From the subjective perspectives of those who participated in these productions, he charts how cosmopolitanization and national identity have evolved in different forms in different historical epochs. In the earlier era, cosmopolitanism on the part of the Japanese line producer was deployed in the service of national interests and to resist foreign domination. In the contemporary era of globalization, the Japanese line producer's sense of identity as a cosmopolitan independent filmmaker overrides concerns about the national interest.

Finally, the ethnographic approach is most clearly developed in Ae-Ri Yoon's study of the animation industry in South Korea. Based on participant observation and interviews conducted in Korea and Japan, Yoon's research charts how the appreciation of animation has changed in Korea from the unique perspective of the animators themselves. She details the conflicts and dilemmas they face, and contextualizes their experience against larger questions of how culture contributes to national economic power within the region and the world. For the animators drawing cells in Seoul, is the call for original creation a welcome opportunity to shake off the humiliation of outsourcing, or is it just a new stage of entrenchment in a global order where survival makes it the only way forward and demands new self-sacrifice?

Discourse, Crossing Borders

The next set of essays focuses on the consumption of cultural products. The three chapters start from highly varying methodological positions. First, Laikwan Pang brings the radical engagement of a Cultural Studies perspective to bear on the regionally popular cultural phenomena of animation culture. Not taking the rhetoric of intellectual property rights at face value, she asks us to question how the illegal reproduction of Japanese animation culture in China creates new forms of circulation and consumption practices of copying and sharing. In an essay that strikes right at the heart of questions concerning alternative forms of politics — "an anti-politics" that challenges the current global knowledge economy — she argues that such acts are subversive to the dominant system of the information society based on the privatization of intellectual property.

In contrast, Shinji Oyama analyses his topic of the East Asian brandscape both from high theory and from the ground up — or to be more precise, the ground floors of the department store where the cosmetics sections are located. This double approach enables him to move away from the dominant focus on brands as national cultural epistemologies to an ontology of brands that gives order to Appadurai's otherwise disjunctive "-scapes" (media, economy, law, technology, and so on), and that shape the complex power relations of globalized consumerism and consumer knowledge. To be specific, where many of us think of brands in national terms, Oyama deconstructs their image with information about ownership, marketing, and other features of the transnational corporate era to demonstrate that brands are no longer confined to the nation, but rather they deploy the national as part of the transnational operations.

Finally, Rowan Pease's study of Korean pop music in China shows where Pang's and Oyama's seemingly divergent approaches to consumption converge. Through her grounded analysis of Chinese fan writing and art about Korean pop music, she describes how the popular cultural market, nation, region, and discourses of gender and sexuality, ethnicity, and nationalism are negotiated by the consuming subject. Just as Pang and Oyama argue that national power is neither omniscient nor omnipotent, Pease demonstrates how regional and global enterprise may be subverted in unexpected ways by the unpredictable and maybe uncontrollable activities of local fans on the ground. Crucially, then, Pease describes a complex, often ambiguous relationship that exemplifies how popular culture does not correspond with easy binary structures of producer and consumer, enterprise and individual. and region and nation.

Nationalism and Transnationalism: The Case of Korea and Japan

At first glance, the last group of essays is the most directly informed by Cultural Studies approaches. However, what is presented here is not simply a set of close textual readings of cultural products. Rather, by expanding the more established concern of how the individual shapes and is shaped by the discursive power of the nation-state to include the transnational, the authors demonstrate how Cultural Studies has a vitally useful and crucially critical role to play in understanding nationalism and the Northeast Asian region. In order to reveal more closely these intersections and negotiations, they take as their focus the particularly difficult relationship between Korea and Japan. The essays presented here have been selected because the varying and diverse perspectives they work from generate a highly salient and deeply thoughtful dialogue that not only produces new and topically relevant insights on this particular corner of the region. By concluding *Cultural Studies and Cultural Industries in Northeast Asia*, they also speak to concerns cutting across Northeast Asia overall.

Nicola Liscutin considers the nationalist backlash against recent attempts to foster the Korean-Japanese relationship by analyzing *Kenkanryū* ("Anti-Korean Wave"), a polemic in manga form against Korean culture, Koreans, and resident Koreans in Japan. Treating its visual representations and rhetorical strategies as a form of "performative history," she explores the issue of historical agency, identity politics, and nationalism as they are shaped and transformed in regional flows of popular culture. She demonstrates that both the "Korean Wave" and the manga that react against it are embedded in the cultural flows enabled by the lowered trade barriers of globalization. The result is a classic example of Appadurai's disjunctures that is ripe for Cultural Studies analysis, and — informed by the critical pedagogy of Henry Giroux — political intervention.

Mark Morris takes us to the other side of the Korean Straits in his examination of how Japan, Japanese figures, and Koreans with Japanese connections are represented in Korean film. At first glance, one might expect Korea's postcolonial cinematic politics of representation to construct Japan singularly as the focus of historical resentment, and superficially, this is the case. Yet, in spite of, or precisely because of, the history of Japanese colonial rule in Korea, the picture that emerges in film is unexpectedly complicated by political confusion, violence, upheaval, and change in the years immediately following World War II to the present. Decolonization and a history of entanglement and dependence clash against each other to produce an agonistic cinematic landscape, whose features are shaped as much by resistance as by complicity.

Finally, in perhaps the most upbeat appraisal presented here of the power of the individual through the regional flows of popular culture, Yoshitaka Mōri considers transnational exchanges of music between Korea and Japan. He adopts and adapts the concept of hybridity to emphasize how such diverse forms of music as *enka* (a "traditional" style of music characterized by melancholy sentiments), alternative rock, and dance music "in-between" Japan and Korea are constructed from their very inception as a blend of influences. In so doing, he demonstrates how this blend is the result of often underground collaborative activities that belie any nationally circumscribed definitions. Are these musicians Korean or Japanese? Does it really matter? As much a modern survey as a critical reading of popular music, Mōri's location of a form of *transnational* cultural production returns us to some of the concerns with Cultural Studies and its role in addressing cultural industries that also animates the first section.

* * * * * *

In a section entitled "Creative Societies, Dynamic Economies" at the OECD Forum 2005, the director of the Marubeni Research Institute, Sugiura Tsutomu declared, "I believe capitalism should be followed by *culturalism*.

> I use the word *culturalism* as the word *capital* is used in *capital*ism. In postmodern economy, capital power is not enough for us to successfully compete in the globalized world. It should be flavored or seasoned with cultural or creative power. In the *culturalism* world, human activities are motivated not by money but rather by cultural attractiveness. All countries, all regions, and all people have their own culture. Every country has an equal chance to become a leading actor in the *culturalism* world. There are no super powers when it comes to culture and happiness.[60]

Sugiura's vision is as ostentatious as it is idealistic. Yet, whether one adopts a "globalist" or "skeptic" approach to the region, his speech highlights how central culture and the cultural industries are to Northeast Asia and perhaps a globalized world overall. It is not just that culture reflects and promotes economic integration, thereby leading on to increasing political co-operation and an enhanced sense of individual affiliation to the region. Rather, the region itself is being constructed discursively, ideologically, and normatively as a cultural entity, one in which welfare is replaced by well-being and quantity of production is superseded by quality of life. Sugiura's, Onodera's, and a host of other visions may simply be paying lip service to what is in the end a social-democratic façade masking very old-fashioned politics, national relationships, social marginalizations, and market fundamentalism.

Cultural Studies and Cultural Industries in Northeast Asia, through the multiplicity of its topics and the diversity of its approaches and assessments, ultimately seeks to question the centrality of culture and the cultural industries in the construction of Northeast Asia. All contributors avoid a simplistic definition of the nation, developing instead a complex understanding that gives primacy of place to the individual as consumer *and* producer, not only of the meaning of cultural products and practices but also to mediate the nation and the region, their respective identities, patriotisms, and chauvinisms. Crucially, all adopt a reflexive approach with the result that this volume not only presents studies of a diverse range of cultural products and practices in their subjective, discursive, normative, and ideological construction of Northeast Asia. It also obliges the reader to ask how we might interrogate our approaches to the study of culture and cultural industries themselves.

I
Reflections on Cultural Studies in/on Northeast Asia

1

Reconsidering East Asian Connectivity and the Usefulness of Media and Cultural Studies

Kōichi Iwabuchi

I remember that, just before I presented this paper under its original title of "On the *Usefulness* of Media and Cultural Studies" at the conference in London, a friend of mine said, "Okay, you are presenting a paper on the uselessness of media and cultural studies." While this was his misreading of the title, I realized it sounded more provocative and perhaps more accurately suggested what I was trying to convey — something about an emergent uneasy sense of doing critical media and cultural studies — and which I am feeling.

I have no intention of generalizing my own sense of frustration. However, I have come to realize the necessity of reviewing what I have done so far and of rethinking the tactic of critical intervention. Over the last ten years or so, what has motivated my academic enthusiasm has been critical engagement with the politics of everyday life through the analysis of media and popular culture. In particular, I have been interested in how to get over the exclusive demarcation of national and cultural boundaries and how to make them more inclusive and dialogic. I have examined these issues especially in the Japanese context and with an attention to media culture connections in East Asia, mostly by looking at people's meaning construction processes in a wider socio-historical context. I have been convinced that I was making sense of the complexity of the ways in which power operates in everyday life through media culture, and this critical study is an *effective* tool to negotiate and contest existing power relations.

However, over the last several years, the optimistic conviction I held in the 1990s has become less certain. Apparently, this is related both to the

increasing concern with border control and national security, especially after
9/11 and, more crucial to the study of transnational media culture flows, to
the escalating penetration of market-fundamentalist corporatism under the
sign of neoliberalism. As is often pointed out, these urgent issues are not
primarily "cultural," and so recently we are witnessing more studies focusing
on political economy issues. This is not to say that the study of people's
meaning construction processes is no longer important or unconnected to
political economy; on the contrary. However, we should more seriously
attend to the operation of political and economic structural restraints on the
process of meaning construction and transborder dialogue. This is imperative
if we do not want to lose sight of "the way in which it [culture] matters —
and hence, its effects — have changed in ways that we have not yet begun
to contextualize or theorize."[1]

In this short essay, I look first at how the logic of corporatism has deeply
penetrated transnational media culture flows and how states are also joining
the game of corporate branding of the nation in ways in which the publicness
of media culture and the possibility of transborder dialogue are severely
hampered by the logic of market profit and national interests. I focus on three
issues: decentering and recentering of transnational media cultural power,
the increasingly systematized connections of national dominant cultures, and
the development of state policies to brand national cultures. Since these
developments are closely related to the prevalent discourses on the pragmatic
uses of culture in neoliberal terms, they inevitably compel us to reconsider
the meaning of usefulness and practicality in regard to our own critical
research, so that we can pursue effective ways, not just theoretically, of
intervention in the realpolitik.

The Reconfiguration of Decentered Power Networks

Let me focus on one of my major areas of research — media culture flows
and connections in East Asia. Studies on intra-Asian media flows and
connections have become active since the mid-1990s, and I am one among
many who have been fascinated with this emerging phenomenon. Cultural
traffic within East and Southeast Asia has indeed been blossoming as
globalization advances. Since the mid-1990s in particular, close partnerships
have been formed in the media industries as companies pursue marketing
strategies and joint production ventures spanning several different markets.
Popular culture from places like Japan, Hong Kong, and South Korea is
finding unprecedented acceptance all over the region, leading to the formation

of new links among people in Asia, especially youth. This trend has shown no sign of letting up. Asian markets have become even more synchronized, joint East Asian projects in film and music have become more common, and singers and actors from around the region are engaged in more and more activities that transcend national borders.

However, more than ten years have passed since I started my research on this issue, and I cannot help but notice corporatist forces becoming more and more robust in the governing of media culture flows. We are no longer naively persuaded by statements such as "Asian media culture de-Westernizes media globalization," but have even become skeptical about it. It is undoubtedly true that the rise of Asian media outflows and intra-Asian flows is a great testimony to the relative decline of American media power. However, the increase in Japanese and other East Asian cultural exports to the global market, and in particular to the markets of East and Southeast Asia, can be seen as a sign that significant changes are occurring in cross-border cultural traffic. Cultural exports have boomed over the past decade, a time when the globalization of culture has accelerated through the integration of markets and capital by giant multinational corporations, astonishing advances in communications technology enabling people in all corners of the globe to link up instantaneously, and the emergence of affluent middle-class consumers in non-Western countries. The complex interaction of these factors has made transnational flows of culture more complex, inconsistent, and unpredictable, at the same time generating a new kind of recentering of power relations.

It would be incomprehensible to deny the enormity of global cultural influence of the United States, but it is also too simplistic to straightforwardly equate globalization with Americanization. It is no longer possible to understand the structure of global cultural power as bipartite, with one-way transfers of culture from the center to the periphery. Cultural power still does matter, but it has become decentralized, dispersed, and interpenetrating. The decentralization of power can be seen in the emergence of multinational corporations from Japan and other non-Western countries as global players, but this does not mean that a new center is emerging to take the place of the United States. Rather, cross-border partnerships and co-operation among media and cultural industries and capital involving Japan and other non-Western developed countries are being driven forward, with the US as a pivotal presence. While the inroads Japanese companies have made into Hollywood and the global diffusion of anime and video games, for example, might look like signs that the US is, comparatively speaking, losing its global cultural hegemony, in reality these phenomena simply illustrate that the pattern of global dominance by multinational media conglomerates centered on the US is becoming more firmly entrenched. Sony's 1989 purchase of a major Hollywood studio was a dramatic demonstration of the breakthrough of Japanese corporations into the global entertainment software business, but this was always a matter of Japanese firms integrating themselves into American cultural power and distribution networks rather than taking the place of America. The spread of Japanese anime and video games throughout the world has also been underpinned by the stepping up of mergers, partnerships, and other forms of co-operation among multinational media corporations based in developed countries, principally the United States. Without US distribution networks, Pokémon (distributed by Warner Bros.) and the anime films of Miyazaki Hayao (distributed by Disney) would not have been released worldwide. What is more, the Pokémon anime series and movies seen by audiences around the world — with the exception of those seen in some parts of Asia — have been "Americanized" by Nintendo of America, a process that involves removing some of their Japaneseness to make them more acceptable to global audiences.[2]

Now that Hollywood has actively incorporated East Asian cultures in the employment of directors and actors, the remaking of Japanese and Korean films and co-production with Asian film industries, this tendency has become ever more deeply structured. A worldwide recentering of media productions, especially films, is going on as the marketing range of media culture has become more and more international than before. Cultural power in the age of globalization is not concentrated in the place where the culture originates. The structure of global cultural power is being reorganized from a pattern of rule with the centralization of power in the dominant country to one that is highly dispersed and ubiquitous, spearheaded by multinational corporations based in developed countries.

The new configuration of decentered power networks also exploits locally specific meaning construction in a particular manner. It is widely argued that globally disseminated cultural products and images are consumed and reconfigured through a process of hybridization in each locality. American popular culture is exported to countries throughout the world, but the cultural products that perform best are those that mix in local elements while absorbing American cultural influences. Meanings are negotiated locally, resulting in the creation of new products that are more than mere copies. Yet we should not forget that this increase in cultural diversity is being governed by the logic of capital and organized within the context of globalization.[3] Globalization does not destroy cultural differences but rather brings about a "peculiar form of homogenization" while fostering them.[4]

The global spread of American consumer culture has led to the creation of a series of cultural formats through which various differences can be adjusted. These formats could be described as the axis of the global cultural system. In this sense, one could say that "America" has become a base format that regulates the process by which modern culture is configured around the world. As multinational media corporations press ahead with global tie-ups and partnerships, they are also trying to raise their profits by tailoring this axis to every corner of the world while promoting cultural diversity in every market. The world is becoming more diverse through standardization and more standardized through diversification, but its cultural dynamic is driven by the marketing logic of multinational corporations, which tend to foster dominant stereotypes of national cultures and to disregard unbeneficial cultural differences.

Regional media culture flows in East Asia are not free from this decentering-recentering force either. As exemplified by Star TV, owned by News Corporation and MTV Asia, global media giants are penetrating regional media flows by deploying localization strategies. It should also be noted that the activation of regional media flows is based on the rise of regional hubs such as Japan, Korea, Hong Kong, and Taiwan, and their corporate alliances. Major media corporations are forging transnational partnerships and facilitating mutual promotion of media culture. Co-production and remakes of films are becoming more common, with the aim of targeting multiple markets in the region, which can be seen as the emergence of "Asiawood."[5] These decentering trends in the region indicate the activation of multidirectional flows. However, in reality, the mode of media production is being recentered through the alliance of major media corporations in East Asian countries. This development engenders a new international hierarchy in production capacity, with Japan, Korea, Hong Kong, and Taiwan in the top tier. In this sense, how and whether East Asian media culture flows are actually alternative imaginaries to American ones is not clear.

Here, it should be noted that emerging transnational connections through popular culture are predominantly ones among media and cultural industries in urban areas of developed countries. The more intensified media culture flows become, the more obvious this tendency appears. While the circulation of made-in-Asia texts are becoming more common in many parts of urban spaces in East Asia, the kinds of text circulating are mostly restricted to commercially and ideologically hegemonic ones in each country. Here we are now witnessing exchange among the dominant cultures of East Asia and a loose network among East Asian media industries that produce, distribute, and market nationally dominant "Asian mass culture," which does not do justice to cultural differences, inequality, and marginalization in each society in gender, sexuality, race, ethnicity, region, class, migration, and so forth.

Needless to say, this is not to dismiss the significance of various kinds of people's decentering cultural practices that try to express alternative and resistant views. Yet, we need to do something more to prevent these visions and practices from being uncritically absorbed into the everyday and to rearticulate them in order that they might effectively persuade a wider public.[6] We need to consider how to transform them into "a systemic counter to corporate destructiveness" that subtly depoliticizes such resistant activities and practices in a way to render them "an irritant."[7]

Reflective yet Uneven Consumption

These emerging structures of uneven transnationality in the field of media culture have cast a shadow on the possibility of transborder dialogues and connections. Many studies have shown that media consumption has brought about new kinds of relationships, mutual understandings, and reflexivity about one's own society and culture.[8] In Japan, high hopes have been held out for popular culture's potential to facilitate cultural dialogue, particularly in its capacity to improve Japan's reputation and transcend Japan's historically constituted problematic relations with other East and Southeast Asian countries. Certainly, the dissemination of enjoyable Japanese contemporary culture has introduced the sociocultural issues and concerns that many young people in the region share. Furthermore, my own research demonstrates that the consumption of Hong Kong or Korean media cultures in Japan has somewhat destabilized a historically constituted belief in Japan's superiority over the rest of Asia — a kind of thinking that, while accepting that the country belongs geographically and culturally to Asia, at the same time makes a distinction between Japan and Asia.

The mediated encounter with other Asian modernities may make Japanese people realize that they now inhabit the same developmental time zone as people in other Asian regions and that the peoples of Asia, washed by similar waves of modernization, urbanization, and globalization, have experienced these phenomena in similar yet different ways in their own particular contexts. Considerable numbers of people are also actually visiting other Asian cities, meeting people there, starting to learn local languages, and reading something about Japan's colonial history. Most notably, media connections have dramatically improved the relationship between Japan and Korea as the people have come to hold much better images of their neighbors.

This may prove an opportune moment for Japanese people to critically review the state of their own culture, society, and historical relationship with other parts of Asia. As popular cultural flows are becoming more multilateral and regular, they might also be significantly furthering cultural exchange and mutual understanding among youths in East Asia on a large scale that has never been observed before. Undoubtedly, there is a great possibility of cross-national dialogues engendered by media culture flows, as the personal is always political, and everyday mundane meaning construction through the media is an indispensable part of the public participation.[9]

At the same time, however, there is much imbalance, not just in the quantity and the vector of the flows but also in the perception and appreciation of spatio-temporal distance or proximity, as discussed above. As East and Southeast Asian media culture prospers and triggers regional exchange, it is also reproducing views of other Asians as not-quite-modern and leading to structural unevenness. An awareness of "familiar" cultural differences in East Asia developed through the consumption of popular culture, for example, does not necessarily lead to the kind of shared sense of contemporaneity that promotes cultural dialogue on equal terms. Indeed, flows of popular culture from other Asian countries into Japan are also arousing a contrasting sense that these countries still lag behind Japan, albeit slightly. As Asian culture is consumed more widely in Japan, Orientalist thinking that attempts to understand Asia's present by equating it with Japan's past good times has insistently reared its head.[10]

Again, the new connections being forged through popular culture in Asia, because they are based on globalized consumerism, are reinforcing discriminatory practices of inclusion and exclusion of certain groups. The links brought about by popular culture consumption are above all the ones among the relatively affluent people (in the case of TV dramas, particularly women), most of whom live in urban areas. They thus exclude a tremendous number of places and people. When the Taliban government was chased from Kabul in November 2001, Japanese newspapers carried as a symbol of peace a picture of Afghan children having fun playing Japanese-made video games. But one cannot compare the way children in Kabul who had just escaped a war devoured these games while sitting outdoors with how children in the safety of their homes in Tokyo or Hong Kong fool around with them. This is not to totalize and essentialize the division between people by place of residence and class. The development of media communication technologies and their increasing accessibility have blurred social boundaries and division and promoted "no sense of place."[11] However, we need to remember that such blurring practices have brought about not just cross-boundary connectivities but also cross-boundary divisions such as the widening gap between haves and have-nots and the uneven economy of attention. East Asian connections forged through popular cultural consumption are underpinned by the power of multinational corporations and capital (and the absolute US military strength that supports this system); these bodies benefit some and exclude others, while acting freely beyond the confines of national frameworks in accordance with the fundamental tenets of consumerism.

Brand Nationalism

In relation to this unevenness, we should not dismiss the persisting relevance of the framework of the nation-state in the new configuration of uneven media culture connections. While the main corporate actors of cultural globalization disregard the rigid boundaries of nation-states, their national origins are limited to a small number of powerful nations, including Japan. Furthermore, transnational corporations still operate most of their transnational business from their home country. As a result, their profits are enjoyed largely within national boundaries.[12] Cultural commodities and images are predominantly produced by a small number of wealthy countries, including Japan, and many parts of the world still cannot even afford to produce substantial local media cultures. Sreberny-Mohammadi's argument about the continuing importance of the nation-state, made about fifteen years ago, is even more imperative now that the framework of the nation-state, both as a spatially controlled entity and as a discursively articulated geography, is not losing its prominence in the analysis of uneven global cultural flows.[13]

This point has become even more salient as states have become eager to see the creation and promotion of "cool" national brands. In the 1980s and 1990s, "culture" extended its role to other spheres and became a useful vehicle for various social actors, including marginalized people and NGOs, to pursue their own political and economic interests.[14] Today, however, it is the alliance of the national governments and private (transnational) corporations that most powerfully uses "culture" in the promotion of national brand cultures in media texts, tourism, fashion, food, and so forth. For states to maximize national interests and beat international competition, culture has come to be regarded as important politically to enhance "soft power," and as important economically for attracting multinational capital and developing new industries in which creative industries play a significant role. Here we are witnessing the rise of brand nationalism.

Perhaps "Cool Britannia" is the most famous state policy of this sort, but many national governments in East Asia are also eager to pursue this kind of policy. It is well known that the Korean government engaged with this policy in the 1990s and that this contributed to the Korean Wave. Following this Korean success, the Japanese government has actively also sought to develop cultural policy. "Cool Japan" products are expected to become another Japanese core export commodity, and the Japanese government has organized several committees to discuss what policies need to be implemented. Many Japanese universities have also established programs to train professional creators by inviting the participation of prominent film directors and animation producers, including the internationally renowned film directors, Kitano Takeshi and Kurosawa Kiyoshi.

Politically, it is anticipated that media culture will improve the image of Japan in East Asia to such an extent that the historical memory of Japanese colonialism will be eradicated in the region. The need to export Japanese media culture is being even more eagerly discussed with the recent rise of anti-Japanese feeling in China and Korea vis-à-vis historical and territorial issues. Following a recent survey that revealed that Korean youth who consume Japanese popular culture tend to feel more empathy with Japan (*Asahi Shinbun*, April 27, 2005), the imperative to step up the export of media culture to Asian markets has been even more stressed. This strategy is viewed as strengthening Japan's cultural diplomacy as it presents, from a Japanese perspective, an opportunity to enhance Asia's understanding of a postwar "liberated" and "humane" Japan.

While the importance of using media cultures for enhancing national interests may seem unequivocal, discussion of Japanese cultural exports tends to be confined to a narrow context at the expense of wider public interests. Media culture's potential to stimulate transnational dialogue should certainly not be dismissed out of hand; it has promoted new kinds of mutual understanding and connections in East Asia. However, even though mediated cultural exchange may improve the image of the nation and enhance a sense of empathy and belonging in its audiences, history and the memory of colonialism cannot be easily erased. Historical issues necessitate sincere dialogue with the broad involvement of all citizens, which cultural policy should try to promote.

A preoccupation with market-oriented and international policy concerns will fail to give due attention to marginalized cultures and to the issues (re)generated by transnational cultural flows. There is an urgent need to discuss and develop policy agendas on various issues, such as the high concentration of media ownership in the hands of a few global companies; intellectual property rights; and the transnational, international, and intra-national division of cultural labor.[15] It is also worth reiterating that the new connections being forged through media culture are reinforcing practices of inclusion and exclusion of certain groups in society. In East Asia, transnational links have been developed between the dominant media industries and between dominant media cultures of metropolises. The rise of brand nationalism does not give due attention to the promotion of "unprofitable" cultural expressions and marginalized voices, and even discourages the public discussion over such issues in the name of national interests. These uneven market-oriented transnational flows and connections are furthered by collaboration between nation-states and the private media sector in the branding of the nation.

Useful Media and Cultural Studies

Finally, let me get back to the question of the usefulness of media and cultural studies. There is an optimistic view that the media are stimulating cosmopolitan awareness among the inhabitants of the "global village," but this view seems less feasible now. A series of political and economic developments at the beginning of the twenty-first century has again revealed how economic disparities around the world are growing to desperate levels and how discourses about "them" — those savage rogues that threaten "us" — are being replicated worldwide. As states intensify their alliance with (multinational) corporations, whereby the borders clearly dividing nations and cultures are being more tightly controlled, the power structure is ubiquitously recentered, and exclusion and imbalance are being institutionalized on a number of levels, one of which is East Asian media culture traffic. In this situation, it is indeed imperative to engage critically with the pragmatic administration (of cultural transnationalism) that strives to use media culture for narrow-minded national interests, and which significantly constrains the possibility of transborder dialogues. Critically attending to how Japanese and other East Asian media industries and their products are collusive in producing cultural asymmetry and indifference has become more crucial than ever before. A key question is how we can cultivate social imagination that would encourage people's mutual engagement beyond national and cultural divides with various aggravated social and cultural issues of our time.

However, for this to happen, we also need to tackle the questions of how to institutionalize critical insights into the politics of media and culture in everyday life that have been developed by various media and cultural studies practitioners, and how to convince the public that cultural issues still do matter even when a concern with hard politics, conflicts, and neoliberalism seems to dominate the world we are living in and highly sophisticated cultural theories are perceived as out of touch with people's everyday feelings and experiences. I do believe that media and cultural studies still retains its impulse to critically intervene in realpolitik and that its relevance is even intensifying, but, as Ien Ang rightly argues, we are now urged to face more seriously the challenge of how to reconcile the "critical" and the "practical."[16] While academics are also under strong pressure to produce immediate results and contribute to institutions and society, we should contrive our way of being practical in knowledge production. This is not to say that researchers should work within an ivory tower. As researchers, our task is to address awkward normative questions by charmingly and intelligibly demonstrating that the usefulness of critical cultural research is "stretched beyond the level of immediacy," because "keeping questions open is actually useful, that thinking more complexly and reflexively about issues is actually practical, if not here and now then in the longer term" and to convince the public that nothing is more practical than critical engagement with the way things are organized, "to offer better descriptions and accounts that do not shy away from complexity, contingency and contestation to open up new possibilities."[17] Being useless at the level of immediacy is often more practical in the long-lasting pursuit of a more democratic use of media culture.

At the same time, I would suggest that, if the logic of immediate production of results has so deeply penetrated in our society, we should make an extra effort to make our version of "usefulness" reach a wider public and persuade them of its practicality, rather than just being satisfied with its good circulation and critical discussion within the academy. Some means to achieve this could include contriving pedagogical practices inside and outside schools, working with public and private institutions that administer cultural policy and production, and writing more to the public through the mass media. In any case, we need to make a pragmatic critique within, not from outside of, existing institutional formations to balance dominant discourses on cultural issues "against the less instrumental engagement of critique," even though we all know that this is rather a risky business for academics.[18]

At the 2006 conference of the International Association for Cultural Studies in Istanbul, we discussed the image of the intellectual. Chris Healy, from Melbourne University, concluded that it was an "ethical aunt." In his discussion of the representation of intellectuals, Said (1994) argues for an image of "amateur" who is motivated and committed by worldly issues in the society and contesting sincerely against the oppressive authority.[19] At the same time, intellectuals seem now to be required to strive more than ever to facilitate transborder dialogues of various kinds. The duty of academics is not just confined to offering an interpretation and analysis of the complexity of what is happening in an intangible manner and making a sound criticism against authority. The image of the "ethical aunt," like that of organic intellectuals, represents the role of the intellectual as going between the state and the civic, between corporatism and public-ness and between people who are divided by various boundaries. The image of the "ethical aunt," however, shows the necessity of engaging with the mundane labor of the go-between more consciously and effectively to work not just "for" but "with" institutions, corporatism, and people, with a determined will to promote the creation of "common culture" that promises people's democratic participation in public dialogues.[20]

Having said this all, I do not have a ready-to-hand method for it. But no worries; be optimistic. After all, my sense of frustration might be derived from my sense of compulsion that I need to engage with cultural issues in a way to bring about an immediate change to society. This may be to fall into the trap of neoliberal discourse by accepting its rules for contesting its very logic. For now I would rather commit myself to working hard and steadily at what I can do in everyday life to generate dialogues among citizens of the world for the construction of a more open and inclusive society in the future. For this purpose, media and cultural studies is still useful to me.

2

Asian Cultural Studies:
Recapturing the Encounter with the Heterogeneous in Cultural Studies

Michael Dutton

I want to discuss the radical potential of an Asian Cultural Studies. But, before I can do that, I must firstly address another question. Can one really even speak of an "Asian Cultural Studies"? After all, between the two fields of Asian Area Studies and the parallel universe that is Postcolonialism, there appears to be little geographic or theoretical room to constitute such a field. Despite this, that is precisely what appears to be happening with the emergence of journals such as *positions, Traces* and *Inter-Asia,* projects such as this one, and, perhaps most significantly, the emergence of strong centers of Cultural Studies outside the usual Anglo–American world. From Seoul, to Hong Kong and on to Taipei, Shanghai, Beijing, Tokyo, and Singapore, new centers of Cultural Studies are making their appearance and producing work that throws up a set of potentially challenging questions that could redefine Asian Area Studies in the West. This challenges the hegemonic position of Western voices speaking authoritatively about Asia and, even more radically, challenges the epistemological assumptions that underpin that work.

We are, therefore, beginning to see the slow and somewhat shaky appearance of a new field we could call "Asian Cultural Studies." I say slow and shaky because, intellectually, this new field is being pulled by Area Studies and Postcolonialism in two distinct directions as both attempt to claim sovereignty over it. For the moment, then, Asian Cultural Studies is less a new field than a disputed territory where questions of intellectual sovereignty are yet to be settled. Let me endeavor, if not to settle these disputes, then, at the very least, to figure out what is at stake here.

The largely US-dominated field of Asian Area Studies would, with some validity, see a Cultural Studies approach as being its wayward child. It is, for area studies, both a thing of youthful intellectual exuberance and promise within "the field," but also something that is regarded as suspiciously trendy, light, postmodern, and Marxist. It is not, therefore, an area of serious intellectual or policy pursuit. For Postcolonialism, Cultural Studies is less a sub-area than a kindred spirit. The postmodern, Marxist, literary, and cultural bent of postcolonial scholarship cements this link even though the themes of hybridity, difference, and the centrality of the question of the colonial legacy tend away from many of the themes central to the constitution of Cultural Studies. Moreover, the geographic shift of the field, away from a single largely American-centric focus to one that is now established across an array of Asian centers, opens onto questions that potentially decenter the knowledge not just geographically but also intellectually. In both Asian Studies and Postcolonialism, then, the ownership claims over an Asian Cultural Studies, while not without validity, are far from being claims to full ownership. While Postcolonialism has proven to be a crucial intellectual precursor to an Asian Cultural Studies and shares with that field a certain theoretical "family resemblance," the connections between the predominantly Western Area Studies and this new Asian-centric Cultural Studies are, intellectually far more fraught and raise far greater anxieties.

For Western Asian Area Studies knowledge, there is a latent anxiety about the worthiness of the notion of culture central to the constitution of Cultural Studies. The reason is that Western Area Studies is, in many ways, the social science turn of Oriental Studies. As such, it drew away from Oriental Studies but still picked up from that discipline a set of assumptions about culture that are in many ways, antithetical to the notion of culture in Cultural Studies. This was hard for Area Studies to avoid, as this Western tradition of Oriental Studies was a field almost defined by the question of culture. In Western Oriental Studies, however, "culture" meant "high culture" and an understanding of this was thought to be crucial to any appreciation of the past great civilizations of the Orient. Oriental Studies was, in the main, interested and only interested in the "great civilizations" of the East.

Emerging in the West at the moment of supremely confident empire, Oriental Studies displayed what Raymond Schwab once called a "condescending veneration" toward Oriental civilizations' past.[1] Operating within an enlightenment tradition of progress, Oriental Studies formed an illuminated two-way mirror that shone upon the greatness of "other" [read Asian] past civilizations only to further illuminate the greatness of the contemporary West. Through science, technology, and industry the West, after all, had conquered most of the known world and established empires in which the reason of civilization was transformed into the white man's burden. As an intellectual domain of the latest and greatest civilization, Oriental Studies in the West believed their approach situated them on an Archimedean point enabling the truth of formerly great societies of the non-West to shine through. As reason and science played such a critical role in the construction of this narrative, great weight was placed upon the scientific method, and gradually one discovers that this not only spread to scholars in the non-Western world but also to those scholarly endeavors concerned with the geographical space monopolized by Oriental Studies scholarship.[2]

This single-minded emphasis upon unearthing past great civilizations began to fade as (social) scientific knowledge of the non-West spread. Asian Area Studies, in superseding Oriental Studies, offered the promise of a new, more (social) scientific approach while maintaining a recognition of the importance of (high) culture. In place of questions of past civilizations lost, Asian Area Studies employed modernization theory and other versions of positivist social science to recast the problematic of intellectual engagement with the non-West.

No longer would the intellectual spotlight be upon the greatness of the non-Western civilizations of the past but would instead turn the focus toward the contemporary failures of these non-Western societies mired in backward traditions. Focusing on the problems of the present and armed with a Parsonian-inspired certainty in scientific method, modernization theory constantly coded difference as lack and lack as a deleterious effect of cultural tradition. Thus, despite this "scientific" refocusing of concerns, Oriental Studies made a backdoor reappearance. Asian Area Studies maintained the privileging of Western knowledge and society that was once central to the development of Oriental Studies, but the focus on past great civilizations and high culture of this latter knowledge form were now understood as "tradition." With Area Studies, however, the "condescending veneration" of Oriental Studies gave way to a darker understanding of tradition as that which was blocking the development of the modern in the non-Western world.

There is less faith in modernization theory these days, but one still finds, in myriad micro-level ways, the seepage of this idea of a "cultural tradition" operating more discretely as a framing device for contemporary Asian Area Studies intellectual concerns. In Western studies of Chinese politics, for example, one still finds a tendency to focus upon elite factional infighting, upon the laws of the state, and upon the bureaucracies that enforce that state's power. While addressed in the language of social science, the focus, questions, and concerns of this subfield still force us back into what is little more than a new way of thinking through the category of Oriental despotism.

In Chinese politics, not only does this enable an almost unquestioning and homologizing analysis of Mao as emperor surrounded by a court, but perhaps more perniciously and certainly more generally, it helps bolster a view that politics in China is primarily about questions of the struggle of the people attempting to break free of the yoke of a despotic, totalitarian and, as it so happens, Oriental state. If the political focus of the subdiscipline of Chinese politics centers on the question of despotism, then in relation to the fields of art and literature, the great civilization narrative tracks toward the continuation of the search for high art and great literature, while in intellectual history it reinforces the focus upon the intellectual elite who are said to have always been important because of the Chinese cultural tradition of literati-officials. In other words, Area Studies has, on the whole and in the main, tended to continue to operate around an understanding of the operation of the state that is drawn from the same wellspring of the great civilizations/ Oriental Despotism discourse.

It is this that is potentially threatened by more recent social and cultural theory. While the focus of Cultural Studies upon questions of "the everyday" and "the popular" challenge the "high cultural" focus of this approach, theoretical questions arising from the new humanities, postmodern social theory, and psychoanalysis that have come to inform Cultural Studies tend to problematize the unity of notions such as the "Orient" and the despot. There should be little need for me to point to the political consequences of these two theoretical and conceptual moves other than to say that they share a certain kinship with the development of the Subaltern Studies School on the one hand, and Edward Said's devastating critique of the link between Orientalist knowledge and colonialism on the other. Nor, perhaps, is there a need for me to show that the logic of deconstruction (or psychoanalysis) leads to a formal questioning of concepts like the despot, the totality, and the law of the father. It is, however, important to note that, in shifting attention from "high culture" to "the everyday," Cultural Studies also, albeit more indirectly and for different reasons, challenges these understandings.

Shifting its focus away from the law of the father towards the fashions of the son meant that Cultural Studies intrinsically questioned the singularity of the notion of "culture" at the same time as it disinterred the occluded heterogeneity of the everyday. In turning its gaze away from the despot and casting an eye upon the popular, Cultural Studies refocused intellectual concerns upon the vernacular-speaking, popular, and everyday world. It naturally meant a focus on the heterogeneous. The shift in the empirical focus then forced certain changes to take place at a theoretical level.

In Britain, for example, the radical turn affected by the Birmingham School had, as its most obvious indigenous progenitor, the 1930s sociology of the Mass Observation movement, but its intellectual influences were drawn from rather more heterodox sources. Certainly, its most obvious and direct influence came from the British Marxist tradition in general and Raymond Williams's work on culture in particular. But as British cultural studies grew and Marxism itself became a radical political and social movement drawing theoretical inspiration from continental sources, Cultural Studies also developed a more European and philosophical orientation.

Political activism opened directly onto continental Marxist thought, feminism, Lacanian psychoanalysis, and a little later postmodern theory. As a consequence of these influences, Cultural Studies would be drawn toward broader and older theoretical inspirations. Bahktin's group on language and the carnival, the Lacan Circle on psychoanalysis, Bataille's College of Sociology's interest in excess, not to mention the radical turn occasioned by feminist theory, all played some part in influencing the questions being posed and the research approaches being adopted toward popular culture. Perhaps the most contested and problematic continental influence came from the Frankfurt School.

Theodor Adorno's elitist dismissal of popular culture crushed the chances of any full engagement with this, leading Kate Soper to suggest Cultural Studies had little by way of a "direct bequest" from this school. Despite this, it has to be acknowledged that much of the critical vocabulary through which British Cultural Studies began to think anew questions of popular culture came from this legacy.[3] There is, of course, one exception to the general dismissal of critical theory and that comes in the figure of Walter Benjamin, who has been described as Cultural Studies' favorite son.[4]

It is, perhaps, in the work of Walter Benjamin that the philosophical possibilities of Cultural Studies was laid out most clearly in what he once called his monadological method. This method reversed the order of philosophy so that intellectual endeavors would focus not on the universal but on the concrete and the particular. Whereas traditional philosophical theory, according to Benjamin, "drains objects of their concrete plenitude," the monadological approach "burrows into the material thicket in order to unfold the dialectic of the essential." With this, says Kracauer appreciatively, "ideas jump between one another like electric sparks rather than being formally 'sublated' into a formal concept."[5] Despite Benjamin's resurrection within Cultural Studies as the philosopher of the pavement, his ideas held no monopoly on contemporary Cultural Studies approaches and there was always, within this field, a theoretical counter-tendency holding out the prospects of a much more conventionally sociological approach.

This clash of approaches is perhaps most evident today in the desire for a cultural policy approach. This, however, is just the latest edition in a much longer debate that takes us back to the West and to the thirties. Indeed, early developments that were to help found Cultural Studies as a distinctive endeavor were, in part, derived from the culture–policy clash that emerged as a result of Theodor Adorno's involvement in Paul Lazarsfeld's Princeton "Radio Research Project."

Begun by Lazarsfeld in 1937, this project was the first empirically grounded overview of a new cultural event: radio listening habits. This was at a moment when the power of radio upon the population was raising a series of social, political, and economic concerns. It was feared that its potentially edifying, educational value was being squandered in trivial pursuits sponsored by a rapacious advertising industry or alternatively hijacked for totalitarian political ends.[6] Lazarsfeld's study was part of a project to rescue radio so that it could bring "serious radio listening" to the American public. Lazarsfeld's aim was to promote the use of radio so that it could function like a serious book — with all its edifying and educational effects — upon the radio listener. Yet if the project is remembered at all today, it is remembered for only one thing: it was Theodor Adorno's meal ticket into the United States.

So why would Paul Lazarsfeld, who is arguably the founder of modern empirical sociology, be interested in someone like Adorno?[7] Essentially, the reason is Adorno's highly critical and elitist assessment of jazz. For Lazarsfeld, Adorno offered to broaden the theoretical parameters of the music research project. Essentially, Lazarsfeld hoped to wed Adorno's theoretical approach to a set of empirically grounded and field-research-based questionnaires and interviews. This attempt to translate Adorno's work into an empirically assessable set of research questions proved to be something of a disaster, not least because of Adorno himself.

Because of complaints about his interview method being random and unsystematic, his talks with radio personalities biased and distorted, and his discussions with American jazz musicians (who claimed that through radio they were disseminating culture to American high school children) resulting in Adorno labeling them all "idiots," Lazarsfeld carpeted him. Writing to him of the need for a major revision of his research methodology, Lazarsfeld summarized his own views into a series of points:

"My objections can be grouped around three statements," he would write to Adorno. These are:

> [1] You don't exhaust the logical alternatives of your own statements and as a result much of what you say is either wrong or unfounded or bias;
> [2] You are uninformed about empirical research work but write about it in authoritative language, so that the reader is forced to doubt your authority in your own musical field;
> [3] You attack other people as fetishist, neurotic and sloppy but you show yourself the same traits very clearly.[8]

To bring Adorno to heel, Lazarsfeld proposed an alternative approach. Focusing on an empirically grounded "typology of listeners" that could be tested and verified, he called upon Adorno to mend his ways. But Adorno responded to this call for a typology of listeners with a "typology of emotional types" in which, he insisted, crying would be his most significant object of analysis!

Today, few would remember this "radio project," but who in Cultural Studies would not know of Adorno's contribution? Indeed, Adorno's (in)famous work on the culture industry was to find one of its earliest expressions in his trenchant criticisms of the American music industry, which were a direct result of his involvement in this radio project. The American music industry's penchant for standardizing songs, wrote Adorno, made these cultural products "pre-digested." Its promotion of a pseudo-individualization, he insisted, created a false sense of freedom and this whole cultural system, he concluded, was complicit in the process of commodification that reduced people to things. In other words, Adorno's work on the "radio project" led to what is arguably the founding document of the (relatively) new field of Cultural Studies. It could do this, however, only by freeing itself of the encumbrance of Lazarsfeld's approach.

Adorno and the Frankfurt School's struggle to find an alternative way of approaching popular culture is remembered here, not so much because it was one of the first explicit attempts to bring theory and policy together but because it shows the incommensurability of the critical theory approach with the empirically driven, quantitative approach of Lazarsfeld's, that Adorno so derisively labeled "administrative research."[9]

It is this incommensurability captured not in "The Culture Industry" essay itself but more generally in Adorno's "style of thought," that would set him apart from Lazarsfeld and show what was actually at stake for Cultural Studies in this dispute. Leaving aside the easily made claim of snobbishness — a claim, I might add, which is as applicable to Adorno as it is to Lazarsfeld

— what is actually at stake here is, I believe, a particular "way of doing." This particular "style of thought," I would somewhat contentiously argue, opens onto the possibility of a much broader critique of Western knowledge systems, and this broader critique actually comes to threaten the concept of reason that underpins critical theory's broader project of resurrecting the enlightenment project.

So what was this style of thought upon which I am placing so much weight? Adorno's objections to the underlying philosophical foundations of Lazarsfeld's study sum up well his "style of thought": "I reflected that culture was simply the condition that precluded a mentality that tried to measure it."[10] If culture is a condition that refuses measurement, if it is accessible only by a typology of emotions, does it not, in turn, come to border that rather strange world that Georges Bataille once labeled the heterological? After all, as Bataille himself notes, "An object of an affective relation is 'necessarily *heterogeneous*'."[11] If, then, culture defies measurement and is accessible only via the realm of tears, joy, excitements, and other forms that require an understanding of emotions, it is transformed into a key to an understanding of that side of us all that Bataille labeled the heterological world of the erotic, the excessive, the passionate and the immeasurable and stands in contrast to the homogeneous world of science, production, and technics. Is there not, then, in this moment when Adorno looks aghast at Lazarsfeld's positivism, the possibility of opening onto a form when critical theory's entire enlightenment project is, itself, forced to blink? Perhaps I am placing too much weight on this single statement of Adorno's and on his alternative, a typology of emotions. Nevertheless, in emphasizing (or even inventing) this side to Adorno's thought, I am able to cast a stronger light upon the possibilities of a radical form of Asian Cultural Studies that takes the world of gods and spirits seriously.

Let us, however, move away from Adorno to another style of thought that offers another equally challenging and, if anything, more politically charged possibility. I am thinking here of Edward Said's seminal work on Orientalism, in which he speaks of Western approaches to other cultures as being founded upon a particularly colonialist "style of thought" that ontologically and epistemologically privileges the knowledge base of the West over that of the rest.

"They cannot represent themselves but must be represented," Said argued, stealing a line from Karl Marx.[12] In an argument that takes us from early Oriental Studies right through to contemporary Area Studies, Said shows the way in which this field of Oriental and later Asian Studies constituted a key example of Foucault's idea of power/knowledge.

While Said would recognize shifts within Asian Area Studies away from Oriental Studies, this did little, he claimed, to alter the general argument that these fields produced knowledge forms and effects that reinforced what could be called a colonialism of the mind. Notwithstanding the validity of this overarching argument, what Said's method inadvertently does is flatten the two fields and occlude the possibility of opening on to a very different "style of thought" that could well have flowed out of some of the romanticist tendencies of Oriental Studies that took seriously the possibilities of the sacred to open onto the heterogeneous.

In other words, just as one might reject Adorno's elitism but still recognize the theoretical import of noting the immeasurability of culture and a typology of emotions, so too one might reject the inherent intellectual colonialism of much of traditional Oriental Studies while still hanging onto aspects of its (overly romanticized) claim about the immeasurability of non-Western cultures and the sacred realm within them. In arguing that the approaches of Oriental and Area Studies were both Western ways of colonizing knowledge of the non-West, the differences between the two are occluded. Yet it is in these differences, I would suggest, that the possibility of breaking with the dominant Anglo-American epistemology lies. To appreciate this, I must rehearse what was at stake in the battle between Oriental and Asian Area Studies.

Oriental Studies — which was built around the concerns of language, culture, and "civilization" — began, in the West and in part, as a Christian-inspired and philosophic-theological search for the original languages of Adam. By the time of its demise, Oriental Studies had become a mere ancillary of Asian Studies departments with realist policy imperatives. While the former, warts and all, offered a window onto what Bataille might call the heterogeneous world, the latter not only closed this window but bricked it up with a methodology based on a positivist approach to science, reason, and technics. Asian Cultural Studies has the opportunity of reopening this window and challenging dominant Western forms of reason by showing that the difference of non-Western cultures speaks not just to questions of "local diversity" but to the limits, silences, and occlusions of Western forms of reason that cannot see much less address the radical differences of the non-West. Moreover, the multicentered nature of this new field, wherein scholars are located throughout the world, means that it is potentially more attuned to the power of difference and heterogeneity. Yet Asian Cultural Studies can only turn this heterogeneity and difference from an empirical fact into a theoretical form by avoiding the temptations of identity politics and extending the already existing critique of Asian Area Studies that challenges its very theoretical foundations.

Identity politics does little to rupture the dominant Western ontological-epistemological frame of reason that underpins Area Studies insofar as it is easily incorporated into this framework. With identity politics, non-Western scholarship can all too easily be recast as an albeit wayward version of the "native informant." What is critical is not the identity of the scholar but the theoretical approach. On this front, even critical Asian Area Studies has very little to say. Over the years, critical Area Studies has mounted a compelling case to demonstrate the link between the operation of power and the development of the Western-dominated field of Area Studies. Critics have highlighted the way the Cold War and its security needs have run in tandem with the development of the Asian Studies field. If this critique is to be believed, and I have no reason to doubt it, Asian Area Studies is a field of applied knowledge that is joined at the hip with the colonizing process. Indeed, as these critiques acknowledge, the very founding moment of this particular interdiscipline was inextricably linked to servicing the Western state's Cold War policy and security needs. The state needed analysis that was utilitarian, pragmatic, and empirically grounded.

With the social science turn away from the romanticism of Oriental Studies, Asian Studies offered the promise of a new positivist and scientific understanding of the non-West. Area Studies gained protean life in its applied knowledge framework that was, in turn, geared largely to servicing the policy needs of the state. Policy goals, not a search for those points of immensurability and incommensurability, would propel this interdiscipline. So, with this original Mark of Cain scarring its body, the root cause of the field's theoretical poverty, it has been suggested, could be sheeted home to its proximity to power.

While I am persuaded by this argument, I wonder whether its politically inspired attempts to damn Area Studies by its close working association with and sponsorship by state power actually helps us understand its lack of wonder; its desire, in the language of Bataille, to bring the heterogeneous world into the realm of the homogeneous. Like identity politics, this critique is also all too easily incorporated into the dominant Western way of seeing, for it can simply lead to a claim that, to be genuinely "objective," it needs to free itself of the encumbrances of state. Once freed, science is then free of the temptation to bend the facts to state ends.

If, however, we begin instead by noting that the sponsorship of Asian Area Studies by state power was largely because it was a "style of thought" that localized and repressed the incommensurable, immeasurable and excessive elements of culture and allowed the "Other" to be "calculable," then we come to see the problematic nature of their relationship slightly differently.

Thus, the Orientalism inherent in Area Studies does not just emanate from its proximity to state policy and power but from its "style of thought."

Strangely, I am drawn back to the Frankfurt School to speak of the error of this conflation of theoretical method and state sponsorship. If Asian Area Studies was theoretically reduced to realist (homogeneous) questions and methods merely because of the demands of state, why then, I would ask, wasn't the Frankfurt School similarly reduced to theoretical poverty after its arrival in America and its heavy involvement with the US security apparatus, the OSS?

It is now something of a forgotten fact that it was not *Dialectic of Enlightenment* that lit the flame of the Frankfurt School in the US but Franz Neumann's now largely forgotten 1942 text *Behemoth*.[13] Neumann's text not only secured him a professorship at Columbia University but it also brought the work of the institute as a whole to the attention of the US academy and government. Neumann's trenchant critiques and startling analysis of the Nazi totalitarian regime caused a sensation at this time and proved crucial in moving the Frankfurt School from the margins of the US academy onto center stage. More than that, it secured for this group a seat at the table of power.[14] Neumann's analysis formed the basis of the empirical work undertaken by the Research and Analysis Section of the OSS. Indeed, as one scholar has noted, in relation to the influence of *Behemoth*, the OSS researchers did "little more than attempt to elaborate on its main theses and make them palatable to government officials otherwise unfamiliar with twentieth-century radical thought, let alone known for their Hegelian-Marxist sympathies."[15]

Surely, if the Frankfurt School was sponsored by the same state apparatus that would, six years later,[16] bring us Asian Studies, then the argument that links the theoretical poverty of the latter field to state sponsorship alone needs reexamination. After all, there may be many complaints leveled at the Frankfurt School, but theoretical poverty is not one of them! One may object and say that, when the postwar focus of the US government shifted from Nazism to communism, the conditions that had enabled America to embrace *Behemoth* vanished. This is undoubtedly true, but it ignores the fact that the question I am posing is not about a manifest political Left/Right split but rather a latent form of politics articulated around the very possibilities of taking the heterogeneous world seriously.

The latent political problem that I am referring to here is perhaps more compellingly rendered through the binary division thrown up under the banner of Postcolonialism and famously named by Edward Said as Orientalism. As Said so poetically informed us, "Europe and its Other" is much more than a geographic description of spatial difference. It is an ontologically and epistemologically informed "style of thought" for the appropriation of the non-West into Western knowledge frames. Its principle (although by no means sole) site of operation used to be Oriental Studies, the precursor to contemporary Asian Studies. Where Asian Studies is a march to the social sciences, Oriental Studies is humanities based. Yet this humanities-based scholarship, as I have tried to suggest, had another side that offered the possibility of rejecting the "objective" knowledge forms that were intimately linked to the colonial project, and provides an opportunity for taking the world of gods and ghosts seriously. Once Area Studies began what Tani Barlow has called the Cold War intellectual mapping of the world, any possibility of shining a light on questions of incommensurability vanished.[17]

That is why Adorno's reading of culture as impossible to measure is worthy of recollection, for it is through this that the whole question of incommensurability, and the radical intellectual potentiality of an Asian Cultural Studies, becomes clear. That is also why Said's work proves critical, for it not only pushes us to address the theoretico-philosophical question of representation and examine our own enunciative modalities, but in raising this under the banner of the all too familiar philosophical category of "otherness," it also draws us toward the very limits of translatability and measurability. Said's intervention, in other words, offered a more directly political turn to a cultural debate that once saw Lazarsfeld and Adorno at each other's throats. Yet the challenge thrown up for Asian Cultural Studies is to renew the possibilities opened by this debate and offer a way to address latent forms of political and social expression that refuse incorporation into the dominant social science framework.

It is in the heterodox otherness of popular non-Western culture that a number of theoretical opportunities for creative, critical intellectual work are opened before us. This double move on culture enabled by Asian Cultural Studies — a move that would point to the popular as well as to a radical otherness from the West — should be viewed as an opportunity to reengage with a philosophical tradition that avers both identity politics and mere description. This double otherness of Asian Cultural Studies, when read in this way, leads not to a politics of identity but to an engagement with the heterogeneous. For Adorno, it led to negative dialectics, for Benjamin to the monadological method, and for Bataille, to *dipense*. Yet in all three cases, it points away from a body of work that could be assimilated into the world of applied "objective" knowledge. This approach would then broaden out and refocus our conception of politics and culture so that the heterogeneous remainder within both would become an obstacle halting any easy assimilation into positivist discourses. It would threaten to radically disrupt the dominant ontological-epistemological framing of Western knowledge, but only if it could avoid the temptation of assimilation. A politics of identity is the easiest way in which such assimilation could take place. To avoid that temptation is the radical political choice and that, in turn, points to a focus on that which can never be measured or incorporated.

3

How to Speak about Oneself:
Theory and Identity in Taiwan

Mark Harrison

"What is this nation called Formosa?"

(Ko Kiansing, 1965)[1]

Taiwan jiayou! Taiwan jiayou! [Go Taiwan, go Taiwan!]
(Protesters, Hand-in-Hand Rally, 2004)[2]

In the life of nations, people address themselves and their collective identity in historically specific and changing ways. There are styles and registers with which people talk about themselves as a coherent group. Identities are addressed with certain valorized narratives and themes and legitimized with epistemologies under which people know themselves, and know that they know themselves. These ways of speaking about identity have a politics and a sociology, expressing changing social circumstances as the changing registers of national address.

In Taiwan, as its politics have transformed over fifty years, "theory" in forms such as Cultural Studies and postcoloniality has become a key globalized language for addressing Taiwanese identity among the Taiwanese, folding its own assumptions in the mode of social knowledge it produces into Taiwan's own politics and epistemologies of identity. Cultural Studies retains certain features: an attentiveness to the contingency of language and its relationship to power in social and cultural formations, and an awareness of the self-reflexive and self-consciousness nature of representation and identity. The political history of Taiwan forms a specific set of socio-political conditions in which theory has found a fertile ground in shaping the language of Taiwan's social life. These conditions were established under Taiwan's authoritarian rule, when language in public life was wholly distorted by the features of Taiwan's military government, and have been propelled forward since the lifting of martial law in 1987 by enabling the establishment of a self-conscious identity movement. The crisis of Taiwan's politics and identity has placed the crisis of representation at the heart of its problematic. Within this socio-political context, the task of doing "theory" in Taiwan has fallen to a community of academics and commentators for whom theory energizes relationships to specific globalized modes of address to identity, and places them in specific relationships to Taiwan's changing political life.

The purpose of this essay is to recover continuities in Taiwan's martial law and post-martial law period, and show how the elaborate theoretical innovations of contemporary social and cultural theory are part of an ongoing crisis of representation for Taiwan and a complex outcome for the cultural studies project. The way the Taiwanese speak about themselves is an appeal to the possibility of an identity, an object in suspension, and Cultural Studies has offered the Taiwanese a globalized academic language in which to make such an appeal. At the same time, the relationship between theory as a global discourse and Taiwan as a marginal inchoate nation-state remains a challenge for theory, as it operates within the brute realities of real, empirical power between China, Japan, and the US.

Writing History: Taiwan as Nation

Taiwan, like many other places in Asia, has a history fractured and layered by the ascendance and decline of imperialism, colonialism, and neo-colonialism. Into this history have entered the different ways the Taiwanese have come to know and address themselves as "Taiwanese." Perhaps more so than elsewhere, in view of Taiwan's contested statehood, it produces an intensely politicized discourse of its own identity.

The Taiwanese write their history with geopolitics: Taiwan's first recognizable modern government was a Dutch colonial administration in the mid-seventeenth century. Through the eighteenth and nineteenth centuries, Taiwan was a frontier of the Manchu Qing empire, inscribing the Eastern boundary of a sino-centric notion of the "civilized" and the "uncivilized."[3] In the first half of the twentieth century, following the Sino-Japanese War of 1894, it became a colony of Japan, whose expanding empire drew new boundaries across Asia. Rather than civilized or uncivilized, Taiwan was transformed by the mechanisms of Japanese colonial modernization expressed in modern medicine from a "sick" region to a "healthy" one.[4] After World War II, Taiwan passed to the Republic of China of the Chinese Nationalists (KMT). Beset by corruption and economic collapse, the Taiwanese initiated an abortive uprising known as the 2-28 Incident[5] before the Nationalists lost the Chinese civil war to the Communists and relocated the national government to Taipei in 1949. From 1950, Taiwan fell under the aegis of the United States,[6] through yet new sets of defining boundaries, as a part of the "Free World" as "Free China," against "Red China" and Communism, as a bastion of anti-communist resistance in Asia, and a model of the corporatist, militarist development state.[7]

At the same time, under these hegemonic statist discourses of Taiwan's history and identity over more than 100 years have been a multitude of oppositional political and nationalist counter-narratives. In these, writers, artists, and political and community activists have addressed Taiwanese identity in art and literature, political manifestos, and local politics. Taiwan has been the marginal subject of the provincial and the colonial; in counter-hegemonic anti-Chinese nationalism, it has become both an appeal to an authentic, essential Taiwan and a counter-appeal to a pluralist Taiwan; and it has been self-reflexively theorized by the Taiwanese as the postcolonial. In the late 1980s, following the bitter decades-long political struggle of the democracy and Taiwanese nationalist movements, martial law under the KMT was lifted, democracy enabled, and these narratives have become the material for a self-conscious project of nation- and identity-building.

From the late 1940s, in the immediate aftermath of the 2-28 Incident, a generation of Taiwanese nationalists, such as the US-educated brothers Liao Wen-yi and Liao Wen-kuai, articulated a Taiwanese identity in ways that drew upon some of the prevailing forms of the internationalized address of nationalism of the period. They wrote Taiwanese history as a national history, constructing a teleology of the historical realization of the "truth" of the nation — in the case of Taiwan as a nation forged in a struggle against Manchu, Japanese, and Chinese oppression. They also drew upon the conventional appeals of nationalisms to identity as an essentialist, undifferentiatable sign, to the people of Taiwan as wholly and uniquely "Taiwanese."[8] Living on the boundary of China, this was an ambiguous move. Early Taiwanese nationalists at once appealed to the indivisible sign of "Taiwan" but made that sign meaningful in reference to the military dictatorship of the Chinese Nationalists and the threat of the Chinese Communists by its differentiation from "China" and the Chinese. In Tokyo in 1962, the exiled nationalist Liau Kianliong stated this baldly: "Formosan people are different from Chinese people ... a momentary glance, even at a distance, is enough to recognize whether a person on the road is Chinese or Formosan."[9] Taiwanese nationalists implicitly understood the production of identity by differentiation but refused the recursive, iterative nature of identity's endless possible differentiation. Liau did not proceed to identify the many ways that some Taiwanese people are different from other Taiwanese people, such as the differentiation between Taiwanese Aborigines, Hakka, and Minnan, or the multitude of other possible pluralisms.

In any case, such a reductionist nationalist rhetoric of Taiwanese identity never traveled very far in Taiwan. It rejected too explicitly the complex interplay of the respective legitimacies of the cultural formations which were identified as "Taiwanese" and "Chinese." This was especially so in the context of the social tension created by 2-28 and the arrival of 1 million Nationalist refugees on the island in 1948–49 at the end of the Chinese civil war. The mass migration into Taiwan produced the divisive social categories of "Mainlanders" and "Taiwanese," or *waishengren* and *benshengren*,[10] in a quasi-colonial relationship ideologically reinforced by the KMT party-state's sinicization of Taiwanese social life, which maintained effective hegemony over addressing identity on the island itself. The political logic of early Taiwanese nationalism of the exclusion of *waishengren* and rejection of Taiwan's Chinese identity formations defied the basic political and economic pragmatism of those who found themselves living together in postcolonial Taiwan under the hegemony and political oppression of the KMT.

Instead, under martial law, ways of speaking about Taiwan emerged in two alternative ways. First was in its oppositional politics in the 1960s and 1970s as a part of the pro-democracy movement. These were appeals to a Taiwanese identity in the campaign for a democratic Taiwan under principles of national self-determination, and which echoed rather more liberal and pluralistic registers of national address, especially in the global context of decolonization and the liberal attempts to elaborate multicultural bases for nationhood. The Presbyterian Church in Taiwan, which was a vociferous supporter of human rights and democracy, issued a *Statement of Our National Fate* in 1971 that addressed identity as a function of subjectivity, as the acceptance of Taiwan's pluralism and a subjective commitment to life on the island: "We the people on Taiwan love this island which, either by birth or chance, is our home. ... We are all well aware of our different backgrounds and even conflicts, but at present we are more aware of a common certainty and shared conviction."[11] By "birth or by chance" acknowledges the bitter legacy of the 2-28 Incident and the divisions between *waishengren* and *benshengren*. Out of these circumstances came a contingent pluralism, an improvised counter-appeal to both the Chinese nationalist sinicization policies of the KMT and to the renunciation of a Chinese identity by the emigré Taiwanese nationalists. The Presbyterians and other liberal voices articulated that learning to live together within a democratic and independent Taiwan was the only option for its people, however deep the social divide and animosities.

Second, there was the (re-)emergence of nativist literature in the 1970s, in which social identity was addressed by power and social justice as a function of marginality. In a complex alignment with Taiwanese nationalist politics, the democracy movement and the legacy of China's May Fourth Movement, the effects of Taiwan's industrialization and modernization on Taiwan's rural life became the material for constructing social identity as an appeal to the authenticity of the disempowered.[12] In nativism, the "real" Taiwanese were the poor in the village or the rice field living traditional lives, a traditionalism defined by their marginalization and disappearance in the face of Taiwan's industrial "miracle" economy.[13]

However, as meaningful and important as these oppositional political and cultural attempts to articulate the form of a social identity on Taiwan were, they were overlaid and overwhelmed by a highly dysfunctional regime of signification under martial law. It is this regime and its complex effects that created the conditions for particular ways for the Taiwanese to speak about Taiwan in the 1990s and later.

Under martial law, the mechanisms of political control in Taiwan were as direct and brutal as any dictatorship but also operated as a rhetoric of address to identity politics in public life. The KMT party-state invoked a national mission to "fight communism and recover the mainland" (*fan gong fu guo*)[14] and referred to the "Communist bandits" (*gong fei*)[15] of the ruling Chinese Communists on the mainland in meaningless quotidian slogans that were reproduced in the discourses of the media and public life as ritualistic acts of subjugation before KMT state power.

Such enunciations were a dimension of the structuring of socio-political relationships on Taiwan by the state's authoritarianism yet were operating in a discourse in which public language was in a constant crisis of legitimacy. On January 1, 1979, the very day the United States revoked diplomatic recognition of Taiwan in favor of the People's Republic of China, signaling the final ignominious end for Nationalist China, President Chiang Ching-kuo, the son of Chiang Kai-shek, gave a speech in which he "resolutely reiterated the determination to fight Communism and recover the mainland"[16] and simultaneously generated multiple layers of tacit social knowledge about who really believed this language of Nationalist governance.

Similarly, the media in Taiwan under martial law used specific rhetorical strategies which self-consciously intervened in the discursive effects through which it regulated the forms of social and political knowledge it produced. The newspapers used quotation marks in their texts to delegitimize the enunciation of certain expressions of identity politics. References to Taiwanese independence (*taidu*) as a political position or movement became *suowei* "*taidu*" (so-called "Taiwanese independence"),[17] adding a layer of sarcasm to the meaning of the phrase. Through such a layer, the state-controlled or managed media invoked a Taiwanese reading public as an imagined and constructed interlocutor who would share in the newspaper's derision for the notion of an independent Taiwan. So-called "Taiwanese independence" became a mutual, knowing joke among the public, the press, and the state.

But like the tacit social knowledge about politics, political commitment, and opposition created by the public recitation of the slogan "fight communism and recover the mainland," such textual practices in newspapers produced at the same time a potentially unruly discursive space. Even as the quotation marks delegitimized the notion of Taiwanese independence as a viable political position, equally they expressed the ultimate limits of the regulation of the reading public that they invoked. The Taiwanese public, imagined by quotation marks to be derisive of the notion of an independent Taiwanese nation, might have stripped them away in their reading practices and read "Taiwanese independence" with a full commitment to the term.

In this confused and contested discursive space in Taiwan, therefore, the political crisis of its quasi-colonization by the Chinese Nationalists after 1945 meant a crisis of representation of the nation. Under martial law, and a public language distorted by KMT ideology and the pretense of Taiwan as the "Republic of China," the Taiwanese lived with the reality of the contingency of the relationship between language and power in the way they spoke about themselves as Taiwanese. In the registers, narratives, and ideologies produced in the context of Taiwan's authoritarianism were multiple layers of the possible meanings of a social identity, with a wholly ambiguous legitimizing regime of what people might have *really* meant when they addressed "Taiwan" as a social and political object.

This complex regime of state and oppositional politics and their attendant signification formed a preamble to 1987, when martial law was lifted after forty years. As a result of the removal of overt restrictions on the media and publishing, and a recognition by both the state and the public that authoritarianism was at an end, a torrent of writing was released — political, scholarly, and commentary — which addressed social life in Taiwan. Identity politics became part of a complex expression of social and political change, which included the commodification of identity politics, when the media was suddenly liberated from direct and indirect state control and became caught in a frantic market for readers who wanted to understand what it meant to be "Taiwanese."

The crisis of representation of the martial law period gave way with democratization to the promise of a resolution of Taiwan's address to its own nationhood. At least within the epistemological framework of Taiwan's post-martial law nation-builders, there was an aspiration that the objectively invoked Taiwanese nation would be aligned with the rhetoric of address to that nation in public life. Instead of Taiwan as "Free China," and the recitation of Chinese Nationalist slogans, Taiwanese activists hoped that, with democratization, an appeal to "Taiwan" would finally mean Taiwan.[18]

In the late 1980s and into the 1990s, the key issue that would realize this aspiration was the 2-28 Incident. It became the center of a project to rewrite the history of Taiwan as a "Taiwanese" history, written against the Chinese history of the KMT, from which 2-28 had been erased. At the outset, this project was done fully cognizant of the politics of history-writing, and by 1988, 2-28 was already a self-conscious political memorialization movement. It was folded into Taiwan's identity politics at the center of a self-reflexive demand to engage publicly with Taiwanese history and social life in which the politics of memory were far more fundamental than any empirical historical details of the events being uncovered.

In 1988, Chen Yongxing, the chairman of the 2-28 Peace Day Promotion Committee said, "For the past forty years on the island of Taiwan, no-one has dared publicly discuss the 2-28 Incident. No-one could assuage the injustice to the souls of the dead victims. The government authorities would not face making the truth of its history public."[19] In this political process of rewriting history, he hoped to normalize Taiwanese social life, making what has become a common appeal to a "Taiwanese" future by politicians, commentators, and academics. With the recovery of the memory of 2-28 into a Taiwanese history, Chen called for "vigorously establish[ing] a Taiwanese society of mutual love and respect, and tolerance and peace."[20]

These early debates about the recovery or discovery of the 2-28 Incident in the late 1980s have become an ever-shifting array of issues, controversies, and social movements in the 1990s and 2000s, structured around the broader identity question. Cross-straits relations, education, language, indigeneity, feminism, and the environment have become themes with which to narrate the explicit contestation of the attempt to render as natural and self-evident an identity formation for Taiwan as "Taiwanese."

However, despite the appeal by Taiwanese nationalists and activists for democratization to lead to the "rectification" of the Taiwanese address to themselves and a new national consensus, such hopes have been unfulfilled. Especially since the election of Chen Shui-bian (known colloquially as A-Bian) as the Democratic Progressive Party president of Taiwan in 2000 and again in 2004, Taiwan's identity politics have become more, rather then less, bitter, vitriolic, and divisive. This reached a low point in 2006 with the attempt to create a mass public campaign to unseat the elected president with former democracy activist Shih Ming-teh as its figurehead. During the campaign, the artist Chu Ge wrote calligraphy proclaiming that "If A-Bian does not step down, then Taiwan has no future," and the singer Lu Lili appropriated a traditional Taiwanese song and rewrote the lyrics to read, "A-Bian step down, and save Taiwan."[21]

In its fraught democratic socio-politics, Taiwan's address to its nationhood after 1987 might be understood as an inversion of Ackbar Abbas's notion of a *déjà disparu* in Hong Kong. Abbas proposed that Hong Kong had an identity that became visible just at the moment of its disappearance at the Hong Kong handover to China in 1997 and was expressed as nostalgia or memory of an identity that Hong Kong never knew it had:

> This is *dis-appearance* . . . the binarisms used to represent Hong Kong as a subject give us not so much a sense of *déjà vu*, as the even more uncanny feeling of what we might call the *déjà disparu*: the feeling that what is new and unique about the situation is always already gone, and we are left holding a handful of clichés, or a cluster of memories of what has never been.[22]

In 1987 in Taiwan, just as punitive state restrictions on public discourse were lifted, its identity became an active and self-conscious rewriting of history to create a new, naturalized Taiwanese history, to articulate and secure as it were its inchoate memories and national truisms. However, by its very politics, this project denaturalized the discursive processes of its naturalization. Instead of nostalgia for an identity which it had never known, Taiwan's identity became an appeal to the future possibility of a singular, naturalized, unifying identity even as the attention by the Taiwanese to the need for an active discursive process for the creation of that singular identity revealed its very impossibility in its self-conscious exposure of its political and ideological mechanisms. As a result, Taiwan has been addressed by the Taiwanese as an object in suspension, in a self-conscious and self-reflexive act of (re-) writing of the possibility and imperative of identity itself. Indeed, the central theme in the discourse of Taiwanese identity after 1987 has been the problematic of Taiwanese identity. That is, the most important topic of Taiwan's identity debates is an object called "Taiwanese identity."

In this way, a writer such as Yang Qingchu can deploy the language of identity politics in an unsatisfactory appeal to a resolution of the crisis of Taiwan's national address by self-consciously appealing to mechanisms of identity-making:

> Taiwan must internationalize, and internationalization should be the direction for the cultural pluralism of every ethnicity on Taiwan. No matter if it is "localism" or "place-ism," this is the way Taiwanese subjective consciousness must go. But without "localism" or "place-ism" from which to jump to internationalization, is to be without a personal history or culture, and so be rootless.[23]

These self-reflexive "theorized" attempts to naturalize a discourse of Taiwanese identity are also in the language of Taiwan's competitive party politics. In 2004, the ruling Democratic Progressive Party institutionalized such contemporary modes of address to identity in Taiwan in its policies, with the release of the *Resolution on Ethnic Pluralism and National Unity*: "to promote the strength of the national culture, and enable the different ethnic groups in the new nation to contribute to prosperity, the party should further deepen the party's principle of pluralism, establish mutual acceptance between each ethnic group, to participate together in the construction of the nation's civil society."[24]

Therefore, the crisis of representation that characterized the martial law period up to 1987 was made visible, even absurd, both within Taiwan and outside, by the unique strangeness of its historical and geographical particularisms and the implausibility and illegitimacy of the politics of Nationalist China on Taiwan. The visibility of that crisis made visible the need for a self-conscious project of identity-building. Yet that very visibility has exposed the processes by which identities are made, and left impossible the task of making a singular, coherent, and self-evident Taiwanese identity that legitimizes itself by naturalizing the task of its own formation.

Theorizing Identity

Just as Liao Wen-yi and Liao Wen-kuai and other Taiwanese nationalists from the late 1940s drew upon the globalized language of right-wing nationalism (and Wilsonian internationalism) in their opposition to the Chinese nationalism of the KMT, so too have contemporary cultural and political practitioners in Taiwan drawn upon a new global rhetoric, the self-conscious rhetoric of identity politics and "theory," to both respond to and express the current identity crisis that Taiwan is experiencing. Notions, explicit or implicit in the rhetoric of democratic Taiwan, such as *hybridity, pluralism, performativity*, fully elaborated and theorized by global Cultural Studies and postcolonialism, have been applied to find a way forward to deal with the identity question in Taiwan's post-KMT, post-quasi-colonial society and the crisis of representation at the center of Taiwanese identification.

The political and cultural need to address the suspended object of Taiwanese identity emerged at just the time when globalized Cultural Studies, broadly imagined, became a key language of social knowledge in Taiwan. It has been exemplified in the work of Chen Kuan-hsing, Ping-hui Liao, Chiu Kui-fen, Chao Ting-hui, and others, who have been part of the Asian project to translate, and deal with the problems of translation of, Cultural Studies out of the Anglo- and Francophone academies into non-Western settings. These academics in departments of literature and cultural studies, notably at Tsing Hua University in Hsinchu, south of Taipei, are US-educated, usually bilingual and, wielding the language of theory, operate fully within the global academy, in parallel with their Taiwanese colleagues in political science and international relations, and the natural sciences.

In a complex alignment of identity and history-writing and the reform of Taiwanese politics, Cultural Studies has offered the epistemological tools to both subjectively address Taiwan's social life and objectively understand the process of its remaking, becoming a theoretical language which has shaped the way Taiwanese speak about themselves. The features of Cultural Studies, its attentiveness to politics and the politics of culture and its apprehension of the contingent relationship between language and power, have given it a productive basis for theorizing Taiwan, so that in Cultural Studies in Taiwan there has emerged a conjunction between Taiwan's social knowledge of itself and its crisis of representation and the crisis of representation as a problematic associated with deconstruction and the linguistic turn in the production of social knowledge.[25] From national and issue-based political rhetoric, to popular cultural criticism and academic social research, there is a process of identity-formation which negotiates the global deconstruction of identity in theory as it self-consciously works to reconstruct a basis for Taiwanese identity.

Within the Cultural Studies scene in Taiwan, Ping-hui Liao has self-reflexively identified this specific voice in the articulation of Taiwan's identity debates in the 1990s, that of the theoretically informed academic or activist, created by "expanding transnational network and new educational system of global and 'hegemonic' forces, images, codes, styles, and technologies"[26] who has worked to develop a post-nationalist identity discourse in Taiwan: "These bilingual intellectuals trained in Europe or the United States and returned to Taiwan or were local writers with easy access to foreign symbolic or cultural capital."[27] They created designated critical spaces which Liao refers to as:

> neither global nor local. As 'neither-nor', with an insider-outsider view of the complex micropolitics of location and memory which is beginning to flourish and interact with the changing realities . . . Among the topics discussed are the unstable mixtures of new ideas . . . with local politics in Taiwan or China; the resurgence of indigenous and traditional cultures in relation to modernization; oppositional projects of ethnic identity and cultural location ... emergence of new cityscapes and urban social relations; forms of cultural production and consumption.[28]

The "insider-outside" voice that Liao describes suggests the location from which appeals to Taiwanese identity as a suspended object are made. These are neither claims on the unmediated authenticity of the essentialized national subject of a Taiwanese nationalism nor simply an "anthropological" view of the processes of nation-building in Taiwan, but a self-reflexive subject position which deconstructs its own subjectivity in the process of trying to construct it. These subjects fit appropriately into a socio-political scene in which the basis of their address to their collective identity as Taiwanese is a self-conscious and self-reflexive exposure of the mechanisms of making that address. What Hall refers to as the "theoretical noise" of the origins of Cultural Studies in the Centre for Contemporary Cultural Studies at the University of Birmingham[29] finds an appropriate expression in the political and social "noise" of Taiwan's fraught appeal to its own sense of itself, especially in the Chen Shiu-bian era after 2000.

The arrival into the identity debate in Taiwan by a "transcultural public sphere" of theoretically informed academics or activists has therefore become a structuring language for Taiwan's discourse of identity, both within the academic field and in public. On this basis, the mass circulation broadsheet newspaper *Ziyou Shibao* can publish a detailed piece by Academia Sinica academic Shan Te-hsing about Edward Said and the role of the intellectual in contemporary society, with appropriate references to Said's later work in the context of Taiwan's identity debates: "In *The World, the Text and the Critic*, Said contrasts 'affiliation' and 'filiation', the latter as congenital, natural, determined, physiological, an unchangeable blood relationship. But Said emphasizes 'affiliation', the kind of forward-looking, cultural, flexible, active, enabling subjective will and dynamic identity and power relations."[30]

More proscriptively, with an acknowledgement of her career in politics, Tsai Ing-wen, political scientist, former head of the Mainland Affairs Commission and then vice-premier, and chairwoman of the Democratic Progressive Party, published an article in the journal *Zhengzhi Kexue Luncong* (*Political Science Review*) applying the work of Bhabha and Derrida to self-consciously elucidate the objective problematic of what is her own subjective identity as Taiwanese. She valorizes the performative and pluralistic aspects of identity that can be drawn from Bhabha's work, arguing against conservative forms of nationalism for an understanding of identity as the "doing" rather than the "being," and acknowledging the basis of identity as relational. She writes: "individual and collectivities pursue association on the basis of legitimized distinctions, but at the same time, those attempts to establish political and cultural identities in the basis of difference rely on flexible and negotiated boundaries."[31] On contemporary Taiwan, Tsai says: "Looking at this phenomenon in a positive way, we can say that Taiwan's socio-political situation in the post-martial law period has moved towards 'pluralization'."[32] Tsai's objectification of her own subjective identity — objectively explaining one's subjective social identity — is what Homi K. Bhabha describes as the "double writing" of the pedagogical and the performative,[33] but one in which Bhabha does not anticipate his own role as a producer of explanatory theory being deployed as a rhetorical device in the objective explanation of a post-colonial Taiwanese nationhood.

These are examples of the textualization of public discourse in Taiwan, creating a "metatopical" discourse in which Taiwanese commentators, scholars, and politicians adopt a distanciated subject position from which to critique their own identity as Taiwanese. For Liao, this is a discursive process in which social life becomes self-reflexive:

> Cultural criticism columns in Taiwan's newspaper literary supplements have functionally converted the public sphere in the world of letters, a sphere held together by the medium of the press with its serial literature and institution of the reading public, into a public domain of professional criticism within which 'the subjectivity originating in the interiority of the conjugal family, by communicating with itself, attained clarity about itself.'[34]

Liao is identifying a mode of address for social discourse in Taiwan. In his notion of "communicating with itself" and "attain[ing] clarity about itself," there is an apprehension of the nexus of a national subjectivity and the objectively invoked nation which characterizes the contemporary national.

The national addresses his or her own subjective national identity as an object, "Taiwanese," as if it has an objective existence outside of and separable from its subjective experience.

These gordian formulations intersect with the specific way, after Abbas, that Taiwan's address to its own identity was expressed earlier. Deploying the rhetoric of Cultural Studies, the Taiwanese deconstruct their own nationhood, to make visible the discursive process by which they are trying to naturalize the discourse of Taiwan. For Yang, confusingly, it must be internationalized but also retain a connection to its pluralistic culture, which is also based in the authenticity of the local. In this way, the Taiwanese can be seen to have created a necessary self-reflexivity in response to the legacy of the crisis of their representation under martial law, which renders them marginalized from their own discourse of their sense of themselves as Taiwanese.

In the processes of communicating and achieving "clarity" has been a social history of a changing array of themes, issues, and controversies within which have come these self-reflexive appeals to the possibilities and promise of Taiwanese identity. Over the past twenty years, certain tropes have been valorized and others marginalized to establish a structure for the themes that the Taiwanese have appealed to in order to generate a possibility for what Taiwanese identity might "really" be: 2-28, Taiwanese independence, Taiwan consciousness, and so forth. The discourse is also historicized by those who appeal to its naturalization. In the late 1980s and early 1990s, the appeal to a naturalized Taiwanese identity came in one form as the notion of an "identity complex," articulated most comprehensively in a piece by Yin Zhangyi in the journal *China Tribune*, "Analyzing Taiwan Consciousness," which applied Erik Erikson's psychoanalytic notion to theorize a "Taiwan complex" and a "China complex" to describe Taiwan's identity as a national neurosis that would resolve as Taiwan matured as a nation.[35] Since then the notion of a Taiwan complex has faded from debate, replaced by more up-to-date topics, like the issue of education in the *Renshi Taiwan (Understanding Taiwan)* high school textbook controversy of the late 1990s[36] or more recently instrumental issues such as the dangers to Taiwan's nascent national integrity from excessive dependence on the mainland Chinese economy,[37] and the contentious presidential election of 2004, with the endless appeals to resolve Taiwan's ongoing Blue-Green political crises and "solve" Taiwanese identity.[38] The Taiwanese government promoted the "rectification of names" in which old Chinese Nationalist state and corporate institutions that included the title "China" or "Chinese" were renamed "Taiwanese," appealing to the very foundation of a national address and to the pliable, political contingency of national histories. The renaming of the Chiang Kai-shek Memorial, the large public square in central Taipei, as the National Taiwan Democracy Memorial Hall, was undertaken as a wholly self-conscious act of history writing, and the accompanying vitriolic public debate explicitly articulated the contingent remaking of the nation through institutions and the language of the state.[39] Acknowledging the architectural encoding of Nationalist state power by the existing structures in the square, the political historian Chen Yi-shen called for replacing the main memorial with something like the Edo Museum in Tokyo, to elaborate a Taiwanese history that takes in "everyday life, work, ethnicity, conflict, to mold the historical memory of the community."[40]

In this form of the decoding of the social, cultural, and political life of the nation, the Taiwanese readers, who are themselves imagined by the institutional practices of the media, read the narrative of their own national identity in the daily press and can envision their future as "Taiwanese" people in the criticisms made in social commentary on an ever-changing array of issues on their present. Taiwanese identity is as much about the process of narrativization as elaborating a coherent substance to the content of a Taiwanese national consciousness.

According to Ping-hui Liao, this is a function of the commodification of Taiwan's identity discourse in a competitive media market. It "generate[s] the desire to decode public culture in an industrialized and commodified cultural knowledge: a desire for the simple formulation of social circumstances, in order to experience and perceive the everyday as mediated."[41] The notion of the commodification of Taiwanese identity in its cultural production adds a useful critical dimension to how it may be understood; however, the emphasis here is on a theoretically inflected rhetoric as a response to the crisis of representation from the martial law and post-martial law periods. As argued above, this rhetoric has found an alignment with the demand to remake Taiwanese identity after democratization. Therefore, the operation in Taiwan of this "transcultural public sphere" has developed in a complex and multilayered trajectory from both the earlier forms of liberal democratic debates about Taiwanese identity in 1960s, the political appeals to nativism in the 1970s, as well as the crisis in Taiwan's self-address under the KMT's authoritarian rule.

While the broad Cultural Studies project might have found a receptive set of socio-political conditions on Taiwan, it is a wide-ranging body of work that produces certain elisions and emphases in how it informs Taiwan's identity-making. On the one hand, the rejection of essentialism implicit in the linguistic turn of Cultural Studies aligns the theoretical impetus of Cultural

Studies with the response to KMT authoritarianism by liberal nationalists and democracy activists who described a subjective basis for Taiwanese identity. The Presbyterians in the 1970s could appeal to the notion of love: "We the people on Taiwan love this island," and in the 1990s the famous democracy activist and politician Lin Yi-hsiung could offer the simple formulation that "the Taiwanese are people who are prepared to make their homes on Taiwan."[42] These are vernacular expressions of the kind of theoretical formulations offered by Cultural Studies that identity, to paraphrase Judith Butler, "is not a noun . . . [it] is always a doing, though not a doing by a subject who might be said to pre-exist the deed."[43] The "doing" is loving the island or making a home on a "Taiwan" that is always already there, regardless of when and from where an individual literally arrived. This is in contrast to the Formosan nationalists who appealed to a politically (and culturally) unviable objective differentiation between Chinese and Taiwanese in their articulation of Taiwanese nationalism and a post-2-28 Taiwanese political project.

At the same time, Cultural Studies has also been described by Chen Kuan-hsing as emancipatory and politically motivated, and this too gives it legitimacy in Taiwan's identity formation in the post-martial law era:

> Cultural Studies . . . has always recognized that "theory" is not a universal set of formal propositions but an analytical weapon generated out of and in response to local-historical concerns . . . At the same time, the belief in producing organic intellectual work has put Cultural Studies in touch with the currents of social conflicts. Concerns of and interaction with social and political movements . . . have not only produced undeniable tensions which kept the energies of Cultural Studies alive, but forced Cultural Studies to recognize the "common" structures of domination: capitalism, patriarchy, heterosexism, ethnocentrism, neocolonialism, etc.[44]

For Chen, Cultural Studies grew out of the worldwide decolonization movements, with a legacy of the Marxist tradition of the attempt to integrate theory and political practice in its activities. Chen suggests that, in the current era of globalization, as a result of new flows of capital and culture, Cultural Studies remains one of the few intellectual traditions willing to theorize and intervene epistemologically and politically in these new potential forces of global domination.

As well as the liberal pluralistic national imaginings of the democracy activists both during and after martial law, these emancipatory political goals of Cultural Studies that Chen emphasizes places it in a relationship with the development of nativism or localism, first in the 1970s in literature, and then in the post-martial law era as the more wide-ranging localization movement, or *bentuhua*.

As indicated earlier, the political dimension of nativism as a literary movement in the 1970s gave it a similarly emancipatory political project. Sung-cheng Chang underscores the political impetus of the nativist writers of the 1970s, who, one could suggest, either reinvigorated the May Fourth tradition of the politically engaged intellectual, or alternatively articulated a specifically Taiwanese cultural imagining, but in either case explicitly sought out an emancipatory literary form that expressed the experience of the marginalized in Taiwanese society, especially the rural poor.[45] The 1990s version, *bentuhua,* which can echo Formosan nationalism of the 1950s and 1960s, is also a contender for a rhetoric of nation-building in Taiwan but has little of the complex elaborations of Anglo- and Francophone theory or the cultural criticism described by Ping-hui Liao. It is an emotive national cultural language, incorporating a Taiwanese national historiography and appealing ultimately to the idea of a Taiwan as an undifferentiated sign, or transcendental signifier. *Bentuhua* has developed a notion of an authentic or "real" Taiwanese subject found in Taiwan's local cultures and language, producing, after Americana, a kind of "Taiwanana." But more politically, it also constructs an imagined ahistorical rural past for Taiwan as a function of Taiwan's changing social power relations through the political struggles against the political oppression of the Manchus, the Japanese, the Chinese Nationalists, and now the Chinese Communists, as ongoing struggle for Taiwanese self-determination. In *bentuhua*, authentic Taiwanese local culture is a form of resistance. Li Hsiao-feng, a leading proponent of *bentuhua,* writes: "In the period of foreign control of Taiwan, local culture was the grain which sustained the dignity and life of the nation. Its special quality is the basis of the search for our history, and the sadness of many of our songs."[46]

Therefore, nativism and Taiwanese nationalism presage some of the political concerns of Cultural Studies — the valorization of the subaltern and the politicization of culture as resistance — that from the 1970s have used appeals to authenticity as a counter to KMT cultural hegemony and have continued to make that appeal as part of Taiwan's competitive democratic political rhetoric and commercial cultural market. However, the specific theoretical impetus of Cultural Studies is antithetical to the essentializing imperative of the nativist and nationalist cultural movements in Taiwan.

Chen Kuan-hsing has been specifically critical of the limits of nativism. He argues that it is ultimately merely a response to or a product of colonization, framed by the politics of colonialism so that ultimately the nativist pursues an authentic identity that is merely the mirror of that of the colonizer, as a form of colonial mimesis. He argues that "the rediscovery of the self in is no way bounded by the nation-state. It can go in any direction where a tradition of 'difference' (from the colonizer) can be discovered."[47] Similarly, Chiu Kui-fen has explicitly contrasted the goals of post-colonialism as originating in the Western academy and localism in the literary debates of the early 1990s, but equivocated on the theoretical limitations of nativism in literature, and its links to old-fashioned notions of "Third World literature," as well as the hegemonic potential of the introduction of postcolonial theory from the West.[48]

As a part of his broader project of the cultivation of a politicized form of Cultural Studies in Asia, Chen Kuan-hsing has proposed a "critical syncretism" to avoid the hegemonic potential of nativism or nationalism as counter-colonial politico-cultural movements, and as a more sophisticated response to the limited rhetoric of "pluralism" or "hybridity" which characterizes much of Taiwan's identity debates in the 1990s and 2000s and remains a staple, following Bhabha, of postcolonialism. Chen recognizes the hegemonic potential of nativism in the ideologies of Taiwanese identity and the failures of the pluralistic model, and proposes an active process of identity-making across the boundaries of the postcolonial, so that subjects "becom[e] others, to actively interiorize elements of others into the subjectivity of the self so as to move beyond the boundaries and divisive positions historically constructed by colonial power relations, patriarchauvinism, heterosexism, nationalistic xenophobia, etc."[49]

Chen's theoretical elaborations are celebrated and his status as a leading global practitioner of Cultural Studies cannot be questioned. But the ambivalent relationship that Cultural Studies has both to the notion of *bentuhua*, via commonalities in their politics and to the liberal and pluralistic national imaginings of some parts of the democracy movement, suggests that the infusion of theory into the self-reflexive making of Taiwanese identity in the 1990s elides a complex politics of its own.

Another way to look at Cultural Studies is as not merely a resistive response to post-imperialisms and the hegemonic potential of global capital but an aspect of globalization itself. This is precisely what Liao suggests when he refers to the "neither-nor" or "insider-outsider" voice that narrates contemporary Taiwanese social life and to Cultural Studies in Taiwan as a product of transnational global networks, and what Chen elides in his belief that Cultural Studies remains a key intellectual project for tackling the injustices of globalization.

Such an assertion means dissolving the presumption of Cultural Studies to "speak about" and recognize that, even as its rhetoric informs the address to a Taiwanese identity in the post-martial law era, it remains a voice that speaks from a distanciated position of authority, using a global rhetorical style legitimized by the globalized institution of the academy. Such recognition is demanding of it that it follow through on its own assumptions and acknowledge its own epistemological implication in processes of globalization, and deal with issues of positionality: who speaks, to whom, and about whom.

Controversially, Ping-hui Liao has observed that the Taiwanese subjects who are producing the "transcultural public sphere" in which the rhetoric of theory is the language with which Taiwan is "generating its eternal self-generation" are US- educated Taiwanese returnees or local academics steeped in the language of Euro-American cultural theory, and largely second-generation *waishengren*.[50] Such an observation, anecdotally supported by my own in Taiwan, is on the face of it a serious, even audacious, statement, but beneath the fraught Taiwanese social distinction of *benshengren* and *waishengren* is an acknowledgment of the status of symbolic capital in the production of Taiwan's discourse of identity. *Waishengren* as a group could be argued to have benefited most from the construction of the quasi-colonial polity under the KMT after 1945, in the context of the state's marginalization of the "local" in its institutional distribution of symbolic capital.[51] In the post-martial law period, the deployment of a certain kind of rhetoric of identity in Taiwan expresses continuing access to symbolic capital, no longer expressed by the KMT rhetoric of "Free China" but now found in the globalized flows of culture and capital that Cultural Studies should be especially well placed to intervene in.

The question of who does Cultural Studies in Taiwan reintroduces politics into the kind of self-reflexive theorization of Taiwan address to its identity proposed earlier. It suggests that Cultural Studies might be antithetical to certain forms of resistance. As a part of the globalization of the academy, Cultural Studies might be implicated in certain specific political circumstances in which it becomes itself a political response by certain kinds of Taiwanese to alternative claims over identity on the basis of political and cultural resistance. That is, in the instance of Taiwan, Cultural Studies offers a theorization, and critique, of nativism and localist cultural movements that lay claim to legitimacy on the basis of claims of authenticity and essentialism and appeals to fluid, unbounded, and even globalized identity formations which transcend the political limits and strictures of the colonial, postcolonial, and national through a highly elaborated global theoretical language. That impetus to critique the essentialism of localism and nationalism in Taiwan suggests a wider struggle for legitimacy in Taiwan's identity politics among the Taiwanese over how that identity is defined and by whom.

Therefore, the question to ask with respect to Cultural Studies in Taiwan is whether, rather than part of practices of resistance and the self-reflexive remaking of a post-martial law discourse of identity, it is itself a practice of hegemony. Are the objects of analysis of Cultural Studies not being valorized but rather being appropriated or deployed as part of a wider process of the expression of the global socio-cultural capital of those who do Cultural Studies? Cultural studies is part of a global culture, implicated like all others in the global flows of capital, both material and symbolic, that structure social, political, and cultural life in the post-Cold War era.

Such an assertion identifies Cultural Studies in Taiwan as a form of practice and locates it within global discursive structures of power, and indeed Cultural Studies is itself uniquely placed to theorize its own implication in globalized discourses as they are expressed in Taiwan. As a form of critical scholarship, Cultural Studies is directed towards exposing the effaced operation of power as it constructs subjectivities and shapes cultural formations. This essay is self-reflexively drawing upon the theoretical language of Cultural Studies to both attend to the register of Taiwan's address to its identity and cautiously directing it at Cultural Studies itself as part of that analysis.

Such critique is nothing less than should be expected of the theoretical elaborations made possible by the globalization of Cultural Studies through the 1990s. It has entered a regime of identification in Taiwan that takes in a complex self-reflexive discourse of sophisticated theorization, populist political rhetoric, culture, and the invocation of authenticity in *bentuhua*, all of which have occurred as Taiwan's economic and cultural life have been drawn into the amorphous phenomenon known as "globalization" in the post-Cold War era. None of this can be separated, however, from the context of Taiwan's marginal place as an autonomous, identifiable polity. Mainland China continues to exert both a belligerent military and political threat over Taiwan as well as an economic allure, and China's economic power is reshaping global geopolitics in ways that leave Taiwan marginalized in the international community. Taiwan's location on both a fault line of contemporary geopolitics and of modern Asian history makes for a sharpening of the effects of real, material power, of the policies of governments, of military force, and of hundreds of billions of dollars of trade. While sophisticated theoretical elaborations might offer paths forward for Taiwan's identity problematic, for all its flaws and for all the misdeeds done in its name, it is the appeal to the nation that remains the key geopolitical formation with which the Taiwanese are resisting the hegemony of the People's Republic of China and their geopolitical marginalization. While Cultural Studies may be rightfully reluctant to rehabilitate the nation as a viable site of identity, it also needs to recognize the material practices of power in the region, the 1,000 missiles that the PRC has pointed at Taiwan from across the Taiwan Straits, and engage directly with the moral and political implications of those brute political realities and take seriously the political and cultural responses to them.

II

Cultural Industries in
Northeast Asia

4

Placing South Korean Cinema into the Pusan International Film Festival: Programming Strategy in the Global/Local Context

SooJeong Ahn

Since Venice under Mussolini, film festivals have played a significant role in introducing national film culture within a global exchange system. Enmeshed in a set of cultural politics aimed at promoting cultural diversity, they importantly help to brand films nationally and circulate them across the borders of the nation-state. Despite the growing interest and importance of film festivals as a scholarly topic, research has tended to focus on high-profile European festivals, such as Cannes, Venice, and Berlin. Little primary empirical research has been conducted to date on the subject of non-Western film festivals. As a result, the existing scholarship on this topic has largely failed to comprehensively acknowledge the different social and cultural contexts of non-Western film festivals. In this respect, the recent proliferation of film festivals in East Asia, such as Pusan, Singapore, and Bangkok, is of particular interest and requires attention, since the role of film festivals within the ongoing globalization of the region emerges from and creates a distinctive cultural-political context. For example, whereas film festivals in Europe were established as part and parcel of postwar projects to promote regeneration, the recent phenomenon of film festivals in East Asia seems to be bound up with the new international spotlight on "Asian cinema" centered on this region and the rise of East Asia as an important economic region.[1] In this context, the Pusan International Film Festival (PIFF) in South Korea is of particular importance, since its distinctive approach to cultural politics in East Asia demonstrates the ways in which the festivals more generally have begun to negotiate and renew their roles and identities between the national, the regional, and the global.[2] This essay aims to reveal that PIFF's regional — as opposed to a purely national or globalized — approach towards East Asia, synergized by the global visibility of South Korean cinema, displays a distinct agenda and sociocultural context different from that of Euro-American film festivals.

The international recognition of Korean cinema[3] has mainly been achieved through the festival circuit in the West and the remarkable growth of the national film industry since the 1990s. In conjunction with the new global visibility of Korean cinema, PIFF has established in a relatively short period since its inception in 1996 a firm position in East Asia to serve as a showcase for Asian cinema. Recent scholarship not only tends to agree on the key role that PIFF has played in promoting Korean cinema, but its status within the global economy is fundamentally interrelated with the evolution of PIFF itself.[4] However, despite the presumed importance of PIFF in its close link with Korean cinema, existing scholarship has given little sustained attention that is grounded in empirical observation to this relationship. As a result, a number of crucial questions remain unanswered, ones which this essay seeks to address. First, recognizing that PIFF has played a role in promoting Korean cinema, how specifically and to what extent has the festival functioned over the past decade? Second, how did it correspond to individual Korean filmmakers' self-positioned strategies aimed at breaking into the global film market? And finally, how does PIFF relate to the concept of "Asian identity," a concept that acts as the focus of the festival's identity?

This essay seeks to reveal some of the institutional dynamics of film festivals by focussing on the programming sections at PIFF between 1996 and 2005. Specifically, it aims to illustrate how the programming of local sections is closely tied to the current political, economic, and social interests of the institution. While PIFF has served as a showcase for Asian films by evoking Asian identity as a regionalization strategy, the festival has equally striven to promote the local film industry by showcasing some Korean films in prime high-profile sections which act as a gateway to the global film circuit. In this respect, a close examination of these key local sections — "Opening" and "Korean Panorama" — provides a useful baseline to understand the overall complex situations characterizing the contemporary Korean film industry within the local/global context.

As observed at its tenth anniversary in 2005, recent momentum towards the establishment of PIFF as a representative of East Asia reflects the festival's change of focus in approaching the global film market. In this sense, globalization has served as a force to prompt local initiatives that have resulted in the rapid growth of the Korean film industry. This in turn has led to the production of regional cultural developments such as the "Korean Wave."[5] However, because these trends contest narrowly defined national values in East Asia as they impact upon and challenge political, historical, and economic contexts, it must be noted that global forces have also resulted in ambivalence concerning the politics of regional/national identity. For instance, the Screen Quota movement[6] and the lifting of the ban on Japanese cultural products[7] are clear examples that demonstrate the contradictions and complexities that the Korean film industry has faced. This essay explores how these new complexities have forced PIFF to establish alternative approaches including, especially, the promotion of regionalization according to a new transnational framework of globalization. Importantly, changes made by PIFF have had far-reaching impacts on festivals in East Asia, for example in Hong Kong and Tokyo, which have attempted to reconstruct their status and identities. Ultimately, this essay considers, through its examination of PIFF, how the cultural politics of cultural industries in East Asia may be transitioning from a focus on the national to the regional as they increasingly target the global market.

Opening the Festival with a Korean Film

Between 1996 and 2005, three Korean films were shown in the "Opening" section: *Peppermint Candy* (*Pakha satang*, Yi Ch'angdong [Lee Chang-dong], 2000), *The Last Witness* (*Hŭksusŏn*, Pae Ch'angho [Bae Chang-ho], 2001) and *The Coast Guard* (*Haeansŏn*, Kim Kidŏk [Kim Ki-duk], 2002).[8] *Peppermint Candy* is of particular interest, since this film provides a discursive site that demonstrates how the Korean film industry has substantially transformed in the last decade.

Despite the acknowledged significance of the role that festivals can play, there has been little research on the "programming" of local sections. "Programming" refers to the slot where a film is placed in a film festival. This slot often determines its relative position and importance, and it indicates the way in which each film is circulated and interpreted in the global market. In this light, films placed in the "Opening" section are significant, since they not only attract more attention to the festival in marketing, but they establish — as the first encounter audiences including journalists and professionals have with the festival — the festival's image.[9] In this sense, placing a new local title into the "Opening" slot reflects a desire to place special emphasis on national film production.

Overall, PIFF's program consists of nine sections: "Opening/Closing," "A Window on Asian Cinema," "New Currents," "Korean Panorama," "World Cinema," "Wide Angle," "Special Programme in Focus," "Korean Retrospective" and "Open Cinema."[10] As shown in the chart below, films in the "Opening" section largely feature some combination of Asian directors and films. The main exception to this trend is Mike Leigh's *Secrets and Lies* (1996), which opened the very first festival in 1996. Although it did not match the festival's identity as "the platform of Asian cinema," Park Kwang-su who, as deputy director of the first festival, was instrumental to the film-selection process, explained that programmers were desperately looking for a "big, quality film" that could represent the event that year.[11] Moreover, because the first PIFF was launched suddenly and unexpectedly,[12] preference was given by programmers to a safe choice rather than on taking a risk with a less acclaimed film. *Secrets and Lies* had won the Palme d'Or in competition at Cannes a few months earlier and had already gained a Korean distributor.

Table 4.1   Opening films in PIFF 1996–2005[13]

	Year	Title	Director	Nationality
1	1996	*Secrets and Lies*	Mike Leigh	UK
2	1997	*Chinese Box*	Wayne Wang	France/UK/USA
3	1998	*The Silence*	Mohsen Makhmalbaf	Iran/France
4	1999	*Peppermint Candy*	Lee Chang-dong	South Korea
5	2000	*The Wrestler*	Buddadeb Dasgupta	India
6	2001	*The Last Witness*	Bae Chang-ho	South Korea
7	2002	*The Coast Guard*	Kim Ki-duk	South Korea
8	2003	*Doppelganger*	Kurosawa Kiyoshi	Japan
9	2004	*2046*	Wong Kar-wai	Hong Kong/China
10	2005	*Three Times*	Hou Hsiao-hsien	Taiwan

Since 1997, the "Opening" section has tended to show new titles of prominent Asian directors such as Wayne Wang, Mohsen Makhmalbaf, and Hou Hsiao-hsien. However, it was not until its fourth year that PIFF chose to open the festival with a Korean film, *Peppermint Candy*. Significantly, this second feature-length film of Lee Chang-dong engages with themes of historical trauma and recovery in Korea by dealing with events like the Kwangju Uprising, the IMF (International Monetary Fund) crisis, and military dictatorship since the 1980s. Opening the fourth PIFF with this film, the programming committee ambitiously asserted:

> This year's festival celebrates Asian cinema, with the Korean entry
> *Peppermint Candy* as its curtain raiser. Lee Chang-dong, whose acclaimed
> *Green Fish* (1996) exposed the essence of Korean society, captures the
> process of recovering lost time with a new cinematic form. [. . .] Simply
> put, this film is a personal history of Young-ho. Through his character,
> however, we experience twenty years of Korean history. The changes
> in Young-Ho echo the turmoil in our society.[14]

Drawing plaudits from foreign guests and local audiences, this film was highly
acclaimed during the festival. In a press conference after the world premiere
screening, Lee said, "I am honoured that this film was selected as the opening
film. Without PIFF, it would be impossible to screen Korean film including
my film to many film professionals from the entire world."[15] Spurred on by
its success in PIFF, *Peppermint Candy* went on to win multiple awards at the
Karlovy Vary International Film Festival in the Czech Republic, including
the Don Quixote Award, the Jury's Special Prize, the *NETPAC* (Network
for the Promotion of Asian Cinema) Award, as well as the Grand Bell Award
for best film of 2000 in Korea. In addition, the film was invited to the Cannes
Film Festival Directors' Fortnight.[16] On top of this critical acclaim, the film
was successful at the national box office when it was released to general
audiences with huge media support on January 1, 2000.[17]

The success of *Peppermint Candy* marked a turning point in PIFF's
programming and subsequent direction.[18] Indeed, it gave PIFF — not to
mention the Korean film industry — self-confidence in the ability of Korean
films to appeal globally. Reflective of this new-found confidence, PIFF
selected another Korean film, Bae Chong-ho's *The Last Witness*, to open the
festival in 2001, and a year later, in 2002, Kim Ki-duk's *The Coast Guard*.
Importantly, these three films engage with the history of South Korea in the
latter decades of the twentieth century, focussing especially in their cinematic
construction of the national narrative on how individual identity is brutalized
by institutional repression.[19] In *Peppermint Candy*, the innocence of the
protagonist Yŏngho is destroyed by police and military brutality during the
1980s and 1990s, while Private Kang in the *Coast Guard* goes mad as a result
of the hair-trigger atmosphere to which he is exposed when guarding the
volatile border between North and South Korea.[20] The tragedy in *The Last
Witness* emerges in the depiction of the political division of the nation and
the issue of prisoners of war in the Korean War. Despite their specific
contextual differences, these three films crucially suggest the way that PIFF
presents and promotes national films to the global market. In short, the
thematic similarity of these films reveals a desire specifically to explore the
history of a divided nation.

Furthermore, in relation to film production and financing, it is necessary to point out that there was an attempt at blockbuster filmmaking in both *The Last Witness* and *The Coast Guard*. To veteran director Bae, a leading filmmaker of the 1980s, *The Last Witness* represented an ambitious comeback to commercial filmmaking. In a rare instance of local government funding, the film received financing from Kŏje City in Korea and Miyazaki Prefecture in Japan, which amounted to around twenty percent of the film's total budget.[21]

In *The Coast Guard,* Kim also attempted something very different in scale and form from his previous films, by casting big-name star Chang Tonggŭn (Jang Dong-kun) and invoking a strong political message. Significantly, however, the film failed to become a commercial blockbuster in Korea despite the considerable reputation it should have garnered for itself having opened PIFF in 2002.[22] It seems that several extremely provocative scenes involving the depiction of brutal rape and miscarriage were unbearable to audiences.[23] In fact, such scenes, which British film critic Tony Rayns describes as "sexual terrorism," are typical of Kim's style.[24] Ironically, it is partly because of this aspect that his films have been praised and have received awards at major Western film festivals such as Venice and Berlin even though they are turned away by local audiences.[25] As the example of *The Coast Guard* demonstrates, PIFF's choice of opening film can give rise to controversy, conferring in the case of Kim a sort of official ratification of a film which may be nonetheless "ostracized"[26] by the local film industry.

It could be argued that, by mixing national history with popular genres, *The Last Witness* and *The Coast Guard*, by being shown in the "Opening" section, reflect and recognize a larger trend prevalent in contemporary Korean films since the late 1990s, as exemplified by Kang Chegyu's (Kang Je-kyu) *Shiri (Shwiri,* 1999) and Pak Ch'anuk's (Park Chan-wook) *Joint Security Area* (2000). As Chris Berry points out, recent Korean films since the late 1990s have drawn on an interest in local political issues, while utilizing recognizable Western aesthetics such as the blockbuster model to appeal to global audiences.[27]

Of course, the strategy can backfire. As was seen in the case of *The Coast Guard*, opening screening in PIFF does not necessarily confer success, and in some cases, it can result in negative media coverage of the festival itself. Film critic Yang Yunmo, for example, complained in a major local newspaper on the choice of *The Last Witness* to open PIFF:

> PIFF made a critical mistake in selecting *The Last Witness* as an opening film, since the film was full of cliché. The film discouraged local

enthusiasm for the Festival and Korean films alike. The Festival committee, in particular, must not be influenced by personal relationships in the film industry or a certain reputation of a filmmaker.[28]

Journalist Pak Ŭnju was equally critical:

> It is doubtful that such a high-budgeted blockbuster like *The Last Witness*, whose production cost amounted to a staggering four-billion Korean won [approximately US$4 million], could incorporate the Festival's spirit concerning Asian cinema. The committee needs to be aware that it is not obligated to screen a Korean film as the opening selection of the Festival.[29]

These criticisms reveal and confirm the dilemma PIFF has in programming local films. While the festival committee has tended to rely on established or globally recognized directors in the "Opening" section, the Korean film industry has begun to evolve and grow rapidly both in industry infrastructure and creativity.[30] For example, in 2001, when *The Last Witness* was shown at PIFF, Korean audiences were exposed to huge box-office hits such as *Friend* (2001), *My Sassy Girl* (2001), *Kick the Moon* (2001), and *My Wife Is a Gangster!* (2001). Whereas the success of this string of films can be attributed to a variety of novel themes and cinematic approaches, *The Last Witness* and *The Coast Guard*, as the last runners of this blockbuster boom period, were seen as merely following the existing trend of Korean blockbusters. As such, they failed to appeal to local audiences.

As illustrated, an examination of Korean films in PIFF enables us to consider the particular conditions, considerations, and criteria that shape programming decision-making processes and, in particular, the ways that the festival attempted to promote Korean cinema to the global film market. However to understand more clearly the importance of PIFF to the Korean film industry, we must also consider this industry's transformation since the 1990s. To demonstrate this, let's consider *Peppermint Candy* again, since this film poses an interesting problem: why was this film singled out at a time when there were so many new local titles that year such as *Lies* (1999), *Chunhyang* (2000), *Barking Dogs Never Bite* (2000), *The Isle* (2000), *The Virgin Stripped Bare by Her Bachelors* (2000), and *Die Bad* (2000)? To answer this question, we must look at a number of multilevel factors that shaped the selection process.

The year 1999 is significant, since it was in this year that the first Korean blockbuster was released — Kang Je-kyu's *Shiri*.[31] The commercial success of this film and the subsequent large amounts of capital invested in filmmaking quickly transformed the structure of the local film market. The emergence of PIFF became an important part of the local film industry, which was looking for a route into the global film market. Because it marks the beginning of a crucial period of substantial transformation of the Korean film industry,[32] the positioning of *Peppermint Candy* within this situation was significant.

First, this film was financed by UniKorea, a new investment firm founded in 1999 that is of particular importance[33] because it was created by actors and filmmakers in order to support creative diversity outside of the mainstream.[34] *Peppermint Candy* was the first film that UniKorea financed.[35] As the founding of UniKorea indicates, there was great potential to open up a space alongside the blockbuster and other popular genres of the Korean film industry for the development of niche products such as *Peppermint Candy*. The influence of UniKorea is best explained by the presence of its cofounder, actor Mun Sŏnggŏn (Moon Sung-keun).[36] Moon starred in such works of New Korean Cinema as *Black Republic* (1992) and *A Single Spark* (1995) which were directed by Pak Kwangsu (Park Kwang-su). He also served as vice-chairman of the newly launched Korean Film Council (KOFIC) in 1999.[37]

Alongside changes in the structure of capital investment in the film industry, there was a considerable struggle between the so-called "old" and "new" generations in government film policy. When the former Korean Motion Picture Promotion Corporation (KMPPC) was replaced by KOFIC, the new leadership formed by members, including Moon, was challenged by older film professionals such as the former KMPPC president Yun Ilbong (Yoon Il-bong) and Kim Chimi (Kim Ji-mi), head of the Korean Motion Picture Artists Association. Although Moon had to resign due to resistance from the older generation of leaders, KOFIC successfully took the initiative to play a key role in establishing cultural policy at the governmental level around this period.[38] The unique position of UniKorea and these changes directly influenced the status of *Peppermint Candy* to ensure that it was differentiated from other local films.

At this point, we should turn our attention to the position and status of director Lee Chang-dong. Following the screening in 1996 of *Green Fish* in PIFF's "New Currents" section, which serves to promote emerging film talent in Asia, and subsequently *Peppermint Candy* in the "Opening" section in 1999, Lee completed his third film, *Oasis* (2002), with the financial support of the Pusan Promotion Plan (PPP). The PPP is a "project market" through which selected Asian filmmakers can pitch new projects to potential producers. This film was subsequently nominated for a Golden Lion at the Venice Film Festival and received the Special Director's Award in 2002. Having been supported by and closely involved with PIFF in these various ways, Lee has become an established representative of the Korean film industry. The fact that he worked as Minister for Culture and Tourism between 2003 and 2004 confirms the status that he has gained in Korean society. This case demonstrates how the festival, through its programming, engages with particular filmmakers to create and enhance its brand. It further shows how the interests of individual filmmakers and institutions can be brought together.

Another significant point that must be considered is that *Peppermint Candy* is the first Japanese-Korean co-production, one that was followed by theatrical release in both countries. Considering that there were still restrictions on cultural exchanges and collaborations at that time, this project is noteworthy since it attracted financing from NHK (*Nihon hōsō kyōkai*, the Japanese national broadcasting corporation), a novel development that attracted media attention and helped to determine the film's distinctive position in the local film industry. It must be emphasized that, despite the geographical contiguity of Korea to its neighbors, there was little cultural exchange before the 1990s with other East Asian countries and especially Japan, due to the legacy of its colonial past. As mentioned, Japanese cultural products were banned in Korea. The position and success of *Peppermint Candy* must be considered within this sensitive political and historical context, a fact that the *Hollywood Reporter* stressed:

> Confirming its groundbreaking role in Asian cinema, the Pusan International Film Festival will open October 14 with the first Japanese-Korean co-production to be released in South Korea, organizers said Thursday. *Peppermint Candy*, directed by Korea's Lee Chang-dong and financed by Japan NHK, will premiere at the huge 5,000-seat outdoor theatre as the first of more than 200 films to be shown at the ten-day festival. According to NHK, it will be the first co-production to be screened in South Korea since the country's president, Kim Dae-Jung, announced a gradual lifting of the ban on Japanese cultural products last year.[39]

In the opening ceremony of the 1999 festival, a special message on the importance of "cultural exchange" between Japan and Korea from President Kim was delivered on the big screen. After PIFF, this film was also screened in Japan in the opening section of the Third NHK Asian Film Festival in December 1999, under a huge media spotlight. All these rhetorical and political circumstances precisely mirror the transformation of the local film industry and show how these factors affect its relationship with PIFF.

The final point regarding PIFF and *Peppermint Candy* is the contradictory symbolism of the Screen Quota system. Physically occupying PIFF Square in Nampo-dong Street in Pusan during the festival, local filmmakers fervently argued in favour of the system, claiming that, without it, Hollywood products would completely dominate the local film market. Newly emerging members of the local film industry such as Lee Chang-dong, Myŏng Kyenam (Myung Kae-nam) and Moon Sung-keun were always at the head of these demonstrations. Ironically enough, these events, which supported an apparently nationalistic agenda, occurred in the same place where Japanese films — now expressly permitted as a result of PIFF's screening of these films — were enthusiastically received by young audiences. Consequently, as a new public sphere, the space where PIFF is located symbolizes a complex and contradictory interplay between the local and the global. PIFF screening of *Peppermint Candy* in 1999 should be read with these complex transformations of Korean society in mind.

Putting "Korean Panorama" into a Global/Local Context

Whereas Korean films screened in the "Opening" section over the past decade have mirrored some of the ways in which institutional dynamics interact with the local film industry, "Korean Panorama" offers a key to understanding how individual filmmakers have responded to these institutional dynamics. Since its emergence in the late 1990s, PIFF has become an important part of local cinema. For instance, there was recognition that films shown and spotlighted at PIFF frequently paved the way for global distribution. However, the role of the festival has been gradually forced to shift, and many new local titles find a direct route into the global market without the mediation of local institutions such as PIFF or KOFIC.

Within the festival program structure, local programs generally tend to receive less attention.[40] The main exception to this is "Korean Panorama," which has been continually spotlighted by both foreign guests and the local audience since its inception. "Korean Panorama" aims to showcase a spectrum of the latest Korean films by featuring approximately twelve to fifteen films each year. In common with a number of international film festivals that have utilized their own national cinema sections to achieve overseas visibility, PIFF has attempted to manipulate "Korean Panorama" in order to break through to the global film market. The powerful position of this section can be attributed to the relatively strong potential for global distribution it can create. Consequently, the local film industry has come to believe that PIFF can guarantee the exhibition and distribution of its products. Furthermore, because it became increasingly difficult to be selected for the "Opening" or "Closing" sections since there were so many more local titles being produced, "Korean Panorama" has become the only available section for the Korean film industry to exhibit films to the global market before cinematic release.

However, in recent years, many new titles have begun to be premiered in other prestigious international film festivals such as Cannes, Venice, and Berlin. As a result, PIFF began to lose its special position for showcasing Korean movies in 1999, and since 2003 it has failed to stage the world premiere of any major local titles. Let's consider some examples. Of the films selected for "Korean Panorama" in 1999, the majority had already been shown abroad prior to PIFF. In September of that year, *Lies* (Jang Sun-woo [Chang Sŏnu]) was entered for competition at the Venice Film Festival. In July, Yi Chaeyong's (E Jae-yong) *An Affair* won the grand prize at the Fukuoka Asian Film Festival, while Song Ilgon's (Song Il-gon) *The Picnic* won top prize at the 1999 Melbourne Film Festival. Also, Park Kwang-su's *The Uprising* (*Les Insurgés*, 1999) was screened in competition at Locarno. As Stephen Cremin notes, overseas guests no longer seemed to visit Pusan to watch — "let alone discover" — Korean cinema. Indeed, in May 2006, in addition to the world premiere of Pong Chunho's (Bong Joon-ho) *The Host*, Cannes Festival attendees could catch over twenty Korean films in the market.[41]

Meanwhile, there has been much criticism of "Korean Panorama" because of the number and diversity of films in the section. For instance in 1999, "Korean Panorama" featured eleven local films made throughout that year. Derek Elley, senior critic of *Variety*, commented that this section failed to encompass "the full breadth" of current Korean production.[42] Tony Rayns also complained that "there are many people who mainly come here to see Korean films, so they want to have a good panorama. Panorama should mean panorama, it should mean wider view."[43]

As seen in the examples above, "Korean Panorama" was unable to offer the first showing of Korean films since several filmmakers continually sought, by themselves, to establish an international reputation for their artistic achievements. A clear example is the case of Park Chan-wook, whose films recently gained a high reputation in the global film market. Although almost all films from *The Trio* (1997) to *Sympathy for Mr. Vengeance* (2002), *Old Boy* (2004), and the recent *Sympathy for Lady Vengeance* (2005) were screened in "Korean Panorama," not one had a world premiere in Pusan. As the case of these films illustrates, individual filmmakers and distribution companies have begun to present many local titles directly to the global market without the institutional support of PIFF, often through entry into the competition section of global festivals such as Cannes, Berlin, and Venice. Aware of this difficulty in premiering Korean films in this section, PIFF has striven to find a way to adapt to a more competitive film festival environment by strengthening its Asian identity and remapping Asian films.

Building up Regional Identity as a Regionalization Strategy

In fact, the world of film festivals is always in "a state of flux."[44] Some older festivals vanish while new ones flourish. The Karlovy Vary Film Festival, one of the most important international venues within the "Eastern Bloc" since the 1950s, was put at risk by an attempt to replace it with a new one in Prague between 1995 and 1996.[45] The Hong Kong International Film Festival (HKIFF), once one of the top festivals in East Asia, has been upstaged by its young and dynamic counterpart in Pusan since the late 1990s. More recently, the position of the Tokyo International Film Festival is being threatened by its domestic Tokyo counterpart FILMeX, initiated in 2000.

Considering these circumstances, PIFF's self-generating, self-reflexive regional identification to differentiate itself from the rest of East Asia is notable. In fact, the emphasis on regional identity was prevalent in the region. For example, the HKIFF, established in 1977, had maintained a high international profile as a platform for Asian cinema during the 1980s. On the tenth anniversary in 1986, Hong Kong was clearly aware of its status and identity as a premier film festival in East Asia. In the "Foreword" of the program, Albert Lee commented: "Over the decade, the festival, apart from presenting recent European and American films, has also put much effort into showcasing Asian and Hong Kong cinema. This has given HKIFF its uniqueness among films festivals all over the world."[46]

Significantly, whereas PIFF asserted surprisingly similar rhetoric at its tenth event in 2005, recently the HKIFF seems to have redefined its festival identity in a different way. Celebrating its twenty-fifth year in 2001, the festival organized a special program that integrated three types of ethnic Chinese cinema, including mainland China, Taiwan, and Hong Kong.[47] In the subsequent year, the HKIFF deleted the key section called "Asian Vision," which showcased fourteen to sixteen contemporary Asian films. Instead, in order to differentiate its Asian section from Pusan's "A Window on Asian Cinema" and "New Currents," films produced in the Asian region were now allocated to the "Global Vision" section and a new section named "Age of Independence: New Asian Film and Video," which takes the form of the Asian Digital Competition. These examples reveal the struggle over its status and identity and its self-conscious attempts at differentiating itself from its counterparts in the region.

In this context, it is significant that, while PIFF has responded to local imperatives through local programs, it has always stressed its position as an East Asian "hub." As Korean scholar Kim Soyoung states:

> Pusan, evoking its geographic proximity to the rest of Asia, claims the region as its main focus. The highlighted programme *A Window on Asian Cinema* is an attempt to locate the city of Pusan as a new focus for Asian cinema in competition with the Hong Kong and Tokyo international film festivals. With rising interest in the Asian region and Northeast Asia in particular, Pusan selectively promotes Asian identity to reach out towards the global.[48]

Put simply, PIFF has deployed its Asian identity as a regionalization strategy that works beyond the nation-state rather than situating its festival identity within the national framework. In order to be a platform for Asian cinema, PIFF has become more demanding of world premieres in its competitive "New Currents" section for Asian films. The festival has also specifically used its tenth anniversary to reestablish its strong identity. The Tenth PIFF can be considered a significant moment in its overall structure, identity, and position within a local, regional, and global context. This event has been accompanied by a promotional crusade, involving a massive 31 screens, 307 films from 73 countries, including 122 Asian films, the launch of the Asian Film Academy, and the announcement of the new Asian Film Market from 2006. By aggressively and extensively programming Asian films in the name of "Remapping Asian auteur cinema: Asian Pantheon," the festival has claimed itself to be a critical hub in Asia, upstaging in the process the existing Hong Kong and Tokyo festivals to become the "portal" of first contact with the other "new" Asian cinemas.[49]

In regards to the Korean film industry, PIFF has created the PPP, a so-called "pre-market," where new Asian feature film projects can seek co-financing and/or co-production partners from all over the world. PPP is one of the most distinctive marketing strategies of PIFF, and it represents a direct response to the dramatic transformation of the local/global film market as discussed earlier. Since its establishment in 1998, PPP has positioned itself as the gateway to Asian film projects by proving that a number of its projects have been completed, awarded at prestigious festivals, and distributed to the global audience. For example, the following films which have been spotlighted at global film festivals were completed with PPP funding: *Platform* (Jia Zhangke) in 1998; *Beijing Bicycle* (Wang Xiaoshuai), *Circle* (Jafar Panahi) and *Address Unknown* (Kim Ki-duk) in 1999; *The Bow* (Kim Ki-duk) and *Oasis*

(Lee Chang-dong) in 2001; and *Woman Is the Future of Man* (Hong Sang-soo) in 2002.

Spurred by its initial success, PPP has carved out a major network within Asia's rapidly growing film production sector. Moreover, PIFF and the KOFIC launched the Asian Film Industry Network (modelled on the European Film Promotion Network) and announced a film market in 2006 in which PIFF and South Korea was established as "a prime regional mover."[50] The success of PPP also demonstrates that global-scale film festivals are emerging as a new kind of "global producer" through their powerful involvement with the creative production process via project markets, and newly functioning as a crucial means of production as well as exhibition and distribution. Responding to the transformation in the local film industry and to survive the more competitive environment in the global film market, PIFF has positioned itself as a strong business-oriented film festival by reconstructing Asian identity both in programming and PPP.

5

Global America?
American-Japanese Film Co-productions from *Shogun* (1980) to *Lost in Translation* (2003)

Yoshi Tezuka

> We must now, I believe, talk about a banal cosmopolitanism, in which everyday nationalism is circumvented and undermined and we experience ourselves integrated into global processes and phenomena.[1]

> Here [in developed countries in Asia], cosmopolitanism degenerates into a set of strategies for the biopolitical improvement of human capital. It becomes an ideology used by a state to attract high-end expatriate workers . . .[2]

In their study of how Hollywood's global domination works, Miller et al. argue that exploitation of the "New International Division of Cultural Labour" (NICL) through foreign location production is a key mechanism of its hegemony. According to Miller et al., "Hollywood is global, in that it sells its wares in every nation, through a global system of copyright, promotion and distribution that uses the NICL to minimise costs and maximise revenue."[3] Hollywood thrives on the creative differences and cheap labor offered by foreign talent and location shooting.

Similarly, Goldsmith and O'Regan have investigated the development of a global infrastructure that caters for international English-language film production across the world, in places such as Australia, Canada, the Czech Republic, England, Ireland, Italy, Mexico, Romania, and South Africa. Their study suggests that "this global dispersal of production is best understood as an unstable and unequal partnership between a footloose international production economy and situated local actors and intermediaries."⁴ The strong economic incentives that Hollywood blockbuster projects pose for local industries mean that local actors across the world are driven to invest in studio infrastructure and training of English-speaking crews for global film productions.

How does the Japanese film industry fit into this development of the global film service industry to cater for English-language productions emanating from the US? On the surface, it hardly fits at all. First, the soaring foreign exchange rate in the late 1980s made Japan one of the most expensive countries in the world, and so there was no obvious economic incentive for foreign producers to shoot in Japan. Second, the self-consciousness about Japanese cultural differences prevented Japan from developing a film industry that would attract foreign filmmakers, and a shortage of English-speaking film crews made it very difficult to organize international productions. Third, since the demise of the studio production system in the 1970s, the filmmaking infrastructure had become severely dilapidated.⁵ The Japanese studio facilities and equipment were hopelessly outdated by the 1980s. As result, Japan as a film location built a reputation as a place that was expensive to shoot in, where nobody spoke English, and only inadequate studio facilities and equipment were available. Therefore, structurally speaking, Japan is hardly a part of the worldwide network of what Goldsmith and O'Regan call "The Film Studio," which serves Miller et al.'s "Global Hollywood."

Nevertheless, numerous foreign films have been shot in Japan over the last few decades, and Japan is being integrated into Global Hollywood. This essay discusses the experiences of filmmakers and crews who worked on two international co-productions filmed in Japan: the film and TV series adapted from James Clavell's *Shogun* (Jerry London, 1980) and Sofia Coppola's *Lost in Translation* (2003). Produced over twenty years apart, a period of radical global change separates these two films. Both projects were initiated by English-speaking producers and filmed entirely on location in Japan with different degrees of Japanese financial, technical, and creative participation. Through the analysis of how differently the Japanese and American filmmakers and crews experienced these two international film productions in Japan in each historical context, this essay aims to illustrate the changes in the subjectivities of filmmakers and crews, as well as changes in filmmaking practices before and after the economic globalization that took place in the late 1980s and 1990s. While the primacy of national identity and allegiance to one's national filmmaking community was usually taken for granted in the pre-globalization days, loyalty to a transnational network of filmmakers and meeting with globally accepted — usually American — norms and standards of filmmaking practice has become a professional imperative for those who work in the film industry of the global age.

Economic globalization has engendered a "banal cosmopolitan reality" in which everyday lives of local individuals have become integrated into the global market economy. As a significant "unintended consequence" of economic globalization, Ulrich Beck argues that "banal cosmopolitanism" is changing and undermining the conventional ways we conceive ourselves as national subjects; we all are becoming cosmopolitan in one way or another without knowing it. According to Beck, unlike philosophical or normative cosmopolitanism, "*really existing cosmopolitanization*" in today's world means "latent cosmopolitanism, *unconscious* cosmopolitanism, *passive* cosmopolitanism which shapes reality as side effects of global trade or global threat such as climate change, terrorism or financial crisis"[6] (italics in original). In our banal cosmopolitan reality, he states: "My life, my body, my 'individual existence' become part of another world, of foreign cultures, religions, histories and global interdependencies, without my realizing or expressly wishing it."[7]

By recognizing that subjectivity is a product of disciplinary mechanisms, techniques of surveillance, and power-knowledge strategies in the Foucauldian sense, I believe Beck's observations about the way that the cosmopolitan subject is constituted in the global age are useful for understanding the process of subjectification and subjection of those individuals who work on transnational film production and engage with cultural difference as part of their professional practice. Therefore, I regard their experiences as cases of *really existing cosmopolitanisms*. Most individuals in film industries are becoming cosmopolitans of one kind or another, due to their professional imperative. They develop a technique of the self that requires self-entrepreneurship in the context of "advanced liberalism"[8] in the global age, in which "one constructs one's self with a view to marketability and value-adding propensities."[9]

The political economist Leslie Sklair observed the emergence of "the transnational capitalist class (TCC)," the new ruling class of the global age.[10] One of its main characteristics is that the "TCC seek to project images of themselves as citizens of the world as well as of their places and/or countries."[11] Unlike in classic class theory, the TCC includes not only those who own capital and control major corporations, "but also other groups whose resources and actions are deemed vital to the process of globalization: neo-liberal bureaucrats and politicians, assorted professionals and technocrats, advertisers and the mass media."[12] If we identify the TCC within the context of the global film industry it includes a wide range of people who promote and benefit from the process of globalization, including executive producers in Hollywood, or high-flying independent filmmakers like Sofia Coppola, the director of *Lost in Translation*. Cosmopolitanism's complicity with capitalist accumulation is an age-old truism as Marx points out: "cosmopolitanism is realized as exploitation on a world scale through international commerce and the establishment of a global mode of production."[13] On one hand, Global Hollywood strives on commodification of local differences and cheap labor. But on the other hand, Global Hollywood provides opportunities on a global scale to a small number of local filmmakers and producers who join the TCC, or become local affiliates of the TCC.

I have chosen *Shogun* and *Lost in Translation* as my case studies because they are well-known film productions, which, I believe, represent a certain ethos of the time. Also, they bookend the years before and after economic globalization in the late 1980s and 1990s, leading me to expect that they would show historical difference. The main focus and the key source of my information is the experiences of Japanese line producers. Fujii Hiroaki was in charge of the production of *Shogun* and Inoue Kiyoshi was in charge of the production of *Lost in Translation* in Japan. I carried out semi-structured in-depth interviews with both of them in the summer of 2005. Since I had known both Fujii and Inoue personally for a few years through my film industry contacts, and they knew me as a producer in the UK, the interviews took the form of informal peer conversations.[14] Interviews with James Clavell and Sofia Coppola, as well as members of the American film crew that worked on these two projects, are taken from various existing archives and published materials, including newspapers, film magazine articles, and promotional materials.

The main function of the local line producer in such international co-productions is to act as an interface between the American production team and the local Japanese crew. Both Fujii and Inoue were responsible for managing the budget and organizing Japanese casts, crews, locations, studios, and sets — virtually everything the American production needed for filming. The function of the line producer is absolutely crucial for the production to operate effectively as a coherent team. However, being a mediator is not an easy task, and the line producer is often on the frontline of conflict. The line producer is constantly put in the position of having to mediate and negotiate different loyalties and interests between the two parties.

The main aim of the in-depth interviews was to gain insight into what it was like for the Japanese film crews to work with their American counterparts on these productions, rather than simply obtaining factual information about the productions and confirming archive research. I was interested in knowing how Fujii and Inoue saw the differences and similarities between the American and the Japanese crews and their ways of doing things; how they managed to bring the two sides together to work as a team or how they failed to do so, and what it was like to be mediators as line producers of projects that demand such transcultural practices. In other words, I was interested in studying how they made "cultural distinctions and classifications"[15] through their articulation of nationalistic or cosmopolitan cultural values in their speech. Studying cultural distinction is a way to study "culture": "Within the Birmingham School, where the concept of 'cultural studies' originates, the concept of culture has been taken to refer to something like *collective subjectivity* — that is, a way of life or outlook adopted by a community or social class."[16] In this sense, my main goal was to gain insights about the culture of the Japanese filmmaking community in 1980 and 2003, before and after economic globalization, with particular reference to how they dealt with the Western otherness of American film crews.

The study of cultural distinction concerns how individual interviewees construct reality via studying how each conveys her or his story. A great deal of attention is paid to "how the views or ideas expressed are being produced through different distinctions and classifications"[17] rather than on the factual validity of what is being said, since the study aims to "find out the individuals' inner conceptual world or the motives for their actions."[18] Because I carried out both interviews in the same year, 2005, my two interviewees have different distances from the events in their memories. Moreover, they have different power relations to the dominant discourse of the time in the filmmaking community. While Fujii had to go back twenty-five years to recall his memories, Inoue had only two years, meaning the factual information provided by Inoue may be more accurate than Fujii's. But more importantly, twenty-five years' time lag has given Fujii a critical distance on the dominant discourse of his time, while Inoue did not have such an advantage, being interviewed only two years after the event.

My interviewees belong to different generations and have very different professional backgrounds. Hence, they belong to different filmmaking communities within the Japanese film industry. Fujii is about thirty years older than Inoue and he started his career in a major film studio in the heyday of the Japanese film industry.[19] Inoue started his career in low-budget independent films after the demise of the studio system. Although Fujii and Inoue are both cosmopolitans of their respective generations, I expected their views and attitude towards Americans and transnational practices would be different from each other. I was particularly interested in how they would differ in their openness towards otherness and their attachment to Japanese ways of doing things and feelings.

The Production of *Shogun* (1980)

Shogun was a twelve-hour TV mini-series made for the American network NBC and based on the 1,200-page best-selling novel by James Clavell. The novel was inspired by the real story of an English navigator who reached Japanese shores in 1600. The navigator, William Adams, was given a Japanese name and made a samurai by the *Shogun* (the overall ruler of feudal Japan). He built Japan's first Western-style sailing ship and became a high-ranking officer and adviser on Western matters for the shogun. The film version of *Shogun* concentrates on the subjective experiences of this English navigator, named John Blackthorne, who came into this land of striking otherness and eventually learned a way to respect this seemingly barbaric, foreign way of life.

James Clavell's novel *Shogun* was published in May 1975, and it remained at the top of the best-seller list for thirty-two weeks. Seven million copies were sold in the first five years alone in the US. It was translated into over twenty languages across the world. Outside Japan, *Shogun* probably remains the most widely read novel set in Japan to this day. When *Shogun* was aired on American network television for five days in September 1980, the *New York Times* reported that over thirty percent of American households with television sets watched the series on average, and this hit forty-seven percent in San Francisco.[20] The result was "*Shogun* fever" among the American public, during which Japanese food, *sake*, kimonos, and more sold like hotcakes, and learning a few words of Japanese became a fad.[21] A number of cultural commentators in both Japan and the US linked this phenomenal success of *Shogun* to the rise of the Japanese economy, a rapidly shifting economic power balance between the two countries, and the underlying tensions and anxieties of the American public.[22] In retrospect, this extraordinary reception of *Shogun* was a cultural symptom of the coming "trade war" which led Japan to pursue *Kokusaika* in the 1980s — the opening of the Japanese domestic market and the diminishing of its "cultural uniqueness."

Shogun was Clavell's third novel following *King Rat* (1962) and *Tai-Pan* (1966).[23] His first novel, *King Rat*, was based on his experience as a Japanese prisoner-of-war in Changi Prison near Singapore, one of the harshest POW camps, where he suffered greatly at the hands of his Japanese captors. According to Clavell, the weight of the world shifted from Europe to America after the war, and then "we lost it in the West" and the weight of the world shifted again to the Pacific area. In the Western media in general, *Shogun* was seen as pro-Japanese, a sympathetic portrayal of the strikingly different culture and tradition of the country and people.

Shogun was the first major co-production involving major Japanese financial participation since the small boom of American and European films about Japan in the 1950s.[24] The consortium of Japanese media companies allegedly paid US$7.5 million[25] of a US$22 million budget,[26] in return for the rights to create their own Japanese theatrical version. Tōhokushinsha was in charge of the location shoot in Japan, Tōhō Studios distributed a special Japanese two-and-a-half hour version in cinemas across Japan, and TV Asahi broadcast the television mini-series later.

The shooting of *Shogun* took place over a six-month period in 1979. All the key production personnel — the producer, the director, the cinematographer, the production designer, and the sound mixer — as well as all the key crew plus gaffers, grips, and chief assistants came over from the US. In all, the American crew formed a group of over fifty people. The Japanese crew and cast exceeded 100 on most of the shooting days.[27] In Japan, the production of *Shogun* was publicized as an epic-scale American-Japanese co-production, and an unprecedented cultural event.

However, the filming of *Shogun* was not at all easy for the American crew, and the problems were attributed to "the clash of cultures" between American and Japanese ways of making films. The film director Jerry London states:

> Some of the American crew went home. I had an assistant director, a production manager, a prop man; they just said: "It's too hard. I can't get what I want easily", and left. We had to replace them. It was a tough job, because of the fact it was not a normal way of living. You are living with an entirely different group of people. And, they have their own way of doing things, as we do . . . [28]

It was not that Americans were inexperienced in filming abroad or even that they were inexperienced in filming in Japan. Many American films had been shot without much difficulty in Japan before. In fact, one of the American production managers on *Shogun* had spent years in Japan as part of the occupation force immediately after the war. He was very experienced and knowledgeable about Japan, but things were different this time.

The Japanese Line Producer of *Shogun*: Fujii Hiroaki

My main interviewee for this case study, Fujii Hiroaki, was born in 1929 and was a student during the war. Upon graduation from a prestigious private university, he joined Daiei Motion Picture Company, one of the Japanese major studios that produced many international prize-winning films such as *Rashōmon* (Akira Kurosawa, 1950), *Ugetsu* (Kenji Mizoguchi, 1952) and *Jigokumon* — *The Gate of Hell* (Teinosuke Kinugasa, 1953). The president of Daiei Motion Picture, Masaichi Nagata, led the internationalization of Japanese cinema in the 1950s.[29] Daiei had facilitated numerous foreign productions such as *The Tea House of the August Moon* (Daniel Mann, 1956); *Hiroshima Mon Amour* (Alain Resnais, 1959); and *Flight from Ashiya* (Michael Anderson, 1964). Fujii has a reputation of being a cosmopolitan type in the Japanese film industry, because he has had experiences shooting films abroad and facilitating foreign film crews in Japan[30] Like the majority of the educated class of his generation, Fujii reads English but is not comfortable in spoken communication. According to Fujii's regular interpreter, Fujii is actually quite competent in English but he prefers to speak through an interpreter.[31] As far as I know, Fujii was the most cosmopolitan Japanese film producer available in 1980. In fact, I do not know of a single Japanese film producer of his generation and caliber whose English is fluent enough and who is confident enough to communicate with Westerners without an interpreter.

As the Japanese line producer, Fujii was in charge of organizing all the production requirements for the American production team. *Shogun* was not an easy operation and many crew members were hired and fired, which would have been very unusual on a Japanese production. Unlike Americans, who were used to working on weekly contracts, Japanese crews were normally employed for the entire period of a production. They did not leave or got fired, except under extraordinary circumstances. Nevertheless, Fujii found the *Shogun* production intolerable and left halfway through. He was in what he felt was irreconcilable disagreement with the executive producer, James Clavell.

According to Fujii, the nature of the problem on the *Shogun* production was apparent from the very beginning. It was the American lack of trust in the Japanese team and lack of understanding about the ways things work in Japan. During the pre-production period, for example, the American production team came over to scout for the main locations. They brought over the American production manager, an ex-air force lieutenant who had spent years in Japan as part of the occupation force. He tended to command the Japanese production team in the "occupation force" manner. He was trusted as a "Japan expert" by other Americans, and the location scouting was organized based on his memory from thirty years ago. However, Fujii pointed out that it would probably have been much easier and more efficient if the Americans had trusted the Japanese and consulted their local knowledge, instead of just issuing orders. Fujii felt the production of *Shogun* was reminiscent of the military occupation: "Thirty years after the occupation, they still treated us like twelve-year-olds, just as General MacArthur had done."

There was a short period during the occupation when the Japanese media often referred to the Japanese population as "the children of MacArthur" and enthusiastically celebrated the liberty and democracy that the occupation had brought over. They fantasized about being part of Western modernity along with America, but disillusion came when General MacArthur made a famous speech in the American Congress that compared the mental age of the Japanese to that of "a boy of twelve." The speech made it blatantly clear that the Japanese did not belong to the same modernity as the Americans and that they would never be conceived of as equals. This disillusion inscribed deep shame, resentment, and impotency within the postwar Japanese psyche.[32] Thus, at the bottom of the trust problem and communication difficulties was the stigma of the war and occupation, which resurfaced as Japan regained its confidence as its economic power grew.

A similar point was made by Adachi Chiho, the 26-year-old bilingual secretary to James Clavell, who had spent part of her life in the US. Adachi stated that one of the Americans had been in Japan just after the war. At that time, the Americans took the role of teachers:

> I think he had the same image 30 years later. . . . We are going to Japan again to teach these people how to make a film. And he influenced the rest of the crew. It was like, "We're going to be the teachers and they're going to learn, and we are going to do it in our way." But as you know, Japan has come up in the world since then. They have their own ways, and they are set ways. It was hard for them to accept that here are these Americans coming in and ordering them around and if they said anything, the Americans would just reject it.[33]

As a result, there were constant conflicts during the production of *Shogun* and Japanese crew members often felt degraded. However, this was financially well compensated. Before he left the production as the line producer in charge of the budget, Fujii had negotiated the Japanese crew rates according to the old studio union agreements. The Japanese crew were paid handsome overtime, double-time over the weekend, and so on, even though none of this was the practice in the Japanese film industry anymore.

The Japanese film labor market was rapidly shifting towards flexible specialization — short contracting on a job-to-job basis — during the 1970s, and freelancers were not unionized. Only some of the Japanese crew working on *Shogun* were members of Tōhō Studios' union and the majority were freelance.[34] Nevertheless, the rates of crew payment for all Japanese crew on *Shogun* were based on the studio union agreements, including all the extra charges stipulated in the old union rules. This made jobs on *Shogun* well paid. According to Fujii, there were several reasons for this. First, extra incentive was necessary to recruit high-quality professionals. Second, even with all those extra charges the Japanese labor costs were still low by Hollywood standards, and so the American producer accepted them without much quibbling. Even the extra cash per diem payments for location expenses that were not in the Japanese union rules were paid in accordance with the normal American practice. Fujii stressed that he was just doing his best to make sure his Japanese crew was treated as fairly as possible. Indeed, his reputation for being a cosmopolitan is partly based on his negotiation skills with foreigners.

Fujii decided to leave the production of *Shogun* halfway through, even though the job was very well paid. The discord with the American production team, and executive producer James Clavell in particular, became unbearable for him. Fujii described Clavell as "solemnly pompous." I found Fujii's reaction a little emotional, so I asked him if he thought the problem was something to do with Clavell being a survivor of Japanese war atrocities; it is well-known that Clavell survived one of the worst Japanese camps, where fourteen out of fifteen prisoners died.[35] Fujii was not sure if that had something to do with his problems with Clavell, but he was certain that both American and Japanese attitudes and relations were still affected by the war.

The Production of *Lost in Translation* (2003)

Economic globalization, or, what was then called *Kokusaika* — "internationalization" — in Japan in the late 1980s and 1990s, banally cosmopolitanized the life of the Japanese middle classes. *Kokusaika*, the Japanese configuration of economic globalization, refers to "The switch from export-led to domestic demand-led economic growth, the gradual diminution of Japan's 'uniqueness,' and the sharing of the burdens of maintaining free trade and a growing world economy together with the United States and the European Community."[36]

Kokusaika was about the moderation of Japanese cultural exceptionalism and the beginning of attempts to integrate alleged Japanese "uniqueness" into the emerging global economy in the post-Cold War constellation of powers. In practical terms, *kokusaika* was a consumption-based project that purported to open the Japanese market further for foreign goods, symbols, and labor. It was in this economic and cultural milieu of *kokusaika* in the 1990s in Tokyo that the director of *Lost in Translation*, Sofia Coppola, found a successful professional career as a fashion designer and photographer, the experience of which became the basis for her film.

Lost in Translation is about two Americans, a young woman (Scarlett Johansson) and a middle-aged actor (Bill Murray), who are stuck in a Tokyo hotel. She is newly married but left alone in a city where she knows nobody and has nothing to do. The actor is earning easy money by appearing in a whisky TV commercial. However, his stay has been accidentally extended, so he is also stuck in a city where he knows nobody and has nothing to do. They form a sort of comradeship and explore the city together, and become romantic and introspective in turns.

The director, Sofia Coppola, states that it is about the two characters "going through a similar personal crisis, exacerbated by being in a foreign place."[37] The Park Hyatt, a high-tech designer hotel frequented by Western celebrities in Tokyo, and the floods of neon signs on the streets, which look so beautiful but do not mean anything to these characters, provide an ideal setting for this romantic tale of being lost in a cosmopolitan environment.

The story is said to be based on Sofia Coppola's personal experiences in Tokyo. She visited Tokyo frequently when searching for a new career direction in the 1990s. Her acting career had gone into a steep dive after *The Godfather: Part III* (1990), a film directed by her father, Francis Ford Coppola, in which her "portrayal of Mary Corleone was widely attacked and ridiculed."[38] Sofia Coppola found herself being treated much more seriously in Japan. She published a book of her photographs and created a clothing label called Milk Fed with an old school friend in 1995. Coppola states that, although "Milk Fed is now sold almost exclusively in Japan, where the clothes are produced . . . the clothing company does well enough that I don't have to make money from movies."[39] She often stayed at the Park Hyatt Hotel, where she filmed *Lost in Translation*, when she was in Tokyo. Tokyo and the Park Hyatt Hotel are special places for Coppola, because there she found new professional success and a grown-up identity.

Lost in Translation was filmed entirely on location in Tokyo. The twenty-seven days of filming took place in autumn 2002, and its modest budget of US$4 million, of which approximately US$1.7 million was spent in Tokyo, was financed independently with some Japanese participation.[40] About a dozen key crew and cast flew from the US. The film was intended to be a low-budget production by American standards and based on the independent spirit of location filmmaking, meaning that a minimal crew with minimal equipment would go to the location and shoot, sometimes even without permits. The American producer, Ross Katz, indicated that it was Coppola's philosophy not to impose the American way of doing things on Japan. She wanted to learn and to adapt to how the Japanese crew made films. Her intention was to collaborate.[41]

Nevertheless, the production was not without real crises. For example, in the second week of the shoot, when a Japanese location manager and an assistant director declared that they were quitting because the situation was out of control and they had had enough, a gap began to open up between the two sides that brought the production to a halt. This happened after a day of shooting in a busy *shabu-shabu* hotpot restaurant. The location was available only on condition that they would abide strictly to a time limit, and the Japanese location manager had given a personal guarantee to the owner of the restaurant in order to make filming on that day possible. However, the day went slowly and filming went on much longer than anybody had expected. Coppola and her cameraman kept shooting despite the repeated warnings and pleas from the Japanese location manager and the assistant director. They had gone beyond the time limit by "hours" and the restaurant owner was fuming. Eventually, the location manager had to physically pull the plug — cut the electricity.

At the end of the long shooting day, Inoue, the line producer, summoned everybody — the Japanese location manager and assistant director, Sofia Coppola, Ross Katz and the cameraman — for a meeting to talk over the problem. Later, Coppola recalled that night, to answer a question from an American journalist, "How did you get over the language barrier in Japan?"

> You can offend people without knowing you are. We were shooting late at one location, we were only about ten minutes late — totally normal for American shoots, but there we had totally disrespected them. So it was definitely a challenge getting through all that.[42]

In some situations, what feels like "only about ten minutes" for one person feels like "hours" for others. Eventually though, a reconciliation between the Japanese location manager and Coppola and her cameraman was effected in the meeting, so that business went on as usual from the next day again. However, Katz, Coppola, and her cameraman had to go to apologize to the restaurant owner to save the face of the Japanese location manager. Inoue reckons that Katz and Coppola were palpably not comfortable offering apologies for a problem that they did not really acknowledge. But Inoue was glad they did it anyway, because their gesture helped a great deal to smooth feelings over, and he managed to talk the location manager out of quitting.

The Japanese Line Producer of *Lost in Translation*: Inoue Kiyoshi

Inoue Kiyoshi started working in the low-budget independent sector of the Japanese film industry in the early 1980s, while he was still a college student.[43] After years of working in the impoverished conditions of the Japanese film industry, he decided to go to the US. According to him, the reason was that he thought "speaking English and communicating with foreigners would be essential for the work in future. And I wanted to learn the American way of filmmaking." Being a freelance assistant producer and director, Inoue was not earning very much, and he did not have rich parents. But still it was possible for him to study in the United States, because of the strength of the Japanese yen and social conditions under *kokusaika* that encouraged young Japanese to study abroad. The dollar came down to 125 Japanese yen in 1988, making a dollar worth half what it was worth before the 1985 Plaza Agreement that allowed the dollar to depreciate against the yen. Also, "banal cosmopolitanization" was taking root.

Inoue spent two and a half years studying English and filmmaking in Los Angeles. Then, in 1991, he met the producer Doug Claybourne, who was preparing location filming in Japan for *Mr. Baseball* (Fred Schepisi, 1992). Inoue was hired as a production assistant for *Mr. Baseball*, and he came back to Japan as a part of the American production team. Inoue's spoken English is not perfect; he speaks with a rather heavy Japanese accent. But he is willing and confident enough to communicate in English on most production matters and he seems at ease among Westerners.

Unfortunately, *Mr. Baseball* became another American production in Japan that suffered from the so-called "clash of cultures" between Japanese and American crews. However, in Inoue's view, the main cause of the problems was less to do with "cultural differences" than with the clash between big Hollywood movie-making culture and smaller, non-Hollywood, ways of making films. According to Inoue, "Japanese locations are not suitable for big Hollywood productions: if they want to shoot in Japan it is better to adopt more independent ways of filmmaking."[44] Inoue's point is the scale of the production and the materials necessary to sustain the grandeur of Hollywood productions make location work in Japan impossible. For instance, the number of vehicles the Hollywood production demanded made moving from one location to the next through narrow Japanese streets painfully slow. Finding parking spaces anywhere near the location was impossible, because of the general lack of space in Japan. The number of crew and cast members and the amount of equipment that the Hollywood production demanded was impossible to accommodate in most of the Japanese buildings, and so forth.

Hollywood productions demand the same scale and standard wherever they go in the world, just as if they were shooting in California. However, according to Inoue, working on *Lost in Translation* was a very different experience from working on *Mr. Baseball*, mostly because *Lost in Translation* was an independent production. For Inoue, the borderline that marks the real cultural difference is not about national culture but about differences between Hollywood and independent filmmaking cultures:

> Independent filmmaking is far more flexible, and independent filmmakers share similar problems everywhere in the world. Since I came from the independent background myself, I enjoyed working on *Lost in Translation* much more than I did on *Mr. Baseball.*[45]

Inoue identifies himself as an "independent film producer" transnationally, and this occupational identity appears to override his loyalty to the interests of other Japanese film crew members to a certain extent. Inoue became involved with *Lost in Translation* through Stephen Schible, a Japanese-speaking co-producer of *Lost in Translation* in New York. They had come to know each other through a low-budget Japanese independent film shot in New York called *Artful Dodgers* (Takuo Yasuda, 1998). Inoue estimated the Japanese part of the production budget for the producer, Ross Katz. He gave a very competitive estimate, which included an offer to set up Lost in Translation Ltd in Japan, and operate all finances through this company. In this way, the American production company could avoid paying production mark-ups. These would usually be between ten and fifteen percent of the expenditure in Japan, and paid to a Japanese production service company.

Lost in Translation was made on a tight budget, and Inoue is proud that the production was managed cost-effectively. He insists that *Lost in Translation* did not cost any more than a Japanese independent film of similar size would have cost. He negotiated everything on the basis of what a low-budget Japanese independent film production would pay. Moreover, Inoue admits the crew labor costs were kept at the lower end of the scale even by Japanese independent standards. Inoue thought this was appropriate, because *Lost in Translation* was an independent film on a tight budget, even though it was American. Having seen the global box office success of *Lost in Translation*, however, Inoue now feels that perhaps he should have paid his Japanese crew a bit better. But, of course, this is something he could have never known in advance. To be a good independent line producer, he just had to do his best to be as competitive as possible.

Comparing the Japanese Line Producers Fujii Hiroaki and Inoue Kiyoshi

The contrast between the cultural distinctions that the two Japanese line producers, Fujii Hiroaki and Inoue Kiyoshi, made in their interviews also indicates a discursive disjuncture between 1980 and 2003. For Fujii, the primacy of national identity comes naturally and he showed no hesitation in identifying himself as a "Japanese producer" who belonged to the history and tradition of the Japanese cinema and film industry. In his thinking, respect for national culture is the precondition for international cooperation. Therefore, he was more or less saying that, if Americans come to Japan to make films about Japan, they should trust the Japanese and follow Japanese ways. In contrast, for Inoue, who started his filmmaking career after the demise of the Japanese studio production system and its tradition, his sense of belonging to the Japanese cinema and film industry is far more ambiguous. Inoue sees himself primarily as "an independent producer" and defines himself almost in resistance to both the Japanese majors and Hollywood production alike. His occupational identity seems to come before national identity, and he expressed a strong feeling of affiliation to the independent filmmaking community that is supposedly transnational. Inoue stated:

> I like working on independent films and I like working on international projects. It used to be the case only major film companies were involved in international projects, but not anymore. Like *Lost in Translation,* independent filmmaking has also become international. Producing independent films is always a financial struggle, but I find the experience more rewarding.[46]

The difference between Fujii's and Inoue's ideas about what a good line producer should be and where his loyalty should lie is manifested most clearly in the ways they handled Japanese crew rates. For Fujii, it was important and necessary to pay all Japanese crew, including freelancers, impartially. Here, the normal division in the Japanese labor market between the studio employees and freelancers was erased against the external otherness of the American employer. Fujii mentioned the friendship he developed with American crew members of *Shogun* and the respect he gained for their expertise. However, when he had to take sides, loyalty seemed to lie naturally with the Japanese crew.

In contrast, Inoue set the crew rates at the same level as for Japanese low-budget independent productions, which means that the rates on *Lost in Translation* were on the lower end even for by Japanese standards, despite the fact that the Japanese film workers' rates are already much lower than American rates. The reason is that the Japanese labor market for film workers had been fully flexibly specialized by the late 1980s, they were not unionized, and they had no means of group negotiation or wage protection.[47] At one point during the interview in his office, he pulled out the actual budget and cost report of *Lost in Translation* from a bookshelf and showed it to me. This openness surprised me, because producers are normally very secretive about actual numbers, even if there is no reason to hide them. Inoue showed me the budget. It was compiled using standard American production budget software, which is rarely used in Japan. Furthermore, he was keen to demonstrate the transparency of his budget and the way he ran the production according to internationally accepted norms and standards, the so-called "global standard." He showed a few signs of regret when he talked about the level of wages he paid to the Japanese crew, but that was the nature of the global film business and there was nothing he could do about it.

As Beck cogently points out, the "*really existing cosmopolitanism*" (emphasis in original) is often "deformed cosmopolitanism . . . because it is sustained by individuals who have very few opportunities to identify with something greater than what is dictated by their circumstances,"[48] like financially struggling local filmmakers and producers who venture into transcultural projects. The comparative case study of the two Japanese line producers, I believe, clearly demonstrates the transition from "national" to "cosmopolitan" discursive regimes, which shapes their subjectivity. Inoue's case signals the emergence of Japanese transnational identity which identifies with a transnational community. It also shows the extent to which TCC ideology has permeated self-proclaimed "independent" filmmakers.

6

In between the Values of the Global and the National:
The Korean Animation Industry

Ae-Ri Yoon

> "Globalization" is on everybody's lips . . . For some, "globalization" is
> what we are bound to do if we wish to be happy; for others
> "globalization" is the cause of our unhappiness. For everybody, though,
> "globalization" is the intractable fate of the world, an irreversible process;
> it is also a process which affects us all in the same measure and in the same
> way. We are all being "globalized" — and being "globalized" means
> much the same to all who "globalized" are.[1]

Globalization is indeed on everybody's lips and it may be *the* concept of
our time, as quoted above. We are often told that the world is interconnected
and operates interdependently in economic and political terms; technical
developments have compressed time-distance,[2] so that the shrinking world
is described as a "global village." Consequently, there is a myth-like belief
that homogeneous global culture is emerging.[3] However closely
interconnected the world seems, it is clear that globalization is not balanced
or fair to everyone. Bauman clearly states that globalization can mean either
"happiness" or "unhappiness" to different people.[4] Indeed, globalization is
a complicated process of various "political, economic and cultural flows"[5]
among the global, the national, and the local, and therefore may not make
everybody equally happy. Furthermore, when global discourses are combined
with local knowledge, or rather when a local tradition encounters a global
newness, disharmony is predictable. There must be conflict, dilemmas, and
struggles, followed by negotiation.

Negotiation occurs where we live, work, and pursue happiness. Therefore, a full understanding of globalization cannot neglect personal and intimate experience. Yet little empirical research into such areas exists. I want to emphasize that only a focus on "today's personal experiences" can grasp the very problematic globalization process of the present. However, the majority of current debates about globalization are distant from the reality of ordinary life. An example is the debate on globalization using historical data, which Friedman himself recognizes as "'big structures and huge processes' that are decidedly 'experience far'."[6] However, believing that "experience near"[7] empirical work should be taken equally seriously to help our understanding of globalization, I propose turning our attention to those who are marginalized and often overlooked. How differently do people in different places react to and experience globalization on the basis of their history, culture, and personal experiences? How do they manage to balance the different influences of the global and the national? What are the consequences, or to be more precise costs, they have to pay for pursuing the values of both spheres? To answer these questions, it is fundamental to examine the globalization process from people's lived experiences and emotions, because these may capture significant differences that reveal another important stage of the globalization process that I call "critical negotiation."

Therefore, this essay presents the stories of animators in South Korea (hereafter Korea), who experience the negotiation process of globalization both in their work and daily lives and feel them deeply. For the past forty years or more, the Korean animation industry has widely been known as a subcontractor for foreign production companies, mainly in the US and Japan. However, today's Korean animation industry is experiencing a cultural transition driven by the logic of global capital. In response, the industry as a whole is trying to throw off the shackles of being a subcontractor and is aiming for creative agency. This has also caused various changes in the Korean public's perception of animation. My findings show that, in this cultural transition, due to Korea's particular historical and cultural circumstances (explained later), the Korean animators are encountering contradictory situations that are leading them into numerous negotiations between the values of the global and the national. These negotiations are as ambivalent and complicated as the tangled historical web of Korea itself.

This case study is part of a larger research project with empirical data collected during fieldwork, including personal interviews with forty participants in the Korean animation industry, and observation at a Japanese OEM animation production company.[8] Throughout this study, I strive to convey the situation that the Korean animation industry faces. But more important, I pursue a wider understanding of the Korean animators' struggles as they tackle their transitional status, and I do so with their own voices rather than through institutional analysis or by making assumptions on their behalf.

It is easy to see negotiations between different cultures as spaces for creating new cultural representations (as theorized, for example, through hybridization and glocalization), or for witnessing the coexistence of a number of cultures (as theorized, for example, through multiculturalism and cultural pluralism). The particular forms of negotiation that the Korean animators have been experiencing cannot accurately be analyzed using such established theoretical concepts. Therefore, to capture the animators' subjective and complicated experiences and their different realizations of the globalization process, in this research I use "in-between" as a central concept.

"In-between" in this essay is an analytic tool enabling us to perceive how the negotiations experienced by neglected individuals challenge our understanding of the globalization system. My use of the term "in-between" is not that of Homi Bhabha — though there may be similarities in matters of hybridity — but rather derives from a technical term in animation production.[9] Here, "in-between" indicates the numerous small movements that connect one key frame to another; the animators who do the drawings to produce these movements are called "in-betweeners." This process is to make the characters' movements as smooth and aesthetically natural as possible to the viewer, though it requires intensive labor. Appropriating this term, here I define "in-between" in two ways. First, it refers in the case of the Korean animation industry to numerous conflicting transitional stages between being subcontracted laborers and becoming creative and autonomous agents. Second, on a larger scale, it refers to the unavoidable negotiations between the local and global animation spheres that are often neglected but, in fact, are reflected in other fields and industries in their globalization process. This "in-between" experience happens in many parts of the world differently on the basis of different histories, cultures, and social contexts. What this research tells us is that globalization is a problematic process that involves conflict and dilemmas in various forms that have to be negotiated when the local encounters the global. Although I have found several different in-between stages (occurring between the pillars of the global and the local), in this essay I focus on the negotiation that mirrors the animators' struggles between Korean traditional ideology and the newly found industrial values of animation.

Prior to the main investigation, I briefly analyze the past and present situation of the Korean animation industry as seen against particular conditions in Korea that accentuate the inevitable "in-between" state.

Korean Animation: The Past and the Present

Korea as a nation has gone through various political and historical upheavals. From the beginning of the twentieth century to 1945 it was under Japanese colonial occupation. The Korean War from 1950 to 1953 eventually divided the country into North and South. These national tragedies injured national pride and fuelled a competitive spirit. Most important, the basic struggle for survival focused the nation on economic development to feed its people. So, for Korea's government, economic power became the major way to unload the burdens of the past, build Korea's new image, and receive global recognition.[10] This is clearly reflected in the political manifesto of the former president, Park Chung-hee:

> My chief concern, however, was economic revolution. One must eat and breathe before concerning himself with politics, social affairs, and culture. Without a hope for an economic future, reforms in other fields could not be expected to yield fruit.[11]

The desperation to overcome poverty and famine was sublimated into complete devotion to industrial and manufacturing development, later championed as "the miracle on the Han River."[12] During this time, animation was a marginalized media genre. It was regarded as fit only for children to watch, but also, ironically, as harmful to children's morals.[13] It was seen as both "too cheap to appreciate as culture" and "too luxurious to spend money on" at a time when making ends meet was the main priority. As a result, it was cold-shouldered by the Korean public from the 1970s until recently. Despite these problems, Korea has become a major international producer of animated film and ranks third in the world, after the US and Japan.[14] How could this be possible? Its massive output is created by countless subcontractors, production companies both big and small. Known in the industry as OEMs, they are normally responsible for the "in-between" process discussed above. However, this process does not require creativity, because most OEM commissions come with firm guidelines. In other words, Korea has been a hidden production force as a "surrogate mother"[15] and "back office"[16] for foreign animation production such as *The Simpsons* (US), *Batman* (US), and *Spirited Away* (Japan).[17] An anonymous provider in the global division of cultural labor under democratic capitalism, Korean animators' efforts are not particularly recognized or appreciated either inside or outside the country. Instead, they are often heavily criticized for "lack of creativity."[18] Moreover, Kim Joon-Yang argues that the majority of Koreans consider that OEM "was new imperialism in the territory of animated film" and regard it as a "national disgrace."[19] Considering Korea's colonial history with Japan and the politically complicated involvement of the US in the Korean War, such an account is not an overstatement. Indeed, it shows the national sensitivity about being victimized by strong foreign countries.[20] However, the animators' inevitable choice of OEM work should be considered in relation to the then-poor national economic situation, rather than subjected to harsh criticism. They have their own explanations.

Veterans of more than twenty or thirty years and who are animation experts hold different views and had different reasons for working in the OEM industry. "Mr Big Smile" (39 years old) has worked with numerous animators and is the author of a book about Korean animation history. He explains:

> In the 1970s, purely because of economic hardship, we had to take OEM work. There was no correct model for the Korean animation industry to follow from the beginning. In the end, this has led to absence of creativity in Korean animation history. Without money, what can you do? What can you create?

A similar scenario was outlined by "The Boss" (52 years old), whose career in animation has spanned more than thirty years. He now runs his own OEM animation company. His account tells us how difficult conditions were in the 1970s and how hard animators had to work to make a living:

> We had to do OEM work. There was no choice. We had to live. It was such a hard time. We had to keep deadlines and stick to them! For twenty years, I never had a vacation. Never! I don't have any memory of having a break, even during national holidays and weekends. I only went home five days a month, and that was only if I was lucky. Otherwise, I stayed working non-stop in my office. The average working day was fifteen to sixteen hours, and the maximum twenty hours.

The above statement shows that the expression of "hanging on by one's fingertips" was the cruel reality of Korean animators then. Economic rewards may not "inspire creativity"[21] by themselves, but they may help, especially in modern society where income can be the best motivator for productive action. It seems that, during those difficult economic days, the animators might also have believed that monetary rewards and financial stability would inspire future creativity. "The Boss" went on to explain that it was possible for him to bear the hard times in the past, for he had a dream that one day he could create his own work. Many of my informants expressed a common view, regardless of how long they had worked in the industry: working in the OEM industry was and is only a steppingstone and training period for their future creative work. Therefore, many young animators start as an in-betweener at OEM animation companies despite the extremely low wages and poor living conditions. They are hungry for chances to expose their artistic instincts, creativity, and skills, and monetary reward is only a small motivation. The promising changes in today's Korean animation industry may be what these animators have been waiting for. In recent years and particularly since the mid-1990s, animators and the animation industry have suddenly come under an enormous cultural spotlight.

> For a long time Korea was seen as a place where Europeans could make their cartoons in a cheap way. When slowly the makers found an even cheaper place in China, Korea started to develop its own *anime*. Korean films [should] earn more attention than they get now. They have their own style.[22]

I suggest three main reasons why Korean animation is being recognized. First, however severely criticized, the long history of OEM work has undeniably resulted in huge improvements in Korean animators' ability to take on board new styles, techniques, and drawing skills. Second, having achieved a technical base and skills, today young Korean animators have begun to realize the long-time ambition of producing their own creative animation work. As a result, many examples of Korean animation are now being recognized as original enough to attract world audiences. The fantasy animation *My Beautiful Girl, Mary* (*Mari iyagi*, 2001) by Yi Sŏnggang, which can be described as a fairytale for adults, won the Grand Prix at the Annecy International Animated Film Festival in 2002. At the same festival in 2004, Sung Baek-yeop's *Oseam* (2003), based on a Korean Buddhist folktale, also won the Grand Prix, one of the animation world's most prestigious awards. Pak Sejong's *Birthday Boy* (*Pŏsŭdei poi*, 2004), the story of a small boy in the Korean War, was nominated for an Academy Award for Best Short Subject in 2005. An educational animation, *The Birds & the Bees — a Secret You Shouldn't Keep* (*Aidŭri sanŭn sŏng*) by Kwak Yŏngjin and Kim Yŏngbŏm, 2005), and Ch'oe Hyŏnmyŏng's graduation film, *Walking in the Rainy Day* (*Pi onŭn narŭi sanchaek*, 2005), also won awards in the 2006 Annecy Festival.

Parallel to the increasing world recognition of Korean animators' creativity has been the increasingly positive attitudes of Korean audiences. Public perceptions of animation are changing from seeing it as a "children's medium" to appreciating it as a tool of cultural economic power. This is the third reason for the recognition of Korean animation. Reportedly, it was prompted by the successful model *The Lion King* (Roger Allers and Rob Minkoff, 1994) by global media tycoon Disney. The film grossed US$312,855,561 in the US and almost US$768 million worldwide,[23] while merchandising (videos, DVDs, toys, and so on) generated almost US$450 million in revenue.[24] Clearly, animation can contribute to national wealth and increase economic power. For a nation like Korea, whose past fifty years have been solely devoted to economic growth and national development, the example of *The Lion King* came as a surprise and a challenge. It was a great opportunity to break the shackles of animation's negative image and redeem it as a "golden goose": "Animation is a golden goose industry, a pollution-free industry with no chimneys, and an intellectual/knowledge industry for an era of infinite competition."[25] These astonishing changes confirm that a cultural transition is occurring in the Korean animation industry and that it has been initiated by the dynamic forces of globalization and contested Korean nationalism. Figures 6.1 and 6.2 represent well how Korean animators feel about the current state of the Korean animation industry.

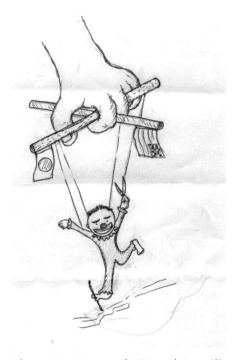

Figure 6.1 Puppet of USA and Japan?[26]

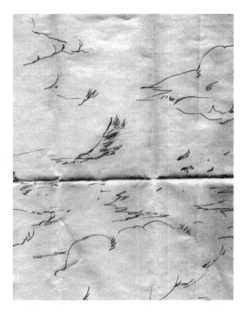

Figure 6.2   Be Free and Creative!!![27]

How are Korean animators coping with these sudden changes? Examining these questions will show how globalization has influenced and shaped Korean animators' daily experiences.

Traditional Ideology and Animators' Struggles

One of the most important factors behind Korea's accelerating economic growth is the power of education, rooted in traditional Korean Confucianism.[28] Its ideology is based on "adoration for literature and contempt for arts," and such an attitude continues for animators. In today's Korea, "string pulling"[29] through the education system, which Bourdieu points to as "social capital,"[30] helps people to succeed in various ways. Networking through one's old schools can help build social bonds, which Winch aptly expresses as "norms of trust prevalent within a society."[31] Admission to high-ranking Korean universities became a successful way out in a competitive society characterized by "examination hell" and "examination mania."[32] Given this social context, it is easy to understand why animators would have low social status, because they are assumed to be "less academic." As well as such an emphasis on literacy and education in Confucianism, family values that accentuate blood ties operate significantly in Koreans' minds. Responding to parents' expectations is regarded as filial affection and virtue. From the research results, it was possible to grasp that these national values shape both the animators' position in society and their own decision-making processes before entering the industry. The consequences are represented in the form of individual educational and career detours.

"Rough Rabbit" (29 years old) did his first degree in electronics and used to work as an engineer. But, out of his desire to become a 3D animator, he quit and started learning animation. He told me how hard it was to make his mind up:

> [While working at the company] I was not able to do my own creative [animation] work there. So I left. My mother was furious. She did not understand why I left the job and started a master's degree in animation. She often asks me why I am wasting my specialist knowledge and education.

A similar episode was shared by "Mr Gentle" (45 years old). He has worked in the animation industry for twenty years and now is an established animation director. He recalled the time when he had just started in animation:

> When I was young, it was common that people who drew got less attention, and an artist was probably the least favored occupation for most parents. Anyway, my father didn't like it. I liked to draw, but somehow I majored in electronics at university. It was a spur-of-the-moment decision that I quit a company job and got into the animation industry. I did not have any income whatsoever at the beginning because I was still a trainee animator. So, it was no surprise to see my entire family in total shock, and they yelled at me, "What on earth did you leave your job for? Are you out of your mind?"

It is not only the parents' generation that looks down at animation as a profession; such attitudes are also common among the younger generation. "Baby Face" (23 years old) did not go to university and started her career as an animator right after high school. She explained, clearly upset,

> [With other animators] all we talk about is animation and comics day and night . . . but people [in Korea] think that only kids watch animation. That's why I cannot communicate with the average person . . . they are not interested in us and keep their distance. If I started a conversation with someone who has such fixed ideas, we would end up snarling at

each other. So, normally I don't talk about animation with people outside the office.

All this indicates that, for Koreans, and especially for the parents' generation who experienced famine and poverty in the 1950s Korean War, the persistent demands to pursue higher education are mostly related to financial concerns. In this sense, being an animator is not an ideal profession; only a small percentage make big money and many trainees and low-ranking in-betweeners make very little. In most cases, animators start their career as in-betweeners and experience financial hardship for many years. During my interview with "Baby Face," she saw my new MP3 recorder and asked the price, which led her to talk about her wages and financial hardship:

> I worked overtime for more than twenty-eight days last month, and can you guess how much I earned from it? Total US$367![33] I was broke, a total beggar! How sad is this life, huh?

To my surprise, her monthly income was less than the price of an MP3 recorder. Many animators undergo hardship, and such financial instability is often seen as "falling behind the modern competition."[34] As a result, animators feel obliged to compensate for their parents' disappointment and, by working hard, strive to prove that their decisions to work in animation were right. "Yellow Giant" (35 years old) started as an in-betweener the year he finished high school, despite his mother's persistent demand that he go on to higher education. After sixteen years, he has become an art director. He explained that his mother's disappointment was unbearable when he started as a trainee in-betweener at an OEM company:

> To make up for her disappointment with my decision, she bought me a nice suit to wear at work. Everybody in the office gave me a funny look. (Laughs) I started as an in-betweener in 1990 and in my third month, I earned US$965. I drew 2,000 pages that month, day and night, and that was how I made that amount. It was a big sum in the 1990s. After seeing so much money, my mother stopped scolding me and started encouraging me.

"She bought me a nice suit to wear at work" in fact represents Korean parents' very last act of unyielding self-respect to keep their child from "failing" in the social competition.[35] These social and cultural attitudes are an inescapable part of the milieu that animators inhabit, and this may be why Confucian family values have such a large impact on animators. Nevertheless, especially since the 1990s, globalization has entered Korean society and the animation market, and Korean animators as well as the general public have been more exposed to global discourses. For animators, this occurs through their own subcontracting work, American and Japanese comics and animations they look at, and the computer skills they acquire for their work. For audiences, it happens through television and film, Internet downloading, and DVDs. Factors from global discourses add to Korean animators' existing struggles and problems caused by national values and lead them into new dilemmas and challenges, producing further in-between struggles for them.

Newly Found Industrial Values Challenge Animators

In some ways, Korean animators have experienced benefits from globalization because it has given them a means to make a living. However, the old helpful aspect of globalization is becoming a challenge. Today's foreign companies are shifting their sites in the global division of labor to even cheaper locations elsewhere, such as China, the Philippines, India, and Vietnam. Those with global power have more mobility than do local laborers. As Bauman states: "capital can always move away to more peaceful sites if the engagement with 'otherness' requires a costly application of force or tiresome negotiations. No need to engage, if avoidance will do."[36] Global production companies exploit local labor and leave, locust-like, for another field. This is the so-called game of "global pick and mix." This leaves the local animators with great concerns as well as new challenges.

"Mrs Colorful" (45 years old) has been working as a producer at a Japanese OEM animation production company for almost twenty years. She said:

> It is worrying that so much work is going to China or the Philippines because they are cheaper. Korea has been the number one for the OEM animation industry for the past twenty years but the current situation is very unstable. We don't get as much work as before.

Logical and rational as it may seem, the above comment clearly indicates how the process of globalization and its economic strategy has become a cruel reality and a struggle for the local animators. They possess relatively less power than their counterparts in the foreign production offices. Being in the weaker position, for them the nature of modern capitalist democracy under "time-space compression" feels different from the way it feels for those on top. An animation art supervisor, "Miss Captain" (37 years old), who mainly supervises the most labor-intensive "in-between" department, shared her deep discontent with foreign production companies:

> Sometimes, I get upset by looking at difficult cuts that we have to draw (for low payment). Nothing I can do, though. We are physically so far away from those foreign countries doing the ordering. Not a word of complaint can be made at all! If we did complain, what would happen? They would simply say, "We could send the work somewhere else!" That's a scary thought. Especially because the Chinese animation market is growing bigger and bigger and more work is being sent to them, we have to do our best to *please* the foreign companies to keep our work. No point bellyaching. After all, it'll be no one's loss but our own.

"Miss Captain's" comment, "physically so far away," indicates that globalization does not seem to fully compress the distance between the weak (local animators) and the strong (global/transnational production company employers). What we see here is a clear line between the powerful and the weak that globalization has created under the seemingly merciful name of democratic capitalism. Thus, however elided time and space may seem in the globalization process, for foreign employers, Korea is only regarded as "the offshore low-wage assembly."[37] The distance between the two may even have widened from the local animators' standpoint. In this sense, globalization seems to be the Janus of the current era. Janus, as the most powerful god in Greek mythology, paradoxically loved peace and war at the same time. He closed the door of his garden during peacetime and opened it during wartime. However, as is widely known, the door was closed only once. In other words, there was endless war. As Janus-faced globalization has turned once "friendly others" to "threatening others," for the local animators it has become another challenge. The (globalization) door, which had been closed during peacetime of OEM work as stable source of income, is now wide open and pushing the Korean animators out into the battlefield of competition. Having been called upon to compete in the world market by the invisible forces of capitalism, the Korean animators are currently experiencing downsides of globalization as they lose work to other cheap locations like China, leading to increased unemployment and decreases in income. This suggests that, in the face of the ever-changing global environment, the local must react sensitively and rapidly to minimize the negative impact of the subtle shifts in the cultural labor force as seen above. One of Korea's immediate responses to such changes was to encourage domestic animators to produce highly original "Korean-made" or "Korean-branded" animation to differentiate them from others, a process encouraged by positive economic results not only in the form of the animators' immediate income but also in animation's potential economic contribution to national income. Indeed, almost everyone with whom I conducted interviews names the same fuel that ignited the engine of Korea's cultural industries: "It all began with *The Lion King!*"

Today's Korean animation industry is clearly in an in-between state caused by the powerful force of globalization. In this condition, current changes in Korea, such as the positive appreciation of animation, the growth of animation education courses, and governmental support in the form of animation cities and museums, can be regarded as results of the negotiation between the global and the local. As a result, the Korean animation industry is preparing to compete and negotiate with global others, following the path of in-between despite the painful costs paid along the way. Ironic and hypocritical as globalization may seem, Korean animators have indeed tasted its bittersweet process. It is hard to resist the charming seduction of globalization's economic potential when the entire nation has witnessed and understood this dream. Perhaps this is why it is even more inevitable that Korea's animators will continue the agonized struggles of being in-between.

Tensions between global and traditional values and consequences such as those experienced by the Korean animation industry are happening in many parts of the world as part of the globalization process. However, these are overshadowed by the seemingly positive experiences that a small number of strong nations have had of globalization. It must always be remembered that globalization creates differences and various in-between stages. In order to see a more complete picture of globalization, we need to pay attention to those marginalized people who battle every day on the rim of the in-between.

III

Discourse, Crossing Borders

7

The Transgression of Sharing and Copying:
Pirating Japanese Animation in China

Laikwan Pang

Sharing and copying are two very fundamental human activities, but they face fierce opposition in today's knowledge economy, which is fueled by the privatization and the management of originality and creativity. In fact, the current knowledge economy exploits creativity not only as a commodity for profit but also as capital itself, making creativity, like labor and raw materials, a major factor in late-capitalist production. As a result, creativity is highly fetishized, and it is directly associated with wealth and power. Any activities that might diffuse the values of creativity, like sharing and copying, would be condemned. Creative industries have become an important part of this new knowledge economy.[1] As one of the most prominent creative industries in the world, the Japanese cartoon industry has yet to consciously turn itself into a full member of this new economy. In this essay I want to examine its ambiguous position in relation to the new global cultural environment. I choose to portray this industry from an alternative angle: instead of directly explaining how the industry functions, I examine "peripheral" activities — pertaining to sharing and copying — to analyze the relationship between the reception of the Japanese cartoon and the global knowledge economy. Sharing and copying may be very different activities with regard to the consumption and the production of cultural products, but both are acts related to the establishment of human relationships, and both are criminalized in the global legal regime of Intellectual Property Rights (IPR). Analyzing the sharing and copying activities related to the Japanese cartoon culture in East Asia, we might be able to gain a more pertinent view to understand the specificity of this culture and, more broadly, the antagonistic relationship between knowledge economy and societal bonding.

I believe we can identify many practices within the current global knowledge economy that harm that same economy in most forceful ways. However, in order to identify these alternative practices, we must resist theorization at the universal level, precisely because these practices are localized, particular, and are results of and responses to dominant discourses. The more subversive, I believe, are the effects of those parasitical activities corroding the dominant power from within, and the most destructive actions are often "anti-political" in nature — they are not consciously constructed as oppositional politics but as everyday embodied experiences that transcend and overwhelm the structures that engendered them. The analysis of sharing and copying activities as ambiguous or even destructive by-products of creative industries, as this essay shows, provides one perspective from which to analyze how the knowledge economy might be interrogated.

In this essay, I study pirated Japanese cartoon materials circulated in China, to demonstrate how this kind of "sharing" challenges creative industries, and I examine animation as a creative industry in itself to understand the intimate relationship between creativity and copying. I also show that sharing and copying interact extensively in popular culture. As Henry Jenkins reminds us, there is always a creative and subversive side to fan culture, because fans often poach (interpret, recycle, and appropriate) original sources in imaginative and socially embedded ways;[2] but the fan culture I address herein is even more indeterminate, because the texts themselves are highly amorphous and their popularity in China is mainly realized through piracy and the culture of online sharing.

Sharing: The Fan Culture of Anime in China

One of the major incidents marking China's open-door policy was the signing of the Sino-Japanese Treaty of Peace and Friendship on August 12, 1978, and one result was the selective introduction of Japanese television programs to China. Among the first imported programs broadcast were Tezuka Osamu's *Astro Boy* (1963) and *Kimba the White Lion* (1965–66).[3] As happened in many other East Asian countries, Japanese anime soon became vastly popular in China. Recent research shows that more than eighty percent of Chinese youths prefer Japanese anime to any other cartoon form.[4] However, no feature-length Japanese anime films have been shown on official Chinese screens.[5] In China, the importation of foreign cinematic content has been much more strictly limited than has television content; and the quota of imported revenue-sharing films has been almost entirely filled by Hollywood and Hong Kong blockbusters.[6] Most importantly, Japanese studios have not shown much interest in the Chinese market; domestic and, to a lesser degree, Western markets are of primary concern — a point I revisit later. A few anime films have been shown in festivals; e.g., Oshii Mamoru's *Innocence* and Shinkai Makoto's *The Place Promised in Our Early Days* were shown at the 2005 Shanghai International Arts Festival.[7] The enormous popularity of Japanese cartoons and the scant number of anime films publicly screened in China are by no means proportional.

In fact, piracy culture carries Japanese cartoon culture, both anime and manga, in China. The availability of two new forms of circulation — disc or print piracy and online sharing — provides venues for Japanese cartoons to reach the vast population of Chinese youths. By piracy, I mean those copyright-infringing activities mostly with commercial interests at stake, most commonly seen in the forms of disc piracy of animation (anime) and reprints of comic books (manga). As a result of the wide implementation of digital technology, there is a burgeoning network of disc piracy developing in Asia.[8] Japanese anime occupies an incredible share of these mass-produced pirated discs. However, more traditional print piracy has not disappeared; new digital-printing technologies have facilitated more efficient and higher-quality mass reprinting of manga.[9] While these pirated materials are manufactured to be sold for profit and are therefore easily criminalized, online sharing, which is mainly a social and leisure activity with no financial reward, cannot be viewed directly from an economic perspective. An incredible amount of material is distributed online free of charge, ranging from anime and manga to all kinds of peripheral information about Japanese cartoons, with the aid of specific peer-to-peer (P2P) applications or large servers.[10] This is not unique to Japanese cartoons; we are witnessing the rise of a new culture online, in which netizens diligently upload, download, and classify various cartoon materials. The criminalization of this new culture has given rise to many legal and moral disputes worldwide.[11]

The online vs. offline distinction is increasingly problematic, particularly in Japanese cartoon culture. In general, disc piracy and online sharing overlap a great deal. Although abundant materials can be freely obtained online, pirates sometimes repackage them as new commodities for profit. These activities range from reselling online materials in print or disc form, to popular magazines and periodicals collecting material online without citing proper references. While online materials can be sold offline for profit, pirated materials can also be distributed free of charge through the Internet. Many current Japanese television programs are available online immediately after their broadcast in Japan — sometimes with Chinese subtitles already added, thanks to the generous efforts of some bilingual and technologically informed viewers. Some online materials are remakes of existing anime or manga adapted by their appropriators. With the aid of new digital technologies, piracy has become a much more adaptable and widespread activity that is immanent in the everyday lives of many people.

To my knowledge, there are no official distributors of Japanese anime or manga in China. In fact, if an anime available online or on disc has Chinese subtitles, it is almost certainly a bootleg. According to some Japanese sources, about 2.1 trillion yen worth of pirated anime are sold in China each year.[12] Although television was the only channel through which to propagate anime in China in the 1980s, the Internet and piracy are now responsible for further propagating this culture.[13] Manga, in contrast, has always been pirated, in print in the past and on the Internet today. Without piracy and online sharing, the two major means by which Chinese youths reach the outside world, Japanese popular culture might have a very different face in China.

What does this "pirated" popular culture look like? I recently purchased a volume published in mainland China in a bookstore in Hong Kong: *The World of Miyazaki Hayao,* by Fei Yuxiao (Figure 7.1).[14] The book came with eight bookmarks and a pirated soundtrack of *Howl's Moving Castle,* and its retail price was 35 RMB (US$4.30). The price is extremely low by Japanese or Western standards, of course, but it is on the expensive side for the general Chinese readership, and it is targeted to a market of young upper-middle-class urbanites.

Obviously this commodity is a counterfeit product, and it comprises many levels of piracy. The CD was copied directly from a legally produced disc, and the many images collected in the book were captured from different sources. The author compiled the text by consulting different online and print materials, without citing his sources. As mentioned, none of Miyazaki's films has ever been screened in official Chinese theaters, and his works have become popular in China largely through pirated discs. We can safely infer that customers are attracted to this book because they have watched pirated Miyazaki movies. Ironically, the copyright page ascribes copyright to Fei Yuxiao, and indicates that no one can copy or appropriate materials from the book without the author's consent (p. 4) (Figure 7.2).

Many of the images collected in this Miyazaki book are captured from different sources: some directly from online pages,[15] some from Japanese anime magazines,[16] some (more crudely) from discs or television,[17] and some from Chinese sources which themselves are pirated materials.[18] The pictures

Figure 7.1 Cover page of *The World of Miyazaki Hayao*

Figure 7.2 Copyright page of *The World of Miyazaki Hayao*

are not only a collage of attractive images, but they are also carefully selected, illustrated, and juxtaposed, and obviously much editorial effort was involved. The information provided is rich and diverse, including standard promotion materials like film descriptions, film analysis, interviews, and behind-the-scene reports. It also provides detailed biographies of those involved with the films, including not only important associates of Miyazaki, such as film producer Suzuki Toshio (p. 197), music score composer Joe Hisaishi (p. 199), and publisher Tokuma Yasuyoshi (pp. 202–3), but also the likes of Jonathan Swift, the eighteenth-century British author whose work inspired *Castle in the Sky* (p. 53), and Miyazaki's late follower Kondō Yoshifumi (pp. 189–91). There is also an elaborate description of the famous Ghibli Museum Mitaka, which features Miyazaki's works and which has become a minor tourist attraction in Japan.

Of course, the text cites no original sources for such a rich set of information, and it is not my intention here to figure out where the materials came from. But I can say that many of these materials came directly from Japanese sources, both online and in print, although the author has also freely made alterations and added information for Chinese readers. For example, in the section introducing Miyazaki's environmentalist thinking, the author discusses the theories of the Japanese botanist Nakao Sasuke, who allegedly heavily influenced Miyazaki (pp. 131–3). The section is clearly copied from an article available online, *"Nausicaa of the Valley of Wind* to *Princess Mononoke*: The Thirteen-Year Collaboration of Miyazaki Hayao and Studio Ghibli" by Kanō Seiji.[19] But the Chinese translation is not precise. Perhaps due to the absence of copyright concerns, the author seems to feel free to add ideas anywhere and anyway she or he likes. For example, in a passage describing the food the ancient Japanese loved, the Chinese author adds that this eating practice is very similar to that of the Yunnan area, a comparison not mentioned in the original article. This connection echoes the ancient Japanese-Chinese cultural connection that this book draws on and continues, and Miyazaki's own works are also characterized by such transcultural tendency. This book was published when Sino-Japanese relations were at their worst since World War II; anti-Japanese demonstrations were seen everywhere in major Chinese cities. Thanks to these online and alternative networks, cultural connections between the two countries can no longer be single-handedly manipulated by political discourse.

This Miyazaki collection involves the actual selection and manipulation of materials produced by the official Miyazaki industry, but they are also heavily rearranged and reassembled. Although delicate editorial work is evident in the pirated volume, the editor is also erroneous at times. Mistakes and confusions abound, making reading not effortless. There is, for example, an unexpected combination of typesetting styles found in this Miyazaki book. In general, Japanese typesetting follows the traditional Chinese way of arranging words in vertical lines from right to left. But contemporary typesetting in mainland China follows Western practice: horizontal lines from left to right. This pirated book oddly combines both practices. The overall typeset design is a modern Chinese one, but there are a few pages deliberately modeled after the original Japanese. Since the front and back covers were similar, I was confused as to where to begin reading the first time I flipped through the pages: Do I read the book like I would a standard mainland Chinese book, or like a (pirated) Japanese one? After some effort deciding where the beginning was, the following reading experience was an odd one. After finishing the section on Joe Hisaishi in modern Chinese typesetting (pp. 198–201) (Figure 7.3), I was thrown completely off by the section on Tokuma Yasuyoshi that followed, because it was set in Japanese style (pp. 202–3), and the first sentence begins at neither end but the middle of the two-page layout (Figure 7.4). Ironically, Tokuma is a publisher-tycoon, backing not only Miyazaki's works but a large part of the country's print and cartoon industries. This typesetting mistake makes Tokuma, of all figures introduced in this book, the most "incomprehensible" person of all.

Figure 7.3 The pages on Joe Hisaishi, typeset horizontal left to right

Figure 7.4   The pages on Tokuma Yasuyoshi, typeset vertical right to left

The use of Japanese typesetting might be mimicry, in an effort to evoke the experience of reading authentic Japanese magazines. The careless typesetter is so keen on producing Japanese effects as to have committed such a serious editorial mistake as the juxtaposition of different typesetting styles. This kind of editorial mistake can probably be seen only in hastily published pirated materials, and it most unexpectedly destabilizes the information that this book tries to offer. Information is no longer transparent or pleasurable to take in. I appreciate the editor's efforts in collecting, editing, and even fabricating materials from divergent sources, but I am most amused by the careless mistakes that resulted from the typesetter's hurried appropriation of these different materials.

Today, knowledge is intimately associated with consumerism: the more consumers are educated about specific products, the more fervent their desire to consume them. The Miyazaki collection shows us that entertainment is no longer easily distinguishable from information, and the popularity of Japanese anime in China is accompanied by a large amount of fan knowledge available online and offline, so that fans are able to obtain a wide range of information about the texts and their producers. The side products included in this collection — soundtracks and stationery — might be as important as the films in forging culture and fandom. Tie-ins, as this collection demonstrates, are given much weight in creative industries because they form myriad networks in which the commodity can signify and circulate, and they tremendously enrich the cultural value of the commodity through association with other objects, subjects, and affects.

Although the Japanese cartoon industry has never been concerned with the Chinese market, anime are tremendously popular and widely pirated. Such popularity cannot be controlled and managed. "Counterfeit" fan culture is a challenge to the knowledge economy partly because piracy redistributes and re-presents knowledge and information in ways that copyright owners and distributors have no way to control or even anticipate. This Miyazaki collection is a juxtaposition of tangible and non-tangible materials, and online and offline piracy, yet this creative combination of materials is considered enemy to "true," that is, profitable, creativity.

Copying: The Production of National Identities

Piracy and sharing are subversive in two ways: they redistribute human expressions and creativity that are already privatized, and they form alternative practices and circulation networks outside the mainstream globalization hierarchy. The two hegemonic systems, the IPR legal regime and the global commodities distribution networks, work for each other; privatized intellectual properties must be circulated within the dominant global network, so that the capital accrued can be safely guarded within the hegemonic structure. Piracy challenges both systems at the same time.

However, we cannot assume that IPR offenses necessarily constitute anti-globalization or anti-capitalism, as most of the time copyright infringement does not lead to actual economic and cultural flows that subvert the dominant networks. In fact, it is often the opposite — counterfeit products prepare "underdeveloped" markets for their acquiescence to the commodity and the promotion of the brand name. While counterfeit tie-in products like this Miyazaki collection are clearly situated outside the IPR order, the pirated book does not signify alternative transnational reception networks. Obviously, Chinese readers are learning to consume Japanese products through this sharing, so the cultural hierarchy of production and reception in which Japan is center is not challenged but is further promoted by these illegal practices. The Miyazaki volume in fact demonstrates a reification of the author function conjured up by creative industries — the author being both Miyazaki and Japan. The book might have breached Miyazaki's copyright on many levels, but it does not challenge the basic reception structure in which Chinese viewers consume and admire Miyazaki and Japanese culture.

National identity continues to matter in transnational cultural flows, both in national economy and affects in identification. We might better understand the subversive effects of piracy if we juxtapose piracy with creative industries' production of national identities. National interests produced by creative industries rest both on ideological and economic grounds, which overlap and contradict. On the populist level, one can easily find in Chinese online forums condemnation of the consumption of Japanese popular culture as anti-patriotic, but these emotions densely intertwine with various, less noticeable, economic concerns. Creative industries have largely been a policy product and are intimately related to national economies, and there is a strong tendency among creative industries to produce and protect national identities. A burgeoning animation industry is developing in China with such nationalist baggage.

The overwhelming popularity of Japanese anime in China forces the government to curtail the fervor by implanting a protectionist quota system: regulations now stipulate that no more than forty percent of the animation broadcast in China can be foreign productions.[20] In order to occupy the remaining sixty percent of the airtime, local industries are trying very hard to satisfy a television audience that instead craves Disney and Japanese anime. The Chinese government also recognizes the importance of the development of a national entertainment industry to reduce the economy's heavy dependence on manufacturing.[21] The city of Hangzhou, home to sixty cartoon and animation enterprises employing 10,000 people, is currently being groomed to be the capital of Chinese animation.[22]

Complicating the nationalist project is the offshoring phenomenon. Animation is an extremely labor-intensive industry, and Chinese artists are in fact responsible for the actual production of many Japanese animations. Currently, more than eighty percent of Japanese anime is outsourced offshore,[23] and we might say the entire Japanese anime industry relies on the labor of adjacent countries — mostly South Korea, the Philippines, and China. If creative industries are often associated with nationalist pride, providing offshore creative labor is not; however, the former is often fueled by the latter. Today's nationalism cannot be analyzed without taking globalization into account. South Korea has developed a national animation industry as a result of the offshore-labor training it has received from Japan,[24] and China is following closely on its heels. As if to supplement offshore-labor training, Chinese academics are also sent directly to Japan to study cartooning, so that they can come back to teach Chinese students and establish a cartoon industry based on the highly successful Japanese model.[25] Major national universities such as Beijing Film Academy and Renmin University of China have recently established their own animation departments to train animators at the university level, following the government's agenda to develop China's animation industry.

Because the national creative industry is largely a result of global capital and labor flows, the establishment of the national creative industry as a reverse hegemony does not challenge, but rather supports, the global knowledge economy. For example, the first Sino-Japanese co-produced anime film *Silver-haired Agito* was announced in China as the first step of the development of the Chinese animation industry, but according to the end titles, the Chinese contribution was largely the labor-intensive portion. The nationalist protective agenda contradictorily encourages the importation of foreign cultural products and the exportation of Chinese labor. The rise and the fall of such national industries is not only tolerated but encouraged by the new global economy, as long as the interests of the dominant powers are not too severely challenged. Also, animation is an extremely labor-intensive industry, and the animation industries in both Japan and Korea are notoriously exploitative.[26] The development of animation as a competitive national industry in China will inevitably produce another type of sweatshop. The current affinity between creative industries and nationalist interests would ultimately lead to the submission of creativity to specific economic or political agendas; nationalist industries are therefore a devastating way to promote creativity. Piracy might be an indirect, if feeble, way to challenge such kinds of nationalist projects, which associate culture with national pride and exploitative national economy. To put it another way, piracy upsets the dominant system of control, and given the availability of pirated discs and publications of Japanese anime, the Chinese government will never be able to gain full command of its national animation culture or industry.

The relation between animation and national identity can also be approached from the perspective of representation. There seems to be a very strong cultural identity attached to Japanese animation. But this association between Japanese national identity and anime, I believe, is largely forged. Cartooning is a visual form closely associated with copying. In its original meanings, a cartoon is a drawing made on paper as a study for another drawing, so a cartoon is always itself a copy. It is therefore very difficult to differentiate between creative copying and plagiarism in cartoons. The notion of originality and identity in cartoons is not only weak but alienating.

The cartoon culture's strong affiliation with copying enormously complicates any national identity produced thereby. For one thing, its pictorial form facilitates an emphasis on collective identity, which is particularly apt to exaggerate values and ideologies related to the human body that are generally difficult to realize in photographic form. For example, it is easier to represent and legitimize exaggerated masculinity and heroism in animation than in any live-action fantasy, because animation has the capacity to render figures indestructible.[27] The same logic can be applied not only to gender identity but also to cultural identity, as cartoonists can also easily provide common bodily traits to people. This is particularly the case for Japanese anime, which does not value individualistic traits. A major difference between Japanese anime and Disney is the lack of "personality animation" that American animators value. In Disney works, the appearances and the voices of the characters, as well as their activities and even mannerisms, differentiate one character from another.[28] In contrast, Japanese cartoon characters look very similar to each other, so that it might be easier to identify a single collective image in Japanese anime.

However, "Japaneseness" in pictorial form is difficult to clearly define. In fact, ethnic and racial identities are seldom clearly demarcated in Japanese animations, unlike in many American cartoons. While gender identity is reinforced in certain cases, Japanese anime is also famous for its transgender tendencies.[29] There are clearly Japanese values, Japanese tastes, and in some cases specific Japanese social concerns structured in the texts.[30] But these divergent factors and concerns are too diffuse to mark the Japanese identity. Many Japanese animators, particularly Miyazaki, set their stories and design their characters based on foreign models, and it is difficult for viewers to differentiate Japanese characters from foreign ones. We also cannot take a certain Japanese animation style for granted. Although there seems to be a common form — rich and dynamic drawing, doe-eyed characters with feminine features, and expressive and exaggerated color schemes — there are too many exceptions to claim a unified style. Since by nature animation is free from any indexical burden and can be produced and received without any cultural identification, the cultural/national identity of Japanese animation could be both easily constructed and easily evaded.

Because animation is essentially a culture of copying, the relationship between representation and reality is most dynamic. The kind of mimesis that is the basis of animation is structured not only through similarities but also differences; we enjoy animation precisely because it is not reality. Animation could be conceived as being structured by the dynamics between the aesthetics of imagination and the aesthetics of copying — between abstract and realist models.[31] If our modern visual culture is largely characterized by the desire for photographic realism and the creation of the illusion of dynamic reality, animation might be a major exception that can afford to play with reality and highlight the complex similarity-qua-difference mechanism of mimesis.[32] Among other forms of representation, animation might be the one most resistant to claims of essentialist cultural root, allowing Disney to appropriate and exploit folk culture, and to situate its works within a forged timeless tradition. Animation in general has been shown to be a culture of appropriation.[33] This is also the case with Miyazaki, who quite freely appropriates stories and visual materials from different historical periods and cultures, with an aim to situate his works in a "supra-cultural" plane that supposedly belongs to all children of all cultures.

While it is ultimately futile to try to detect national identity through pictorial forms, could we locate a national identity in anime forced through diplomatic coercions, as in the case of Hollywood, which is backed up by the American government?[34] The level of political interference is an important index to demonstrate the relationship between creative industries and the new global knowledge economy, which the Japanese cartoon seems not yet to have joined. While Japanese manga and anime are popular and widely pirated in Asia and around the world, unlike the American cartoon industry or the Japanese electronic industry, which carefully protect their copyrights, the Japanese cartoon industry has shown little interest in IPR. Scholars have identified at least two reasons. First, due to the relatively low damage incurred by these mostly fans activities, it is not economically rational to bring these suits. Second, the Japanese comic industry has not developed an elaborate global distribution system.[35] As Kōichi Iwabuchi argues: "The most serious shortcoming of the Japanese animation industry, despite mature production capability and techniques, is its lack of international distribution channels. Western (American) global distribution power is thus indispensable to make Japanese animation a part of global popular culture."[36] As some critics also argue, the Japanese animation industry has not progressed very far from its roots as a cottage industry of sensitive artistes, and domestic competition is simply too strong to allow them to explore other markets, to say nothing of "nonexistent" ones like mainland China.[37] As part of the new global economy, national IPR consciousness is often directly related to the exportation efforts of creative industries, which have yet to become fierce in the Japanese animation industry. However, the situation has been gradually changing over the last two years. In the face of Japan's declining economic power, the Japanese government has recently moved to "brand" Japan. Beginning in 2004, in the name of cracking down on piracy, the Organization for Promotion of Overseas Distribution of Content began affixing a "Made in Japan" trademark to Japanese animation and video game packaging.[38] Implementing new IPR efforts, whether the Japanese cartoon culture will become a full-fledged member of the knowledge economy remains to be seen. But I find this relative ignorance of global exportation to be a unique feature of the Japanese cartoon industry thus far, which is in clear contrast, for example, to Disney's reception around the world being dictated by IPR terms.

If it is futile to locate the Japaneseness in its representation, is there a national readership that makes the Japanese cartoon culturally unique?[39] Japanese cartoon culture engenders a unique fandom, which began in Japan and is currently spreading among anime and manga fans all over the world through the Internet: there is heavy participation in creative fan fiction — *dōjinshi,* which refers to a fan's self-published works that mainly copy and transform already published materials. As the flourishing *dōjinshi* culture attests, Japanese manga is mainly a culture of copying and sharing; fans not only consume the materials passively but actively contribute to their production and expansion, generally without any direct financial interest at stake. A major centripetal force of *dōjinshi* culture is the fans' loyalty to the originals: their reproductions must closely follow the plots, characterizations, and sentiments of the originals. But *dōjinshi* fans also draw for the sake of drawing differences, characterizing the dynamic interactions between identity and difference inherent in the *dōjinshi* culture.[40] I believe it is this communal bonding developed through copying that most uniquely distinguishes Japanese animation from other cartoon practices. But it does not mean that this unique identity is "Japanese," because, first, the *dōjinshi* culture is practiced among fans all over the world, particularly on the Internet. More importantly, the spirit of *dōjinshi* is adaptation and transformation, which therefore both fortifies and resists identity construction. This is most obviously seen in the new cosplay phenomenon, which is flourishing among Japanese cartoon fans not only in Japan but other Asian communities. Cosplay fans dress as cartoon characters of their liking in public, and they perform and transform themselves through such public rituals. The strong connotations of performance inherent in cosplay mock any naive national identification associated with Japanese cartoon culture.

While the Japanese cartoon industry is such a successful national cultural industry, it also facilitates transcultural copying and sharing, and therefore is resistant to both the logic of privatization and of national identity. This is something the current IPR logic is not yet able to comprehend, as the American Creative Commons advocate Lawrence Lessig asserts that the tolerance and respect for copying demonstrated in the *dōjinshi* culture is beyond the imagination of American creative industries and the US legal environment.[41]

Iwabuchi also points out the contradictory manifestations of the popularity of Japanese cultural commodities in Asia. On the one hand, in order to avoid cultural discount effects, the Japanese cultural presence is deliberately de-emphasized in certain commodities, such as cultural technologies and animation; on the other hand, "Japaneseness" is much more visible in many other cultural products, like popular music and television programs.[42] Iwabuchi does not give us an answer to understand this inconsistency, and only claims that globalizing forces "make transnational cultural flow much more disjunctive, non-isomorphic, and complex than what the center-periphery paradigm allows us to understand."[43] The *dōjinshi* culture might demonstrate more clearly the intricacy of this inconsistency — that "Japaneseness" is both desired and rejected in transnational cultural consumption. In a way, the presence and the absence of distinct cultural identity do not cancel but support each other in the logic of global capitalism, because this economy is based on both mass and niche markets, both the rejection and the fetishization of "newness." At the same time, uniqueness and sharing do not necessarily contradict. The sole emphasis on originality as demonstrated in today's IPR logics fails to understand the importance of sharing even in contemporary culture.

This brings us back to the Chinese Miyazaki collection I discussed earlier, which not only reflects the current *bricoleur* state of the Japanese anime culture in China but is also a recreation of the Japanese fan culture, which is not ruled by IPR concepts and shows little concern for notions of "originality." I would argue that it is the book's affiliation with the Japanese *dōjinshi* practices, instead of the actual information collected in the book, that makes this Chinese publication so akin to both Japanese popular culture and animation. Although the Chinese Miyazaki book does not include new creations modeled after Miyazaki's works, the rearrangement and new interpretations of Miyazaki also produce effects similar to those of *dōjinshi,* diffusing but also unifying the collective identity of Japanese anime. This collective imaging could be highly subversive to the pseudo-individualization of today's post-Fordist products conjured up by commodity culture and protected by IPR.

To sum up, there may be many reasons for and efforts contributed to the Japanese identity of Japanese animation, but none of them is definitive. In view of the pictorial form, the weak exportation impulse, and the wide regional consumption, the national identity produced by the Japanese cartoon is marked not in the texts, in policy, or in its reception. We must recognize that the seemingly distinct national identity in Japanese cartoons can easily be changed or copied by others. And this dilution of Japanese identity is particularly probable in the age of globalization, now that Chinese and Korean artists are hired to produce anime, fans can easily obtain and change related graphics on the Internet, and products are circulated widely in official and pirate markets. As Judith Butler reminds us, alterity is inherent in every identity.[44] Without romanticizing piracy as conscious revolutionary acts against capitalism, we can, however, through cases like the circulation of pirated Japanese anime in China, develop a mode of critical thinking on cultural alterity. This is relevant to both our new global economy, in which all cultural differences are equalized and relativized through money, and never-ending international conflicts, as shown in the age-old mistrusts between China and Japan. I believe that the Japanese cartoon culture has secret spaces in which to reactivate a vibrant dimension of copying and sharing that is increasingly repressed by our current creative industries; whether these spaces can be maintained depends largely on that industry's refusal to join the knowledge economy and protect its IPRs.

Acknowledgements

I am grateful to the research assistance of Amy Li, whose enormous commitment in the Japanese culture enlightens my understanding of the magic of this popular culture, which has helped youths around the world to find and escape themselves.

8

The East Asian Brandscape:
Distribution of Japanese Brands in the Age
of Globalization

Shinji Oyama

For Marx, writing in the age of the manufacturing economy and imperialism, wealth appears as an immense accumulation of commodities.[1] Yet in the age of the information economy and globalization, wealth appears as an immense accumulation of brands. There should be little doubt that global brands have become one of the most visible signs of globalization. Powerful and ideologically charged images — such as the long queue for the first McDonald's in Moscow or Starbucks in the Forbidden City in Beijing (now closed) — seem to point in one irreversible direction: global homogenization. Or at least this is the image popular journalism likes to draw: all-powerful Western brands engulf non-Western worlds, annihilating local cultures in the process. However, this simplistic discourse has itself provoked growing dissatisfaction and some resistance, as documented in Naomi Klein's *No Logo*.[2]

Globalization is as much a process of heterogenization as of homogenization, and often it rearticulates historically determined and preexisting power relations.[3] This is demonstrated particularly well by the marked presence of Japanese brands in the postcolonial geography of East Asia. In addition to the globally recognizable Japanese brands in the high-tech or automobile sectors, such as Sony or Toyota, one finds a great diversity of Japanese brands in the region in those sectors generally considered to be more cultural, ranging from clothing, beverages, and packaged foods to cosmetics. In East Asia, we see Japanese brands such as Pocari Sweat (a Japanese sport drink) or *non-no* (a Japanese women's fashion magazine) sitting alongside

Coca-Cola or MTV. The ubiquity of those "lifestyle" brands contrasts sharply with their lesser presence (or absence) in the non-Asian market, and it points to the growing difference the East Asian region makes.

In this sense, there are fluid but distinctively East Asian flows of brands constituting what I call in this essay the "East Asian brandscape." This essay is an attempt to analyze East Asian brandscape as one paradigmatic manifestation of the distribution of cultural power in the age of globalization. It draws on Appadurai, who characterizes globalization as "disjunctures" among five scapes: the ethnoscape (constituted by the movement of people), the technoscape (constituted by the movement of technologies), the financescape (constituted by the movement of capital and money), the ideoscape (constituted by the movement of ideologies and state politics), and the mediascape (constituted by the movement of images and the capacity to produce such images).[4] I understand the brand not so much as another flowing object but rather as a multilayered and complex object that cuts across these different scapes, driving *and* putting an order to otherwise chaotic flows. The brandscape seen in this way is not the distribution of national cultural power, as it is usually imagined, but an organization of disjunctive and globally dispersed forces.

Brandscape as Distribution of Cultural Power

The East Asian brandscape has drawn attention both outside and inside academia from those attempting to explain the phenomenon. Just as the ubiquitous presence of American brands has long been seen as a part of Americanization, Japanese brands in East Asia have been associated with "Japanization," the intense circulation of Japanese cultural products, such as pop music or television dramas, throughout Southeast and East Asia.[5] This phenomenon has been received in Japan as a sign of its long-awaited soft or cultural power, which may signify the transformation of Japan from a faceless economic animal to a "cool" cultural power.[6] One influential business magazine, *Nikkei Business*, elatedly claims that Japanese popular culture has changed "the very foundation of sensory ratios, structures of feeling, and aesthetics" of young East Asian consumers. It goes so far as to acclaim the rise of "the Greater East Asian *Atsuzoko* (or Japanese super platform-shoe) Sphere," spanning from Seoul to Bangkok, and waiting to be inundated with Japanese brands.[7] The hope is that this might be as geographically extensive and economically profitable as Japan's expansive empire during the 1940s — the Greater East Asian Co-Prosperity Sphere.

Leo Ching criticizes this born-again regionalism. For him the Japanization discourse signifies the latest phase of Asianism. Asianism, imagined through primordial religions or aesthetics, had "critical valence" because of its radical potential for resistance to Asia's "common colonial legacy and anti-Eurocentrism" until it was tarnished by colonial vision of the Greater East Asian Co-Prosperity Sphere.[8] As soon as popular culture and consumer brands become "the fundamental form in which the putative unity of Asia is imagined and regulated, the internal contradictions of Asianism [the Asia of Asianism] are suppressed for the sake of commensurability and compatibility within the global distribution of cultural power."[9]

In other words, Japanization and a phenomenon like the East Asian brandscape is nothing more than the way capitalistic cultural power is distributed in East Asia following certain cultural commonalities. While I agree with Ching's skepticism about new Asianism, my interest lies in analyzing the actual process and structures through which the distribution of cultural power occurs through a form such as the brand. This almost has not been analyzed at all, even in East Asia. Instead there seems to be an assumption, both in the celebration and critique of Japanization, which equates the cultural power of the brand as an ideological national cultural power and the brandscape with the organized distribution of such national cultural power. In this context, the question about the East Asian brandscape can be productively re-asked as a question about the "distribution of cultural power" in the rich Media and Cultural Studies tradition of tackling this issue.

Although very little attention has been paid to brands per se, many have tried to address the issue of the global distribution of cultural power in Media and Cultural Studies. The earliest and most persistent form of such criticism may be found in the discussion of cultural imperialism. Scholars in this tradition such as Schiller conceive of the global distribution of cultural power as an unequivocal unidirectional process, whereby global — mostly American — culture in tandem with economic, political, and military forces dominates vulnerable local cultures.[10] Japanization discourse shares a great deal with this line of thinking in the way it poses cultural power as representing ideological domination by a powerful nation-state.

Recent scholars provide more nuanced discussion, arguing instead that such a process is better explained by a complementary and mutually constitutive relationship between the global and the local.[11] In this view, globalization leads not to homogenization but to heterogenization through the production of structured rather than random differences.[12] Robertson captures this dynamic eloquently with the concept of glocalization, which refers to "the tailoring and advertising of goods and services on a global or near global basis to increasingly differentiated local and particular markets."[13] The concept's potential strength lies in its capacity to identify the ways in which globalization is, in the broadest sense, structured. However, subsequent works have reduced this capacity to the analysis of localization at the level of representation, such as how global brands like McDonald's localize their advertising or products.[14] As a result, glocalization fails to make sense, for example, of the way in which Coca-Cola increasingly relies not just on advertising but on the development of local brands, such as Inca Cola in South America, or the covert way in which the French giant Groupe Danone (owner of Evian and more) has proceeded by acquiring a controlling stake in one of China's best-known brands, Wahaha.[15]

However useful they might be, these models do not go very far in explaining the brandscape. As I will explain, the brand needs to be understood not only by the representation of advertisements but also by the multilayered ontological existence of the brand, which cuts across hitherto analytically separated domains such as economics, culture, and law.[16] There is a danger in privileging representation, for example through the semiotic analysis of represented Japaneseness in advertisements, as a relative determining force that precedes other forces. To do so would direct analytical attention away from the structures that govern distribution of cultural power and from the ways that a brand's cultural power operates relatively autonomously from the semiotic of its representations. Drawing on Appadurai's idea of scapes, I argue that the brandscape should be understood as a dynamic organization of dispersed and disjunctive global forces rather than as a distribution of national cultural power. To illustrate this, here I use the concrete example of the luxury cosmetic industry. I look first at how cosmetics brands appear and are distributed on the ground floors of premier retail spaces in several East Asian cities, as well as in London. I then go on to explain the complexity of contemporary brands and come back to shed new light on the same ground floor spaces.

The Ground Floor

In 2006, the combined sales of the world's top 100 cosmetics companies are estimated to have been approximately US$140 billion. Among companies specializing in fragrance, makeup, and skincare luxury cosmetics, Paris-based L'Oréal (US$19.8 billion) leads the industry by a wide margin, followed by New York-based Estée Lauder (US$6.8 billion), and Tokyo-based Shiseido (US$5.8 billion).[17] This industry is a trendsetter in the use of cutting-edge marketing techniques, particularly in advertising and promotion. Cosmetics brands dominate not only the most expensive time and space of commercial media but also premier real estate space, such as duty free shops or high-end department stores, making them a significant part of the urban landscape.

The juxtaposition of brands in department stores constitutes a series of concrete spaces in which the brandscape flow becomes visible. Let us map these spaces by the generally perceived place of origin of the brands in Tokyo, Taipei, Hong Kong, Seoul, and — for comparative purposes — London. Of the forty brands on the ground floor of Tokyo's trendsetting Isetan department store (in Shinjuku), twenty-four are Western (mostly American and French), and eleven are Japanese. The Western to Japanese ratio becomes twenty-six to eight in Sogo Causeway Bay in Hong Kong; fourteen to five in Shin Kong Mitsukoshi in Tianmu, Taipei; and twenty-two to five (along with four Korean brands) in Lotte in Myongdong, Seoul. In London's Selfridges, it is thirty-two to two.[18] Brands originating in a few Western nations are still hegemonic on a global scale. Nevertheless, in an industry that has been long associated with and dominated by Western and racialized ideas of beauty and modernity, the strong position of Japanese brands in Asia is a significant marker of what makes the region different in the otherwise globally homogeneous market.

Understanding the significance of this regional difference needs some further elaboration. The three largest Japanese cosmetics companies, Shiseido, Kosé, and Kao, have varying degrees of presence in the luxury segment of Western markets.[19] However, in such markets, these brands develop their position and identity according to global standards: typically, they use Caucasian models and generic designs at all levels of their branding effort. To use Iwabuchi's influential concept, these brands become "culturally odorless." The idea of cultural odor captures the moments in the process of consumption when widely disseminated symbolic images of producing countries, such as racial or bodily signifiers of a national way of life, become associated positively with the products being consumed. The global success of American brands is inseparable from American cultural odor, or constructed Americanness.[20] Iwabuchi argues that, in contrast, Japanese cultural products such as the Sony Walkman are largely culturally odorless, consciously deprived of any signifier of Japaneseness, and thus are not generally perceived to evoke a specifically "Japanese" lifestyle.[21]

What marks the difference of Japanese brands in East Asia and helps to constitute the East Asian brandscape is a higher intensity of cultural odor. With Shiseido Maquillage, one of Shiseido's pan-Asian regional brands, the advertising and promotional material designed for the Japanese market has been used in eight countries with very little localization. Consumers from Thailand, Malaysia, the Philippines, Singapore, Indonesia, Hong Kong, Taiwan, and Korea are exposed to identical messages, sounds, and images that routinely feature Japanese celebrities such as Misaki Itō or Yuri Ebihara, who are hardly known outside the region.[22] The plethora of Japanese female bodies and overwhelming cultural odor contradict the commonly held perception that Japanese cultural goods are culturally odorless more or less everywhere, with a greater emphasis on glocalization in general.

These quantitative and qualitative differences could give the impression that the East Asian brandscape is, in fact, unambiguously a site for the distribution of national cultural power, Japanese brands sitting next to French or American brands and so on. There can be little doubt that Japan exerts some degree of cultural influence as a regional cultural center. However, it is also this obviousness — the seemingly unmistakable representations of Japanese bodies — that directs analysis away from the complexity of contemporary brands and the complex economic exchanges that make brands key drivers of globalization. In what follows, I analyze in some detail what contemporary brands have become, and then return to look at the ground floor of department stores from a different angle.

The Brand: A Complex Object

The original function of a brand was to make it possible to distinguish otherwise undistinguishable goods or livestock, to identify their producers, and to guarantee quality. As capitalism has evolved, however, branding has become a strategy of differentiation that operates increasingly on the basis of intangible values.[23] The growing reliance of brand value on intangible and abstract qualities enables the brand to become complex object. As the global brand consulting firm Interbrand puts it:

> A brand is a mixture of attributes, tangible and intangible, symbolized in a trademark, which, if managed properly, creates value and influence. "Value" has different interpretations: from a marketing or consumer perspective it is "the promise and delivery of an experience"; from a business perspective it is "the security of future earnings"; from a legal perspective it is "a separable piece of intellectual property."[24]

It is in this context that Celia Lury draws attention to the "multi-layered character of a brand's ontological existence."[25] It is ontological in the sense that a brand exists as an object autonomously from our subjective conception of it. Brands, in other words, cannot be reduced to the meaning people understand them to have, because they also evoke the objective existence of a whole set of institutional organization and practices.[26] It is at the intersection of such objective institutional supports and practices that brands, although remaining intangible and abstract, exert very tangible effects on, and realize their value and influence in, a global cultural economy.

With all its complexities, the brand is first and foremost a cultural object that provides a basis for the production of other values. Because advertorials or product-placement are more rampant than ever, brands appear in media both through advertising and as content in their own right. This generates a complex mediascape in which brands become omnipresent cultural resources, enabling consumers to appropriate them for signifying practices and the construction of identities.[27] Although the significance of advertising has always been overrated, advertising has always been a part of overall branding, simply involving the use of media to herald the arrivals of goods or services, branded or otherwise.[28] The more fundamental difference between branding and advertising is suggested by Interbrand's definition of it in the quote above as "experience" rather than, for example, "text."

From Advertising to Experience

Experience is a contentious concept, intensely discussed in philosophy and cultural theory. Here, I deploy a less specialized dictionary definition of the term: first, it consists of practical contact with and observation of facts or events; second, it is the knowledge or skill acquired by such means over a period of time; and third, it is an event or occurrence that leaves an impression on someone.[29] Thus when one says, "you never understand the brand until you experience it," it implies a way of knowing that is different from reading or decoding a text. There is a sense of immediacy that is fundamentally physical and kinesthetic. This can be seen in the messages posted on www.lovemarks.com — a website set up and managed by the global advertising agency Saatchi and Saatchi — by (presumably) loyal customers of the cool professional makeup brand M.A.C. Cosmetics:

> The whole experience of the MAC shop makes me feel like I am a little girl and [*sic*] the lollie shop. The girls are inspirational and the products are devine [*sic*]. I went from wearing no makeup to being a MAC only girl. And when you get a make over you feel like a movie star, way to go MAC. (Alannah, New Zealand, December 6, 2005.)[30]

> I am absolutely in LOVE with MAC's lipglass! The variety of colours and
> finishes is amazing, the texture of it is perfect — not tacky, and the smell
> and taste of it is so familiar and comforting. I would be absolutely
> devastated if MAC ever took lipglass away from me. (June, Singapore,
> September 19, 2004)[31]

What is at stake for brand managers is not solely sleek advertising or
effective logos. Rather, it is absolutely every interface consumers have with
the brand in space and time and through which they "experience" brands.[32]
Many such interfaces are outside the control of brand managers. Very little
can be done about journalistic comments, critical academic works, everyday
conversations, or various forms of interactive communication, like blogs or
social network service sites such as Myspace, which retain a great degree of
autonomy.[33] What branding managers do have control over are such interfaces
as products; package design; advertising and promotional visuals; visual,
auditory, or olfactory presentations in retail space; call centers; staff uniforms;
websites; and sponsored events, be they fashion shows, concerts, or club
nights. Luxury cosmetics brands rely very heavily on lavishly designed counters
for the delivery of experience. The M.A.C. Cosmetics counter seems designed
to reproduce the excitement of a fashion photo shoot with a studio-like
setting, imposing umbrella strobes, pumping house music, and multiracial
poly-sexual staff.[34] For brands like M.A.C. or shu uemura, which have done
very little advertising in traditional media, the experience at the counter plays
a decisive role.[35] If the products or store staff fail to live up to the promise,
much research testifies, then even the sleekest of advertising does little to
salvage disappointed experience.[36]

This more "holistic" view of brands directs analytical attention away from
the ocularcentric privileging of the visual, the rational, and signification
evident in mainstream Media and Cultural Studies. The ways in which
consumers experience brands includes the semiotic, rational, and interpretative
pleasure derived, for example, from the brand's origin. But it also includes
the "affective," such as the "smell and taste" of lipgloss. Registered at the
level of the physical body, the affective or unprocessed sensations precede
the production of meaning. In other words, in the experience of a brand,
the culturally odorless and cultural odor are inseparable. The two do not occur
autonomously from each other but in a nonlinear process of resonance
through which intensity of experience is either heightened or dampened.[37]

Branding involves the management of these spatially dispersed and
temporary discrete interfaces — the very material and immaterial medium
of brands — in such a way that each relates to the other in a sort of mutual

excitation to produce a consistent and at times synesthetic experience that is more than the sum of its parts. Each qualitatively different interface must somehow flow from or communicate the brand's memory or identity, or better its virtuality. The virtuality of the brand should not be understood in opposition to the real or material but to the actual. The brand as the virtual is something potential that can be actualized in a great number of interfaces — such as the ground floor counters in department stores — and a great number of products.[38]

It is this virtuality of the brand that is now legally protected as "a separable piece of intellectual property" valued and exchanged because it provides "security of future earnings" on the global market. The economic value of the brand was highlighted when a senior Coca-Cola executive commented that, even if the Atlanta company lost all of its tangible assets, its representatives could walk into a bank and receive credit sufficient to replace the entire global infrastructure, as long as it still had the exclusive legal right to the use of its brand, whose value is estimated to be around US$60 billion or two-thirds of its capitalization.[39] Not surprisingly, the Coca-Cola company has such legal rights, as most countries in the world now recognize that a brand — distinctive logo, fonts, color schemes, symbols, or even scents registered as such — constitutes intellectual property and confers monopoly rights on the owners of such a property.[40] The prominence of intellectual properties in the global "ideoscape" is so great that, in recent American foreign policy, and particularly in America's negotiations with China, it seems to dwarf Enlightment-inspired concepts such as freedom and democracy.

Recent decades have seen various forms of brand-driven economic exchange, and without these the brandscape cannot be properly understood. First, there has been a growing number of brand-motivated mergers and acquisitions. In the realm of cosmetics this has sent most brands into the hands of a very few groups. For example L'Oréal was a decidedly European company until the Welshman Lindsay Owen-Jones was appointed CEO in 1988. He steered the group into globalization through a series of cross-border acquisitions, including not only such French brands as Lancôme and Biotherm but also American brands like Helena Rubinstein and Maybelline New York, as well as The Body Shop. L'Oréal also surprised the industry by acquiring the cult Japanese makeup brand, shu uemura, as well as the Chinese brands Mini Nurse and Yue-Sai. Estée Lauder, a brand in its own right, is also a brand-holding company that owns a wide array of North American brands. Until the 1990s its growth was organic, developing internally such brands as Clinique and Origins. When the company went public in 1995, it turned to a more aggressive strategy by acquiring brands such as M.A.C Cosmetics,

Bobbie Brown, La Mer, and Aveda. Shiseido has also undertaken acquisitions, to which I return shortly. In all cases, the acquisition prices were for the brand value, and this was well in excess of the value of the tangible assets producing the commodities themselves.[41]

The second important form of brand-driven economic exchange is brand licensing. Simply put, this is the leasing by a brand owner (licensor) of the use of a brand to another company (licensee) in return for payment of royalty fees. This allows a brand licensor to access resources that are otherwise not readily available and a brand licensee to have access to the virtuality or potential of an already proven brand. Although the conditions imposed on licensees can be strict, it is increasingly common now to find licensees taking a greater role in key decisions, including those concerning advertising, promotion, or product design.[42] Large cosmetics groups all team up with fashion brands, particularly on their fragrance lines. L'Oréal has license agreements with the Italian fashion label Giorgio Armani and the American label Ralph Lauren; Estée Lauder has license agreements with such American designers as Tommy Hilfiger and Donna Karan; and Shiseido has agreements with the eccentric French designer Jean-Paul Gaultier, a promising Cuban American designer, Narciso Rodriguez, and an established Japanese designer, Issey Miyake.

Brands used to be largely nationally bounded and characterized by monogamous relationships between brands and their owners. This is becoming increasingly uncommon, as more companies rely on a number of brands or a "brand portfolio" that is truly transnational.[43] When brands become the virtual, legally protected and exchanged in global markets, the various layers composing brands are no longer mapped neatly on top of each other.

Back to the Ground Floor

It is this complexity of contemporary brands that must be brought to bear on the analysis of the ground floors and the East Asian brandscape. As we have seen, L'Oréal, Estée Lauder, and Shiseido are in fact not merely brands but also brand-holding companies, boasting between them a great number of luxury brands. These groups dominate the luxury cosmetics world, together with another formidable French group, LVMH (Moët Hennessy Louis Vuitton), the owner of Parfums Christian Dior, Guerlain, and Kenzo Parfums. These four groups, together with Kosé and the Japanese toiletry giant Kao, own twenty-six of the thirty-six brands in Isetan Tokyo, twenty of the thirty-five in Sogo Hong Kong, fifteen of the twenty in Mitsukoshi Taipei, and twenty-two of the thirty in Selfridges in London. Transnational brands in these groups enjoy unimaginable advantages in finance, technologies, marketing, and human resources. It is these groups and certainly not nation-states that negotiate terms with department stores and media companies, making them the meaningful unit of analysis.

These groups usually manage their brand portfolios with a coherent "brand architecture," which specifies the way in which brands are related to, and are differentiated from, each another.[44] Brands may be "endorsed brands," which are sub-brands linked to the corporate brand by verbal or visual endorsement, or "freestanding brands," which are brands the corporate shell serves merely as a holding company for. All but one brand in the L'Oréal group (L'Oréal Paris) and the Estée Lauder group (Estée Lauder) are freestanding brands. This means that, although Lancôme, shu uemura, and Yue-Sai share many resources within the L'Oréal group, the relationship between them remains basically invisible. Shiseido's brand portfolio, in contrast, consists of a large number of endorsed brands and only a handful of freestanding brands. Endorsed brands, such as Shiseido Maquillage and Shiseido Elixir, might derive credibility from their association with the corporate Shiseido brand but also might find that association makes it difficult for them to be differentiated from each other.

Shiseido's endorsed brands are divided into global lines and regional (Asian) lines. The global lines include such flagship brands as Shiseido The Makeup, designed for the global market. Under creative direction from the famed French makeup artist Tom Pecheux, the group gives Shiseido The Makeup a luxurious yet generic identity. This comparatively odorless generic brand identity can be clearly seen in the historical selection of Caucasian models as "the muse" to represent the brand. In contrast, regional brands such as Shiseido Maquillage have been developed primarily for the younger domestic market. Shiseido Maquillage's brand identity is closely linked to the four hottest Japanese celebrities, Misaki Itō, Yuri Ebihara, Chiaki Kuriyama, and Ryōko Shinohara. Shiseido also has freestanding, or "Out of Shiseido," brands that are either "Western" or domestic brands designed to target consumers otherwise indifferent to Shiseido's endorsed brands. These brands are acquired or developed secretly by Shiseido and are not generally recognized as belonging to Shiseido. Western brands include Carita, Decléor, and Nars Cosmetics, all of which are marketed globally. Nars Cosmetics, for example, was created in New York by the legendary French-born makeup artist, François Nars, and is favored (so the website says) by such celebrities as Madonna and Michelle Pfeiffer.

Shiseido's brand portfolio thus enables the company to manage the level of Japanese cultural odor according to regional cultural difference or indeed varying degree of "Japanization." In the East Asian department stores, Shiseido distributes mostly endorsed brands. In Taipei it has a global counter that sells its global line brands and a Tokyo counter that sells regional brands such as Shiseido Maquillage, the latter's sales at almost double those of the former. In contrast, it relies more heavily on freestanding Western brands in non-Asian markets. In Selfridges London, Shiseido deploys three brands, Shiseido Global Line, Nars Cosmetics, and Decléor, which are located next to each other. Its licensed fragrance brands also play a far greater role in European markets, where fragrance can occupy as much as forty percent of the total cosmetics market, as opposed to Japan's meager two percent.

This regional difference can be seen more explicitly with another Japanese cosmetic group, Kosé. Kosé has also developed its domestic brands as Asian regional brands. Like Shiseido Maquillage, these have been promoted on the back of the Tokyo lifestyle through the use of Japanese celebrities. At the same time, its subsidiary Albion has relied upon its licensed brands both in the domestic and international markets. These licensed brands include one American — Anna Sui Cosmetics — and two French — Sonia Rykiel and Paul and Joe Beauté. In my department store case studies, Sonia Rykiel and Anna Sui Cosmetics are found in both Hong Kong and Tokyo, and all three are in Taipei. Likewise, shu uemura is in every one of the East Asian department stores studied. L'Oréal acquired this brand in 2002 and rapidly expanded it into the Asian market, particularly in mainland China. When brands become virtual, protected legally and exchanged in the global market, their layers are relatively autonomous from each other. This gives the department store ground floors in London and Taipei, for example, different degrees of Japanese cultural odor. At the same time, it makes the very notion of Japanese brands increasingly complex.

Difference and Disjuncture

Rereading the department store ground floors demonstrates that the brandscape is more complex than the distribution of national cultural power through semiotics. But what should we conclude about this new complexity? Japanization does point to the convergence of cultural taste among a certain population of East Asian consumers, and this has undoubtedly led to the development of regional brands. However, the exclusive and at times obsessive focus on this as an unmistakable sign of national cultural power, particularly in the case of images of Japanese bodies, does not help explain the complex way the cultural power of brands operates as "branded experience" or the way brands are exchanged on the global market. *Glocalization*, as it has been conventionally used as an analytical framework, is concerned primarily with localization at the level of representation in advertising. Not only is advertising only a part of the brand, but also such a focus on representation directs analysis away from the more complex structures in which differences are managed where transnational brands have been accumulated by large global groups. In either case, representation in advertisements is no longer the primary site where cultural power operates.

The limitations of analytical models that approach brands by representation have led me to Appadurai's model of the scape. The strengths of Appadurai's model include that it goes beyond dichotomies such as the centre versus the periphery, culture versus economy, or local versus global. Instead, it stresses generative interactions between heterogeneous forces (the scapes), which give rise to sociocultural formations in non-deterministic ways. Under Americanization, transnational flows were largely isomorphic, things and non-things alike flowing from Detroit, Hollywood, Madison Avenue, and Wall Street to the peripheries. Instead, under globalization, "people, machinery, money, images and ideas now follow increasingly non-isomorphic paths."[45] This seems to help explain heterogeneous formations like the East Asian brandscape, which has been generated from the disjunctive interactions between scapes: on the technoscape, the narrowing gap in technological capacity among growing numbers of developed nations; on the financescape, the massive flow of capital seeking underleveraged assets (brands); media globalization on the mediascape; and a new set of ideoscapes such as the intellectual property regime and the diminishing nationalistic opposition to the cross-border takeovers in favor of maximization of shareholder value. Appadurai's model has been criticized for ostensibly emphasizing that "nothing is related to anything."[46] Nonetheless, I believe it is an effective analytical framework for exploring the question of "what is related to what" and how in the East Asian brandscape. What is the relationship between scapes? Is there a particular flow prior to and formative of other flows in the East Asian brandscape?

In the emergence of the East Asian brandscape, I suggest, the mediascape is hegemonic over other scapes. Notwithstanding South Korea's ascent to become a regional media powerhouse, the inter-Asian media flow still occurs predominantly from Japan to the rest of East Asia. In particular, many brand managers I spoke to pointed to the significance of the vast circulation of Japanese women's fashion magazines in the region, either to be looked at in the original Japanese version or to be read increasingly in licensed local languages. In the last few decades these magazines have functioned inadvertently as pan-Asian media delivering branded information from Tokyo and contributing to the emergence of the elusive regional cultural commonality.[47] Cosmetics brands dominate these magazines not only with advertising but also with advertorial and tie-in pages. These brands may or may not be available in other markets at the time they appear in Japanese magazines. However, they will be sooner rather than later, as consumers increasingly demand simultaneous access to these brands and marketers quickly respond. In such cases, the mediascape precedes other scapes such as finance or technology in the formation of the brandscape. However, against the nationalistic desires of Japanization advocates, the East Asian mediascape indiscriminately benefits both "Japanese" and non-Japanese brands. Marketers I spoke to were keenly aware of the emergence of an East Asian mediascape and keen to take advantage of it. This adds further disjuncture to the flows, as is demonstrated vividly in the cases of Paul and Joe Beauté and shu uemura.

The fashion brand Paul and Joe was launched in 1995 by the then-menswear designer, Sophie Albou, a native of Paris. Her uniquely colorful and feminine style found devotees well beyond Paris, particularly in Japan. The Japanese cosmetics company Albion approached the designer (who had long been interested in Japanese culture) and struck a global licensing deal for the cosmetics line in 2002. In less than five years, the brand Paul and Joe Beauté, now designed and manufactured in Tokyo in close correspondence with the French designer, has become a popular cosmetics brand circulating globally but most intensively in Asian markets. This demonstrates both the speed and disjuncture with which the mediascape — flowing from France, to Tokyo, to other East Asian cities and beyond — precedes other flows of technologies and capitals. The brand Paul and Joe Beauté represents some aspect of Tokyo culture, as strongly as or even more strongly than some Kosé or Shiseido brands. But it does not do this by carrying signifiers of Japaneseness but rather affective qualities and a position in mediascape similar to those of Tokyo culture.

The Paris company L'Oréal is also more aggressively and resourcefully taking advantage of this increasingly disjunctive mediascape. When it acquired shu uemura, its explicit aim was to bring this brand to the growing Asian market, and particularly China, in order to appeal to Asian consumers who, as its Taiwanese senior brand coordinator in the Tokyo headquarters told me, "appreciate and love Japanese brands." This is particularly well illustrated by CEO Lindsay Owen-Jones's statement:

We didn't just accept to have local brands. We tried to put our brands everywhere. We sell the United States to the Americans, the United States to Chinese, Italian elegance to the Japanese, French beauty to Africans, and Japanese chic to Brazilians.[48]

The brandscape emerges from this new form of the distribution of cultural power, which operates not through ideological domination by the nation-state or through a dialectical relationship between global and local but rather through a more flexible organization of disjunctive forces by increasingly transnational agents such as L'Oréal. The speed and volume of media flows from Japan to Taiwan account for the shape of the brandscape in Taipei, evidenced for example by the abundance of endorsed Shiseido brands, and with it an intense Japanese cultural odor. However, it also includes such brands as Paul and Joe Beauté or Anna Sui Cosmetics, which come with no Japanese cultural odor. In contrast, the reverse may be said about the brandscape in London, where an absence of media images from Japan is complemented by an abundant flow of capital to determine the shape of the brandscape, epitomized by Shiseido's acquisition and deployment of Nars Cosmetics, Decléor, Jean Paul Gaultier, and Narciso Rodriguez.

Nonetheless, brands are insistently talked about — as even I am doing here — by their nationality. Brands are hence quintessential examples of what Appadurai calls "production fetishism," an illusion created by contemporary transnational production relations. This fetishism "masks translocal capital, transnational earning flows, global management, and value-added creative work in the metropolis and often-faraway [manufacturing] workers" with the idioms and ideologies of local, regional or global brands.[49] What is masked is not social relations but a dispersed yet integrated network of global forces that embraces rather than suppresses differences and disjunctures.

Transformation?

Thoroughly commoditized as it may be, we see in the East Asian brandscape the emergence of an elusive sense of regional sensibility, or "East Asian popular culture," in which Japanese culture plays a constitutive role.[50] However, the ways in which brands have been distributed in this affective geography, as we have seen, is complex and contradictory, undermining both the advocates and critics of Japanization.

The analysis of the East Asian brandscape has highlighted a transformation in the notion of cultural power, away from the ideological representations in advertising and the subjective identity to more immediate and perhaps more affective branded experiences. The transformation observed in my small example is hardly an isolated instance but a global phenomenon witnessed in growing parts of the cultural economy.[51] It has been generally acknowledged that most of the world's biggest brands that surround our everyday lives — Microsoft, Nokia, Starbucks, and Mercedes — are primarily customer experience brands that embrace this transformation in one way or another.[52]

In order for Media and Cultural Studies to catch up with this transformation, writes Szerman in a book boldly titled *New Cultural Studies*, it needs once again to "reveal the hidden politics of older forms of cultural criticism . . . through an expansion of the range of what 'counts' as cultural."[53] The task then is to expand the theoretical understanding of the cultural so that we can better analyze proliferating cultural forms, like brands, which have been considered less cultural or culturally odorless, and the process in which they are developed, managed, and exchanged, which has been considered as belonging primarily to economics or management. This, of course, is all the more urgent in Northeast Asia, which is undoubtedly the forefront of this transformation where Media and Cultural Studies seems to be lagging behind the no longer national culture industries.

9

Korean Pop Music in China:
Nationalism, Authenticity, and Gender

Rowan Pease

Authenticity and nationality are closely linked for fans of South Korean[1] popular culture in China, as well for the Korean cultural establishment. Bringing gender into the equation, in this essay I focus on the mainly young female fans of Korean boy bands and idols. It was in 2000 that South Korean pop music became fashionable in China, as part of a regional phenomenon commonly dubbed "Korean Wave" (*Hanliu* in Chinese, *Hallyu* in Korean,[2] a pun on the meteorological homonym "cold current").[3] *Hanliu* first arrived in China in 1997, brought through broadcasts of televised Korean soap operas, which were said to enthral middle-aged women. A proliferation of local and satellite TV channels, such as Rupert Murdoch's Star TV, led to increased exports of foreign programs within Asia, including music television, and through these Korean dance and rap music spread.[4] Increasingly, the Internet gave Chinese youth unprecedented access to music from different cultures, enabling the Korean Wave to spread beyond urban centers. Korean rap group Clon, building on their success in Taiwan, performed in Beijing in November 1999, followed by H.O.T. (High Five of Teenagers) in 2000, and girl groups S.E.S. and Baby Vox. The middle-of-the-road R&B/hip-hop that they performed[5] — with either mildly rebellious or romantic lyrics, including smatterings of English, and slick dance routines — was what Kōichi Iwabuchi has described elsewhere as a "culturally odorless" or "Asianized Western" model of pan-regional modernity.[6] That is to say, there was no element of traditional Korean instrumentation, melodic modes, or compound rhythms, and none of the guttural passion of *ppongtchak* ballads[7] that were ubiquitous in 1970s and 1980s Korea. Korean pop attracted a younger *Hanliu* audience, the most dedicated of whom were dubbed the *haHanzu* (or *haHanyizu*), the "crazed for Korea" tribe,[8] noted for their outlandish clothes and extreme behavior.[9] These fans celebrated their solidarity as members of the tribe, sharing their passion in clubs and online. Defending themselves against charges that they were unpatriotic, they claimed that Korean musicians were more natural and sincere than "commercial" Chinese idols, a quality that could not be imitated. The fans tended to feminize the objects of their adoration, in discussion, artwork, and fiction that was sometimes homoerotic.

In this essay, I discuss the role of Korean cultural industries (including entertainment companies,[10] business conglomerates, and government agencies) in supporting Korean popular music as part of a broader national promotion, and their complex relationship with agencies in China and the fans who reworked it into "an intensely pleasurable, intensely signifying popular culture"[11] that undermined the intended messages of nationalism and regionalism. The conflicting notions of gender, authenticity, and modernity throw up new questions about alterity within East Asia. I draw on the work of Cho Hae-Joang on *Hanliu* discourse,[12] and Iwabuchi's work on fans' self-reflexivity and transnational consumption.[13]

The *Hanliu* Industry in China

There have been several peaks and troughs in China's Korean Wave, its fortunes seemingly dependent on the success of individual idols or of particular TV dramas or films (and hence their original soundtrack sales). For instance, actor Ahn Jae wook [An Chaeuk], star of the TV drama *Star in My Heart* (*Pyŏl'ŭn nae kasŭm-e*), was one of the few Korean stars popular enough to successfully mount a solo concert in a major stadium,[14] while Shin Seung-hun's [Shin Sŭnghun] theme song *I Believe* from the hit film *My Sassy Girl* (*Yŏpki chŏgin kŭnyŏ*, Kwak Jae-young 2001) was a major bestseller, selling 200,000 CDs in China in 2001, and covered by Taiwan artist Van Fan. For many Korean singers, it was essential first to get international exposure through acting in dramas, sometimes co-productions.

During my fieldwork in China in 2003, Korean pop occupied only ten percent of the imported music market (excluding imports from greater China), was disappearing from radio stations and TV, and I (incorrectly) predicted the imminent recession of the wave. The pop idol Rain (a.k.a. Bi, Jung Ji-hoon [Chŏng Chihun]), boy band TVXQ, and TV drama *Jewel in the Palace* (*Dae Changgŭm*) reversed that trend, but even in 2006 Korean and Japanese songs were grouped together in pop charts (*RiHan paihangban*) in which Japanese artists dominated, and neither has ever dented the popularity of music from Hong Kong and Taiwan.

China was a frustrating market for the Korean music industry. As domestic sales shrank,[15] the initial promise of massive sales in China[16] was undermined by piracy at ninety percent and hampered by China's strict publishing controls and high tariffs for legal products.[17] Such problems were by no means unique to Korean cultural products or to music. Anthony Fung has outlined the steps taken by Hong Kong and Taiwanese entertainment companies to overcome the twin barriers of state control and piracy when launching stars such as Andy Lau and Jay Chou in China.[18] An added impediment for the Korean music industry was that the youthful audience for Korean artists had little disposable income to spend on records or concert tickets. For legitimate music companies, the way to earn money from this market was through sponsorship and advertising deals rather than through the traditional business of selling records or rights.[19] Illegal publishing *was* the major driving force behind the distribution of Korean music and hence the market value of their stars. As one media executive told me, "without piracy, there would be no *Hanliu.*"[20] Laikwan Pang has noted the importance of piracy in enabling the distribution of films that would otherwise be censored or unavailable in China, and in challenging the notion of a homogenous Chinese collective by catering to fragmented audiences, and this is pertinent to the diffusion of Korean popular culture in China.[21] Fans expressed distaste for purchasing pirated copies: genuine CDs carried considerable cachet, but these were hard to obtain.

Given the barriers to profitability in China, it is not surprising that Korean entertainment companies were perceived as being ambivalent in their efforts to enter the Chinese market. Perhaps they felt that their efforts would be better rewarded if they focussed on opening the Japanese music market, the second largest in the world, rather than China. While solo idols BoA [Kwŏn Poa] and Se7en [Ch'oe Tonguk] were both making terrific sales in Japan in 2003, one Chinese record company executive complained to me that Korean entertainment companies just "threw" famous artists at the Chinese market rather than analyzing it and laying groundwork as they did for domestic audiences. Another said that, after two years of hard effort placing artists in Chinese television shows, companies had sat back waiting to reap the rewards rather than sustaining their presence. Likewise, a Hong Kong DJ I interviewed in 2003 criticized the lack of supporting material and follow-on that could build on the success of particular songs or TV shows.[22]

Nevertheless, one agency, the SM Entertainment Company, headed by Lee Soo Man [Yi Suman], was widely admitted to be the driving force behind the export of Korean popular music to China. SM was the company behind H.O.T., the greatest of the *Hanliu* stars, and after H.O.T. broke up in 2001, SM continued to manage two former members, Kangta and Jang Woo Hyuk [Chang Uhyŏk], who remained popular in China. A poll on Sina.com's entertainment pages in February 2006 revealed that four of the five most popular Korean singers/bands were SM artists, with Jang in top position and Kangta in fifth.[23] The other, Rain, belonged to the JYP Entertainment stable of artists. Rain's manager, Park Jin-young [Pak Chinyŏng], had already built a large fan base in Japan, and pinned his hopes on opening the US market.[24] His success in China was apparently of secondary importance. Lee Soo Man, in contrast, remained focused on China, which has the potential to be the world's greatest market as soon as piracy is brought under control. He stated his confidence in the regularization and growth of the Chinese music market in an interview in 2005 and suggested that his activities in Taiwan and Hong Kong were a springboard for further expansion there.[25] After H.O.T. split up, Lee struggled to replicate their success with new artists, and for several years he worked on reuniting H.O.T.[26] He also went to China repeatedly from 2001, auditioning artists to recruit to his Starlight Academy and eventually to form a "Chinese H.O.T. or S.E.S"[27] that would surely outstrip foreign artists. Later, his overarching strategy was to form pan-regional bands, as part of a so-called "blue ocean" policy (announced at Hanyang University), or "culture technology" theory.[28] Consequently, appealing to the first generation of *haHanzu*, Kangta formed a singing partnership with Vanness Wu [Wu Jianhao], a member of Taiwanese boy band F4, and two boy bands were launched to appeal to Chinese youth: TVXQ (*Dongfang shenqi*, "Gods Rising in the East") and Super Junior. In a documentary about the band shown on the SBS television channel[29] one member of TVXQ, U-Know, said that "Our name was chosen to make Chinese people feel familiar," while band member Xiah's stage name was reportedly a short form of "Asia," to "reflect his desire to become known throughout Asia."[30] In 2005, Lee Soo Man announced that as part of his "blue ocean" policy of creating a transnational group, he would split TVXQ into two bands, one with a Japanese member and one with a Chinese singer, perhaps chosen through a televised competition. As a result of fan resistance (see below), he abandoned this plan. However, the larger, even cuter and younger boy band, Super Junior, included a Chinese member, Han Kyung [Han Kyŏng; Ch. Han Geng] who graduated through SM Entertainment's auditions and academy. SM also launched a solo Chinese female R&B singer in Korea, Zhang Liyin (K. Chang Ri'in).

Korean State Branding

Chinese media executives may have had some criticisms of Korean impresarios, but during my fieldwork they unanimously praised the investment of the Korean government and large corporations such as Samsung, that were willing to maintain the profile of Korean music through mounting concerts and album giveaways. For companies such as LG and Samsung, Korean artists headed up advertising campaigns that helped them to claim a substantial portion of the Chinese mobile phone and electronics market (for example, Samsung's sales in China increased fivefold between 1998 and 2001, and by 2003 their display screens occupied twenty-nine percent of the Chinese market, and mobile phones nine percent).[31] The Samsung Economic Research Institute in 2005 drew up a report on *Hanliu*, entitled "The Korean wave sweeps the globe," to see how best to sustain and benefit from the wave,[32] and economists credited Korea's healthy export figures to the country's cultural diplomacy.[33] In 2005, South Korea had the world's second largest trading surplus with China (US$42 billion, second only to Taiwan).[34] Not only Korean companies but also Chinese and global companies adopted *Hanliu* idols for campaigns throughout Asia. For example, Ford in 2006 signed up Ahn Jae-wook for its East Asian promotions, and Pantech, the Chinese mobile phone company, was one of many companies that paid Rain to advertise its brand.

The Korean government was likewise keen to capitalize on the economic benefits of *Hanliu*. In 2001, the Korean Ministry of Culture set up the Korean Culture and Contents Agency (KOCCA) — "in recognition of the value of cultural content and its importance as the nation's economic growth factor" — to support cultural industries at home and to facilitate cultural exports and exchange.[35] Besides KOCCA, a major investor in *Hanliu* was the Korean National Tourism Office, which noted the increase of tourism generated by overseas drama fans, and employed *Hanliu* stars, such as Rain, as "goodwill ambassadors." In 2003, the KNTO conducted a *Hanliu* tourism survey in China, Taiwan, and Hong Kong exploring attitudes to Korean culture, publishing the results online. While TV dramas and film were found to have had the greatest impact on visitor figures to Korea, the survey revealed that 27.5 percent of Chinese respondents listed "attend concerts of popular singer" as their "desired purpose of visiting Korea," and fifteen percent cited the "influence of Korean music" in choosing that country for future tourism.[36]

The survey suggested that Korea had found a niche in the market but in no way displaced other cultural imports (for example, although forty-three percent of respondents in Greater China felt Korean culture was very influential, this was below the figure for Hong Kong, American, or Japanese culture). It compared the impact of Korean culture with that of four "competitor" countries (the US, Japan, Taiwan, and Hong Kong), and in the process revealed much about Korea's own political and nationalist concerns, particularly in relation to Japan and America. Six of the eleven options for respondents to the category "reasons I like Korean culture" reflect this preoccupation: "less sexual than Japanese culture," "less sexual than American culture," "less violent than Japanese popular culture," "less violent than American popular culture," "decreased interest in American culture," and "decreased interest in Japanese culture." One other echoes Straubhaar's notion of cultural proximity: "similar in culture."[37] Certainly, Korea's own music media censorship laws (which even in 1997 prohibited the displaying of body piercings, navels, tattoos, "outfits which may harm the sound emotional development of youth," and banned violent or political lyrics),[38] meant that Chinese TV stations could buy in Korean music videos and music TV shows knowing that they were unlikely to upset local censors. However, these questions also reflected a perception that Korea acts as a defender against excessive Westernization and as a guardian of Confucian values within East Asia.

Cho Hae-Joang analyzes discourses about *Hanliu* in Korean scholarship and media, and identifies three main strands: the cultural nationalist (Korean culture is international, it stresses familism rather than violence, it benefits from anti-Japanese sentiment, and challenges US cultural hegemony); the industrialist and neo-liberal (stressing the market rather than culture, giving precedence to mass rather than high culture, youth rather than middle-aged markets, and calling for investment in production and distribution); and the post-colonialist perspective (*Hanliu* is a shallow "B-class" — lowbrow — culture produced by Western capitalist culture "penetrating our bodies";[39] an East Asian cultural bloc should be formed to resist it). Cho argues that these three strands have coalesced into a neo-liberal strand that stresses the economic benefits of *Hanliu*, and that *Hanliu* is indicative of a global shift in which shared East Asian cultures are creating a sense of community that challenges the use of Western "others."[40] It seems to me that this perspective is embodied in Lee Soo Man's pan-regional "Culture Technology" policy and his refusal to measure Asian artists' success by reference to the US market.

Hanliu Discourse: The Chinese Perspective

Elements of the first two strands (cultural nationalist and industrialist) were reflected in writings and in comments on *Hanliu* from the cultural brokers in China. For instance, on Confucian values in Korean culture, Jiao Yan of the Chinese Academy of Social Sciences was quoted in the *China Daily* as saying "We see a purer form of Confucianism and are refreshed by it because we feel a sense of belonging."[41] Such Confucianism, according to a Beijing publisher quoted in the same article, cannot be found in "our own writers and artists." During my fieldwork, Confucianism was not mentioned, nor were family values, though perhaps it is partly that these are not made so explicit in music as in dramas. However, the success of *Hanliu* as an alternative to American and Japanese popular music was mentioned. For instance, on the popularity of Korean hip-hop, Hao Fang, of Starry Sky TV said,

> Hip-hop never got big in China; lots of people think it doesn't fit Chinese language. Chinese don't respect blacks, but they can take Koreans doing hip-hop. . . . they can't totally love Japanese, for historical reasons, and because they feel it's too different.[42]

As for Korean music being international music, on the whole, media executives described Japanese as being more varied, less imitative of the West; for example "In my opinion, Japanese music has already gone past copying the US and Europe."[43] There was a subtext that there was an evolutionary timeline, the West at the most developed end, followed by Japan, and then Korea/Hong Kong/Taiwan. Hong Kong and Taiwan were viewed as being less influenced by Western fashions, according to Robin Pak,[44] because Western and Eastern popular music styles coexisted there rather than fusing. Korea was described as being in an exciting period of development (*penfa*) and specialized in high-quality dance music. One Chinese student, a fan of Western rather than Korean music, made a direct comparison binding fans' social status to their choice of music, saying that the more educated a listener, the more likely the listener was to like Western music. Those with less exposure to Western culture (say, college rather than university students) might find Japanese music interesting, and those with the least exposure (high school graduates) would be satisfied with Korean music.[45]

The industrial perspective described by Cho was more clearly echoed by all those I interviewed. Chinese media executives ascribed the success of *Hanliu* to the packaging and "factory style" production of artists. For example, Ji Lingli, who worked for Baidie Record Company, told me: "SM's packaging is really good. It's really commercial. They don't care if it's rubbish or not; they don't respect art; they just care if they can sell it. Our company is really stupid: we want to do good music, to raise the national standard. Because our boss is a musician, that's our attitude."[46] Gu Hong described SM

Entertainment as a "star-making factory" that closely followed changing styles and rapidly adapted to them.[47] Robin Pak likewise admired the artist creation: the vocal, dance, image, and language training (in Chinese and Japanese). He also spoke of how strictly the artists were controlled both on and off stage during their visits to Hong Kong, as part of maintaining the artist's image.[48]

The Fan Perspective

The discourse about *Hanliu* idols among fans — those who "not only consume a culture, but who translate that consumption into activity, joining a community with whom they share feelings and thoughts about their common interest"[49] — was radically different from that of the Korean and Chinese producers and commentators quoted above.

The stigmatization of *haHanzu* as hysterical, screaming, undiscriminating dupes is a characterization broadly similar to the image of young female fans in the West and elsewhere in Asia.[50] Best known for the sheer volume of their passion, they were hardly the audience that Korean cultural and political elites aspired to attract. The contempt is revealed in this article on the KOCCA website: ". . . the interest of musical value and meaningful content does not extend to the teens."[51] That statement is belied by the wealth of discussion and writing about Korean idols that is to be found in fan sites and forums on the Internet. Likewise, Robin Pak warned me, "If you ask them why they like Korean stars, they won't know . . . They are blind. They'll just say 'like is like,' or that they are handsome."[52]

When I conducted a survey among fans in 2003, "because I do,"[53] love, and good looks *were* common answers to this question, but there were many answers that are pertinent to the issues discussed above.[54] Perhaps not surprisingly, the fans had little interest in comparing Korean music with Japanese or American music, and many enjoyed music of different nationalities, as well as Chinese music. Where K-pop, J-pop, and US-pop fans were put together in bulletin boards there were occasional conflicts, but they were more likely to be about battles between specific artists (for example, H.O.T. versus the Backstreet Boys) rather than issues of nationality. If the "significant others" for Korea were the US and Japan, for the Chinese fans it was Korea that was the other to their Chineseness, that gave them the self-reflexive distance to consider their own culture. In their responses to me, fans never compared Korean music to American, and only one mentioned Japan (and then in passing), in a passage more concerned with Chinese (including Hong Kong and Taiwan) music:

If all those Hong Kong, Taiwan and mainland singers like Andy Lau, Jeff Chang and Sun Nan cover Korean songs, isn't it better to go directly to Korea to listen to the original? And their [Korean singers'] image is more healthy and individual. For example, H.O.T. means High Five of Teenagers. Their behaviour and songs are really a model for youth. Korean singers are fashionable and have vigour, and don't just rely on packaging (in fact, I think Koreans on the whole are very plain). Their dance is the highest level in Asia. We all see that Japanese music is on the wane, while Korean is flourishing. The Chinese mainland is so inferior there is no possibility; the HK/Taiwan singers obviously sing covers for their main songs; their decline is obvious. (IYAH, 30.1.03:9)

Common themes to emerge from the answers to why fans liked Korean artists were that their musical and dance standards were high, that they were vigorous, that they were sincere ("NRG are very natural, they are never artificial" [cjking, 20.9.03:49]), that they showed their feelings ("They are not afraid to cry on stage" [ting 21.10.03:163]), that they were hard-working and creative ("Many people think they are idol singers . . . in fact those five all try to write lyrics and music" [xcandy, 29.8.03:12]), and that their songs covered varied themes. These latter qualities were seen to be in direct contrast to Hong Kong, Taiwanese, and Mainland singers, for example, "That sincere feeling is really hard to see with contemporary Hong Kong/Taiwan music" (ting, 21.10.03:163); or "They're not like the majority of pop music in China, always singing that sort of mm mm chee chee, love you love me romantic song. They always sing about the problems appearing in society or fresh and original themes" (xuxu, 24.9.03: 101).

In an almost complete antithesis to the "industrial" view of Korean and Chinese pundits, for fans it was the absence of commercialism — the authenticity — that differentiated the Korean artists from the Chinese:

When they [Chinese singers] haven't even sung much, they put out "greatest hits" and take our money. It sullies music, and the media spin, so hateful, it's all for money. (rcandy, 21.9.03: 68)

Another complained about the lack of segmentation in the market:

The reason China's music is less exciting is connected to the size of its population (like most of its problems). China overemphasises totality: they want the whole, not parts. Clearly in pop music, if you want to write a song that everyone likes, of whatever status or age, there is going to be less creative power, it's not so rich. (Sun Ho, 14.9.03: 37)

Fans were outspoken in their contempt for the Hong Kong, Chinese, or Taiwanese boy bands that seemed to imitate the style of Korean pop, without embodying its essence. Such bands were described to me as rip-offs (*bianlu pin*), or "meaningless imitation" (holim, 22.9.03: 86). Another fan wrote:

> When I see how many Chinese singers cover Korean songs, it reveals how the Chinese music world lacks creativity. As a Chinese person, I feel really ashamed. Taiwan's latest bands even more so are obviously imitating Korean bands. (IYAH, 30.1.03: 9)

Even Chinese *haHanzu* came in for criticism for inauthenticity from their peers:

> Some of the kids, who wear hip hop clothes and dance on the streets, imitate the appearance of Korean singers, but don't really understand Korean music and don't understand the amount of sweat and diligence behind the bright appearance of these singers. They are not real *haHanzu*. (rabbit27, 23.9.03: 3)

Having noted their hatred of all things commercial, it is not surprising that, within the *haHanzu* community, the greatest enmity was towards Lee Soo Man, who was widely blamed for the demise of H.O.T. and who was seen to be too manipulative. Given this, and their perception that nationality and authenticity are closely linked in Korean music, the fans' response to Lee Soo Man's reported plan to insert a Chinese member into TVXQ was predictable. Here are some of their comments on the rumour from a posting on the Sina *Hanliu* bulletin board which called for a petition:

- Nooooooooooooooooo!!!!
- I don't know how you all feel, but I like the 5 guy TVXQ. If everyone wants to keep our TVXQ, quickly sign up. Thank you.
- Ooooohhhh! [written 555555555555, literally pronounced *wuwuwuwuwuwuwuwuwuwuwuwuwuwuwuwuwu*]
- I was up all night crying
- It can't be. Although I am a Chinese, whatever you say they are a Korean band. Adding in a couple of people from other countries, I feel it would be really weird
- This is just what SM loves doing — H.O.T., Shinhwa, all went that way. Now it's happening again. Kill!
- God! How's that possible? They are one body. How can it be a Sino-Korean joint venture? I'm going to pass out!
- Lee Soo Man has got water on the brain

- If that's true then we Chinese fans [literally "immortal followers"] must go to resist!!!!!
- No matter what happens, you must handle them reasonably. Like us H.O.T fans. We couldn't take it when they split. But now, so many years later, we still support them. I hope you can be like us.

It perhaps reveals that fans understood how the Korean state values *Hanliu* that they decided not to petition Lee Soo Man, who was in their view irredeemable, but the president of Korea, Roh Moo-hyun.[55]

Confucianism and Cultural Proximity

One of the elements that Korean cultural nationalists stress in *Hanliu* is shared Confucian values, and linked to that, the absence of sex in Korean culture. If for Confucian values we read respect for education and elders, for the *haHanzu* this is manifested in the sense of a shared struggle against those elements of Confucianism. For example,

> Many of their songs have expressed our hearts' feelings . . . the pressure at our schools is so high, the H.O.T. brothers' songs give us lots of encouragement. They are our companions in study. (lovewoohyuk, 20.9.03: 85)

In one fan story, "The first person who loves me" by "Hyun&Hyuk," the author expresses frustration through the feelings of H.O.T. member Heejun:

> HeeJun suddenly felt cynical: it didn't matter how many beautiful lives went down this route, in the end the old society, parents and family would drag you back to tradition, the deadest ends, you must marry a girl, have a child . . . this was all mother wanted. However romantic the love, in the end you couldn't get past this oldest wish.[56]

Popular songs by H.O.T. included "IYAH" [Children], which one fan described as "earthshaking": "their song denounced humanity's evils. Their models looked like warriors fighting for humanity" (Sun Ho, 14.9.03: 37). Another popular song was "We are the future," which exemplifies the "classroom ideology":[57]

"We are the future"
Hey Everybody look at me! Now let's overthrow the conventions of the world

I am the new master! Adults' world has already passed.
Old weak things, give up your voice that speaks only rubbish
(The) future is mine. 1, 2 and 3 and 4 and Go!!
Until now we've been in the shade of adults
In a place without freedom, this way, that way interfering, living one day
is exhausting
How long until we finally throw off the adult control
As the days go past, we are so tired we feel faint
I will make my own world myself.
Don't expect the same life as them. I will grow my own century![58]

Other songs from the album continue in this theme, such as *Yŏldŭng kam* ("The End of my Inferiority Complex"), and *Chayu-ropke nalsu ittorok* ("Free to Fly").

Sexuality and Gender

Although explicit sexuality was absent from song lyrics and videos, it was certainly present in the fans' fantasies and implicit in band publicity. The fans playfully overturned gender roles and the power relationship between males and females, stars and fans.

It is helpful here to explore briefly the sexual politics of popular music in China, in order to reveal the extent to which, and especially how, fans' behaviour undermined the status quo. Chinese popular music production and distribution, long under the control of the "masculinist state," is described by Nimrod Baranovitch as male dominated, including in the counter-cultural spheres of rock or rap.[59] The reform and opening of the 1980s and 1990s had allowed gender differences, suppressed by Maoist ideology, to be expressed once again as the image of the ideal "iron girl" gave way to the domesticated, soft, and restrained woman. There is much debate about whether the renewed sexualization of women was a step towards liberation or a return to male–controlled commodification. In mainstream pop, women continued to be objectified in popular songs, exoticized and "othered;" even when songs ostensibly spoke with their voice about their experience, these were mostly written by men "usurping their consciousness."[60] In the 1990s, Baranovitch saw an increasing empowerment of women through their role as consumers of popular music. This, he says, was reflected in "soft" male ballads, expressing romantic love for women, that were "an attempt to compensate for actual experience" of male domination.[61] Nevertheless, "although women do participate in and perhaps even dominate the patronage of soft mainstream music by male singers, the latter are seldom objectified in the way . . . female singers are objectified."[62]

The period when *Hanliu* spread across China saw a further increase in the power of women as consumers. In the early years of the twentieth century, young urban women — constituting 38.1% of the total urban workforce and generally in control of purse strings — became the prime target of marketers, who identified them as ego-, rather than duty-driven.[63] The younger *haHanzu* were economically less powerful, yet finding that the market was unable to satisfy their musical tastes — due to state controls, distributors' hesitancy, and their own avowed reluctance to buy pirated discs — they were able to take some control of distribution through their illegal circulation of music on the Internet. Technology increasingly gave them the tools not only to circulate music but to rework it, creating their own videos and montages, blurring the boundaries between "creativity" and "copying,"[64] and inserting a private, female presence into the public male-dominated production of music.

Unlike the 1990s music consumers outlined by Baranovitch above, the female fans of Korean music were not satisfied with the "inauthentic" romantic expressions of "soft" Chinese stars, and proceeded to objectify their idols shamelessly. On websites such as the Kangta fansite, boy-band members were infantilized and feminized, in the characterization of the star/fan relationship, in artwork and in fiction.[65] Kangta was depicted as a beautiful and idealistic innocent, requiring the fans to protect him from the record companies and the female predators that might exploit him.[66] Similar vulnerable and childlike imagery was found on sites for other idols, for example Super Junior's Han Kyung. There was some collusion from publishers: photographs in the magazine *Yule Wuxian* (*Entertainment Unlimited*) celebrated male beauty in soft focus, semi-naked group shots, while the artwork for TVXQ's *The Another Story of Balloon* [sic] album[67] shows the band members frolicking in cute animal jumpsuits with ears, paws, and tails. In fans' cartoons, band members might be dressed up as fairies, or as sleeping babies with dummies and soft toys.

Other pictures and stories were homoerotic fantasies. Some were taken from Korean or Japanese sites, where this kind of art has a longer history,[68] but others were by Chinese fans. Romantic stories were divided into two genres: love between a fan and the star (*tongren* stories) and stories of love between male idols (*tongtong* or BL — boys' love — stories). Some were suggestive, but others were blatantly pornographic.

Sexuality is fluid, multiply experienced, and not easily discussed with a foreign scholar. I was reluctant to discuss this issue in much detail after my initial questions led the owner of one fansite to remove explicit slash stories, claiming they were unacceptable to some fans. She also suggested that fans couldn't enjoy stories about the idols with female fans, because they would feel jealous. Just one fan wrote about the sheer pleasure of such stories: "Heh heh . . . I also really appreciate the protagonists' stories that tell about fantasy[69] love and their self-loving behaviour" (Sun Ho, 14.9.03: 37). I have therefore looked to secondary sources to consider the Korean star/Chinese fan relationship from several angles.

In classic discussions of Orientalism, the "other" is feminized and infantilized, rendered weak by the gaze of the powerful self. This does not seem a particularly useful model in the case of the Chinese fans and the Korean stars, where the "self" and "other" are, in economic and political power, in a reverse (or at least, more equal) relationship from traditional Orientalist discourse. China may be a greater military power, but South Korea was generally considered more economically developed and "advanced," and the profile of the fans put them fairly low down China's social scale. The work of Iwabuchi on capitalist co-evalness in East Asia suggests that, however equal the relationship between fan and foreign idol, "it still cannot be denied that fans are reducing [Hong Kong] to a convenient and desirable Asian other."[70]

Iwabuchi's study of Japanese fan consumption of Asian popular culture describes the desire for the pre-modern "pure and tender" Southeast Asian boys as a "simple capitalist nostalgia," bringing perceptions of temporality into the equation.[71] And again, more recently, Japanese housewives' desire for the romantic heroes of Korean TV dramas is described by Iwabuchi as expressing nostalgia for a "purity of love."[72] In the case of China and South Korea, fans did not express a temporal distance from their idols — they considered themselves equally modern — making their relationship rather more like that described by Iwabuchi between Japanese fans and Hong Kong idols: "self-reflexive nostalgia for a different Asian modernity."[73]

It is also important to note that ideals of masculinity in Chinese culture during the Qing Dynasty, and possibly earlier, valorized "gifted youth" (*caizi*), with feminine features such as "white skin, red lips, slender fingers and tender airs" rather than the macho ideals of much Western culture.[74] Rather like the modern idol representations, Qing Dynasty romantic heroes had a personality that was "gentle, innocent, timid and even teary," and this "became the model for an eligible and attractive young man."[75] Hence, the (to my Western eyes) feminization of Korean stars may be an affirmation of their masculinity and power, rather than an undermining of it.[76] Continuing the comparison with Qing Dynasty ideals, the more macho characters in Qing romantic fiction are negatively associated with the pursuit of wealth, rank, official life, and public affairs, as "gold-digging toadies," while the feminized male divorces himself from daily practical concerns.[77] The female fans of the empathetic hero Jia Baoyu in *Dream of the Red Chamber* (*Honglou meng*) seem to share much with the contemporary *haHanzu*. Although both the Republican and the Communist governments promoted a more Western model of vigorous masculinity, in retaliation against the "sick man of East Asia" stereotype, Kam Louie argues that both cultured (*wen*) and the martial (*wu*) images of masculinity are seen as desirable and sexy today.[78] It seems that criteria for Chinese masculinity continue to change and are open to negotiation. Most recently in China, androgyny was credited as one of the elements that promoted Chinese "super-girl" singer Li Yuchun to stardom.[79]

Referring to elsewhere in East Asia, sexuality and fandom are discussed by Robertson in the case of the all-female Takarazuka revue, where fans again express the desire for an alternative kind of masculinity to their "boring salarymen" husbands. One actor says: "We look and act like men, but we are always kind and gentle. We understand what women really want."[80] Heather Willoughby suggests that in Korea pop music offers "emancipation from traditional norms" of gender, while noting that this freedom does not translate to audience behaviour.[81]

Finally, Ehrenreich, Hess, and Jacobs's study of Beatles fans, although from a very different time and culture, throws up some interesting similarities. The Beatles' somewhat androgynous sexuality seemed to offer "a vision of sexuality freed from the shadow of gender inequality because the group mocked the gender distinctions that bifurcated the American landscape into 'his' and 'hers'."[82]

The idea of teens being attracted to idols because they are sexually "non-threatening" is still prevalent. In Japan, for example, "the benign rationale was that an all-female revue theatre provided a safe outlet for the budding passions of teenage girls and young women until they were older and their sexual desires had matured and shifted 'naturally' to anatomically correct men,"[83] and in the 1960s, US psychologists opined that "very young women are still a little frightened of the idea of sex. Therefore they feel safer worshipping idols who don't seem too masculine."[84] Such statements have played down the sexuality of teenage fans. The very act of being a *haHanzu* challenges the notion of the non-sexual teenager, as Ehrenreich, Hess, and Jacobs note: "to abandon control — to scream, faint, dash about in mobs — was in form, if not in conscious intent, to protest the sexual repressiveness, the rigid double standard of female teen culture."[85]

It seemed through my reading of the fan sites I analyzed for Kangta, that far from embodying the modern or pre-modern other, Kangta was turned into the self, in his nationality (through the use of Chinese iconography and social structures),[86] age, gender, his status, his idealism. Other fans attempted to become their idol in their appearance, copying hairstyles, makeup, and clothing. Thinking back again over the reasons given for liking the bands, the fans showed a strong identification with the singers and felt a resonance in their songs:

- Because their age is about the same as ours, the music's substance and feeling make us like them. (Xiaofei, 23.9.03:92)
- H.O.T. teach us so much . . . how to be a person. I am so grateful . . . We and the Oppa [brothers] are from different countries, but love closes the distance. (hotfanlj, 20.9.03: 57)
- They don't look down on us. (brina, 23.9.03: 110)

Likewise, on a bulletin board for the idol Rain, members were asked which relationship they would most like to have with Rain. The poll results revealed that forty-five percent said brother/sister, thirty percent said lover, twenty-one percent said friend, and two percent husband/wife.[87] Referring again to Ehrenreich, Hess, and Jacobs,[88] this does not imply that fans do not view Rain, Kangta, or other idols sexually; it is that they want to share their sexuality rather than be an object of it. They want to share the sexual and romantic freedom that they project onto the stars in their erotic fantasies.

Conclusion

Comparing the discourse on *Hanliu* in Korea with that of the fans reveals the extent to which producers and international consumers of Korean popular culture are at cross-purposes. Despite all the efforts and aspirations of cultural gatekeepers in Korea and China, intended messages of regionalism and nationalism were overturned in the fantastic world of the *haHanzu*. The economic side-effects of *Hanliu* were undoubted, but the soft benefits of *Hanliu*, such as the image of Korea as cultured and Confucian, were undermined, by the fans' "uncontrolled" behaviour, by their adoption of the idols as themselves, and by their use of Korean pop as a "nostalgic other" against which to measure China. In the *haHanzu*'s worldview, as described to me, China was the masculine, the commercial, the insincere, the pragmatic, and the convention-bound. This was contrasted with the femininity, authenticity, sincerity, idealism, and passion that the fans ascribed to themselves and to their (imagined) idols. As one fan told me, where they themselves fall short in these ideals they look to Korean artists for support, ". . . the brothers are our models, and we would do our utmost to do good for the brothers we admire" (eugene 3.9.03: 16).

Despite the fans' expressed resistance to the commercialization of pop, and its manipulation by SM Entertainment in particular, there was little negative impact on the sales of Korean music and associated products. Fans still chose to express their loyalty to idols by purchasing legal recordings wherever possible and by using the products that stars endorsed. While the Korean music industry's attempts to enter the Chinese market suffered from bureaucracy and piracy, these factors also limited the growth of domestic competition and thus created a demand for musical imports. Ultimately, Korean entertainment industries may be able to benefit from China's increasing control of piracy and from the global pressure on China to allow greater access to its audiovisual publishing market by foreign companies and to reduce tariffs. However, even should the market ever be completely open, Korean state agencies, record companies, or Chinese media and publishing outlets are not likely ever to be able to control what the fans make of Korean pop.

IV

Nationalism and Transnationalism: The Case of Korea and Japan

10

Surfing the Neo-Nationalist Wave:
A Case Study of *Manga Kenkanryū*

Nicola Liscutin

The year 2005 had been designated "Korea-Japan Friendship Year" by the Korean (ROK) and Japanese governments, to mark the fortieth anniversary of the normalization of diplomatic ties between the two countries. Various joint events and economic, sports, and cultural exchanges were meant to put a positive spin on ROK-Japan relations, which had grown rather tense in the nineties. By March 2005, however, as Shimane Prefecture's assembly passed the "Takeshima Day" bill,[1] Korean protesters rallied around the Japanese Embassy in Seoul in response, and President Roh Moo Hyun declared that "Japanese foreign policy has reached an intolerable point,"[2] it became fairly obvious that the "friendship year" was not proceeding as planned. Anti-Japanese demonstrations, which were occasionally accompanied by violent and spectacular action, the boycott of Japanese goods, and concomitant strong political language, showed no signs of abating in South Korea until well into autumn. While Japanese politicians continued to add fuel to the raging flames of Korean ire, many of their citizens (and business people) felt strong unease in view of the anti-Japan protests in South Korea (and China) and the conflict-laden atmosphere. Once again, the past was haunting Japan-Korea relations and a great many words, actions, and media spectacles were employed on both sides, to foreground not what might bind the two countries but what seemed to divide them. At the same time, by contrast, Japanese fans seemed undeterred in their passion for Korean television soaps, K-pop and their stars: the "Korean Wave"[3] was clearly still booming. Likewise, Korean readers sent Japanese novels up the top of bestseller lists, surpassing the popularity of local authors by a remarkable margin.[4]

The coexistence of, for instance, anti-Japanese protests *and* enthusiasm for popular culture products made in Japan in South Korea or, conversely, of "Korean Wave" *and* anti-Korean sentiments in Japan may seem paradoxical. A paradox that one might be inclined to explain by a generation gap, in which younger generations in both Japan and South Korea actively participate and share in the transnational flows of popular culture products and the regionalizing or globalizing possibilities offered by new media, especially the Internet, and in which older generations might be seen as more concerned with the historical and political determinants (and problems) of Japan-Korea relations. With an eye to younger and future generations, this perspective highlights a reconciliatory power ascribed to cultural exchange and regional flows of culture and consumer products, flows that are facilitated by the deregulation of regional and global markets and the globalizing effects of new media technologies. Likewise, it emphasizes the concomitant positive aspects of hybridizing effects in, and for, cultural practices and the reception/ consumption of transnational cultural products. While there is sufficient evidence to support such a perspective,[5] there is equally — and perhaps not so paradoxically — good reason to argue that those transnational flows and hybridization effects induce or enhance anxieties of losing the seeming certainties of a clearly demarcated national cultural identity and can, therefore, generate neo-nationalist backlashes precisely by way of the means and opportunities that the new global media and visual technologies afford. This chapter is a case study of one such neo-nationalist backlash expressed in popular culture and disseminated through new media.

In July 2005, amid the furore — and informed by both the clashes and the cravings — a hitherto insignificant Tokyo publishing house launched Yamano Sharin's *Manga Kenkanryū*[6] ("Manga The Anti-Korean Wave").[7] As the title suggests, *Kenkanryū* is presented as an oppositional vision to an allegedly blind enthusiasm for things Korean among Japanese followers of the "Korean Wave." It seeks to counteract this infatuation by providing "the truth" about Korea, its history, culture, and Korean claims against Japan for restitution. Putting its premise — "When you know [about] Korea, it's only natural that you become Anti-Korean!"[8] — into action, *Kenkanryū* aims to educate its readers on a wide range of misdemeanours allegedly committed by Korea, which it describes as "thoroughly depraved nation."[9] The manga seeks to demonstrate that "anti-Japan" sentiments and protests in Korea lack any legitimate historical basis, and that "correct" historical knowledge would enable Japanese people to be proud of their country's present and past achievements and thus fortified, to take a firm stance against any kind of "Japan-bashing" by their Asian neighbors. Wrapped in pedagogical camouflage, *Kenkanryū* ventures under the banner of "truth" into an "identity war" between Japan and Korea. As one 18-year old reader put it: "If you read this [manga] and you don't get angry about Korea, you can't be Japanese . . ."[10]

Critics have either dismissed *Kenkanryū* as simply another, of several, neo-nationalist pop-culture products or denied it any attention at all, an understandable stance given that the manga makes for fairly unpleasant reading. To my knowledge, one of the first in-depth critical analyses of the manga and the corresponding blog hype was the 2007 article by Rumi Sakamoto and Matt Allen posted on *Japan Focus*.[11] While my textual analysis of *Kenkanryū* pursues similar lines of criticism, I want to make a case for examining the educational power ascribed to the manga. In view of an emerging "youthful"[12] Japanese nationalism that appears to spread by means of visual technologies and new media, it seems crucial to gain a critical understanding of popular culture phenomena such as *Kenkanryū* and the "cultures of circulation"[13] within which they emerge. In particular, I am keen to understand the ways in which these new sites of pedagogy "generate forms of knowledge" that are "mediated through specific social relations and mobilize select ideologies, histories and memories"[14] in response to what is considered an "identity war" between Japan and Korea.

Kenkanryū became an instant bestseller and topped the Amazon Japan ranking for several weeks. The second volume was published in February 2006, and the third in August 2007. Again, each of these publication dates coincided with significant political and historical dates.[15] To date, the combined sales of the *Kenkanryū* volumes have reached a total of around 800,000 copies,[16] which is a fairly impressive figure when compared to the sales figure for other manga in book format. The breathtaking impact of *Manga Kenkanryū* is demonstrated less, however, by its sales figures than by the extensive pro-*Kenkanryū* movements that rapidly spread on various Japanese and global Internet sites, such as the Japanese 2channel (*ni-channeru*) or the English-language blog site Occidentalism.org.

Anti-Korea sentiments began to appear on Japanese blog sites from around 2002, in the wake of the Soccer World Cup and the North Korea abduction affair.[17] But the manga seems to have accelerated dramatically the dissemination of Anti-Korea ideas and fuelled, in turn, the discussions on those Internet sites, with the effect that the "Anti-Korean Wave" quickly transformed into a spectacular mainstream trend. The rapid development of this phenomenon points to significant changes in the ways in which a text like *Kenkanryū* is circulated through new sites of knowledge production and dissemination that are created by the new media. From the start, *Kenkanryū* was designed to participate in these "new sites of learning:"[18] The manga draws explicitly on and promotes specific Internet sources and blog sites, and gestures implicitly towards the efficacy of these joint forces in enabling an "Anti-Korean Wave." To this end, and similar to its related Internet sites, the manga manipulates quite effectively existing distrust in the mass media and school education. It presents itself as a young, subversive educational force in opposition to those traditional sites of learning and knowledge transfer, and promises to provide information that those established institutions allegedly seek to suppress. *Kenkanryū* thus offers its readers the thrill of breaking taboos along the lines of "what you always wanted to know about Korea but were afraid to ask!" (Or rather, "what you always thought about Korea but never dared to say!") Arguably, part of the pleasure that *Kenkanryū* — and other revisionist narratives like it — affords its readers, lies in it "flaunting a feigned oppositionality."[19] In the process, *Kenkanryū* apparently succeeds in presenting itself as a reliable source of knowledge about Japan-Korea relations. It is truly astonishing how many readers and bloggers pay tribute to the manga in their comments, as opening their eyes about the "true" nature of Korea, or providing them with information on Korea they could not find elsewhere.[20]

My analysis is inspired by Henry Giroux's concepts of "public pedagogy" and "the spectacle." Giroux has highlighted the centrality of the new media as both "a political and pedagogical force that has become a defining feature of the culture of fear" and "as a new technology for redefining the very nature of politics itself."[21] It is the task of the critical pedagogies he envisions "to rupture the force of the spectacle" and to engage the possibilities of these new public technologies "as a democratic political and pedagogical force . . . for positive intervention and change."[22] This would involve, among other things, learning to read the new visual technologies and "to translate and negotiate their attempts to construct particular identities, flows of experience and social events, past and future."[23]

Thus, my examination of *Kenkanryū* as manga *and* pedagogical practice is guided, primarily, by three interrelated questions: what are the visual and rhetorical strategies employed in the manga, how does *Kenkanryū* construct an impression of historical truthfulness, and what notions of identity are promoted by the manga? After the textual analysis, I return to the issue of the interface between manga and new public technologies.[24]

Structural and Visual Aspects of *Manga Kenkanryū*

Let me begin with a brief introduction to the central structural and visual aspects of the manga. The main character of *Kenkanryu¯* is Okiayu Kaname (Figure 10.1), an "ordinary" high school student who is not particularly interested in history but has the "vague understanding that Japan has done bad things to Korea."[25] His best friend in high school is a Resident (*Zainichi*) Korean with the Japanese name Matsumoto Kōichi and a troubling identity crisis (Figure 10.2). Initially, Kaname is shown to be a bit of a "softy," because he is overly perceptive to issues of discrimination against Koreans. However, the 2002 World Cup Soccer co-hosted by Japan and Korea, and the words of his dying grandfather concerning his experiences in colonial Korea, lead Kaname to question his own perceptions, and form the initial impulse for his desire to learn "the true history" of Japan-Korean relations. And what better place to study the "surprising truth about Korea and its history" than the "Far East Asia Investigation Committee" towards which Kaname is steered by his school friend, the cute but tough Aramaki Itsumi (Figure 10.3), when they enter college.

Figure 10.1 Okiayu Kaname, main protagonist. Yamano (2006a), front cover.

Figure 10.2 Matsumoto Kōichi. Yamano (2006b), 44.

Figure 10.3 Aramaki Itsumi. Yamano (2005), 39.

The committee consists of four second- and third-year students. There is the "cool"[26] rich kid Sueyuki Ryūhei, who plays the role of the tutor and intellectual figurehead (Figure 10.4). Ironically, he could be mistaken for a cartoon version of "Yonsama" [actor Pae Yongjun], the star of the Korean TV soap *Winter Sonata* and the "Korean Wave." Then there is the striking, reserved Soeuchi Tae, who, as chair of the committee keeps the group together; Yagami Tetsuya, who is "an expert on anti-Japanese mass media;"[27] and Kaneda Yasuhiro, a "naturalized Japanese" of Resident Korean origin, who believes that he alone is in a position to establish "real friendship"[28] between Koreans and Japanese (Figure 10.5). In *Kenkanryū 2*, the group is joined by Miyako, Ryūhei's devoted little sister, and Tinshia Ryū, an exchange student and "anti-Korean Taiwanese beauty obsessed with Japanese *manga* and anime."[29]

Figure 10.4   Sueyuki Ryūhei. Yamano (2005), 97.

Figure 10.5   From left: Yagami Tetsuya, Soeuchi Tae, Kaneda Yasuhiro. Yamano (2005), 198.

The visual representation of the characters in *Kenkanryū* follows the principles of traditional Japanese manga iconography and moves on a scale ranging from "cartoony" to "realistic" design. The simple, abstract "cartoony" design (Figures 10.1 and 10.2) with its cute, childlike features serves to facilitate a reader's identification with the protagonist(s).[30] By comparison, all figures of Korean descent, friend or foe alike, are depicted with pronounced cheekbones and thus, allegedly more realistic (Figure 10.2). Likewise, opponents of the committee (Figure 10.6) — whether they are Japanese or Korean — are drawn in an exaggerated "realistic" or even grotesque manner with the effect that these characters are "objectified" and "their otherness from the reader" is emphasized.[31] Finally, the depiction of "real-life" figures such as Tokyo Governor Ishihara Shintarō is done with "photographic" realism. Crucially, the visual representation of the characters aims to align readers with the student protagonists' perspective and to see opponents through their eyes. This also means that the only "agreeable" standpoint from which to read this manga is the one defined as a patriotic Japanese *national.*

Figure 10.6   Example of grotesque depiction of antagonists. Yamano (2005), 47.

The first volume of *Kenkanryū* (289 pages) is divided into nine "proper" manga episodes, which are interspersed with "columns" contributed by well-known historical revisionists such as Nishio Kanji[32] and Ōtsuki Takahiro, who is associated with Fujioka Nobukatsu's "Liberal Historiography" (*Jiyūshugi shikan*) group. These columns are supposed to lend the manga intellectual weight and authority. There are furthermore six "files" organized as short conversations between the protagonists, which are used to provide additional evidence for, or comments on, topics addressed in the episodes.

The manga's episodes follow one of two rather simple plotlines: a history lesson or a debate with a group of Korean or Japanese opponents. The narrative structure underlying both types of episode is that of a contest — a structure common to various genres of manga. In the more frequent lesson-type episodes, the senior students of the committee enlighten their juniors about a topic. For example, there are lessons dealing with "the history of how Koreans came to live in Japan: . . . the myth of 'forced deportation,'"[33] "Korea steals Japanese culture,"[34] or with the "fact" that "Koreans are disliked all over the world."[35] Episodes such as these form one of the battlefronts, Korean views of history, on which *Kenkanryū* attacks. All of these episodes aim to refute Korean criticism of Japan and to demonstrate Japan's purity of motives and benevolence in practice vis-à-vis Korea in both the colonial and postcolonial periods. This so-called "truth of Korea and its history"[36] is told entirely from a Japanese-identified perspective, while Korean voices are repeatedly silenced.

Episodes such as "the threat of Anti-Japanese mass-media" are targeted against a second group of "enemies," Japanese NGOs working for reconciliation with both North and South Korea, as well as "Anti-Japanese mass media" such as the *Asahi* newspaper or the TBS television news program. An intriguing feature of the manga is that the parental generation is denied any authority and trustworthiness to teach history to the younger generation. It appears only in form of left-wing school teachers, journalists, and NGO representatives. They are depicted (Figure 10.7) as the threat from within, whose "aim it is to destroy the Japanese nation-state."[37] For example, teachers organized in the Japanese Teachers' Union are represented as communists and brainwashed into "anti-Japanese" thinking,[38] from whose "evil hands" children must be protected.[39] NGO activists and journalists are dismissed as being under direct North Korean influence and seeking to impose their biased, "anti-Japanese" messages upon an unsuspecting populace.[40] So, what in academic circles would probably be regarded as critical thinking is here consistently coded as "leftist thought" and represented as pathological, a *Kenkanryū* version of an "axis of evil," so to speak.

The learning and teaching of history in *Kenkanryū* thus takes place in a closed world, that of the student-led "Far East Asia Investigation Committee." Paradoxically perhaps, readers are granted privileged access to this world. But, as the narrative develops, the logic becomes clear: it is the revolutionary, sacred mission of the committee students and their followers and readers to rescue Japan from ideological self-destruction and turn it back into a strong, proud, and "beautiful nation."[41]

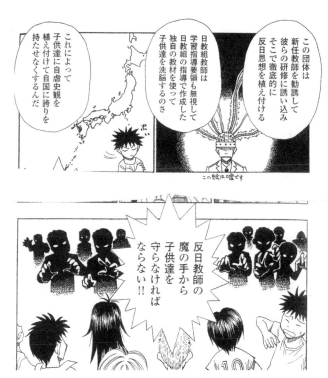

Figure 10.7 "Brainwashed Anti-Japanese" teachers – a "threat" to Japanese children. Yamano (2006a), 136, 139.

The manga works with a set of fairly crude strategies through which groups of people are differentiated, and included or excluded from understanding and teaching history. These strategies emanate from one central, if ambiguous, notion which defines the *Kenkanryū* rhetoric, that of historical "truth." "Truth" is only to be found in distinguishing between "correct" and "false" versions of history and not, as in standard historiographical practice, in researching a historical issue from different perspectives. Even though this distinction is continuously stressed in *Kenkanryū*, no explanation is given as to how to arrive at the "truth," how to discern a "correct" representation of the past or how to recognize another version as "fiction." The implication presented as self-evident in *Kenkanryū* is that "true" history is that version of the past which is resolutely pro-Japanese, positive about the nation-state, and staunchly patriotic. Accordingly, the manga operates within rigid binary opposites: Japan versus Korea, us versus them, truth versus fiction, good versus evil and so forth.

Identity War and Its Weapons

The "truth," that is the "correct," knowledge of Japanese-Korean history proves its power in the debate-type episodes. Take for example the debate-contest with a group of visiting "elite students"[42] from famous South Korean universities, which has as its topic Japanese-Korean history since the Japan-Korea "merger," which refers to the Japanese annexation of Korea in 1910. Significantly, the committee is represented on this occasion only by its smart female members, Soeuchi Tae and Aramaki Itsumi. The debate revolves around the issue of Japan's policies in colonial Korea and begins, as is usual in the episodes of *Kenkanryū*, with a disclaimer by the Japanese representatives: "Firstly, the idea often stressed by Koreans that 'Japan robbed Korea of various resources' . . . is nothing but fantasy!"[43] The halo-like light emanating from Tae (Figure 10.8), and other senior members of the committee whenever they make a particularly strong point, is a conspicuous visual marker repeatedly employed in *Kenkanryū*. These halos are designed to show the protagonists, quite literally, as enlightened, and symbolically, to endow their utterances with authoritative "truth."

Figure 10.8   Halos of "true" knowledge. Yamano (2005), 213.

The girls then set about proving how much Japan exerted itself in modernizing Korea, for example, by building a modern infrastructure, introducing modern [Western] medicine, setting up a proper school system and so forth. The necessary resources for these modernization projects were all provided by Japan and, as Itsumi asserts, "the Japanese taxpayer was made to sweat" for this.[44] These frames (Figure 10.9) illustrate two interesting visual strategies that are frequently employed in *Kenkanryū*. The first is a close-up shot on the eyes of the committee members, in this case Tae, suggesting the clarity of their intellectual vision and their superior command of history. The second is the manipulation of the background of the frame: invariably in *Kenkanryū*, a black background symbolizes non-existence, in this case the alleged lack of roads, education system, and so forth in Korea, before Japan modernized the country. Superimposed on this black "nothingness" are, in white script, Japan's "gifts" to Korea: modern medicine, electricity, emancipation of slaves, and so on. This line of Tae's argument culminates then in her powerful statement that it would not be an exaggeration to say that today's Korea had been created by Japan (Figure 10.10).[45] Their arguments never fail to create a stir in the audience, while their Korean opponents, unsurprisingly, blow up in outrage (Figure 10.11).

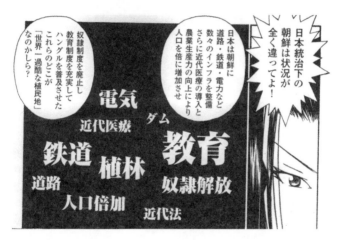

Figure 10.9 Examples of visual strategies: close-up and background manipulation. Yamano (2005), 214.

Figure 10.10 "Present-day Korea was created by Japan." Yamano (2005), 217.

Figure 10.11   Response of Korean students. Yamano (2005), 203.

We then come to a central rhetorical strategy of *Kenkanryū*, whereby evidence is provided through the use of allegedly historical photographs. Here the photos are used to demonstrate the Korean situation before and after Japan's annexation of the country (Figure 10.12).[46] Photographs are presented as indisputable historical proof. To stress their "truth value," the photographs are complemented by corresponding cartoon frames, in this particular case showing the Korean contestants grinding their teeth, as if they were conceding victory to the arguments of the Japanese side. But the *Kenkanryū* logic stretches further: if photographs do not exist — for example of Koreans being forcefully deported by truck[47] — that means that the event did not take place (Figure 10.13). Likewise, if the term *kyōsei renkō* did not exist at the time, this means that forced deportation did not exist.[48]

Confronted with such logic, the Korean opponents are depicted as showing one of two reactions (Figure 10.14): they are grinding their teeth, sweating, downcast, and voicing nothing more than a few grunts; or they blow up in anger. Through its grotesque and exaggerated depictions, the manga parodies Korean feelings of anger and renders them ridiculous for the amusing consumption of its readers. At the same time, the Korean participants are granted only a couple of small frames and a few sentences for their response. Not once does the manga allow the Korean side to develop its argument or

Figure 10.12 Issue of historical evidence: photography. Yamano (2005), 221.

Figure 10.13 Alleged lack of historical evidence. Yamano (2005), 85.

Figure 10.14 Stereotypical representation of opponents' reactions. Yamano (2005), 213, 216.

to present its evidence. On the pages of *Kenkanryū*, it is the turn of the Japanese to talk and nobody is going to stop them. More to the point, it is up to the Japanese side to teach the Koreans their own history, because they are allegedly either ignorant or brainwashed.

Whereas the Korean students are reduced to uncontrolled, hysterical rage or silence, the Japanese side is shown to be rational, knowledgeable, well-disciplined, and eloquent. *Kenkanryū* mobilizes here old-fashioned Orientalist stereotypes and binaries, that of the superior power being rational and masculine, and the inferior "other" being hysterical and marked as feminine. That the Japanese side is represented by female figures, while the Korean contestants are in the majority male, only intensifies the intended effect of celebrating Japanese victory over the humiliated Koreans.[49]

Kenkanryū unabashedly promotes a vision of Japan as a superior civilization and culture by making a spectacle out of the Korean defeat. And it is precisely from this spectacle of Korean defeat and Japanese "truth" that *Kenkanryū* appears to draw its educational force. Not a few readers begin their fan letters by stating proudly, if anonymously *"watakushi wa kenkan desu"*[50] (I am anti-Korean!).

It is thus not without rather obvious sarcasm that the debate culminates in Itsumi's assured statements that firstly, "emotional arguments and masochistic or expiatory approaches to history only obstruct the view on true history (*hontō no rekishi*)," and that secondly, "during the 35 years of annexation the people of Japan and Korea worked together, hand in hand, for Korea's modernization. *This* is the history which ought to be transmitted to following generations!"[51] With Itsumi's final statement, the debate ends, and the story of the first volume comes full circle. Now, it is no longer Kaname's grandfather but the grandchildren's generation that has come to own and propound the "true" history of Japan-Korea relations. This version of history has become an integral part of their "Japanese" identity, and their victory in arguing for the "truth" of that history apparently imbues them with a strong sense of self-esteem. The committee members seem to embody the ideal of a young Japanese as envisioned by neo-conservative thinkers and politicians: diligently learning to be patriotic, committed to the nation-state and its future, rejecting "masochistic" approaches to Japan's past, on the whole well-behaved, cute looking and successful in her or his career after graduation. To be sure, there are no *freeters* or *neets*[52] among the Japanese protagonists of this manga, and it might be for this reason that *Kenkanryū* also appealed to older generations of readers.

However, self-esteem is caught up in a system of competition, which also happens to be the defining structure of *Kenkanryū* as narrative. Self-esteem relies on the evaluation and recognition of one's achievements by an "Other."[53] By its nature, the results of such evaluation are fragile, as they can easily be reversed. Moreover, this sense of self-esteem depends, crucially, on the gaze of yet another — the West — whose presence makes itself felt but is conspicuous by its absence as a character in *Kenkanryū*.[54] In a similar way, "Japaneseness" seems to depend on the recognition by this "Other," the potential, threatening loss of which engenders a persistent anxiety. To keep that fear at bay, *Kenkanryū* operates within rigid binary oppositions that are employed to solidify the protagonists' and, by extension, the readers' "Japanese identity."

The Place of *Zainichi* Koreans in *Kenkanryū*

To be Japanese, according to *Kenkanryū*, means to be a Japanese national, positive and proud of Japan's past, ready to defend the nation and its history against any form of attack. Proper history, in this framework, is what is good for Japan, the nation-state. In this representational regime, Korea becomes the radical "Other," the negative image. However, by drawing and continually reinforcing such clearly demarcated national boundaries, the manga does not allow for any kind of "in-between-ness" or for alternative voices. This raises a crucial question: What, then, are the place and function of *Zainichi* Koreans in the imagined community of *Kenkanryū*?

As mentioned, two *Zainichi* Korean figures are crucial for the manga's narrative: Kaneda Yasuhiro, the "naturalized Japanese of Resident Korean descent" (Figure 10.15), and Matsumoto Kōichi, the unassimilated Resident Korean. By representing Yasuhiro as a full, respected member of the nationalist committee, the manga feigns a politics of integration defying any notion of discrimination against ethnic Koreans. Likewise, the pivotal role given to Kōichi in the narrative suggests on the surface an attitude of tolerance of *Zainichi* Koreans by the Japanese, albeit a tolerance that the readers are asked to reconsider.

Figure 10.15   Kaneda Yasuhiro's transformation from Korean to Japanese citizen. Yamano (2006b), 60.

A particularly disturbing episode in *Kenkanryū* deals with the alleged "theft" of Japanese cultural property by Korea, in which Japan appears as a helpless victim of Korean greediness for "origins":[55] the claim that the martial art of kendo originated in Korea sparks off an intensive discussion among the committee members about Korean attempts to appropriate every tradition held dear by the Japanese, from kendo to sushi and origami, even popular culture such as manga. The discussion returns obsessively to Korea's alleged ambitions to lay claim, in an international arena, to the origins of cultural practices and products that are seen as essential ingredients of Japan's cultural identity. The fear — what if the world were to believe Korean claims? — runs like a red thread through this episode and leaves the team lost for ideas of counter-measures. The only solution offered by the manga as such is to "brand-name" all that cultural property as unmistakeably Japanese and to promote it globally as national products. The underlying concern is that Japan needs to improve significantly its self-promotion, as it seems at risk of losing out to Korean efforts in the international arena. In this episode, *Kenkanryū* plays so effectively on this apparently latent fear of its Japanese readers that several have begged the publisher Shinyūsha to arrange for the manga's translation into English.[56]

To allay the fears of other Japanese students, Kaneda Yasuhiro volunteers to explain how Koreans use history solely as "a tool to prove their nation's superiority" (Figure 10.16).[57] Koreans, in Yasuhiro's stern words, are bending and distorting historical facts endlessly, in order to make their country look better. *Kenkanryū* represents Yasuhiro, who has consciously "chosen the path to live as Japanese," as the embodiment of a successful naturalization process.[58] His identity is constructed as *totally* "Japanese," a process by which his ethnic identification seems to have been eradicated. Except that he acts as an "insider-informant" and, more to the point, fierce critic of Korea. The character of Yasuhiro, with his firm loyalty to the Japanese nation–state and its identity, is advocated as the ideal model of assimilation to which every *Zainichi* Korean should aspire.

Figure 10.16 Yasuhiro's lecture on Korea's abuse of history. Yamano (2005), 118.

   But precisely because Yasuhiro is so well assimilated, his character offers little in development for the *Kenkanryū* narrative.[59] For its pedagogical practices, then, the manga requires an opposite to Yasuhiro: Kōichi, the *Zainichi* Korean. Whereas Yasuhiro speaks Korean fluently, knows as much about Korean as about Japanese history and puts his knowledge at the service of the Japanese, Kōichi is presented as not very clever and with hardly any knowledge of the Korean language. He is, as the leader of the South Korean student group accuses him, *panchoppari* (neither-nor): neither Korean nor Japanese, not even half (Figure 10.17).[60]

Figure 10.17   The "real" Korean and "neither-nor" Kōichi. Yamano (2006a), 194.

   As a contrasting figure, Kōichi and his behavior are constantly measured against Yasuhiro's internalized "Japaneseness." And much energy is spent to impress upon Kōichi that, for him as well, naturalization is really the best path to pursue. He is arguably the most intriguing character in the manga, as he brazenly and bravely struggles to find a "Third space"[61] in which he could live an "in-between-ness." Needless to say, *Kenkanryū* denies him such a happy end: there is no "happy hybridity" available to him. According to *Kenkanryū*, you are either with us Japanese, or you are against us, though the *Zainichi* Korean may stay silent and invisible. The manga also demonstrates that South Korea does not offer a home to the *Zainichi* Korean: Kōichi has nowhere to go but to tread the path to naturalization.

Frequently, Kōichi bursts onto the scene seeking to remind his old pal Kaname and the antagonistic members of the committee that discrimination against Koreans is still rampant in Japan. He functions as the spark and fuel for the lessons of the group. The narrative needs the figure of Kōichi to enact its educational objectives as much as the committee students need him in their narcissistic desire for esteem. *Kenkanryū* exploits the figure of Kōichi relentlessly: he is put on a kind of catwalk through the manga, where he is to show off every possible stereotype hung on young *Zainichi* men: hot-tempered, ever ready for a fistfight, ignorant of Japanese social and linguistic hierarchies and thus bad-mannered, radical in his complaints about discrimination, fundamentalist in his attachment to Korean ethnic identity, and militant in his commitment to *Zainichi* organizations (Figure 10.18). However, Kōichi shows, in sharp contrast to the other self-assured Japanese students, moments of deep insecurity and self-reflection, which make him a

Figure 10.18 Representation of *Zainichi* Korean temper. Yamano (2005), 74, 30.

rather endearing figure (Figure 10.19). And precisely because *Kenkanryū* uses the figure of Kōichi, the *Zainichi* Korean, as the object on which to exercise its mechanisms of exclusion, his figure exposes, if unwittingly, the anxieties and claustrophobic nature that come with the new solid "Japanese" identity which the manga seeks to promote.

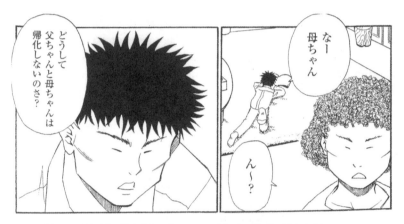

Figure 10.19   Kōichi reflects on his family's *Zainichi* status.
Yamano (2006a), 66.

Modes of Address and the "Culture of Fear"

If *Kenkanryū* sounds eerily familiar in its ideological tenor and chauvinistic rhetoric, this is no coincidence. Yamano Sharin confesses on his web page great admiration for Ishihara Shintarō, the outspoken politician and man of *The Japan That Can Say No*[62] fame, former Prime Minister Abe Shinzō and the nationalistic manga artist Kobayashi Yoshinori.[63] And their influence makes itself clearly felt in the manga. He furthermore borrowed generously from the neo-nationalist ideas of the aforementioned Nishio Kanji and his *Tsukuru-kai* as well as Fujioka Nobukatsu and his "Liberal Historiography." Whether it is the attack on an allegedly hegemonic "masochistic view of Japanese history," the rewriting of Japanese imperialism into the liberation of Asia, or of the colonization of Korea into an altruistic measure to modernize the country, the tenets of these historical revisionists are faithfully regurgitated, often verbatim, by the protagonists of *Kenkanryū*.

More importantly, the manga mobilizes the same fears of a loss of national identity and international influence, of alienation and of an external or internal threatening "Other," that is, the same feelings of anxiety and resentment, with which Fujioka, Nishio, et al. in their various revisionist writings appealed so successfully to their readers. Survey results of the last five or six years show a dramatic increase in "threat perception" among Japanese, which has increased support for stronger defence policies, and "intensified Japan's hostility toward" China, North and now South Korea.[64] Giroux's warning can to a certain extent also be applied to Japan, that a "culture of fear" and the spectacle of ubiquitous threats through "rogue states" and terrorism have paved the way for nation-states to become more authoritarian, for the public sphere to be collapsed into the nation-state, and everyday life to be militarized. New emergency laws, the revaluation of the Japanese Self-Defense Forces, the establishment of a formal Ministry of Defence, the discussion about Article 9 of the Japanese constitution,[65] or the musings of government representatives on a legal framework for preemptive attacks, suggest that military might "has become a central motif of national identity."[66] Particularly pertinent to my analysis of *Kenkanryū* is Giroux's observation that, within a culture of fear, "language . . . and image lose their critical functions as they are turned into weapons to combat an enemy."[67] With fairly blunt, but apparently no less effective, visual and verbal weaponry, the manga attacks those citizens groups as "unpatriotic" who oppose nationalist education, constitutional revisions, or remilitarization, defames their representatives, teachers, and journalists as "brainwashed," and ultimately, seeks to debase critical thinking in the name of a "true history." Has, as Guy Debord once feared, "the most elaborate machinery of forgetting" now been built, which could make the past "fully tractable to power"?[68]

Conclusion: Surfing the "Anti-Korean Wave"

Apart from the ideas of these well-known historical revisionists, Yamano Sharin has apparently drawn for *Kenkanryū*'s lessons on postings on 2channel, where he once acted as a moderator. Korea-related boards on 2channel, which is regarded as the largest Internet forum worldwide,[69] emerged in 2002 in the wake of the Soccer World Cup and especially of the North Korean abduction affair. These seem to have turned ever more aggressive in reaction to the 2005 Anti-Japan protests in South Korea and China. Statistics for the summer of 2005 show that several other Anti-Korean blog sites, which "billed themselves as . . . antidote for the Japanese 'mass media's tendency to beautify Korea,'" made it into the top twelve of Japan's most popular blog sites.[70]

Alongside the Anti-Korean boards on 2channel, the site "Choose (what you believe) Carefully! Information on Korea" came sixth; on seven we find "Japan's Outrageous Asian Neighbours;" and in twelfth place "The Truth about Asia — what the mass media doesn't tell you about China and Korea." Blog-site rankings for spring 2007 showed that, in the "Social and Economic Affairs" category, several anti-Asian and anti-Korean blogs continue to rank among the top ten.[71]

Because of the short "lifespan" of blog threads, it is very difficult to ascertain retrospectively which — and how many — bits of information and opinions from the Japanese "blogosphere" went into the making of *Kenkanryū*. But as the narrative and visual format of manga is based on mechanisms of fragmentation and reductionism that are similar to the dialogue structure of blog sites, the transfer of a blog entry into a manga-bubble seems relatively straightforward.[72] Internet-wise readers of *Kenkanryū* have commented that, for *netā* (blogger), the manga is little more than a collection of information available on the Internet, though presented in a visually appealing narrative. Precisely because it is a manga, *Kenkanryū* is seen as an "excellent introduction" and "education" for Anti-Korea "beginners" who do not have access to, or knowledge of, Internet sites and blog culture.[73] In exchange, as it were, *Kenkanryū* teaches its readers — for instance, in one of the "files"[74] — how to become Internet literate.

There is, however, a crucial difference between blog sites and manga: while the blog entries conceal the identity of the blogger, *Kenkanryū* personalizes the Anti-Korean message by giving its protagonists the faces of cute, cartoon characters. These "cartoony" protagonists function as a focalizer transforming hitherto vague or scattered Anti-Korean sentiments into one spectacular narrative of "shock and awe." The success of *Kenkanryū*, thus, seems to lie in it contributing a specific visual grammar and a concise, pungent rhetorical vocabulary to existing "Anti-Korea" Internet discussions. The manga condenses, as it were, historical information dispersed over various sites (digital and printed) and transforms it into a visual narrative of some coherence and narrow delineation. The manga has, moreover, a much longer shelf life than entries on blog sites and is more akin to textbooks or encyclopedias published in comic-book format, with which many Japanese from their teens to their forties are already familiar. *Kenkanryū* thus reaches a much larger section of Japanese consumers: while blog culture could still be regarded as subculture, the manga helped to make the "Anti-Korean Wave" mainstream.

The main Japanese broadsheets, with the exception of the neo-nationalist *Sankei Shinbun*, refused to put ads about the publication or reviews of *Kenkanryū* on their pages, which served only to reinforce bloggers' view that

Japanese mass media were biased towards Korea. However, international news media — ranging from *The New York Times*,[75] the British *Times*[76] to *Al Jazeera English*[77] — reported on the manga and its popularity. The strong international attention given to the manga forced Japanese newspapers and TV news programs to eventually join the debate.

As mentioned, discussions about the manga spread also to English-language Internet sites, such as Occidentalism.org, which boasted about being "the most highly ranked site for Kenkanryu [*sic*] on google after the publishing company itself."[78] Occidentalism.org targeted, in particular, critical reviews of the manga in international news media such as *The New York Times*. Similar to *Kenkanryū* and related Japanese blog sites, it uses the "ethnicity card" to determine whether a review is "correct." Thus, Norimitsu Onishi, who reviewed the manga for *The New York Times*,[79] is attacked and declared as not trustworthy with the following argument: "It is well documented that Norimitsu Onishi is a second-generation [*Zainichi* Korean] who . . . has a penchant for praising all things Korean and speaking ill of all things Japanese. He was famous in Japan for his outward support of the Communist party as well as his time spent in school in [North] Korea. His father was a pachinko parlour owner in Kyushu."[80] Bloggers consider him of the same detestable calibre as "Korean trolls" who are accused of spamming blog sites with their views.

Kenkanryū and the blog sites offer a system of "Anti-Korea" representations, in which neo-nationalist language, rhetoric, and images become crystallized, as it were, and are then, by one click of the mouse, circulated and further disseminated. The educational and political force of the "Anti-Korean Wave" rests largely, as I have tried to suggest, on the synergy effects in knowledge transfer which manga and blog sites together create, the representational regimes and modes of affective address they employ to fashion and promote specific forms of agency and identity, the cultures of circulation within which they operate, and the ways in which they spectacularize the alleged "identity war" between Japan and Korea.

But the prominence, which the "Anti-Korean" discourse achieved through manga and Internet sites, can also be explained by the notable scarcity of critical, alternative sites of learning in Japanese cyber- and manga-space.[81] It seems thus all the more essential to face, as Giroux urges, the challenge posed by the centrality of the new media and the large array of pedagogical sites they have created, and to engage with the question of "how these new technologies might be used to put into place modes of identity, subjectivity and agency that expand and deepen the possibilities of democracy rather than shut it down."[82]

11

Melodrama, Exorcism, Mimicry: Japan and the Colonial Past in the New Korean Cinema

Mark Morris

In his recent reassessment of Italian neo-realist cinema, Mark Shiel has recalled that "one of the presumptions of the national cinema approach is that while films make an interesting object of study in themselves, their ultimate utility lies in the ways they produce a 'collective narrative' of a people and a national culture." He goes on to note that "a balance must be struck between approaching . . . national cinema as a unitary phenomenon, the expression of a discrete and stable national culture, and recognising that on close analysis any national culture is bound to reveal itself to be 'eclectic, fragmentary and contradictory'."[1] I do not think that any student of modern Korean history or of contemporary South Korean film would argue that Korean national culture has, throughout the twentieth century and now on into the twenty-first, been anything but eclectic, fragmentary, and contradictory.

This essay first refers to a number of different films that have appeared in the last handful of years, ones that apply a variety of mainstream generic conventions to stories that touch on Korea's former colonial master, Japan. It then looks in some detail at a film that is perhaps more art house than multiplex in its ambitions: Im Sangsu's *The President's Last Bang* (*Kŭ ttae kŭ saram-dŭl*) from 2005. Throughout, the things I have to say are geared towards the political and historical as well as the cultural. I hope to suggest the usefulness of keeping a certain postcolonial critical consciousness[2] alert when dealing with products of any "new cinema" emerging in a region such as northeast Asia once shaped by colonialism and empire — one that sometimes come from Europe but, most significantly for the future of the region, sometimes from next door. For it is a striking feature of the contemporary popular culture of East Asia that optimism about the increasing flow and circulation of cultural goods (TV drama, films, a huge variety of music and popular bands, fashion) keeps bumping up against political frictions and ghosts of the not so distant past.

Since the accelerated liberalization of South Korean society and culture from the early 1990s, and since the belated lifting of the ban on Japanese popular culture[3] beginning in 1998 under the presidency of Kim Dae-jung,[4] filmmakers in South Korea have been able for the first time in decades to address aspects of the country's past and present in films about Korea and Japan. Any real freedom of artistic interpretation concerning the colonial era (1910–45) had been put on hold by several factors: first, the political confusion and violence of the immediate postwar years, and then the devastation of the Korean War. Of course, in the decades after the civil war's inconclusive end, many films with Japanese characters were produced. Yet during years of rule by US-backed dictators, South Korean filmmakers could not openly explore the terrain of earlier twentieth-century Korea and the nation's collective implication in the Japanese Empire — not in a country whose military, bureaucratic, and business elite were far too compromised by involvement, often voluntary if not always enthusiastic, with the former colonial power.

In films produced recently, we might expect South Korea's changing relationship with Japan, former imperial master and contemporary regional partner-rival, and its own past to be explored with a freedom presumably only still circumscribed by artistic imagination and commercial pressures. Japan, Japanese figures, Koreans with Japan connections, etc., have in fact emerged as part of a cultural reengagement with the not so distant past. This newly imagined Japan has been expressed across a wide variety of film genres: nostalgic biopic (*Rikidōzan* 2004); martial arts film (*Fighter in the Wind* 2004); historical biopic/romance (*Blue Swallow* 2005). One could add quite a few more titles of films made since 2000: offbeat contemporary Korean-Japanese romance *Asako in Ruby Shoes* (2000), time-travel cop thriller *2009 Lost Memories* (2002), or baseball-genre historical comedy *YMCA Baseball Team* (2002). All of these films, some with fairly large (by Korean standards) budgets, are reasonably well-made efforts at mainstream entertainment; all have scenes or sections that in sheer visual impact are as effective as anything produced on the world market. The technical limitations that plagued filmmakers well into the 1980s have been long overcome.

These films take their place in what has come to be considered the New Korean Cinema. There are many good accounts of the spectacular takeoff of the South Korean film industry since the doldrums of the late 1980s and early 1990s.[5] Recent statistics from the Korean Film Council show how, in the last dozen years, Korean film seems to have carved out a remarkable share of the domestic box office. So where, in 1995, barely 20 percent of actual attendances were for home productions, with foreign films overwhelmingly from the US at almost 80 percent, the market share figures for domestic versus foreign for 2005 were 56.1 percent versus 33.7 percent US (followed by Europe 2.5 percent, Japan 2.2 percent, and China 1.2 percent).[6] Among major developed countries, only France has maintained anything like this sort of domestic market. The peculiarities of the South Korean industry mean that the domestic box office is crucial to the success of any film and to the industry overall; "unofficial" online downloading is a major factor in the dullness of the DVD market so far.[7] Yet Korean film is also part of the regional success story within the East and Southeast Asian cultural marketplace. Film exports in 2002 accounted for less than US$15 million; the figure for 2003 was US$31 million, 2004 US$58 million, 2005 US$76 million. In 2004, almost seventy-nine percent and in 2005 eighty-seven percent of these exports were to other Asian partners in the cultural market.[8] Of course US$76 million would not go very far in Hollywood, and Korean film lags well behind Korean TV drama in regional market profitability and general popularity.[9] Still, coming from an almost extinct domestic market fifteen years ago and no exports to speak of, Korean film seems to be riding the crest of a fairly dependable wave.

Yet, as mentioned, it is hard to know how optimistic one can remain about the future of the regional market and the general ease and speed with which cultural products may continue to circulate between Korea, Japan, the PRC, Hong Kong, and Taiwan. What Chris Berry has recently observed to be true of filmmaking in Taiwan is at least as true in the case of South Korea: "instead of the fading away of the national, our current era seems to feature *both* rising economic globalization *and* rising political national tensions."[10] The political friction between Korea and Japan appears to be increasing at an even more rapid pace than exports of films or TV dramas from the former to the latter: conflict over the tiny Dokdo/Takeshima Islands, Japanese prime ministerial visits to Yasukuni Shrine, the perennial debates about Japan's revisionist history textbooks, the issue of Japanese apologies and compensation for the entire colonial era, or the lack of justice for the thousands of women, Korean and others, forced into sexual slavery during the war — all these issues shadow the positive image of regional flows and other forms of co-operation. Anyone following major news stories during 2007 will be aware of how then-Japanese Prime Minister Abe Shinzō managed to reignite the "comfort women" issue in a dramatic fashion.[11]

If we look back from the fractious present into the turbulent past, it can be taken as axiomatic that, "since Korea's encounter with modernity and its nearly simultaneous colonization by Japan at the turn of the twentieth century, the memory of the struggle for independence has provided a vast reservoir of narrative and discursive practices by which Koreans have come to articulate their modern self-identity. In the modern era" — well before, that is, the omnipresence of the other others thrown up by liberation, civil war and Cold War (the US ally-occupier, the Soviet Union, the Democratic People's Republic of Korea, the PRC) — "Japan became the 'other' of the Korean 'self'."[12] This formulation of Japan as resolutely other to a presumed distinctly Korean self is the premise of much thinking and writing about the colonial past: "The issue of Korean participation in a colonial modernity is finessed in most nationalist histories by isolating the 'true' national form of modernity from any connection to 'tainted' Japanese modernity."[13] The fact is that there were mainly losers: those who actively resisted, the thousands scattered to Manchuria, the maritime USSR and Japan, those forced into Japanese industries or sexual slavery, and the majority of Koreans who still worked the land. There were as well relative winners during the colonial decades. "Long-term colonial rule requires the co-optation of ever larger numbers of the colonized population . . . South Korean officials, business people, and even intellectuals become part and parcel of colonial rule."[14] Most writers, artists, and filmmakers only existed as such to the extent they had been educated, enculturated however reluctantly, and incorporated however marginally into the institutional cultural life of the colony.

Kang Nae-hui has argued that South Korea's thwarted project of confronting the colonial past inhabits three strands of discourse about the nation. One concerns tactical forgetting: "letting people forget the 'painful traumas' of the past. The justification is that reconciliation and unity need to be forged for the well-being of the whole nation."[15] This generally conservative line of argument has, as Kang points out, elements in common with theoretical constructions of South Korea as a postcolonial nation.[16]

Then there is the more straightforwardly nationalistic position of "the strategy of exorcism: It is an attempt to expel the dregs . . . as alien substances or impurities that should not be allowed to mingle with the national culture." The work of exorcism may be "to disprove the worth of Japan" as well as "to expel the evil spirit from the nation and to return to that 'original state' of the nation before the national spirit was injured and corrupted by colonialism."[17] The third discourse is Kang's own, the perhaps utopian attempt to endure the spectres of the colonial past. "To endure ghosts is not to get rid of them but to bear up and resist the afflictions caused by them. . . . How could we deal with ghosts without enduring them?"[18]

In looking below at how the New Korean Cinema has represented the past of Korea and Japan, I adapt Kang Nae-hui's general categories, simplifying and distorting, no doubt, in the process. In examining a first group of films, I take tactical forgetting to be comparable to the melodramatic mode of filmmaking.

Nationalist exorcism is briefly considered with regard to the blockbuster *Hanbando* (*The Korean Peninsula*, 2006) and *2009 Lost Memories* (2002). And while Kang's complex arguments consider a variety of forms of enduring — rather than forgetting or pretending to chase away — the spectres of the colonial past, it is his example of mimicry that seems most appropriate for the film *The President's Last Bang*, examined in some detail below.

Kang redirects the notion of colonial mimicry from the theoretical work of Homi Bhabha[19] to a homely Korean example set in the pre-colonial rather than colonial past. In the *madang guk* folk theatre, it is the figure of *Malttuk-i* the fool who mimicked the actions and pretensions of the noble *yangban*. "*Yangban* struts with his long pipe in mouth; *Malttuk-i* follows him, and uncontrollable laughter immediately comes from the audience. . . . No doubt, there is a shared understanding of the stupidity of the swaggering *Yangban*, between the audience and *Malttuk-i*."[20] We will see below how Im Sangsu sends his actor-*Malttuk-i* through their paces in a cinematic version of colonial mimicry.

Melodramatic Forgetting

Rikidōzan was a moderately successful wrestler in Japan's world of postwar sumo wrestling.[21] According to the trove of legends surrounding him, it was when his progress towards the pinnacle of the sumo ranks, *yokozuna*, was blocked on account of his Korean origins that he went off to the United States, learned the skills and stage-craft associated with pro wrestling, brought them back to Japan and worked to establish the new sport-spectacle as a significant popular entertainment and money-earner. In the new medium of TV, "puro-resu" found its perfect companion. The joint Korean-Japanese production *Rikidōzan* (often listed under the Korean pronunciation of the three characters making up the sumo name, *Yŏkdosan*) tells the rags-to-riches (to emotion-tugging demise) story of a colonial-era immigrant who went on to become not only rich but in a sense more Japanese than the Japanese. It was his success initially in the US, and then against American (or, in a pinch,

Canadian) wrestlers in Japan — whacking away with his patented "karate" chop — which generated an image of Japanese fighting spirit still able to defeat Japan's foes. The actor Sŏl Kyŏnggu had to train and bulk up for the lead role, and learn his lines almost entirely in Japanese. He had a following in Japan based on roles in a variety of films that were critical success in Japan, such as Lee Chang-dong's contemporary classic *Peppermint Candy* (*Pakha satang* 2000), and Japan was clearly a market aimed for.

Rikidōzan contains most of the classical elements of one of the most reliable forms of male melodrama: the boxing film. Shy-but-violent youth, gentle-all-suffering wife, manipulative and sleazy promoters, booze-and-women, too-noble-to-throw-the-big-match last-minute self-realization, sad lonely death, etc. These it transposes to 1950s Japan and the spectacular showbiz of the wrestling ring. The noir-ish male melodrama can, in the East Asian market, sound familiar echoes with a variety of more localized genres, such as *rōnin*, yakuza, or Chinese martial arts films. But even in the case of this rather formulaically structured wrestling melodrama, history got in the way. It was not a success in Korea, and there were problems with the Japanese release. The film had been due to appear in March 2005. "Unlike the previous version, which opened in Korea last December [2004], the new version features many Japanese actors, according to the movie's production company. In fact, Sŏl has recently visited Japan to re-dub his lines in Japanese."[22] Given that nearly all the actor's lines are already in Japanese, albeit pronounced with an accent that the real Rikidōzan may have lost, this need for a re-Japanization of the film suggests that the spirit of cultural exchange can entail hard bargaining. In one of the few scenes in which Sŏl Kyŏnggu has lines in Korean, an old friend asks him if he is still Korean. Rikidōzan replies that Japanese or Korean, it doesn't matter: Rikidōzan belongs to the whole world. It is a sad irony that, whatever the dramatic weaknesses of this film may be, the fictional Rikidōzan should even temporarily be denied his re-entry visa to Japan.

Fighter in the Wind is based on the legend-biography of Ōyama Masutatsu, founder of one of the main schools of Japanese karate. A poor Korean immigrant, Ch'oe Paedal, makes his way to wartime Japan. He intends to volunteer for an air force that is preparing mainly for suicide missions, but is apprehended instead. As Japanese soldiers are about to shoot him and several other Koreans, US planes bomb the airbase, and in the confusion he escapes. He eventually sets out to become a martial arts expert just as the arrival of peace and the postwar era might make that seem an even more eccentric career move. After many trials, and challenges to every master of every martial art he can locate, Paedal fights his way to recognition as the toughest fighter in Japan. A turning point occurs early on, when a Korean mentor offers him a guide to his future path in life: it is in the form of Miyamoto Musashi's *The Five Rings*. This seventeenth-century classic of Japanese Bushidō practice and philosophy seems a rather extreme guidebook to life in a now peaceful Japan. The film shows no sense of irony in sending its protagonist forth with such samurai-like inspiration.

Indeed, to the extent that Paedal is a success, the trajectory of the film seems more mythic than melodramatic: he suffers hardships, turns his back on a loving wife, but faces no temptations of flesh or spirit that can't be overcome through more training and heroic self-abnegation in the pursuit of being the toughest fighter in Japan, and eventually honoured founder of a "traditional" school of karate.

Action sequences are crucial to both of these films, and both display similar limitations (in addition to the problems faced by *Rikidōzan* in convincing the audience that pro wrestling = real fighting). The lead actors can learn enough moves to look good for the typical two–three/five–six-second rapid cuts typical of the action genre. But the rapid cutting itself, jumpy camera movement, heavy-handed soundtrack, etc., can sit uneasily with the slower moments which ought to invite audiences to slow down a minute and find reasons to identify with or to care about the men doing all this frantic action — moments that might allow for a bit of character development. Here, however clichéd the melodramatic style of *Rikidōzan* may be, it at least humanizes its central character in a way the masculinist fantasy of *Fighter in the Wind* does not even attempt. Neither film, indeed, presents its protagonists in anything but a sympathetic fashion; both use narrative form and cinematic technique to invite identification, not judgment. There seems no space within the narrative for an ironical distance, one from which the spectator might seem invited to question these two colonial boys made good as hyper-Japanese heroes. And if their unchallenged mastery of colonial mimicry seems ultimately to betray the rather formulaic narrative and limited intellectual and artistic ambitions of their respective films, that may simply confirm Homi Bhabha's contention that, "in order to be effective, mimicry must continually produce its slippage, its excess, its difference."[23]

Blue Swallow is about Pak Kyŏngwŏn, a pioneering aviatrix whose fame spread in late twenties and early thirties Japan and Korea. A young Korean woman still in her teens goes to Japan determined to train as a pilot. First, an opening sequence shows Pak as an eleven-year-old, watching a column of Japanese troops march towards her village. In her mind's eye, the soldiers transform into a column of marching black-clad ninja warriors, and we follow her CG-assisted imagination as it conjures up images of flying ninja, and then of the girl herself flying. We understand that a dream has taken wing. Pak

Kyŏngwŏn will experience romance along the way; she will challenge Japanese aviators and befriend several; she will only with great reluctance agree to serve the cause of empire as the only way she can undertake her greatest test, a solo flight from Japan, through her homeland and on to the new Manchukuo, all now under the Japanese flag. She will die in the attempt. In female melodrama, as Susan Hayward has summarized it, "there is not necessarily a resolution or reconciliation . . . the female point of view often projects a fantasy that is in patriarchal terms transgressive — and so cannot be fulfilled."[24]

Despite this promising material, and the possibilities of giving historical romance a modern feminist updating, the melodrama managed even before its opening to trigger latent nationalism. The producers of *Blue Swallow* seem not to have reckoned with the very long if selective political memories of their compatriots, some of whom, mainly through the Internet, protested the lavish cinematic treatment of someone regarded as having allowed herself to be made a poster girl for the cause of the Japanese empire. (Press reporting also put into circulation an old rumour that Pak Kyŏngwŏn had been romantically involved with an important Japanese politician named Koizumi, grandfather of former Japanese PM Koizumi Jun'ichirō). *Blue Swallow* ended up one of the costliest failures of 2005–06, selling only some 600,000 tickets for an investment of US$10 million.[25]

All three of the films sketched above make use of Korean and Japanese history chiefly as a colorful, sometimes painful or even violent, background against which the personal dramas, myths, or romances of the protagonists play themselves out. Yet metaphorically, and in some senses literally, once the camera dollies in from a loosely sketched social landscape to focus on medium shots of characters and then moves in closer to frame the emotional turmoil of individual faces in moments of crisis or joy, it never quite pulls back again to reintegrate the personal within the social field — families, classes, regions, nations, histories — from which that personal experience has been abstracted. All that seems halfway forgotten, or merely part of a generalized background setting off the narrative of individuals.

Korean film has a long and complex investment in melodrama, as recent studies of the "golden age" of the mid-1950s to early 1960s have demonstrated.[26] Korean audiences have, until the emergence of the new film industry, been far more avid consumers of Hollywood cinema than of their own, and during the colonial era, not surprisingly, far more likely to see American than Japanese films, until war with the US finally brought imports to a definitive halt.[27] Whatever impact Japanese *Shinpa* melodrama may have had on the makers of early Korean cinema, that of Hollywood prewar melodrama was probably more important for ordinary spectators. But it was during the colonial era itself that cinematic melodrama became both a significant form of popular entertainment and, in the hands of some of Korea's first filmmakers, a focus for attempts to address, however obliquely, the collective fact of domination through the hardships of individuals. Only a handful of films from the period survive, so an assertion that, from its beginnings in 1923 until the draconian censorship policies of the late 1930s, some two-thirds of Korean films (or 84 out of a total 128) were melodramas has to be based on second- and third-hand accounts.[28] Yet enough is known about missing classics such as *Arirang* (1926) or *Ferryboat with No Ferryman* (1932) to show how melodrama could highlight the way in which colonial violence or enforced modernization damaged individuals and families. "The symbolic expressions, such as the use of a madman, the rape of an innocent girl by a pro-Japanese person, and the killing of the rapist were praised [in the Korean press] as an 'ingenious' way to express a national spirit . . . Also symbolic expression was necessary to pass the censorship."[29]

Melodramatic films produced by major players in the New Korean Cinema are no doubt unlikely vehicles for seeking a complex artistic engagement with the experience of the Korean imperial era. The fact that this industry is led by people often only in early middle-age and animated by writers and directors even younger working with actors usually under the age of, say, thirty-two, and producing films mainly for a young audience is no doubt an obvious reason for a lack of anxiety about the past. To take the past or intra-regional sensibilities for granted can, however, have negative consequences for success in the domestic market (*Blue Swallow*) or for a participation in the regional exchange of cultural goods (*Rikidōzan*).

In another sense, these limitations on filmmakers as regards dealing with social and political history seems systemic to cinema itself as mass entertainment, a by now all but ineluctable part of the tacit rules by which commercial films and their audiences negotiate meanings in a melodramatic mode.

> The persistence of the melodrama might indicate the ways in which popular culture has not only taken note of social crises . . . but has also resolutely refused to understand social change in other than private contexts and emotional terms. . . . It has also meant ignorance of the properly social and political dimensions of these changes and their causality.[30]

Nationalist Exorcism

As a result of the rapid growth of the Korean film industry, the stakes have become correspondingly high for the big-budget releases ordinarily geared for the autumn Ch'usŏk festival and summer. During the summer of 2006, posters and TV ads for Kang U'sŏk's blockbuster historical epic *Hanbando* (*The Korean Peninsula*) began appearing in late June. By August it was holding on to the number five spot among the top ten box-office successes, only to fade by September. It still ended up the year as the number eight box-office success — number five among all Korean productions — selling almost 4 million tickets countrywide.

The film is a pro-spective historical, patriotic thriller. Since I have written about *Hanbando* elsewhere,[31] I will keep comments brief. The two Koreas are finally about to move concretely towards reunification via a project to connect the divided nation along the spine of a central railway system. But Japan, villainously claiming legal sovereignty over the former colonial rail system, thanks to its infamous political acquisition of the whole nation in 1910, attempts to wreck the long dream of reunified Korea. A suspense subplot involves a search for the last king of the Chosŏn Dynasty's official seal: if it can be proved that the Japanese diplomats and schemers of a century ago forged their titles to the railways and nation, then their machinations in the present can perhaps be thwarted.

Flashbacks allow for cross-cutting between the near future — in which twenty-first century would-be collaborators seek to rejoin Korea to Japan's economy, even as the Japanese navy sails towards confrontation with the Korean navy — and the past of 1895, when disloyal court officials collaborate in the notorious assassination of the last king's wife, Empress Myŏngsŏng, and the eventual handing-over of the nation to the new Japanese Empire. In this long implausible narrative, there are twists and turns but few surprises. The genuine seal is found in time, the Japanese diplomats are abashed, their documents revealed to be forgeries. One overarching theme concerns bitter differences between pro- and anti-Japan factions within the government. The apparently pro-Japanese prime minister rebukes the reunification-minded president, the prime minister at the very end, arguing bitterly against reunification, fearing economic disaster for the only real Korea, that of the here-and now Republic. Unfortunately, this potentially grown-up political debate (carried on moreover by two of the most respected actors in the industry, An Sŏnggi/President and Moon Sun-keun/PM) is not seriously embodied within the film. Rather, characters on the pro side seem two-dimensional if not truly evil; the Japanese figures past and present are uniformly scowling villains. That they are played by Korean actors speaking only Korean (none of *Rikidōzan*'s linguistic verisimilitude here) adds an extra touch of artificiality to already strained narrative premises.

For the most part, the critics hated *Hanbando*. The *Korea Times*'s staff reporter Kim Tae-jong, writing on July 13, 2006, grudgingly gave it 1½ out of 5 stars: "Although the sensitive theme appeals to Korean audiences, who know the tragic history of Japan's rule, in the end it becomes a propaganda film full of radical nationalism. It lacks cinematic development, reality, and a balanced approach to historical events and the current situation."[32]

Criticisms of the film began before general release. Director Kang U'sŏk (*Silmido, Public Enemy* I & II) had made an early effort to deflect those aimed at *Hanbando*'s crude nationalism. The same reporter observed on July 19 that:

> The film's director Kang Woo-suk doesn't cringe because of such negative criticism. He also does not hide his purpose and openly says that his film aims to criticize Japan. "This is not a film that merely criticizes Japan without reason," Kang told reporters earlier this month after the pre-screening of his film at Seoul Theater, downtown Seoul. "Considering its thoughtless behavior, I really wanted to attack Japan through my film."[33]

Staff reporter/film reviewer Kim noted that "such movies with nationalistic themes, however, didn't translate into automatic success at the box office. There are such commercial flops as 'Phantom, the Submarine' (1999), 'General[s] of Heaven' (2005), 'Fighter in the Wind' (2004) and 'Rikidozan' (2004) and others." Indeed, Kim was able to lay out the numbers to show that of the top ten box-office hits of Korean film coming into summer 2006, five did feature nationalism and patriotism — but all focused on the North-South conflict, including Kang's own 2005 hit *Silmido*.[34]

Hanbando has generally been ignored in Japan. There has been no news concerning a possible Japanese theatrical release — though some brief reports about the film are available in online print media and weblogs — and the film has yet to be offered in Japanese-subtitled DVD. And while the film has appeared in English-subtitled Korean DVD and been picked up for Chinese subtitles by a Malaysian company, it is unlikely to circulate very far or very much within the regional economy. The choice seems to have been to put all efforts into a blockbuster film that might profitably exorcize the demons of the past, depicting all co-operation with Japan past or present as anything from murderous to venial, or at least grievously mistaken. Riding on contemporary frictions and mutual ill will concerning issues real and symbolic between the two countries, *Hanbando,* with its massive advertising campaign and saturation theatrical bookings, seems financially to have just about won its wager. Many people who follow the New Korean Cinema take heart from the huge success — both theatrical and DVD — of rather different films from 2006, such as *King and the Clown* (*Wang-ŭi namja*) and Pong Chunho's *The Host* (*Koemul*), a genuinely international hit on top of 13 million admissions at home.

There is of course more than one way to exorcize a ghost. *2009 Lost Memories* from 2002 is one other film which met a less than enthusiastic critical response upon release. It was, however, fairly successful at home and has sold well in various DVD (English, Japanese, Chinese, French) and VCD versions; at least some of its success outside Korea is due to the regional appeal of model-singer-actor Chang Tonggŭn in the lead role. *2009 Lost Memories* takes an intriguing sort of homeopathic route to the expelling of the colonial past: make it worse in order to make it go away.

The opening scenes of *2009 Lost Memories* begin on October 26, 1909, a century before the film's main action. As is well known to most Koreans, North and South, on this day Korean patriot An Chunggŭn assassinated Japanese statesman Itō Hirobumi on the platform of Harbin Station in Northeast China. Itō, revered in Japan as key founder of the modern nation, is regarded in Korea chiefly as one of the men most responsible for planning the takeover of Korea, finalized after his death in 1910.

And here, in a potentially clichéd bit of nationalist bravado, the narrative springs a surprise. Before An can take careful aim, he is shot by a Japanese soldier in the waiting retinue. Itō is only slightly wounded. There follows a March-of-Time montage sequence, the kind made famous by Orson Wells's *Citizen Kane*: news photos, newspaper headlines and titles tell the story of how history was changed by the thwarted assassination attempt. In this version of history, Itō did become the first governor general of the Korean colony, Japan became a US ally in World War II, the atomic bomb was dropped on Germany, the 1988 Olympics were held in Nagoya and, one final indignity, the 2002 World Cup seems to have been held entirely in a Japan which still incorporated a never-independent Korea. The sequence ends on the photo of a Red Devil striker in a shirt marked with a Japanese *Hi no maru* flag insignia, eloquently robbing a Korean audience of one of the most glorious moments from the year 2002. (The image is calculated to trigger bitter memories of athletes Son Kijŏng and Nam Sŭngyong. Running in Japanese colors and under Japanese names, they famously won the gold and bronze medals in the marathon at the 1936 Berlin Olympics. Son would carry the Olympic flag during the opening of the 1948 London Olympics.)[35]

Only after the flashback and montage sequence does the action shift to 2009. The camera looks out, in extreme long shot, upon a city nightscape, roads crowded with Japanese vehicles and direction signs in Japanese and English. Neon signs seem all in Japanese, no Korean *han'gŭl* in sight. A pan to the left takes in what appears to be a famous central Seoul landmark, the statue of sixteenth-century naval hero Yi Sun-shin. The camera reveals that this is instead, in 2009, a statue of Yi's mortal enemy, the despoiler of mid-Chosŏn Dynasty Korea, Shōgun Toyotomi Hideyoshi. The premise is fascinating if not original: what if? What if Japan had won the war, what if Korea had ceased to exist as an independent nations (or nations)?

As the establishing shots smoothly hand over to the central narrative, the action begins in an art museum, during a party celebrating an exhibition of Korean art. Posters announce that the art objects are about to be relocated to the modern empire's capital, Tokyo. (It is historical fact that during the colonial era, Japanese collectors — including Yanagi Sōetsu, one of Japan's most significant art critics — took a considerable amount of Korea's material culture home with them.) Into this smugly confident soiree bursts a band of Korean resistance fighters. They attempt to snatch a mysterious crescent-shaped stone from among the objects on display. Some interesting lines of narrative imagination start to get tangled up as the film moves into full John-Woo-like mode. One convincing set is soon shot to bits, when the forces of law and order duly arrive, guns blazing.

The JBI — Japanese Bureau of Investigation — joins the Seoul police at the scene. Introduced into the fray are the two leads, the JBI partners played by Chang Tonggŭn and Japanese character actor Nakamura Tōru. Naturally enough, until the JBI capture and question one of the resistance guerrillas, all dialogue is in Japanese. The film eventually explains that the mysterious stone was a key that could open a time-lock, an ancient doorway that allows time travel; the Japanese had discovered it first, gone back to 1909 and stopped An Chunggŭn from carrying out his destiny. After two hours, and many story lines, the climax takes us back into the sepia-toned past. The two JBI partners, one still a loyal Japanese but the other now a born-again Korean patriot, find themselves back in 1909, on the same platform with An Chunggŭn, Itō Hirobumi, and the Japanese soldier whose gun, according to the Japanese recasting of events, had changed history the first time around. The result of this four-way pistols-drawn face-off is not really difficult to work out.

Having endured the imaginary presence of a ghost perhaps worse than the old one, you return to its origins and scatter it into oblivion. Having looked into the face of a future that denied its very existence, Korea gets its history back.

Colonial Mimicry

Im Sangsu[36] is probably not responsible for the rather strange English moniker his 2005 film has been saddled with: *The President's Last Bang*. Yet the dark humour enfolding his often hapless characters is no stranger to the rudeness it displays. The film tells the story of the assassination by the hand of Kim Chae-gyu, head of the notorious KCIA (Korean Central Intelligence Agency), of his long-time ally Park Chung-hee, President of the Republic of Korea from 1961 to 1979. The events take place in the narrative as they did in reality, on October 26, 1979,[37] exactly seventy years after An Chunggǔn shot Itō Hirobumi. Most of the action of the tightly scripted first half takes place during a boozy banquet at the KCIA mansion/safe-house within the presidential Blue House compound; two young women there to entertain Park and his inner circle, hence the crude double entendre of "bang" in the English title.

The Korean title is "*Kǔ ttae kǔ saram-dǔl*," literally "That time, those men;" it involves a more subtle play with language and cultural memory. It quotes the title of a tune made popular in 1979 by singer Shim Subong, "*Kǔ ttae kǔ saram*," "That time, that man." The title is a Korean version of the many variations of the saying "Cometh the hour, cometh the man." Political legend maintains that this song was sung that very evening by Shim herself, one of the two young women actually present at the banquet. (It is still usually listed first on her greatest hits CDs.) The attention to detail, to things such as music and peculiarities of speech, are part of the production's aim to evoke the past as something more than generalized local historical color, as happens in films such as *Rikidōzan* or *Blue Swallow*. For example, Im has added a Japanese song to the Korean songs at the fatal dinner. "*Kita no yado*" (An Inn up North) was an enormous hit in Japan from around 1975, made famous in a recording by the 1960s–70s Japanese diva Miyako Harumi.[38] It is just the kind of Japanese romantic ballad, *enka*, that patriotic Koreans were not supposed to be listening to during those years of the ban on Japanese music, film, and TV programs. Shim Subong is rumoured to have performed songs like "*Kita no yado*" for wealthy patrons in order to supplement her recording earnings, so the narrative fabrication hits a suitable nerve.

More significant, if still only a detail within the overall production, is the use of spoken Japanese at key points in the dialogue. It is here that colonial mimicry works most effectively to undermine the main characters' militantly nationalistic posture. If you don't know Korean or Japanese, this is signalled in the English subtitled version by the sudden appearance at screen bottom, underneath the English words, of Korean translations for Japanese phrases. The first occasion when this takes place is near the beginning, onboard a military helicopter carrying Park Chung-hee and his right-hand men to the banquet. The Park character (Song Chaeho) remarks wryly in Japanese concerning the sexual antics of an absent crony, that a "real man" (Japanese *otoko*) doesn't concern himself about matters down there. In the first cut to Kim Chae-gyu, the KCIA director has just finished a physical examination. To his doctor's stern advice about his ailing health, Kim (Paek Yunshik) retorts that a *samurai* won't concern himself about petty worries. As he leaves the office, the doctor spits the word *samurai* back with contempt. *Otoko* and *samurai:* the two words speak volumes about the past of men such as Park and Kim who, as young men, had fought, or arrested, their fellow Koreans wearing the uniform of the Japanese army or *kempeitai* (military police). Given the predominance of a masculinist discourse of Korean nationalism fostered through the eighteen years of the Park regime,[39] to suggest that the ideal of masculinity half-consciously embraced by Park and his right-hand men was derived from a Japanese model makes for cruelly effective black comedy and mimicry. Latter day *Malttuk-i*, the fictional Park and Kim strut in the linguistic traces left by masters departed a quarter-century ago.

Kim Chae-gyu finally resolves, later that same long night, to kill Park and as many of the cronies at the party as he can; his personal pride has been insulted by them, and he fears that plans afoot to assault anti-government protestors will backfire dangerously. He decides to act. He looks up from his desk, takes his pistol in hand and, spluttering with righteous fury, declares in Japanese, "*Koroshite yaru*": "I'm going to [bloody] kill him/them." Listening outside the office door is Kim's adjutant, Colonel Min. The next shot is of the latter repeating the phrase, and instantly understanding what his boss intends. As with the scene on the helicopter, the scandal is not just that of certain Japanese words in particular mouths but the ease with which they register among the whole class of the politico-military elite.[40]

When finally Kim prepares to deliver the coup de grâce to an already grievously wounded Park, he reviles him in Japanese as a piece of filth, and through clenched teeth calls Park by the Japanese name he had taken as acclimatized colonial subject, "Takagi Masao." Strong stuff in a nation where many older Koreans revere the Park legacy, if not its crueller methods, and where the former president's daughter, and until recently possible future president Park Kŭnhye, remains a powerful figure. "Park's daughter now leads Korea's centre-right opposition party, ensuring that the historically themed *Last Bang* would be read as a comment on the present as well as the past."[41]

Before its commercial release, the Park family took the film's production company MK Pictures to court, claiming defamation of character. Although the film survived largely intact, four minutes of 1979 newsreel footage were suppressed: two minutes' worth which ran behind the opening titles and credits, showing violent protests in Pusan and Masan against the regime's treatment of opposition figure Kim Young-sam; two from the end which showed Park's funeral. The current version runs its opening and closing credits against a black screen. The initial court decision was overturned in 2006. The cut footage will be restored, but MK Pictures, as has been widely reported, has still had to pay some US$100,000 to the plaintiff, Park's son Park Chiman. Park Chung-hee continues to cast a formidable shadow across the political landscape of South Korea. Former President Roh Moo-hyun, his political allies and private research groups, have for several years been exploring the possibilities of reopening the historical books on the colonial era via a variety of truth commissions and committees. It is a difficult, politically slippery issue that may seem to have so far generated more heat than light.[42]

I would not like to leave the impression that *The President's Last Bang* is an intricate art house work of purely auteurist values. It is a good political thriller informed by a sharp-edged sense of political satire and impressive cinematography. The haunting musical score may sound different when the suppressed newsreel minutes are restored: the opening tango theme, for example, will accompany scenes of political protest that the soon-to-die president will spend his last lucid moments planning to crush. The production values are those you would expect of a good, medium-size feature; leading male star Han Sŏkkyu, as Kim Chae-gyu's number three, carries much of the action and narrative links. After the assassination, there is a brief transitional sequence before the second half of the film follows up the fate of the KCIA conspirators. The camera tracks Han Sŏkkyu from above as he moves from the gory banquet room, Park's body now removed, down a hallway to the bodies of Park's two chief bodyguards, now practically floating in pools of their own blood; then the camera travels on to the kitchen and shots of other bodyguards lying dead there.[43] Unlike a less imaginative, more action-geared thriller, this one insists on the aftermath and consequences of the acts of violence which finally prised loose Park's grip on the nation. The long travelling shot noted above seems almost designed to illustrate a dictum often attributed to Godard: "le travelling est une affaire de morale."

The film has none of the ponderousness of a Hollywood-scale assassination conspiracy such as Oliver Stone's *JFK* (1991). One film it might be better compared with is the Korean-Japanese joint production *KT* (2002). Directed by Sakamoto Junji, *KT* (abbreviation for "kill the target") tells in a quasi-documentary fashion the story of the failed assassination attempt and subsequent abduction from Japan of Kim Dae-Jung, Park Chung-hee's most stubborn opponent and ROK president from 1998 to 2003. *The President's Last Bang* uses mimicry against power in a way that allows for laughter at power's expense, without losing the film's overall ethical, critical force.

We know that at least for a time in the aftermath of liberation, Korean filmmakers, writers and actors seemed to have been ready to work around if not yet through the bitter legacies of colonization and war. This latitude, cultural, artistic, and political, would be lost to future filmmakers in the wake of a disastrous civil war and coming of Cold War rigidities and political dictatorships both sides of the 38th Parallel. That is, until the political and cultural sea-changes of 1990s South Korea made it possible for a new cinema to begin to take a fresh look at Korea's eclectic, fragmentary, and contradictory modern history and to make what it can of the intractable Korean colonial past. According to the Korean Film Council's recent annual report *Korean Cinema 2006*, among films currently in the planning stages are one about the doomed Empress Myŏngsŏng and one with the working title "Tokdo Defense Forces." The spectres of old crimes and an awareness of current sources of friction between Korea and Japan will no doubt keep melodrama and exorcism busy in the New Korean Cinema for some time to come.

12

Reconsidering Cultural Hybridities: Transnational Exchanges of Popular Music in between Korea and Japan

Yoshitaka Mōri

Cultural Studies faces a crisis in Japan. About ten years have passed since it was "imported" from the United Kingdom following two key events: Tokyo University's 1996 international conference that included five pioneering British scholars, including Stuart Hall,[1] and the publication by two leading academic journals, *Shisō* and *Gendai Shisō*, of a special issue on Cultural Studies. The term *Cultural Studies* has been acknowledged as a new interdisciplinary domain that draws on and brings together a wide variety of scholarly perspectives ranging from literary criticism to sociology, history, philosophy, anthropology, and media studies. It is true that much fruitful research has been achieved. Indicative of the importance of Cultural Studies, most of its seminal texts have been translated in Japan over the last decade.

However, when looking back over the political and academic situation in Japan, it is undeniable that the political project of Cultural Studies has largely failed. In politics, a number of issues have conspired to give birth to a new conservative and ultra-nationalist regime whose key leaders include the former prime ministers Koizumi Jun'ichirō and Abe Shinzō and the Tokyo Metropolitan Governor Ishihara Shintarō. These issues include the ongoing long-term economic recession dating to the early 1990s, as well as the social instability caused by a series of disastrous events, in particular the 1995 Kobe earthquake, the subway terrorism of cult religious group Aum Shinrikyō, and the militarized global atmosphere emerging in the wake of the bombing of the World Trade Center on September 11, 2001. Importantly, the new conservative politics has gained enthusiastic national popularity thanks to a successful populist mainstream media strategy. By contrast, it is extremely hard to find a critical space from which Cultural Studies practitioners can now intervene.

In the academic world, through the process of neoliberal restructuring under Koizumi's regime, almost all traditional disciplines centered on the humanities — never mind new areas like Cultural Studies — are virtually dying because they are not seen as "useful" either for the government or for industry; and more importantly, students no longer find them very "attractive."[2] Cultural Studies may survive as long as it deals with trendy issues such as globalization, digital culture, animation, TV games, mobile technology and so on, but it can be neither too critical nor political.[3] The university is now subsumed by and subscribes to the logic of market capitalism. For students, it is merely a transitional point where they prepare to go into the business world. In general, the university hardly resembles an independent space where anything, regardless of economic utility and function, can be studied.

In this difficult condition, the "cultural" is gradually coming to be regarded among critical intellectuals in Japan as less important than the political and the economic. For instance, issues concerning an emergent neoliberalist class structure, in which the rich and poor are polarized, dominate policy discussions. In these, the appearance of the *freeter*, the new class of so-called "freelancers" composed of young and poor people stuck in a series of low-income part-time jobs and unable to break into regular employment, are viewed as socially problematic. At the level of global politics and foreign affairs, the military is being reconstructed under the aegis of United States hegemony, and along with it, North Korea and China — the new antagonists — become the target of problem-solving agendas. Not that any of these questions can be ignored, but the exclusion of "culture" in such debates signals a major shift in thinking, one that gives little place for the "critical turn" that approaches like Cultural Studies offers.

In addition to the backlash against the "cultural," there are problems within Japanese — and to some extent Korean — Cultural Studies. First, only a few critical studies of popular culture have been seen so far. Instead, most research focuses on colonial history in relation to Korea, China, and Okinawa, on less-known avant-garde styled literature and films, or on over-theoretical postmodernist/deconstructionist arguments. While I appreciate most of these arguments, I must admit that they are not always open to the public, promoting instead a narrow insider-ism. Second, critical studies of popular culture remain underdeveloped. Most studies of popular cultural genres including manga comics, animation, TV dramas, and popular music are disappointingly apolitical, even though they are sometimes categorized as part of Cultural Studies research.[4] They may deal with contemporary cultural phenomena, but they are easily incorporated into the government's nationalist discourse that tries to promote popular cultural products as a new industrial export through a strategy of national branding.[5]

Third, and most crucially in the context of this volume which interrogates the East Asian region, Cultural Studies in Japan (and in Korea) has not overcome existing national boundaries in its encounters with the nation-state, equating culture instead with monolithic nationally circumscribed cultures. This is especially true when one looks at TV media products such as Japanese TV dramas or the "Korean Wave" (*Hanryū*).[6] Although much scholarship discusses transnational distribution and production, most of it regards cultural products as a kind of national purism. It seems to me that they are unaware that both the Japanese and Korean nation-states are historically made up of diverse races and ethnicities, and as a result, this scholarship unwittingly helps to hide a very real diversity characterizing the East Asian region and maintain myths of national homogeneity.

This essay is divided into four parts. The first introduces the concept of hybridity. It considers some of the problems associated with its use in the context of Cultural Studies in general, and how it is nevertheless an extremely valuable way to explore contemporary Japan, especially the situation concerning *Zainichi* Koreans (Korean residents in Japan) who exemplify one of the "in-between" spaces in East Asia of cultural production and consumption.[7] The next three sections look specifically at popular music but in different historical periods. In the second section, I would like to argue that Japanese popular music is a hybrid production at its very inception and origin, or as I call it, "hybridity-as-origin." In order to understand its character, I introduce two of the most eminent, pioneering composers in Japanese popular music: Hattori Ryōichi and Koga Masao. In the third section, I focus on a more recent music genre, club/dance music, which forms a subcultural phenomenon among young people in Tokyo and Seoul. What I am particularly interested in is the transnational and cosmopolitan nature of East Asian cultural exchange between Japanese and Korean musicians at the production level. In examining this exchange, however, I would like to interrogate to what extent these musicians can or should even be identified as Japanese or Korean. Do these or any other musicians have to be associated with or defined by nationality? Why does nationality even matter? Finally, in the fourth section, through the example of *Zainichi* musicians VERBAL and Wada Akiko, I would like to question the idea of cultural exchange itself, which is often premised conceptually on the existence of national borders.

Ultimately, I would like to explore the way in which popular music is by its nature always hybridized. It is my hope that hybridity, as I argue it here, could wield political potential at a time when chauvinistic nationalism and militant patriotism are becoming increasingly dominant ideologies in political life. My argument may be still tentative, but it will hopefully have a performative impact in what is a difficult condition concerning politics in general and Cultural Studies in particular. In this way, I would like to delineate an alternative transnational cultural trajectory that is able to maintain a critical stance vis-à-vis all nationalist discourses.

Hybridity: Cultural Studies, Japan, and *Zainichi* Koreans

This essay considers popular music *in-between* Japan and Korea. It adopts as its central approach the concept of cultural hybridity in popular culture, which has been used in Western critical intellectual circles since the early 1980s to explain the experiences of second- and third-generation postwar immigrants and what might be identified as their cosmopolitan way of life. In so doing, it has been used to challenge essentialist ideas of race and ethnicity. Following on from Hall's conception of "new ethnicities" by which a crucial shift is suggested from (black/Asian) identity politics to a more fluid, floating, complicated, and mixed sense of identity and political agency, Gilroy, Mercer, Bhabha, and others have, in varying ways, directed the concept of hybridity and related ideas of diaspora and syncreticism to overcoming the Eurocentric tradition of understanding culture.[8] My argument, needless to say, follows their trajectories.

In the age of globalization, it is a cliché to emphasize the importance and possibilities of hybridity to postmodern capitalist society. However, the concept of hybridity, when unexamined, can be highly problematic.[9] Regarding ethnicity and culture, this concept sometimes too easily celebrates the practice of mixing without implying any awareness of what is at stake and, in so doing, it can simply revive a notion of racial essences, namely, parts of an original and essential culture that are being mixed to create a hybrid.[10] In socioeconomic class and status, hybridity may represent only the cosmopolitan experience of privileged middle- or upper-middle-class people in developed countries.[11] In the context of this chapter, we carefully have to distinguish migrant or diaspora culture of displaced peoples from hybrid cultures of cosmopolitans.

Recognizing these problems, however, I would like to employ and develop the term *hybridity* because of its use in exploring the Japanese-Korean relationship. To be certain, this concept has not taken root in Japanese public discourses outside of a small circle of intellectuals, despite their enthusiasm. Indicative of how alien hybridity is to mainstream and popular understandings of Japan, consider the following. In 1986, Prime Minister Nakasone Yasuhiro suggested that black and Hispanic Americans were lowering US literacy and intelligence rates and, as a result, he faced strong criticism from the United States government. It is problematic to me that Nakasone later apologized for his comments by stating that Japan is a nation of one "homogenous race" without any ethnic minorities, the logic implicitly being that Japan therefore does not have any problem with racism as such.[12] The myth of one "homogenous race" survives and has even been strengthened under the recent Koizumi–Abe administrations that inherited Nakasone's neoliberalist policy and racist ideology.[13] The categories of race, ethnicity, and nation are strongly tied to each other, and in most cases they are compatible with the overarching and ambiguous Japanese term *minzoku* (race). The sociological distinction between these terms has never been properly recognized in mainstream discourse.[14] As long as the myth of Japan as a "mono-race" and "mono-ethnic" nation remains the dominant ideology, it is politically necessary to emphasize the importance of hybridity.

The term *hybridity* and its equivalent in Japanese, *zasshusei*, are given specially nuanced meaning because of their zoological connotations. The first character *zatsu* refers to "mixed," "rough," or "wild," hence the original application of *zasshusei* only to animals and plants and not to human beings. Notably, the term in its Japanese rendering refers to a mixed existence whose originary parts remain unidentified or anonymous. The hybrid maintains an undelineated and/or underground relationship with these parts whose origins do not really matter but which nevertheless promote a special ability to survive. While the subversive potential is obviously that the biological association of *zasshusei* contributes to the myth of Japan as one "homogenous race," the "bottom-up" process that it describes, particularly in the context of culture, lends it a popular attractiveness.

However, the importance of cultural hybridity has been largely ignored in Japanese mainstream media, especially in television, which is central to the promotion and distribution of popular music. There are three reasons for this absence. First, the industry is dominated by those who still believe in the myth of a racially homogenous Japan, with the result that there are only a few non-Japanese and people of ethnic minority origin in the television industry. Second, there is an expectation in this industry that audiences are purely "Japanese." Due to a lack of a racial imagination coupled with the narrow logic behind the drive to secure ratings and the advertising market, non-Japanese or people whose "hybrid" backgrounds belie dominant perceptions of racial/cultural homogeneity are never thought of as potential audiences and readers of television's cultural products. Finally, the television industry is subject to the racially defined ideological control of the government which issues broadcasting and business licenses. In short, television tends to exclude non-Japanese both as producers and as audiences because it is basically nationalist. As a means of interrogating and challenging the mainstream media, hybridity should be understood as a political project to discover alternative transnational modes of production, consumption, and distribution.

The concept of hybridity has recently become more significant than ever, because it helps to challenge the logic of the new post-9/11 global militarist order according to which friend-enemy is irresistibly defined by national borders and racial distinction. Under the strong influence of the United States' neo-con ideology, the Japanese government aims to establish a new military alliance with the United States in order to gain hegemonic political power in the East Asian region. Specific policy aims include the establishment of a proper Ministry of Defense and the amendment of Article 9 of the postwar Constitution which forbids the use of war as a means of foreign policy. According to this logic, North Korea (followed by China) is demonized as a potential "evil" enemy in the mainstream media. This contrasts vividly with the image of South Korea, which for the time being is portrayed as a "friendly country," thanks to the "Korean Wave."

Turning our attention to ethnic tensions in Japan caused by the global militarist order, let's consider the situation of *Zainichi* Koreans. Those individuals whose descendents originally came from what in the latter half of the twentieth century became North Korea continue to face serious racial discrimination in everyday life, while people tracing their origins to what is now South Korea are often viewed as friends. Of course, this distinction is unreasonable because most *Zainichi* families came to Japan from a unified Korea prior to its division following the Korean War. Although there has been political tension between South and North Korean *Zainichi*, by and large they had until recently shared the same experiences, particularly concerning racism in Japan. Now *Zainichi* communities are completely polarized in Japanese public representation: good *Zainichi* (South) and bad *Zainichi* (North).

Crucially, this distinction, which ostensibly favors South-originating *Zainichi*, is, from their experience, neither comfortable nor desirable. Consider, for example, the *minzoku gakkō* (so-called "ethnic schools") established by *Zainichi* for their children and where the Korean language and history are taught. The Japanese and Tokyo Metropolitan governments have explicitly and implicitly exerted political pressure in an effort to see these schools incorporated more into the Japanese educational system, which, for its part, promotes *aikoku-shin,* "nationalist" or "patriotic," education.[15] As regards the influence of the recent "Korean Wave," the influence on the Japanese populace is only partial, divided as it is along gender lines: women like the "Korean Wave," but men do not in general. In the sense that the "Korean Wave" helped to change the stereotypical image of Korea and Koreans, it has had beneficial effects. Nevertheless, it often re-essentializes Koreans, imagining them as a unified entity that is then re-projected as Japan's "other."

It is beyond the scope of this work to discuss the *Zainichi* situation in Japan in all its facets. Here, I would like only to suggest that, in the age of globalization, the concept of race and ethnicity is being redrawn to impact on national political borders. One of the important lessons of Cultural Studies I have learned is that national culture is never a unified entity. Instead, it is socially constructed and thus can be challenged, diversified, hybridized, and transformed by different cultures within. By reconsidering the idea of hybridity with specific reference to popular music, I would like to explore and discover some of positive elements characterizing what may be regarded as an emerging cosmopolitan culture.

Japanese Popular Music as "Hybridity-as-Origin:" Hattori Ryōichi and Koga Masao

Let me begin my argument by looking at two famous composers in the history of Japanese popular music, Hattori Ryōichi and Koga Masao. Both of them are distinguished musicians, who are often regarded as the godfathers of postwar music. All the songs they produced are still listened to on TV programs and in karaoke bars, and they are often selected as the best songs in Japanese popular music history. Interestingly enough, both Hattori and Koga spent the early part of their lives in Japanese colonial territories, an experience that overshadowed their subsequent creative careers.

At this point, it is necessary to consider the distinctive character of Japanese popular music as contrasted with its Euro-American counterparts. In the West, the nature of popular music is often understood by ethnic/cultural hybridity. Jazz, rock, reggae, and club music are products of the hybridization of ethnically diverse cultures. Hybridity in the West is further defined when one considers, in particular, "high culture" forms like classical music, which emphasizes the traditional and authentic. Within the Japanese context, however, popular music is distinguished not between "high" and "hybrid" levels, per se, but between Japanese music and Western (mainly

English-speaking) music. "High culture," for its part, is seen as something from the West. The space for hybridized popular music, especially in relation to the Japanese colonial legacy, is further restricted because songs with Japanese lyrics are automatically "nationalized" and labeled as purely Japanese. This particular dichotomy between Japanese (neither Asian nor non-Western) and Western has concealed the "hybridity-as-origin" in Japanese popular music, which, I would argue, needs to be reclaimed.

The quality of hybridity is clearer in the works of Hattori than in the ones of Koga. Hattori, born in 1907, started his career strongly influenced by early jazz. He wrote a lot of hit tunes as a composer for Columbia Records in Japan. One of Hattori's favorite female singers, Awaya Noriko, released several hit songs, including "Ame no burusu" ("Blues in the Rain"), and she was called "the Queen of the Blues."[16] During World War II, Hattori moved to Shanghai to play jazz, which was banned in mainland Japan at that time. He composed and played a jazz-styled symphonic music known as the "Ieraishan Rhapsody." It featured a contemporary trans-Asian hit song, "Ieraishan," sung by a controversial and transnational actress during the Japanese imperial era, Ri Kōran; also known as Li Xianglan in China, Yamaguchi Yoshiko in Japan, and Shirley Yamaguchi in the United States. Returning to Japan after the war, Hattori became a pioneering Japanese popular music composer, rigorously adapting contemporary Western music such as jazz, Latin music, and blues. Hattori's music reminds us that early postwar Japanese popular musical tastes were surprisingly cosmopolitan. The style of his songs could be clearly situated within musical networks, in particular jazz, from Singapore and Shanghai. In addition, his lyrics often touched on his experiences in China and the United States, making it possible for us to situate his music in a global musical map.

Koga's relationship to Japanese colonialism in Korea is much more complicated. Born in Fukuoka in 1904, he moved with his mother in 1912 to Incheon, Korea (his father had passed away in 1908), where he was reunited with his elder brother who had already settled there and who offered to support Koga. He grew up in Incheon and later Seoul for eleven years until he left Korea in 1923. In Tokyo, he entered Meiji University and joined a mandolin club. In 1931, he became a composer for Columbia Records and produced many bestselling records including "Sake wa namida ka tameiki ka" ("Is *Sake* [rice wine] a Teardrop or a Sigh?"), "Oka o koete" ("Go Over the Hill"), and "Kage wo shitaite" ("Following After Your Image").

Koga's music, known as "Koga melody," is often understood as the "music of the heart and soul of the Japanese" (*Nihon-jin no kokoro no uta*), and indeed, the influence of musical styles from abroad on "Koga melody" is much less discernable than in Hattori's. Attributed with rediscovering an ostensibly unique Japanese melody, Koga is recognized as a key contributor to the development of Japanese *enka* music (melancholic Japanese traditional ballads), a major genre of Japanese popular music. His association with Japanese melody has also led to much controversy, since this factor has also been used to explain his nationalist sentiments. Koga's biographer, Sataka Makoto, for example, severely criticized Koga's colonialist tendencies, his right-wing ideological sympathies, and the martial songs (*gunka*) he composed under the theme of *Yamato damashii* (the Japanese spirit) during the war.[17]

In a similar vein, but more alert to the complicated nature of Koga's music in its colonial setting, Korean-Japanese music specialist Kyō Nobuko concurs: "Needless to say, the school in the colony where he studied had music classes in which Japanese songs were taught. Japanese *enka* could be heard everywhere, not only in Japanese towns but also in theaters and films in Korean society." In Kyō's interpretation, Koga was submerged in a Japanese musical environment which was made all the more powerful since, as she argues, Koga was a "homeless" person who had lost his homeland: "He was a young boy who grew up listening to his home country's old music in a foreign colony" and as such he simply lacked "any concern for Korean society."[18] In fact, Kyō is not as critical as Sataka, suggesting that Koga's nationalism, rather than being anti-Korean, emerged from his nostalgic search for his homeland.

As suggested above, Koga's theory was very problematic as regards politics during World War II. From today's viewpoint, we can see that it was completely influenced by the right-wing ideology of that time.[19] Kyō is right to observe that Koga did not recognize that he was on the colonizer's side, but I totally agree that we should be critical of Koga's political stance.

Shifting our attention, I would like to consider more closely what it means to produce culture, by arguing that popular music is made not only by producers, musicians, singers, composers, and record companies, but also by consumers, fans, and those who love the music. Following the development of literary theory since the semiotic turn that Roland Barthes initiated with the statement of "the death of author," all texts have to be understood within the context not in which they are written but in which they are read.[20] The practice of reading is not simply passive but also active in that it produces and reproduces meanings in different contexts. In the same vein, audience theory in Cultural Studies (as developed, for example, by Stuart Hall among many others)[21] suggests that, although TV programs are encoded by producers and then decoded by audiences, audiences do not always react as producers expect. The reading of programs differs according to a viewer's class, race, ethnicity, and gender, and according to his or her particular ideological enclosure. Popular cultural products cannot survive without active audiences who produce their own meanings. Consider, for example, Koga's experience when Korean residents in Japan visited him just after the war. Because they assumed that Koga must be a Korean-Japanese since he spent his childhood on the Korean Peninsula, they asked him, "Mr Koga, please give us your real [Korean] name. We promise you that we will keep it a secret, but we want you to help us." Koga later wrote in his autobiography, "they must have believed that I was Korean-Japanese and been secretly proud of me when they were crying due to the racial discrimination [they suffered] in Japanese society."[22]

I do not try to justify Koga's ideological support for the war but would suggest that "Koga melody" — listened to by Koreans both in Japan and on the Korean Peninsula — impressed and empowered them even if this was not the composer's intention. There is inevitably a gap between the encoding process and the decoding one in cultural production. Koga's experience of music in his boyhood exposed him to a wide variety of different musical trajectories ranging from Western popular music and classical music to Asian continental folk music. For the young Koga, these formed an imaginary Japanese music, a hybridized form that reflected a particular colonial condition. In other words, he may have re-created in the colonial setting a music of the "Japanese heart and soul," but it was only done by collecting together fragments of other genres and styles.

The hybrid character of his music was recognized by the *Los Angeles Times* when Koga traveled in the United States: "Mr Koga's songs themselves are cosmopolitan. While they may contain the rhythm of rumba, tango or waltz, or the fast beat of a march or square dance, they also have the unmistakable lilt of the Oriental song. In other words, he has given the old classic themes modern dress."[23] This comment clearly suggests how Koga's music was accepted by different audiences in different ways that went beyond the composer's intention.

What I would like to emphasize here is that the two composers who are said to be representative of postwar Japanese popular music started their careers influenced by their colonial experiences. This hybridized setting bringing together Japan and the world has often been forgotten and repressed, particularly since *enka* has come to be recognized as a "uniquely Japanese" form of music. However, as the cases of Hattori and Koga demonstrate, we always need to be cognizant of how hybridity lies at the originary center of culture: the history of Japanese popular music is one of the best examples of this phenomenon of "hybridity-as-origin," which in turn created different effects, acceptances, and forms of consumption.

Hattori's and Koga's extraordinary colonial experiences show us how Japanese postwar popular music was hybridized right from the very beginning of its history. The linear historical narrative of Japanese popular music that we know today is, in fact, constructed only by forgetting "hybridity-as-origin." The reconsideration of hybridity in music by the transcendence of national boundaries has great potential since it can provide us with a new way of writing history.

In the Age of Underground Personalized Human Networks

Let us now consider examples of transnational popular culture production today. The relationship between Japan and Korea has become increasingly close over the last ten years, in particular, as a result of the popularity of the "Korean Wave," which completely changed the cultural representation of Korea and Koreanness in Japan. Importantly, the "Korean Wave" helped empower some Japanese as well, since it marked the first moment when many middle-aged Japanese women found their own cultural practices in relation to Korea.[24]

Prior to the "Korean Wave," few Korean musicians were well known in Japan except for some *enka* singers such as Cho Yongpil and Kye Ŭnsuk, and as a result, Korean musicians were, in general, represented as *enka* singers.[25] This may sound strange because in Korea, for example, Cho Yongpil is not only an *enka* singer but a national pop star who sings more sophisticated, westernized music ranging from rock 'n' roll and disco to soul music. In Japan, Cho failed to promote himself as a pop star and is still seen only as an *enka* singer.

Be that is it may, the example of Cho is suggestive in understanding the stereotypical image in Japan of Koreans and the apparently contradictory position that *enka* seems to create between Korea and Japan whereby Korean-styled music has been conventionally associated with *enka* in Japan. Yet the situation is not as paradoxical as it might seem since, although *enka* is also regarded, as suggested above, as the music of the Japanese spirit, the Japanese people look to their colonial "past" and find in it a lost history and a lost identity. As a result, Korea and the Korean Peninsula come to be regarded in a very nostalgic way. By listening to *enka* music from Korea, the Japanese are trying to remember something lost after World War II, what Paul Gilroy might identify as "postcolonial melancholy." Accordingly, people unconsciously try to hold on to what they have already lost, because they do not — and cannot — understand the fact of this loss.[26] This nostalgia is the other side of the coin of prejudice and discrimination against Korean people.

Rather than concentrate and maintain a binary opposition between Korea and Japan in our exploration of *enka*, I would like to develop a different approach. My proposal is to reconstruct a history of *enka* from a transnational perspective according to which this music is understood as a hybrid product and by which we can accept and even share each other's history or experience without any nostalgia or prejudice as though they are our own. Once we understand that even *enka* started as a transnational and hybrid category, we are able to identify different transnational musical trajectories: for example, Cho Yongpil comes to be positioned *in-between* Korea and Japan. Accordingly, the history of popular music is not divided by national borders because transnational music "production," as broadly conceived, precedes national production.[27]

Let us focus on the specific example of cultural exchange in the context of club/dance music, which has gained popularity among young people. This cultural form may not always be visible to the mainstream media, because it inhabits what some cultural commentators would understand as a subculture. Admittedly, the use of the prefix "sub" may look inappropriate today, since the distinction between "mainstream" and "subculture" — or more specifically, major and independent artists/producers — has been increasingly blurred in CD sales.

However, I still want to use the term "subculture" since it pointedly highlights culture which is not conveyed in conventional mass media such as television broadcasting. Instead, these subculture scenes are created by and through new kinds of what I call "people networks," which includes radio broadcasting, independent flyers and magazines, and the Internet. One of my key concerns is how subculture-styled networks become as influential and even as dominant as mainstream culture. In the field of club/dance music, cultural exchange is more active than ever. A considerable number of DJs are traveling all the time between cities such as Tokyo, Hong Kong, Taipei, and Seoul to play music at weekend parties.

One of the most interesting club/dance scenes is *Shibuya-kei* or "Shibuya-style," which is now used to describe a kind of fashionable dance music in the Kangnam area of Seoul.[28] *Shibuya-kei* includes not only underground club music but also some commercially successful groups such as Rollercoaster and the Clazziquai Project. Most of the tunes they have released take the form of well-arranged dance music influenced by different resources ranging from Latin, jazz, and techno, to electronica. It may be difficult to identify this musical style as especially Korean, partly because English lyrics are often used.

To understand why this scene is called *Shibuya-kei*, we need to look to the history of its emergence and development. Regarding the name, Shibuya refers to a district in Tokyo that is renowned for attracting many young people because of its concentration of fashionable buildings, boutiques, restaurants, bars, CD/record shops, and bookshops. Importantly, music in Shibuya is directly related to other cultural forms like fashion, clubs, and restaurants, with the result that the area name refers to a multifaceted cultural concept.

In the early 1990s, the hit charts in CD/record shops in Shibuya were clearly distinct from those in other districts, for example, Shinjuku, which is much more focused on (male-oriented) jazz and rock. In Shibuya, popular groups Pizzicato Five and Flippers Guitar created eclectically fashionable hybrid music influenced by different musical resources from around the world in a way that might be identified as postmodernist. Coined as the *Shibuya-kei* by the media, the cheerful and happy sound was enthusiastically accepted by Tokyo's urban trendsetters.

Shibuya-kei, in fact, coincided with and was influenced by the invention of a different musical category called "J-pop." According to Ugaya Hiromichi, author of *J-pop towa nanika* [*What is J-Pop?*], J-pop was created by FM radio station J-WAVE in the late 1980s when it was seeking to find a new musical category that distinguished Western-sounding Japanese music from exclusively Euro-American music. J-pop was the outcome, and importantly for our purposes, as we will see below, this music made in Japan that sounded like it came from abroad was central to defining the character of *Shibuya-kei* as non-national.[29] I would like to suggest that this character was only possible because of a particular historical and geographical conjuncture that occurred in Tokyo.

One of the most interesting features of *Shibuya-kei* is that it expressly showed "respect" for great musicians from the past and who came from all over the world. *Shibuya-kei* musicians gathered together all kinds of music, and thanks to the prosperity of the late 1980s "bubble economy" that helped make Shibuya area CD/music shops some of the most eclectic in the world in musical genre, they were able to listen to, quote, sample, mix, and dub this music, and eventually create a new hybrid music. In other words, *Shibuya-kei* music was a by-product of consumerism.

How was *Shibuya-kei* discovered in Seoul, Korea? What is the difference between *Shibuya-kei* in Tokyo and its counterpart in Seoul? Yi Ilhwan, a cable-radio producer, suggested that young musicians and directors in Korea, before they entered the music industry, were very much influenced by J-pop in the early 1990s, even though Japanese popular culture was officially banned at that time. They gathered information in a variety of ways, mainly through underground personalized human networks, which I mentioned above.[30] While Korean fans of Japanese music generally listened to more distinctively Japanese music, for example, *visual-kei* rock bands like X-JAPAN and L'arc

En Ciel,[31] people involved in the music industry such as Yi preferred more experimental and cutting-edge music like *Shibuya-kei*. They bought many Japanese CDs at shops including Hyungje, which secretly sold Japanese CDs in the Myŏngdong district, one of central Seoul's busiest commercial areas, or obtained them through those who traveled to Japan. In this way, people like Yi grew up with *Shibuya-kei* music, an influence that shaped their later involvement in the music industry in the 2000s, which included the creation in Seoul of their own *Shibuya-kei* style of music. Seoul *Shibuya-kei* must be understood as a product made by those who consumed *Shibuya-kei* in Tokyo in the 1990s.

New Hybridity through Collaborative Works in Contemporary Music

Building upon the original *Shibuya-kei* cultural exchanges of the 1990s, some musicians in Seoul have recently started to collaborate with *Shibuya-kei* musicians in Tokyo in order to explore a new type of dance music and to make live tours together.[32] For example, VERBAL, a member of one of the most famous rap groups in Japan called m-flo, participated as a DJ/mixer in an album produced by Korea-based Clazziquai. Japanese musicians and DJs often go to Korea to give live performances with *Shibuya-kei* musicians in Korea,[33] while the Clazziquai Project and others regularly go to Japan to organize live events and club parties. Korean club music is now played by FM radio stations and is popular among club people in Japan.

Crucially, when one considers the highly cosmopolitan backgrounds of these musicians, it becomes readily apparent that they cannot be characterized as exclusively Korean or Japanese. DJ Clazziquai, a central figure of the Clazziquai Project, is a Korean who used to live in Canada, while other Korean members of Clazziquai, Alex and Cristina, are still in Canada. Only vocalist Horan lives exclusively in Korea. DJ Clazziquai, moreover, began his career by uploading his works onto the Internet. Only when these tunes gained in popularity online was DJ Clazziquai invited to release his CD in Korea. The story of the Clazziquai Project provides us with a clear example of how digital technology and globalization influence music products and production.

VERBAL from m-flo, which includes Columbian-Japanese vocalist Lisa, similarly, shares in the cosmopolitan experience. Of *Zainichi* origins, VERBAL's real name is Ryu Yŏnggi. He was educated in an international school in Japan followed by study in the United States and is typical of the new generation of cosmopolitan *Zainichi* Korean residents in Japan. In a short autobiographical essay, VERBAL described his complicated identity as follows:

> Both of my parents are Korean. My father is a second-generation Korean and I can speak Korean a little, and I speak both Japanese and English because I was born and grew up in Japan. I have been wondering where my identity is. I always felt like I was homeless and did not have any place to fit in. I wanted to be able to speak Korean, but after a Korean accused me, asking, "why can't you speak Korean even though you are Korean?"' I gave up studying the Korean language. Then I went to the United States to study at a university where I felt I was neither a Korean nor an American, nor a Korean living in the United States: I was just a Korean born in Japan. English is the easiest language for me. I speak English when I have to discuss complicated issues. However, I am different from Koreans who grew up in the United States, since I was not brought up there. I look like a Japanese, behave like a Japanese, but I AM a Korean.[34]

This statement is revealing, since it demonstrates how individuals negotiate many different national backgrounds to create a new cosmopolitan identity that ultimately cannot be affiliated to any one nationality. What interests me is that VERBAL and DJ Clazziquai positively accept these complicated and fragmented identities and, in so doing, they create new flows of people, music, and culture. In the club music scene, experimental and hybrid music is being created through the collaborative works of different kinds of DJs and musicians from Korea, from Japan, and from anywhere.

Admittedly, one can easily criticize these musicians for their privileged upper-middle-class, bourgeois sentiment. However, there is a dark side to this cosmopolitanism that must be considered. For instance, VERBAL's essay opens with a personal story of discrimination when he was four years old: chased by junior high school students, he was called "*Chōsenjin! Chōsenjin!*" (*Chōsenjin* is discriminatory epithet for Korean people). Going to an international school and studying abroad not only represents his privilege, but it is also one of the few ways he could escape severe discrimination in his everyday life.

The new sounds of VERBAL's music demonstrate the significance of personalized human networks, and how national boundaries and discrimination can be overcome. They represent what might be identified as an alternative "Korean Wave," one that is created through the collaboration of *Zainichi* and others in Japan. It not only includes music but also the literature of Korean residents and Korean-Japanese in Japan. Highly acclaimed, this writing has played an important role in Japanese literature and, like VERBAL's music, it is a product of a hybrid culture of diaspora: a taste of Koreanness made in Japan.

Importantly, these new collaborations are not exclusively the products of the younger generation. Consider, for example, the trans-generational collaboration of m-flo and an older female singer, Wada Akiko, who is a television commentator and who is recognized as one of Japan's pioneer soul singers. She began her career as the "queen of rhythm and blues made in Japan" in the late 1960s and released several hit tunes throughout the 1970s and 1980s. Recently, however, her CD sales have dropped. In May 2005, m-flo, who respected Wada for her achievements as an originator of Japanese soul music, released a new collaborative CD club-music single with her called "m-flo loves Akiko WADA."[35]

The following August, Wada controversially came out in a weekly journal interview as a Korean resident in Japan.[36] Although the media had always implicitly suggested that she was Korean, she had never explicitly mentioned it herself. This fact demonstrates the strong sense of taboo that characterizes this issue in the media even today. Japanese celebrities of Korean origin are forced to hide their ethnic identity to protect themselves from racist attacks.

It is not clear how the collaboration with m-flo affected Wada's coming out. What strikes me is that a particular musical form — black music in this case — created both transnational and trans-generational networks. Although Wada has not released any hit songs recently, her music has been increasingly appreciated by young post-*Shibuya kei* DJs and musicians in Japan. For instance, Konishi Yasuharu released a compilation album, "Free Soul Akiko WADA," which featured remixed hit tunes of Wada's from the 1970s.[37] Central to Konishi's successful revival of Wada's former music in the form of contemporary dance/disco music was Japanese "black music," that is, music influenced by American rhythm and blues and soul.

Commercial popular and club music, hip-hop and black music, including soul, R&B, and disco sounds, are sometimes overlooked as merely *apolitical* cultural practices, especially when we compare them to so-called serious music such as rock, punk rock, jazz, and experimental music. The musicians discussed here — Wada Akiko, VERBAL, Konishi Yasuharu, DJ Clazziquai — are by and large regarded only as commercial musicians who are disinterested in politics, and to be certain, it is unlikely that they would make any political comment even if they were asked to do so. They would claim that they are creating neither Japanese nor Korean music, but only "good" music.

However, it would be wrong to regard them merely as *apolitical*. From a traditional Marxist perspective, their music is explained simplistically by and has seemingly been subsumed under the silencing hyper-consumer and profit-driven logic of late capitalism. But when the category of race and ethnicity is taken into account, one easily recognizes in popular music a form of politics that is not accounted for in the Marxist framework. For instance, according to some of the musicians I have surveyed here, there is a certain belief that money never discriminates according to race and ethnicity, a conviction that is incidentally shared in the culture of hip-hop people in the United States and Korean residents in Japan. In the same way, nationality does not matter in creating good music. This particular kind of universalism is activated by racial politics, which the old left has sometimes overlooked. That being said, one should not reduce cultural practices that flow through networks of different nationalities and ethnicities merely to politics in a narrow sense. As I have repeatedly suggested, these musicians only want to make good music, not political music. In other words, one must seek to understand how political effects may be generated in a seemingly *a*political hybrid culture.

Young Japanese musicians' "shyness" and their "aesthetic values" have often confused cultural analysts who have tended to look only at the surface of their activities. For example, Cornyetz regards Japanese hip-hop/black culture merely as a particular pattern of fetishized consumer culture while missing out most of the radical gestures that can be found in underground hip-hop/black culture in Japan.[38] In fact, since the early 1990s, Japanese hip-hop culture has developed its own political language inspired by American hip-hop.[39] *Shibuya-kei* musicians have recently been involved in politics in their own distinctive way. For instance, Konishi Yasuharu (Pizzicato Five) participated in the anti-Iraq War street demonstration as a DJ, and Ozawa Kenji is organizer of a series of anti-globalization workshops.[40] Nevertheless, these musicians are often reluctant to talk about their political activities in public, so much so that they even hide them. I would argue that it is important to find their different politics hidden under their surface.

Conclusion

The cultural trajectories I have drawn in this essay concern a history of transnational exchange in popular culture between Japan and Korea (and to some extent China, in Hattori's case). Although these stories are known in Japan, they are often marginalized from the history of Japanese popular music. My attempt has been to recognize and reconstruct new and alternative histories from a transnational perspective.

By way of conclusion, there are three points I would like to make clear. First, all popular music has political elements even though it may appear apolitical at first glance. Some of this music is so commercialized that it cannot be recognized as a form of political practice in the left-wing tradition of Marxism, which totalizes capitalism and reacts to it like an allergy. Nevertheless, there may often be tactical, if subtle, criticism in this music of a dominant nationalist ideology that sees national culture and even popular culture as though these were racially and ethnically homogeneous entities. The attempts of VERBAL and other *Shibuya-kei* musicians are good examples of this criticism.

Second, the creation of a space for transnational and/or regional East Asian cultural histories presents us with an urgent task. Although Japanese and Korean Cultural Studies have recently tried to look at transnational culture, most only deal with national cultural products such as Japanese TV dramas, the "Korean Wave," J-pop and K-pop. They may be consumed in transnational or trans-Asian markets, but their production is nationally branded. As a result, the development of transnational markets is easily associated with a new strategy of national branding of cultural exports, which are initiated by national governments and cultural industries. I propose two alternative understandings: (1) transnational cultural exchange, and in particular in East Asia, should be regarded as already interwoven in the processes of production as we have seen in the case of music; and (2) because production inevitably incorporates consumption, distribution, audiences, and fandom into its process, we need to recognize and examine the interaction among these different processes of production of popular culture.

Third, hybridity is not an effect of recent globalization. Rather, it constitutes the origins of all popular culture. Koga and Hattori's music exemplifies how hybridity makes a contribution to cultural creation at the very start and how, only later, is this hybrid music then adapted into and adopted as national culture. As I have stated, hybridity cannot always be politically critical. It can, indeed, form the basis of a new cosmopolitan commodity that serves global capitalism. The cultural politics of hybridity may not be able to solve all political, economic, and social problems. Yet, the idea of hybridity offers a different understanding of racial politics in everyday life and culture. I want to put forward the political possibilities of this new transnationalism that is grounded in the recognition of the importance of hybridity, because we are now facing an extremely difficult political situation due to increasingly chauvinistic nationalisms in East Asian countries as well as political and military tensions on the Korean Peninsula. My argument hopes to promote not only cultural exchanges such as those I have introduced here, but also intellectual exchanges which transcend nationally bounded Japanese/Korean Cultural Studies.

Notes

Introduction

1. Jim McGuigan, *Rethinking Cultural Policy* (Open University Press, 2004).
2. Itsunori Onodera, "Creative Industry: A Key to Solidify Bases for Regional Cooperation in Asia" (Speech to Asia Cultural Cooperation Forum, Hong Kong, November 15, 2004). http://www.mofa.go.jp/region/asia-paci/speech0411.html (accessed October 30, 2007).
3. Onodera (2004).
4. Hong Kong Trade Development Council, "Creative Industries in Hong Kong (September 5, 2002)," Hong Kong Trade Development Council. http://www.tdctrade.com/econforum/tdc/tdc020902.htm (accessed October 30, 2007).
5. Government Information Office, Republic of Taiwan, "Challenge 2008: The Six-Year National Development Plan (May 21, 2002)," Government Information Office, Republic of Taiwan. http://www.gio.gov.tw/taiwan-website/4-oa/20020521/2002052101.html (accessed October 30, 2007).
6. China Cultural Industries. "China Cultural Industries," China Cultural Industries. http://e.cnci.gov.cn/ (accessed October 30, 2007).
7. Ministry of Culture and Tourism, Korea, "Culture Industry Bureau," Ministry of Culture and Tourism. http://www.mct.go.kr/english/section/bureau/industry.jsp (accessed October 30, 2007).
8. Antoaneta Bezlova, "From Cultural Revolution to Culture Exports," *Global Policy Forum* (July 28, 2006). http://www.globalpolicy.org/globaliz/cultural/2006/0728china.htm (accessed October 30, 2007).

9. Department for Culture, Media and Sport, United Kingdom, *Staying Ahead: The Economic Performance of the UK's Creative Industries 2007*: 16. http://www.culture.gov.uk/NR/rdonlyres/6EF81987-5187-4B59-BE49-0DC140B99AB0/0/stayingahead_epukci_chp1.pdf (accessed October 30, 2007).
10. Bezlova (2006).
11. *People's Daily Online*, "Creative Industry: New Economic Engine in Beijing," Xinhua (December 15, 2006). http://english.people.com.cn/200612/15/eng20061215_332904.html (accessed October 30, 2007).
12. Hong Kong Trade Development Council 2002, Hong Kong Trade Development Council 2007.
13. JETRO, "Japan Regains its Position as Global Cultural and Trend Leader," *Focus: Gross National Cool* (February 14, 2004). www.kwrintl.com/library/2004/focus32.html (accessed October 30, 2007).
14. Onodera (2004).
15. Mark Berger, *The Battle for Asia: From Decolonization to Globalization* (London: RoutledgeCurzon, 2004), 191.
16. Fu-Kuo Liu, "A Critical Review of East and Northeast Asian Regionalism," in *Northeast Asian Regionalism: Learning from the European Experience*, eds. Christopher M. Dent and David W. F. Huang (London: RoutledgeCurzon, 2002), 20.
17. For further discussion, see Song Hwee Lim, "Is the Trans in Transnational the Trans in Transgender?" *New Cinemas* 5, no. 1 (2007): 39–52.
18. Chris Burgess, "The Asian Studies 'Crisis': Putting Cultural Studies into Asian Studies, and Asia into Cultural Studies," *The International Journal of Asian Studies* 1, no. 1 (2004): 121–36.
19. Mingbao Yue and Jon Goss (eds.), "De-Americanizing the Global: Cultural Studies Interventions from Asia and the Pacific," special issue of *Comparative American Studies* 3, no. 3 (2005).
20. Another crucial volume to consider in this regard would be Ackbar Abbas and John Nguyet Erni's *Internationalizing Cultural Studies: An Anthology* (Oxford: Blackwell, 2005). Noting in their introduction that "a certain parochialism continues to operate in Cultural Studies" they propose their collection of work as an "intervention . . . to clear a space . . . for pluralisation" (2).
21. Chen Kuan-Hsing, "Preface: The Trajectories Project," in *Trajectories: Inter-Asia Cultural Studies,* ed. Chen Kuan-Hsing (New York: Routledge, 1998), xv.
22. Founder of the program Stephen C.K. Chan reflects upon and interrogates the project in "Building Cultural Studies for Postcolonial Hong Kong: Aspects of the Postmodern Ruins in between Disciplines," *Critical Studies* 20 (2002): 217–31.
23. Inter-Asia Cultural Studies Journal. "Homepage." Inter-Asia Cultural Studies. http://www.inter-asia.org/journal/index.htm (accessed January 3, 2008).

24. James H. Mittelman, "Rethinking the New Regionalism in the Context of Globalization," *Global Governance* 2 (1996): 189.

25. Kōichi Iwabuchi, *Recentering Globalization: Popular Culture and Japanese Transnationalism* (Durham, NC: Duke Univesity Press, 2003), 46–7.

26. Jonathan Friedman, "Global Crises, the Struggle for Cultural Identity and Intellectual Porkbarrelling: Cosmopolitans versus Locals, Ethnics, and Nationals in an Era of De-hegemonisation," in *Debating Cultural Hybridity: Mutli-Cultural Identities and the Politics of Anti-Racism*, eds. Pnina Werbner and Tariq Modood (London: Zed Books Ltd., 1997), 73.

27. John Tomlinson, "Globalization and Cultural Identity," in *The Global Transformations Reader: An Introduction to the Globalization Debate*, 2nd edition, eds. David Held and Anthony McGrew (Cambridge: Polity Press, 2003), 271–2.

28. David Held and Anthony McGrew, "The Great Globalization Debate: An Introduction," in *The Global Transformations Reader: An Introduction to the Globalization Debate*, 2nd edition, eds. David Held and Anthony McGrew (Cambridge: Polity Press, 2003), 2.

29. Yeo Lay Hwee, "Realism and Reactive Regionalism: Where is East Asian Regionalism heading?" *UNISCI Discussion Papers* (May 2005): 5.

30. Robert Scollay, "Regional Trade Liberalization in East Asia and the Asia-Pacific: The Role of China" (Paper presented at 2004 Latin America/Caribbean and Asia/Pacific Economics and Business Association Annual Conference, Beijing, People's Republic of China, December 3–4, 2004). http://www.iadb.org/laeba/downloads/WP_35_2004.pdf (accessed October 30, 2007), 6; Berger (2004), 283. It should be noted that bilateralism more generally was, in fact, not novel. However, although flows of trade and capital had been structured bilaterally between the market-oriented economies of Northeast Asia since the 1950s, that bilateralism differed significantly from today's. Emerging out of Japan's piecemeal, nation-by-nation approach to reparations settlements following World War II, postwar- and Cold War-era bilateralism enforced asymmetrical power relations: Japan was positioned as the regional hub and economic leader while its developing neighbors, attached like spokes to the center, were recipients of Japanese foreign direct investment (Glenn Hook, "Japan and the Construction of Asia-Pacific," in *Regionalism and World Order*, eds. Andrew Gamble and Anthony Payne [Basingstoke: MacMillan Press, 1996], 174–84). Of course, this arrangement was central to America's Pacific security order to contain Soviet and Chinese communism. Centred on Japan as the capitalist engine, the coastal defense ring of nation-states stretching from Anchorage to Australia linked defense strategy to economic production. By contrast, bilateralism in the twenty-first century, while still in keeping with America's globalizing conception of a liberalized market-friendly, "low-risk Asia-Pacific," establishes exchange according to legally defined relationships of trade equality in a security

environment that is regionally polycentric rather than globally bipolar (Ngai-Ling Sum, "The NICs and Competing Strategies of East Asian Regionalism," in *Regionalism and World Order*, eds. Andrew Gamble and Anthony Payne [Basingstoke: MacMillan Press, 1996], 215). The United States is still omnipresent in the region, but a relative scaling back of its presence creates room for regional leaders like Japan, China, and, now possibly, ASEAN to modify Northeast Asian and Asian regional organization.

31. Yeo (2005), 1, 9.
32. Christopher M. Dent, "Introduction: Northeast Asia — A Region in Search of Regionalism?" in *Northeast Asian Regionalism: Learning from the European Experience*, eds. Christopher M. Dent and David W. F. Huang (London: RoutledgeCurzon, 2002), 4. See also, for example, Gilbert Rozman, *Northeast Asia's Stunted Regionalism: Bilateral Distrust in the Shadows of Globalization* (Cambridge: Cambridge University Press, 2004).
33. Richard Baldwin, "Prospects and Problems for East Asian Regionalism: A Comparison with Europe" (Paper presented to Research Institute of Economy, Trade and Industry, January 31, 2003). http://www.rieti.go.jp/en/events/bbl/03013101.html (accessed October 30, 2007). A comparison of East Asian regionalism with Europe can be found in Christopher M. Dent and David W. F. Huang's collected volume, *Northeast Asian Regionalism: Learning from the European Experience* (London: RoutledgeCurzon, 2002).
34. Yeo (2005), 9.
35. Sum (1996), 209.
36. The ASEAN nations affirmed in the Declaration of ASEAN Concord II (Bali Concord II) their commitment to establish by 2020 an Asian Economic Community. Its objectives, broadly defined as "economic integration," are to "create a stable, prosperous and highly competitive ASEAN economic region in which there is a free flow of goods, services, investment and a freer flow of capital, equitable economic development and reduced poverty and socio-economic disparities." ASEAN Homepage, "Declaration of ASEAN Concord II (Bali Concord II)," ASEAN. http://www.aseansec.org/15159.htm (accessed October 30, 2007).
37. Yeo (2005), 5.
38. Onodera (2004).
39. Onodera (2004).
40. McGuigan (2004), 35, 122, 130.
41. Government Information Office, Republic of Taiwan (2002).
42. Ministry of Education, Culture, Sports, Science, and Technology (MEXT), Japan, "*Bunka geijutsu shinkō kihonhō*" [Fundamental Law for the Promotion of Culture and Arts]. MEXT, http://www.mext.go.jp/a_menu/bunka/geijutsu/01.pdf (accessed October 30, 2007).
43. Ministry of Education, Culture, Sports, Science, and Technology (MEXT), Japan Homepage, "Culture: Toward the Realization of an Emotionally

Enriched Society Through Culture," MEXT. http://www.mext.go.jp/
english/org/f_culture.htm (accessed October 30, 2007). See also Agency
for Cultural Affairs, Japan, "Building a Society that Values Culture," Agency
for Cultural Affairs. http://www.bunka.go.jp/english/pdf/chapter_01.pdf
(accessed October 30, 2007).

44. Kevin Robins, "What in the World's Going on?' in *Production of Culture/
Cultures of Production,* ed. Paul du Gay (London: Sage Productions, 1997),
38.

45. Roland Kelts, *Japanamerica: How Japanese Pop Culture Has Invaded the U.S.*
(New York: Palgrave MacMillan, 2006), 180.

46. Douglas McGray, "Japan's Gross National Cool," *Foreign Policy* (May/June
2002): 44–54.

47. McGray (2002), 9.

48. Kelts (2006), 5.

49. McGray (2002), 12.

50. MEXT "Culture."

51. "Japan Looks to Play Leading Role in Regional Trade," *Daily Yomiuri,*
September 15, 2006.

52. Robins (1997), 18.

53. Friedman (1997), 81.

54. Yeo (2005), 8.

55. Hook (1996), 200.

56. Wang Xiaoming, "A Manifesto for Cultural Studies," trans. Robyn Visser,
in *One China, Many Paths,* ed. Chaohua Wang (London: Verso, 2003), 279.

57. Wang Xiaoming (2003), 287.

58. Chen Kuan-Hsing, "Why Is 'Great Reconciliation' Impossible? De-Cold
War, Decolonization, or Modernity and Its Tears," Parts I and II, *Inter-Asia
Cultural Studies* 3, no. 1 & 2 (2002): 77–99, 235–51.

59. Mark Harrison, *Legitimacy, Meaning and Knowledge in the Making of Taiwanese
Identity* (London: Palgrave MacMillan, 2006).

60. Tsutomu Sugiura, "From Capitalism to Culturalism" (Speech presented at
OECD Forum 2005, Fuelling the Future: Security, Stability, Development
— Creative Societies, Dynamic Economies, May 2–3, 2005). http://
www.oecd.org/dataoecd/42/61/34825496.pdf (accessed October 30, 2007).

Chapter 1   Reconsidering East Asian Connectivity and the Usefulness of Media and Cultural Studies

1. Larry Grossberg, "Does Cultural Studies Have Futures? Should It? (Or
What's the Matter with New York)," *Cultural Studies* 20, no.1 (2006): 17.

2. See Joseph Tobin (ed.), *Pikachu's Global Adventure: The Rise and Fall of
Pokemon* (Durham, NC: Duke University Press, 2004).

3. Ulf Hannerz, *Transnational Connections: Culture, People, Places* (London: Routledge, 1996).

4. Stuart Hall, "The Local and the Global: Globalization and Ethnicity," in *Culture, Globalization, and the World-System: Contemporary Conditions for the Representation of Identity*, ed. Anthony King (London: Macmillan, 1991), 28.

5. Gregory Beals and Kevin Platt, "The Birth of Asiawood," *Newsweek* (May 21, 2001).

6. Grossberg (2006).

7. Toby Miller, *Cultural Citizenship: Cosmopolitanism, Consumerism, and Television in a Neoliberal Age* (Philadelphia: Temple University Press, 2007), 11.

8. See, for example, Kōichi Iwabuchi, *Recentering Globalization: Popular Culture and Japanese Transnationalism* (Durham, NC: Duke University Press, 2002); Kōichi Iwabuchi, ed., *Feeling Asian Modernities: Transnational Consumption of Japanese TV Dramas* (Hong Kong: Hong Kong University Press, 2004); Kōichi Iwabuchi, "When Korean Wave Meets Resident Koreans in Japan," in *East Asian Pop Culture: Approaching the Korean Wave*, eds. Chua Beng-Huat and K. Iwabuchi (Hong Kong: Hong Kong University Press, 2008); Youna Kim, "Experiencing Globalization: Global TV, Reflexivity and the Lives of Young Korean Women," *International Journal of Cultural Studies* 8, no. 4 (2005): 445–63; and Yoshitaka Mōri, ed., *Nisshiki Hanryū: "Fuyu no sonata" to nikkan taishū bunka no genzai* (Korean Wave Japanese Style: The TV-Drama "Winter Sonata" and the Present State of Japanese-Korean Popular Culture) (Tokyo: Serika Shobō, 2004).

9. Sonia Livingstone, ed., *Audiences and Publics: When Cultural Engagement Matters for the Public Sphere* (Bristol: Intellect, 2005).

10. For more detailed discussion, see Iwabuchi, 2002.

11. Joshua Meyrowitz, *No Sense of Place: The Impact of Electronic Media on Social Behaviour* (Oxford: Oxford University Press, 1985).

12. Paul Hirst and Grahame Thompson, *Globalization in Question: The International Economy and the Possibilities of Governance* (Cambridge: Polity Press, 1996).

13. Annabelle Sreberny-Mohammadi, "The Global and the Local in International Communicationsm," in *Mass Media and Society*, eds. James Curran and Michael Gurevitch (London: Edward Arnold, 1991), 118–38.

14. George Yúdice, *The Expediency of Culture: Uses of Culture in the Global Era.* (Durham, NC: Duke University Press, 2003).

15. Toby Miller and Marie Claire Leger, "Runaway Production, Runaway Consumption, Runaway Citizenship: The New International Division of Cultural Labor," *Emergences* 11, no. 1 (2001): 89–115.

16. Ien Ang, "Who Needs Cultural Research?" in *Cultural Studies and Practical Politics: Theory, Coalition Building, and Social Activism*, ed. Pepi Leystina (New York: Blackwell, 2004), 477–83.

17. Ang (2005), 482.

18. Simon During, *Cultural Studies: A Critical Introduction* (New York: Routledge, 2004), 77.
19. Edward Said, *Representations of the Intellectual* (New York: Pantheon Books, 1994).
20. Raymond Williams, "The Idea of a Common Culture," in *Resources of Hope: Culture, Democracy, Socialism,* ed. Robin Gable (London: Verso, 1989), p. 36.

Chapter 2   Asian Cultural Studies: Recapturing the Encounter with the Heterogeneous in Cultural Studies

1. Raymond Schwab, *The Oriental Renaissance: Europe's Rediscovery of India and the East, 1680–1880,* trans. Gene Patterson-Black and Victor Reinking (New York: Columbia University Press, 1986), 24.
2. I have little space to explain the detail of this relationship here, but for those interested, see Michael Dutton, "Lead Us Not Into Translation: Notes Toward a Theoretical Foundation for Asian Studies," *Nepantla: Views for South* 3, no. 3 (2002): 495–537; or Michael Dutton, "The Trick of Words: Asian Studies, Translation, and the Problems of Knowledge," in *Politics of Method in the Human Sciences: Positivism and Its Epistemological Others,* ed. George Steinmetz (Durham, NC: Duke University Press, 2005), 89–125.
3. On the lack of any direct critical theory legacy upon British cultural studies, see Kate Soper, "Despairing of Happiness: The Redeeming Dialectic of Critical Theory," *New Formations* no. 38 (1999): 141–53.
4. On the question of vocabulary and the favorite son status of Benjamin, see Esther Leslie, "Space and West End Girls: Walter Benjamin versus Cultural Studies," *New Formations* no. 38 (1999): 110–24. Indeed, as Leslie points, Benjamin all too often plays good cop to Adorno's bad cop in that ongoing soapie called cultural studies.
5. Siegfried Kracauer, *The Mass Ornament: Weimar Essays,* trans. & ed. Thomas Y. Levin (Cambridge, MA: Harvard University Press, 1995), 260.
6. It was believed, for example, that Hitler had used the radio in his rise to power when in fact, as Lazarsfeld himself shows, his acquisition of stations happened quite late. See Simon L. Garfield, "Radio Research, McCarthyism and Paul F. Lazarsfeld" (Ph.D. thesis, MIT Political Science), 1987, 26. Cited online at http://www.simson.net/clips/academic/pfl_thesis_ocr.pdf (accessed January 11, 2007). In *Radio and the Printed Page* (New York: Duall, Sloane and Pierce, 1940), 5, Lazarsfeld introduced the concept of "serious radio listening," and asked the question "To what extent has radio increased, or can radio increase, the scope of serious responses beyond the scope so far achieved by print?"
7. Hynek Jerabek, "Paul Lazarsfeld — The Founder of Modern Empirical Sociology: A Research Biography," *International Journal of Public Opinion Research* 13, no. 3 (2001): 229.

8. Rolf Wiggershaus, *Theodor W. Adorno* (Munich: C.H. Beck, 1998), 242.
9. Jerabek, 239.
10. Cited in Stefan Müller-Doohm, *Adorno: A Biography*, trans. Rodney Livingstone (Cambridge: Polity Press, 2005), 247.
11. Georges Bataille, "The Psychological Structure of Fascism," *New German Critique* no. 16 (1979): 69.
12. Edward Said, *Orientalism* (London: Penguin, 1978), frontispiece quote drawn from Karl Marx's essay, "18th Broodmare of Louis Bonaparte," in K. Marx and F. Engels, *Selected Works* (Moscow: Progress publishers, 1950), volume I, 303.
13. Max Horkheimer and Theodor W. Adorno, *Dialectic of Enlightenment*, trans. John Cumming (London: Continuum, 1976); Franz Neumann, *Behemoth: The Structure and Practice of National Socialism, 1933–1944* (New York: Oxford University Press, 1942).
14. By 1943, six members of the institute were in the employ of the US government's security wing. Neumann was deputy chief of the European Section of OSS, and Marcuse was a senior analyst, while Kirchheimer and Gurland were both employed there. Lowenthal was a consultant at the Office of War Information, while Pollock was a consultant with the Justice Department. Only Adorno and Horkheimer (who were both on the West Coast anyway) were not employed in this fashion.
15. William E. Scheuerman, *Between the Norm and the Exception: The Frankfurt School and the Rule of Law* (Cambridge, MA: MIT Press, 1994), 123.
16. I am thinking here of Robert Hall's 1948 report on Area Studies, which is arguably the beginning of Asian Area Studies: *Area Studies: With Special Reference to Their Implications for Research in the Social Sciences* (New York: Committee on World Area Research Program, Social Science Research Council).
17. Tani E. Barlow, "~~Colonialism~~'s Career in Postwar China Studies," in *Formations of Colonial Modernity in East Asia*, ed. Tani E. Barlow (Durham, NC: Duke University Press, 1997), 373.

Chapter 3   How to Speak about Oneself: Theory and Identity in Taiwan

1. Kiansing Ko, "On the Definition of the Formosan," *Independent Formosa* 4, no. 4 (August 1965): 10.
2. Helen Lee, *Gandong 228* (*Touching 228*), DVD (Taiwan National Alliance, 2004).
3. Stephan Feuchtwang, "The Chinese Race-nation," *Anthropology Today* 9, no. 1. (Feb. 1993): 14.
4. This comment is taken from Lo Ming-Cheng's Foucauldian interpretation of Japanese colonialism in Taiwan. See Ming-cheng Lo, *Doctors within Borders:*

Profession, Ethnicity, and Modernity in Colonial Taiwan (Berkeley: University of California Press, 2002), 43.

5. On February 28, 1947, what began as a local riot spiraled into an island-wide uprising against Chinese Nationalist rule of Taiwan. Protests, both violent and institutional, demanded redress for corruption, economic mismanagement, and social engineering, in which the KMT attempted to "re-Sinicize" the Taiwanese after fifty years as a colony of Japan. In March and April of 1947, the uprising was systematically crushed by troops brought from mainland China, killing 20,000 or more people.

6. After forgoing support for the Nationalists against the Communists in January 1950, the Truman administration reversed its position and made the decision to support Taiwan two days after North Korea invaded South Korea on June 27, 1950.

7. For a conservative reading of Taiwan's post-WWII development, see Ezra F. Vogel, *The Four Little Dragons* (Cambridge, MA: Harvard University Press, 1991).

8. See, for example, Joshua Liao, *Formosa Speaks* (Hong Kong: Graphic Press, 1950), and Thomas Liao, *Inside Formosa: Formosans vs. Chinese since 1945* (Tokyo: Publisher unknown, 1956).

9. Liau Kianliong, "Why Formosa Wants Independence," *Formosa Quarterly* 1, no. 1, (July 1962): 6.

10. *Benshengren* or "native Taiwanese" refers to the Taiwanese who can trace their migration to the island from regions of Fujian on mainland China over several generations from the seventeenth to the nineteenth centuries; *waishengren* or "mainlanders" refers to the post-1949 Nationalist refugees and their descendants.

11. Cited in Christine Louise Lin, *The Presbyterian Church in Taiwan and the Advocacy of Local Autonomy*, Sino-Platonic papers, no. 92 (Philadelphia: Dept. of Asian and Middle Eastern Studies, University of Pennsylvania, 1999), 95.

12. Jing Wang, "Taiwan Hsiang t'u literature: Perspectives in the evolution of a literary movement," in *Chinese Fiction from Taiwan: Critical Perspectives*, ed. Jeannette L. Faurot (Bloomington: Indiana University Press, 1980), 49.

13. For a detailed discussion on Taiwanese nativist literature, see Sung-sheng Yvonne Chang, *Modernism and the Nativist: Resistance Contemporary Chinese Fiction from Taiwan* (Durham, NC: Duke University Press, 1993). For an example of the critical tenor of the debate in Taiwan over nativist literature in the 1970s, see Yan Yuanshu, "Dangqian Zhongguo wenxue wenti" (The problems of contemporary Chinese literature), in *Xiangtu wenxue taolun ji* (Discussing Nativist Literature), ed. Wei Tiancong (Taipei: Wei Tiancong, 1978): 763–6.

14. An example of this phrase occurs at the conclusion of the national day speech given by Chiang Kai-shek on the fiftieth anniversary of the founding of the Republic of China. See "Zongtong zui mian quan guo tongbao jizhi

chenglie fu guo jiu min" (The president resolutely urges compatriots of the whole nation to continue towards recovering the nation and saving the people), *Lianhe bao (United Daily News)*, January 1, 1961.

15. "Zongtong zhongshen fangong fuguo juexin" (The president resolutely reiterates the determination to fight communism and recover the mainland), *Zili Wanbao (Independent Evening Post)*, January 1, 1979.

16. "Zongtong zhongshen fangong fuguo juexin," *Zili Wanbao* (1979).

17. "'Taidu' zai Riben gaojifenzi Qiu Yonghan zuo fanzheng gui guo" (The leading "Taiwanese Independence" activist in Japan Qiu Yonghan repudiates his cause and returns to the nation), *Lianhe Bao (United Daily News)*, April 3, 1972.

18. Examples of this kind of appeal following the end of martial law include pieces by the Hakka writer Li Chiao and the well-known anthropologist Chang Mao-kuei. Both called for the renaming of the Republic of China as the Republic of Taiwan, in order to establish a unifying identity consciousness under the name "Taiwan," which would overcome the social division created by martial law and establish an ontologically coherent foundation for national development. See Chang Mao-kuei, "Taidu shi wei toushen guoji de 'zhengming' yundong" (Taiwanese independence means joining in the international movement for the 'rectification of names'), *Zili Wanbao (Independent Evening Post)* April 1, 1992, and Li Chiao, "Taiwan guo gong he shenme?" (What does a Taiwanese nation bring together?), *Zili Wanbao (Independent Evening Post)*, December 12, 1991.

19. Chen Yongxing, "Zou chu lishi yinying jianli hu ai shehui" (Stepping out of history's shadow to build a society of mutual love), *Zili Wanbao (Independent Evening Post)*, February 28, 1988.

20. Chen (1988).

21. "356 Yi wenren gong kai xin yu Bian 'zi ai yin tui'" (356 artists' open letter appeals to A-Bian to "show self-respect and resign"), *Lianhe Bao (United Daily News)*, August 25, 2006.

22. Ackbar Abbas, *Hong Kong: Culture and the Politics of Disappearance* (Hong Kong: Hong Kong University Press, 1997): 25–6.

23. "Huanying Guomindang xinsheng dai zai di hua" (Welcoming the rebirth of the sense of place of the KMT), *Ziyou Shibao (Liberty Times)*, May 4, 2004.

24. Democratic Progressive Party, "Zuqun duoyuan guojia yi ti jueyiwen" (Resolution on ethnic pluralism and national unity). http://www.dpp.org.tw/history/pub/LIT_6.asp?ctyp=LITERATURE&catid=1742, (accessed September 10, 2006).

25. See one version of this argument about the category of gender in Elspeth Probyn, *Sexing the Self: Gendered Positions in Cultural Studies* (London and New York: Routledge, 1993), 1–7.

26. Ping-hui Liao, "The Case of Emergent Cultural Criticism in Taiwan's Newspaper Literary Supplements: Global/Local Dialectics in Contemporary

Taiwanese Public Culture," in *Global/Local: Cultural Production and the Transnational Imaginary*, eds. Rob Wilson and Wimal Dissanayake (Durham, NC: Duke University Press, 1996), 338.

27. Liao (1996), 339.
28. Liao (1996), 340.
29. Stuart Hall, "Cultural Studies and its Theoretical Legacies," in *Cultural Studies*, eds. Lawrence Grossberg, Cary Nelson, and Paula Treichler (New York: Routledge, 1992), 278.
30. "Duihua, jiaotong, fansi, Sayide tanlun saiyide" (Dialogue, communication, remembrance: Said on Said), *Ziyou Shibao (Liberty Times)*, February 16, 2005.
31. Tsai Ing-wen, "Rentong yu zhengzi: zhong lilunxing zhi fansheng" (Identity and politics: A theoretical reflection), *Zhengzhi kexue luncong (Political Science Review)* 8 (June 1997): 51.
32. Tsai (1997), 53.
33. Homi K. Bhabha, "DissemiNation: Time, Narrative, and the Margins of the Modern Nation," in *Nation and Narration*, ed. Homi K. Bhabha (London: Routledge, 1990), 297.
34. Liao (1996), 342.
35. Yin Zhangyi, "Taiwan yishi shifen" (Analyzing Taiwan consciousness), *Zhongguo Luntan (China Tribune)* 25, no. 1 (October 10, 1987): 95–114.
36. "Xinpian 'Renshi Taiwan' jiaokeshu yinqi de zhengyi" (The controversy over the new "Understanding Taiwan" textbooks), *Lianhe Bao (United Daily News)*, June 13, 1997.
37. Myra Lu, "President Adds Weight to Chip Foundry Debate," *Taipei Journal* 19, no. 11 (March 22, 2002): 15.
38. Wang Meishu, "Xie gei qian lü xuezhe pengyoumen" (A note to Light Green scholarly friends), *Ziyou Shibao (Liberty Times)*, June 15, 2006.
39. "Minzhu guan jie pai Bian chi jiu wei quan huohai" (President Chen condemns the damage of authoritarianism at the inauguration of the National Taiwan Democracy Memorial Hall), *Ziyou Shibao (Liberty Times)*, May 20, 2007.
40. Chen Yi-shen, "Zhongzheng miao de zhuangxing shunxu" (Taking steps to remake the Chiang Kai-shek Memorial), *Ziyou Shibao (Liberty Times)*, March 16, 2007.
41. Liao (1996), 344.
42. Lin Yi-hsiung, *Xiwang you yi tian* (I hope there comes a day) (Taipei: Yuwangshe, 1995), 33.
43. Judith Butler, *Gender Trouble* (London: Routledge, 1999), 24.
44. Kuan-hsing Chen, "The Decolonization Question," in *Trajectories: Inter-Asian Cultural Studies,* ed. Chen Kuan-hsing (London: Routledge, 1998), 4.
45. Chang (1993), 149.
46. Li Xiaofeng, *Taiwan, wode xuanze!* (Taiwan, my choice!) (Taipei: Yushanshe chuban, 1995): 1.

47. Chen (1998), 16.
48. Chiu Kui-fen, "'Houzhimin' de Taiwan yanyi" (The post-colonial logic of Taiwan), in *Wenhua yanjiu zai Taiwan* (*Cultural Studies in Taiwan*), ed. Chen Kuan-hsing (Taipei: Juliu Tushu, 2000), 292.
49. Chen (1998), 20.
50. Ping-hui Liao, *Ling lei xiandai qing* (*Alternative Modernities*) (Taipei: Yunchen Wenhua, 2001): 159–61.
51. Thomas B. Gold, "Taiwan Society at the Fin de Siècle," *China Quarterly*, 148, Special Issue: Contemporary Taiwan (December 1996): 1104.

Chapter 4 Placing South Korean Cinema into the Pusan International Film Festival: Programming Strategy in the Global/Local Context

1. Mitsuhiro Yoshimoto, "National/International/Transnational: The Concept of Trans-Asian Cinema and Cultural Politics of Film Criticism," in *The First Jeonju International Film Festival Symposium,* ed. Kim Soyoung (Chŏnju: JIFF, 2000), 61.
2. *Regional* specifically indicates the East Asian region: Korea, Japan, Taiwan, the People's Republic of China, and Hong Kong. I often interchange the term *national* with *local* in order to contrast the *regional* with the *global*.
3. *Korean cinema* designates films made in South Korea, not North Korea.
4. Jeeyoung Shin, "Globalization and New Korean Cinema," in *New Korean Cinema*, eds. Chi-Yun Shin and Julian Stringer (Edinburgh: Edinburgh University Press, 2005), 54–5; Darcy Paquet, "The Korean Film Industry: 1992 to the Present," in *New Korean Cinema*, eds. Chi-Yun Shin and Julian Stringer (Edinburgh: Edinburgh University Press, 2005), 49.
5. The term (*Hanliu* in Chinese and *Hanryū* in Japanese) indicates the sudden influx of Korean popular culture in and continuing since the late 1990s, ranging from television dramas to popular music and films throughout East Asia, including Hong Kong, Taiwan, Singapore, Vietnam, Japan, as well as mainland China.
6. The Screen Quota system is a kind of trade barrier to protect local films. The strictly enforced system, introduced in 1966, requires Korean cinemas to screen local films for between 106 and 146 days each year. It is widely presumed that the Screen Quota system has helped local films to secure screen space and to survive in the highly competitive global film industry. However, this system has been challenged by Hollywood and put under pressure by the dramatic growth of the local film industry since the late 1990s. As a result, controversy has emerged, some advocating a reduction of the quota or the abrogation of the entire system. Korean filmmakers have vigorously fought to protect the system through continuous protest against its abolition. Recently, however, as a result of the Free Trade Agreement

between Korea and the United States on April 2, 2007, the Screen Quota has been reduced from 146 to 73 days.

7. Japanese cultural products, including films, songs, and TV programs, were prohibited following the founding of the Republic of Korea in 1948.

8. Kim Kidŏk, *Coast Guard (Haeansŏn)*, LJ Film, 2002; Pae Ch'angho, *Last Witness (Hŭksusŏn)*, Taewon Entertainment, 2001; and Yi Ch'angdong, *Peppermint Candy (Pakha satang)*, East Film Company, 1999. Korean is transcribed according to the McCune-Reischauer system. The transcription of names often differs in *The Korean Film Database Book* published by the Korean Film Council in 2006 and upon which this research draws. These alternative transcriptions are given on first occurrence in brackets.

9. Liz Czach, "Film Festivals, Programming, and the Building of a National Cinema," *The Moving Image* 4, no. 1 (2004): 76–88. Czach succinctly explores the relationship between the programming process in the Toronto Film Festival and Canadian film industry.

10. Since the first running of the festival, however, these categories have changed with the addition of two new sections: "Open Cinema" added in 1997 and "Critic's Choice" introduced in 2002.

11. Film Director and Director of Busan Film Commission Park Kwang-su, interview by author, January 6, 2006, Seoul.

12. Pusan City's decision to support PIFF was made quite suddenly in 1996 and only a few months before the festival was launched on September 13, 1996. On February 2, 1996, the local newspaper *Kukche Shinmun* reported "Pusan city has suddenly abandoned its long neglect of PIFF and decided to support it, so it can open the event this year to promote the 2002 Asian Games" (Jin-woo Lee, "PIFF Opens in September," *Kukche Shinmun*, February 2, 1996).

13. Figures taken from annual program booklets (1996 to 2005) of the Pusan International Film Festival.

14. Yong-kwan Lee, "Opening Film," in The 4th Pusan International Film Festival, Programme Booklet, 1999, 21.

15. Dong-jin Lee, "To Get the Innocent Dream Back, 'About-turn'," *Chosŏn Ilbo* (October 15, 1999).

16. The Director's Fortnight is an independent section running alongside the Festival de Cannes and organized by the French Directors Society.

17. In addition to its box-office takings, over 300,000 viewed it in Seoul alone (available at www.kofic.or.kr/statistics [accessed June 18, 2007]). A club called "People Who love *Peppermint Candy*" was created by fans who organized a New Year Special Screening which has subsequently taken place every New Year's Day. Although this was initiated as a part of a PR event, it continues until the present, and considerable numbers participate (East Film Company, "*Peppermint Candy* Homepage." http://www.peppermintcandy.co.kr/ (accessed December 13, 2007).

18. Yong-Kwan Lee, interview by author, January 4, 2006, Seoul.

19. David Martin-Jones, *Deleuze, Cinema and National Identity* (Edinburgh: Edinburgh University Press, 2006), 205–19.

20. Moon-yung Hur, "Opening Film," *The 7th Pusan International Film Festival Catalogue*, 2002.

21. Hye-jin Jung, "*The Lasts Witness* Fails to Deliver," *Korea Times* (November 17, 2001).

22. Frank Segers, "Hae an-seon" (*The Coast Guard*), *Moving Pictures* (November 2002).

23. Kim Sugyŏng, "Haeansŏn" (*The Coast Guard*), *Dong-A Ilbo* (November 21, 2002). http://www.donga.com/fbin/output?code=Q__&n=200211210301 (accessed December 13, 2007).

24. Tony Rayns, "Sexual Terrorism: The Strange Case of Kim Ki-duk," *Film Comment* November–December (2004): 51. Rayns coins the expression "sexual terrorism" to characterize the striking scene of fishhooks piercing a woman's vagina and the protagonist's throat in Kim's *The Isle* (1999).

25. In Venice, *The Isle* (1999) and *Unknown Address* (2001) were nominated in competition. *3-Iron* (2004) received the Best Director Award while *Bad Guy* (2002) was shown in competition. *Samaritan Girl* (2003) received the Best Director Award in Berlin.

26. Rayns (2004), 50.

27. Chris Berry, "'What's Big about the Big Film?': 'De-Westernizing' the Blockbuster in Korea and China," in *Movie Blockbusters*, ed. Julian Stringer (London: Routledge, 2003), 217–29.

28. Yunmo Yang, "Olhae pŭrogŭraeming" (This Year's Programming), *Pusan Ilbo* (November 17, 2001).

29. Ŭnju Park, "Hŭksusŏn" (The Last Witness), *Han'guk Ilbo* (November 13, 2001).

30. Darcy Paquet, "The Korean Film Industry: 1992 to the Present," in *New Korean Cinema*, eds. Shin Chi-Yun and Julian Stringer (Edinburgh: Edinburgh University Press, 2005), 44–6.

31. *Shiri* was released in February 1999 and the new edited director's cut was screened in the "Open Cinema" section in the same year at the 4th PIFF.

32. Paquet (2005), 43–9.

33. David Martin-Jones (2006) also points out the importance of UniKorea in his analysis of *Peppermint Candy*.

34. "Mainstream" refers to films intentionally designed to be box-office hits, such as *The Ginkgo Bed* (1996), *The Letter* (1997), *A Promise* (1998), and *Shiri* (1999). Korean cinema entered a boom period with the unprecedented box-office success of many of its films in and since the late 1990s. The key factors explaining this rapid growth are new sources of film finance, increased standards of film production, and governmental film policy prompted by Korean globalization. For an overview of this analysis, see Paquet (2005).

35. UniKorea Culture & Art Investment Co. Ltd. was launched in January 1999 with an initial operating budget of 3 billion won (US$2.5 million). The owner of the company is Yeom Tae-soon, who runs an enterprise called *Aizim*, a fashion brand for young consumers. Its key members are Lee Chang-dong, Moon Sung-keun, and Myung Kae-nam. UniKorea and Aizim were key sponsors of PIFF in 1999.
36. Martin-Jones (2006), 208.
37. The Korean Film Council was established on May 28, 1999, when KMPPC was restructured by the new government of President Kim Dae-jung (1998–2003). KMPPC was founded on April 3, 1973, under the military regime of President Park Chung-hee. Park's government (1961–79) enforced a strict political and ideological agenda that stifled the film industry. For example, KMPPC enacted the Motion Picture Law and frequently revised it to keep the film industry under tight control. For more information, see Korean Film Council's official website: www. koreanfilm.or.kr. and Paquet 2005, 32–50.
38. Following the revision of the Film Promotion Law in 1999, the reform of film policy by KOFIC has changed the structure of the industry. For example, KOFIC has supported "art-house" cinema as well as commercial cinema and tried to restructure the distribution system in order to promote "cultural diversity."
39. Jonathan Watts, "Japan-Korea Team at Pusan," *Hollywood Reporter* (September 17–19, 1999).
40. Czach (2004), 82.
41. Stephen Cremin, "Pucheon Set to Fill Regional Niche," *Hankyureh 21* (August 2, 2006). http://english.hani.co.kr/arti/english_edition/e_entertainment/146041.html (accessed December 13, 2007).
42. Derek Elley, "Pusan Pumps Korean Pic Profile," *Variety* (November 1–7, 1999). However, in response to those criticisms, PIFF in 2004 established an extra section called "Industry Screening" for the guests who attend the PPP to view more Korean films.
43. Su-yun Kim, "British Film Critics Pleased with Improved Facilities at PIFF," *Korea Times* (October 22, 1999).
44. Cremin (2006).
45. Dina Iordanova, *Cinema of the Other Europe: The Industry and Artistry of East Central European Film* (London: Wallflower Press, 2003), 30.
46. Hong Kong International Film Festival Coordinator, Foreword to *The 10th Hong Kong International Film Festival Programme* (Hong Kong: The Urban Council, 1986), 8.
47. Hong Kong Critics Society ed., *A Century of Chinese Cinema: Look Back in Glory: The 25th Hong Kong International Film Festival* (Hong Kong: Hong Kong Film Archive and Leisure and Cultural Services Department, 2001).

48. Soyoung Kim, "Cine-mania or Cinephilia: Film Festivals and the Identity Question," *UTS Review (Cultural Studies Review)* 4, no. 2. (1998): 183.
49. Thomas Elsaesser, *European Cinema: Face to Face with Hollywood* (Amsterdam: Amsterdam University Press, 2005), 85.
50. Derek Elley, "Savvy Moves Boost Pusan Fest Fortunes," *Variety* (October 8, 2006).

Chapter 5   Global America? American–Japanese Film Co-productions from *Shogun* (1980) to *Lost in Translation* (2003)

1. Ulrich Beck, "Cosmopolitan Society and Its Enemies," *Theory, Culture and Society* 19, nos. 1–2 (2002): 22.
2. Pheng Cheah, "Cosmopolitanism," *Theory, Culture and Society* 23, nos. 1–2 (2006): 495.
3. Toby Miller, Nitin Govil, John McMurria, and Richard Maxwell, *Global Hollywood* (London: BFI publishing, 2001), 216.
4. Ben Goldsmith and Tom O'Regan, *The Film Studio: Film Production in Global Economy* (Lanham, MD: Rowan & Littlefield, 2005), xii.
5. For example, the cinematographer of *Shogun*, Andrew Laszlo, stated that "it was not a little culture shock but it was a huge surprise . . . the camera and lighting equipment in Japan was at least twenty years behind what we have in the States," from "The Making of *Shogun*," Disk 5 bonus feature, James Clavell's *Shogun*, directed by Jerry London, DVD box set (Paramount Pictures, 2004).
6. Ulrich Beck, *Cosmopolitan Vision* (London: Polity Press, 2006), 19.
7. Ulrich Beck, quoted in Terhi Rantanen, "Cosmopolitanization — now! An Interview with Ulrich Beck," *Global Media and Communication* 1, no. 3 (2005): 250.
8. Nicholas Rose, *Power of Freedom: Reframing Political Thought* (Cambridge: Cambridge University Press, 1999), 137.
9. Gillian Ursell, "Television Production: Issues of Exploitation, Commodification and Subjectivity in UK Television Labour Markets," *Media, Culture & Society* 22, no. 6 (2000): 810.
10. Leslie Sklair, *The Transnational Capitalist Class* (Oxford: Blackwell, 2002).
11. Leslie Sklair, "The Transnational Capitalist Class and the Discourse of Globalization," *Cambridge Review of International Affairs* 14, no. 1 (2000): 4.
12. Val Burris, "Review: *The Transnational Capitalist Class*," *Contemporary Sociology* 31, no. 4 (2002): 416
13. Pheng Cheah, "Cosmopolitical — Today" in *Cosmopolitics: Thinking and Feeling Beyond the Nation*, eds. Bruce Robbins and Pheng Cheah (Minneapolis: University of Minnesota Press, 1998), 26.

14. I was the managing director of Chimera Films and Communications from 1996 to 2005. The company provided services for Japanese film companies who came to shoot in Europe.

15. Pertti Alasuutari, *Researching Culture: Qualitative Method and Cultural Studies* (Thousand Oaks, CA: Sage, 1995), 63.

16. Pertti Alasuutari, p. 25.

17. Pertti Alasuutari, p. 65.

18. Pertti Alasuutari, p. 69.

19. Most film historians agree that the 1950s was the golden age of Japanese cinema. See, for example, Tanaka Jun'ichirō, *Nihon eiga hattatsu-shi* Vol. 4: *shijō saikō no eiga jidai* (The history of the development of Japanese cinema, Vol. 4: The zenith of the age of cinema) (Tokyo: Chukō-Bunko 1976). Films such as *Rashōmon* (Akira Kurosawa, 1950), *Ugetsu* (Kenji Mizoguchi, 1952), and *Jigokumon — The Gate of Hell* (Teinosuke Kinugasa, 1953) won international recognition through film festival success. Domestically, cinema attendance peaked in 1958 and then went into terminal decline. By the end of the 1970s, none of the Japanese major studios were producing films regularly — apart from Nikkatsu, which decided to specialize in soft-core pornography. See for example, Yomota Inuhiko, "Stranger than Tokyo: Space and Race in Postnational Japanese Cinema," in *Multiple Modernities: Cinemas and Popular Media in Transcultural East Asia*, ed. Jenny Kwok Wah Lau (Philadelphia: Temple University Press, 2003), 77.

20. Chino Keiko, "Shogun *to Karucha shokku*," (*Shogun* and Culture Shock), *Kinema Junpō* no. 797 (1980): 90.

21. Jerry Fisher, "*Shogun* ga beikoku ni uetsuketa 'nihonjin wa chujitsu' 'nihonjin wa kageki' no imēji" (*Shogun* implanted the image that "Japanese are loyal" and "Japanese are extremists" in American minds), *Asahi Journal* 22, no. 46 (November 14, 1980): 22.

22. For example, Mad Amano, "Shogun boom no nazo o toku: hainichi ka hainichi ka" (To resolve the mystery of the *Shogun* boom: Bashing Japan?), *Ushio* no. 260, (January 1981): 106–7.

23. James Clavell, *King Rat* (London: Hodder and Stoughton, 1962); *Tai-Pan* (London: Sphere Books, 1967).

23. James Clavell interviewed by Don Swain in 1986. http://wiredforbook.org/jamesclavell/ (accessed November 5, 2007).

24. Numerous American and European films were shot in Japan in the 1950s, such as *Tokyo File 212* (Stuart McGowan, 1951); *Geisha Girl* (George Breakston, 1952); *Three Stripes in the Sun* (Richard Murphy, 1955); *The Tea House of The August Moon* (Daniel Mann 1956); *Sayonara* (Joshua Logan, 1957); *The Barbarian and the Geisha* (John Huston, 1958); *Hiroshima Mon Amour* (Alain Resnais, 1959). Most of these foreign productions in Japan were initiated by foreign film companies to utilize their Japanese earnings, which they were not allowed to take out of the country because of the foreign exchange

regulations of the time. Thus these so-called co-productions did not require major Japanese financing, and they were not made with Japanese audiences in mind. As a consequence, most of these films were commercially unsuccessful in Japan, and the portrayal of Japanese culture and people in these films were often criticized as insensitive to the Japanese audience. See, for example, Michihiro Kakii, *Hariuddo no Nihonjin: eiga ni arawareta Nichibei bunka masatsu* (Japanese in Hollywood: Representation of Japanese-American cultural conflicts in films) (Tokyo: Bungeishunjū,1992); Takashi Monma, *Ōbeieiga ni miru nihon* (The representation of Japan in American and European films) (Tokyo: Shakaihyōronsha, 1995); Sachiko Masuda, *Amerika eiga ni arawareta 'nihon' imēji no hensen* (Changes in the image of 'Japan' represented in American cinema) (Osaka: Osaka University Press, 2004).

25. Fujii Hiroaki, interviewed by Yoshi Tezuka, August 5, 2005, in Tokyo.

26. "*Shogun* DVD booklet," James Clavell's *Shogun* DVD box set (Paramount Pictures 2004).

27. Fujii interview.

28. "*The Making of Shogun*," Disk 5 Bonus Feature, James Clavell's *Shogun* DVD box set (Paramount Pictures 2004).

29. Nagata advocated the internationalization of Japanese cinema following the success of *Rashomon* (Kurosawa, 1950). He was involved with various international film co-productions, and he set up mechanisms to promote the export of Japanese films to Western and Asian countries (see Tanaka Jun'ichirō, *Nagata Masaichi* [Tokyo: JiJi tsūshinsha, 1962], 123–67).

30. Fujii produced Japanese films shot on location in Italy, such as *The Garden of Eden* (Yasuzō Masumura, 1980). He also produced a film directed by the fashion designer Kenzo Takada, *Dream, After Dream* (Kenzō Takada, 1981), in France, and facilitated the Japanese locations for Joseph Losey's *Trout* (1982).

31. The interpreter, Jun Mori, used to work in my production office in London, and we discussed a lot about Fujii.

32. See, for example, John W. Dower, *Embracing Defeat: Japan in the Wake of World War 2* (New York: Norton, 1999), trans. Miura Yoichi et al. as *Haiboku o dakishimete* (Tokyo: Iwanami Shoten, 2001), 401–29.

33. The Van Ness Organization, *The Making of James Clavell's Shogun* (London: Hodder and Stoughton, 1980): 214

34. Tōhō Studio, where *Shogun* was shot, was the site of the fiercest labor struggles in postwar history, but its labor union was weakened considerably in the 1970s. Sato, Tadao, *Nihon Eigashi 2: History of Japanese Cinema 2* (Tokyo: Iwanami Shoten, 1995), 189–205.

35. The Van Ness Organization, *The Making of James Clavell's Shogun* (London: Hodder and Stoughton, 1980), 23.

36. Chikara Higashi and G. Peter Lauter, *The Internationalization of the Japanese Economy* (Dordrecht: Kluwer Academic Publishers, 1992), 6.

37. "Let's Get Lost: Translation Talk with Sofia Coppola and Ross Katz," DVD booklet for *Lost in Translation,* directed by Sofia Coppola (Momentum Pictures, 2003).
38. Lynn Hirschberg, "The Coppola Smart Mob," *New York Times* (August 31, 2003).
39. Ibid.
40. Inoue Kiyoshi, interviewed by Yoshi Tezuka, August 12, 2005, in Tokyo.
41. Ross Katz, in "Let's Get Lost."
42. Wendy Mitchell, "Sofia Coppola Talks about 'Lost in Translation', Her Love Story That's Not Nerdy," *indieWire* (February 4, 2004). http://www.indiewire. com/people/people_030923coppola.html (accessed November 7, 2007).
43. Inoue worked on *Abnormal Family* (Masayuki Suo, 1983) as an assistant director, the film by Suo Masayuki who later directed *Shall We Dance?* (Masayuki Suo, 1996). Inoue worked on numerous low-budget exploitation films in the 1980s before he went to the US. After the collapse of the Japanese studio production system in the 1970s, these sex exploitation films were one of only a few places from which young filmmakers could gain working experience.
44. Inoue interview.
45. Inoue interview.
46. Inoue interview.
47. For example, based on my own experience, the average rate of pay for a first assistant director in the early 2000s in the US was about US$650 for ten hours a day, whereas in Japan 30,000 yen (approx. US$250) would buy a very experienced first assistant director for a flat day, which normally means over fifteen hours.
48. Ulrich Beck, *Cosmopolitan Vision*, 20 (emphasis in original).

Chapter 6 In between the Values of the Global and the National: The Korean Animation Industry

1. Zigmunt Bauman, *Globalization: The Human Consequences* (Cambridge: Polity, 1998), 1.
2. Harvey introduces the term "time-space compression" in *The Condition of Postmodernity: An Enquiry into the Origins of Cultural Change* (Oxford: Basil Blackwell, 1989), 240: "processes that . . . revolutionize the objective qualities of space and time." This often stresses the rapidity of the exchange of finances, telecommunications, transportation, and more, which are phenomena of globalization, or, in Harvey's view, signs of postmodernity.
3. Marshall McLuhan and Quentin Fiore, *The Medium Is the Message* (London: Penguin, 1967); David Harvey *The Condition of Postmodernity: An Enquiry into the Origins of Cultural Change* (Oxford: Basil Blackwell,1989); Marjorie Ferguson, "The Mythology about Globalization," *European Journal of*

Communication 7 (1992) 69–93; Roland Robertson, *Globalization: Social Theory and Global Culture* (London: Sage, 1992); John B. Thompson, *The Media and Modernity: A Social Theory of the Media* (Cambridge: Polity, 1995).

4. Bauman (1998), 1.
5. Malcolm Waters, *Globalization* (London; New York: Routledge, 1995), 5.
6. Jonathan Friedman, *Cultural Identity & Global Process* (London; Thousand Oaks, CA: Sage, 1994), 15. Here, Friedman uses historical events and previous examples to explain the global process and people's cultural identity. For this reason, he states that his approach is rather "experience far."
7. Friedman (1994), 15.
8. Note that, for reasons of privacy, interviewees' names used in this chapter are pseudonyms. OEM means "original equipment manufacturer," or a company that produces a certain product to order under the brand name of the main company.
9. Homi K. Bhabha, *The Location of Culture* (London: Routledge, 1994). Throughout the book, Bhabha explains in-between in relation to hybridity under colonial conditions.
10. Cho Hae-Joang, "Constructing and Deconstructing Koreanness," in *Making Majorities: Constituting the Nation in Japan, Korea, China, Malaysia, Fiji, Turkey and United States*, ed. Dru Gladney (Stanford, CA: Stanford University Press, 1998), 81. For a more economic approach, see Dong-Myeon Shin, *Social Economic Policies in Korea: Ideas, Networks, and Linkages* (London; New York: Routledge Curzon, 2003), 52.
11. This is a part of the original manifesto of former president Park Chung-Hee's *The Country, the Revolution and I*, cited in Shin 2003, 52 (my translation).
12. GNP per capita was about US$67, and forty-seven percent of the population was engaged in agricultural production. In 1962, GNP per capita grew to US$87, and there were increases in the population engaged in the manufacturing, industrial, and service sectors. National wealth grew continuously and, by 1977, GNP per capita exceeded US$1,000. ECOS — Economic Statistic System, The Bank of Korea, GNP 1953–2000. http:// ecos.bok.or.kr (accessed November 15, 2005).
13. In the mid-1970s, a thirteen-year-old boy committed suicide, believing that he would come back to life like a cartoon character he admired. This was headline news and, as a result, rather negative images of cartoons, comics, and animation were planted in the minds of the Korean public.
14. John A. Lent, "Animation in Asia: Appropriation, Reinterpretation, and Adoption or Adaptation," *Screening the Past* no. 11 (2000). http:// www.latrobe.edu.au/screeningthepast. (accessed February 16, 2007).
15. Ahn Jiwon, "Animated Subjects: On the Circulation of Japanese Animation as Global Cultural Products." Paper presented at The Globalization and Popular Culture: Production, Consumption & Identity Workshop, University

of Manitoba (2001). http://www.umanitoba.ca/faculties/arts/english/media/ workshop/papers/ahn/ahn_paper.pdf (accessed April 30, 2002).

16. Ted Tschang and Andrea Goldstein, "Production and Political Economy in the Animation Industry: Why Insourcing and Outsourcing Occur." Paper presented at DRUID Summer Conference on Industrial Dynamics, Innovation and Development, Elsinore, Denmark (2004), 3.

17. Nelson Shin, the CEO of ACOM, which does outsourcing work for *The Simpsons,* said: "In order to make a 22-minute-episode of *The Simpsons,* 120 staff need to work. In order to make a series, it takes three months to complete and requires 22,000 drawings. As *The Simpsons* requires delicate movements, each character has 27 different mouth shapes" (March 3, 2005, *SportsHanKook;* my translation). This shows that animation requires a labor-intensive production process.

18. Kim Sŏnguk, *Han'guk aenimeisyŏnŭn ŏpta* (There is no Korean animation) (Seoul: Yesol, 1998); Joe Jo, "Overseas Marketing Suggestions for Korean Animation Industry," *Animation World Magazine* 4, no. 12 (2000): 1–3.

19. Kim Joon-Yang, "Critique of the New Historical Landscape of South Korean Animation," *Animation* 1, no. 1 (2006): 61–81.

20. See Lee Sang-Dawn, *Big Brother, Little Brother: The American Influence on Korean Culture in the Lyndon B. Johnson Years* (Lanham, MD: Lexington Books, 2002), 1–19.

21. Keith Negus and Michael Pickering, *Creativity, Communication and Cultural Value* (London; Thousand Oaks, CA: Sage, 2004), 47.

22. Philip Moins, Director of *Anima* 2005, *Kyoto News* (February 5, 2005).

23. Box office data source: http://www.the-numbers.com/movies/records (accessed December 10, 2005).

24. Quoted in Annalee R. Ward, "The Lion King's Mythic Narrative: Disney as Moral Educator," *Journal of Popular Film and Television* 23, no. 4 (1996): 47. For the original source of the data, see Scott Hettrick, "'Lion King' to Video March 3," *The Hollywood Reporter* (January 27–29, 1995): 1, 58.

25. Im Ch'ŏngsan "Manhwa yŏngsang kwallyŏnhakkwaŭi kyoyuk kwajŏng kaebal kwa unyŏng yŏn'gu" (Studies on the development and management of curricula for cartoon and animation courses), *Cartoon & Animation Studies* 3 (1999): 132–93.

26. "Apricot Lady" (29), a female animator who has a university degree in animation from abroad, depicted Korea's animation OEM industry as follows: "We (Korean animators) seem to be a puppet of the USA and Japan by doing their OEM work. I feel unhappy about it!"

27. "Mr Quiet" (26), who interrupted his undergraduate studies in animation for a year and currently works at a Japanese OEM animation company, says: "This bird is us, the Korean animation industry. I hope that one day we will be free and more creative, just like a bird flying high in the sky."

28. Georgie Hyde, *South Korea: Education, Culture and Economy* (New York: St. Martin's Press, 1998), 3.
29. Nick Crossley, *The Social Body: Habit, Identity and Desire* (London; Thousand Oaks, CA; New Delhi: Sage, 2001), 97.
30. Ibid.
31. Christopher Winch, *Education, Work and Social Capital: Towards a New Conception of Vocational Education* (London; New York: Routledge, 2000), 5.
32. Michael J. Seth, *Education Fever* (Honolulu: University of Hawaii Press and Centre for Korean Studies, University of Hawaii, 2002), 14, 140.
33. Korean currency used in this work is converted to US dollars, using http://www.oanda.com.
34. Youna Kim, *Women, Television and Everyday Life in Korea: Journeys of Hope* (London; New York: Routledge, 2005), 157.
35. Youna Kim (2005), 157.
36. Bauman (1998), 11.
37. Robert O'Brien and Marc Williams, *Global Political Economy: Evolution and Dynamics* (New York: Palgrave Macmillan, 2004), 175.

Chapter 7   The Transgression of Sharing and Copying: Pirating Japanese Animation in China

1. I use the term "creative industries" here largely to mean "cultural industries" — ones that produce cultural products. My intent is to highlight its relationship to the current knowledge economy.
2. Henry Jenkins, *Textual Poachers: Television Fans and Participatory Culture* (New York: Routledge, 1992).
3. Li Jianping, "Tashan zhi shi — Riben donghuapian daigei women de sikao" (How we could learn from Japanese animation), *Dianshi Yanjiu (Television Studies)*, no. 9 (2000): 69.
4. Guo Hong, "Beijing, Shanghai qingshaonian donghua diaocha" (Survey of the reception of animation among Beijing and Shanghai youths) (July 2, 2004), http://www.chinanim.com/dh1/newsxx.asp?newsid=4709 (accessed March 13, 2006); Zhao Hua and Xu Yang, "'Sun Wukong' weihe doubuguo 'mi laoshu'?" (Why can't the Monkey King overcome Mickey Mouse?) Xinhuanet.com (August 12, 2004). http://big5.xinhuanet.com/gate/big5/www.ln.xinhuanet.com/wangtan/katong/images.htm (accessed March 8, 2006).
5. *Gin'iro no kami no agito* (*Silver-haired Agito*, dir. Sugiyama Keiichi) was the first anime co-produced by Japanese and Chinese companies (Gonzo and Chinese Film Animation Company [Zhongying Donghua Chanye Gongsi]). It was also the first anime film to be screened in China in March 2006, but, for unknown reasons, it has not yet happened. See "Kaikyo! Nihon anime-

shijō hatsu no Chūgoku kōkai kettei!! *Gin'iro no kami no agito*" ("What a feat! The first Chinese release in the history of Japanese anime: *Silver-haired Agito!!*"), http://www.gin-iro.jp/web/news_html/news_bn.php?REC=18 (accessed February 20, 2006); and Gigi, "Maichu chanye diyibu? Ajide nian'nei shangying" (The first step to the industry: *Agito* will be screened in this year) (March 17, 2006), http://news.myuni. com.cn/content/news/ 21072235562006317103543 59 44484_1.shtml (accessed January 30, 2007).

6. The importation of revenue-sharing foreign films began in China 1994, when the quota was ten films per year. After China joined the WTO, the quota increased twenty, and it reached forty in 2005.

7. Editorial, "'Anime' Subculture Exchange May Bridge Japan-China Gap," Jiji Press Ticker Service (October 29, 2005) (accessed through LexisNexis on March 2, 2006).

8. Laikwan Pang, *Cultural Control and Globalization in Asia: Copyright, Piracy, and Cinema* (London: Routledge, 2006), 80–116.

9. Anonymous, "Zhongguo Dongman Chongman Wenti de 'Chaoyang'" (The rising sun of the problematic Chinese manga and anime) Chinanim. com (October 16, 2005). http://www.chinanim.com/dh1/newsxx.asp?newsid =9856 (assessed March 3, 2006).

10. Vivienne Chow, "Internet Piracy Nightmare for Anime Director," *South China Morning Post* (January 9, 2006).

11. A wave of lawsuits and criminal proceedings against file-sharers is currently instigated by the music industry across the world. In January 2006, the British court for the first time declared illegal file-sharing unlawful and charged two sharers with fines. At around the same time, a new Swedish political party was established, with the clear political aim to abolish copyright laws. For relevant news, see "exis-nexis.com/universe/document?_m =ae1d7f2b4118b30c275a50f5ceee117b&_docnum=8&wchp=dGLzVzz-zSkVA&_md5=575da7cb01edf85bc48466aee00aaac7" File-sharers in Europe face a wave of lawsuits?" *The International Herald Tribune* (April 5, 2006); Jonathan Brown, "Illegal File-sharers Fined for First Time in Britain," *The Independent* (London) (January 28, 2006); Gladys Fouche, "Pirates Pursue a Political Point: A New Swedish Party Aims to Abolish the Copyright Laws that Criminalise File Sharers," *The Guardian* (London) (February 9, 2006).

12. Editorial, "'Made in Japan' Trademark to Fight Anime Piracy," *Mainichi Daily News* (July 3, 2004) (accessed through LexisNexis on March 3, 2006). Such figures are, of course, enormously misleading; Chinese consumers choose piracy partly because official products are so expensive.

13. For example, one can find many Japanese anime on the Chinese "VeryCD" website http://www.verycd.com/ (accessed February 27, 2006). Some major Chinese websites featuring Japanese anime and manga include Comic-Anime Beat, http://www.cabeat.com/pub/index.php?option=com_frontpage& Itemid=1 (assessed February 27, 2006); and TotoroClub.net, http://

www.totoroclub.net/index.htm (assessed February 27, 2006).

14. Fei Yuxiao, "Chuangzao mengxiang yu feixiang de laoren: Gong Qijun" (The world of Miyazaki Hayao), co-published by Dongfang yinxiang dianzi chubanshe and Kuilü wenhua. I bought the book at Idea Bookshop on February 7, 2006. It does not indicate the year of publication, but since *Howl's Moving Castle* was not released until 2004, it is likely to be 2004 or 2005. This author has published similar items about Japanese manga and anime materials.

15. For example, the Korean *Totoro* poster (p. 54) was likely copied from Korean website Cincine.co.kr, http://www.cinecine.co.kr/movie_poster.asp?movie _code=1155&back_url (accessed February 27, 2006).

16. For example, the many manga illustrations in *Nausicaä of The Valley of the Winds* (pp. 26–34) were likely copied directly from the original manga *Nausicaä of the Valley of the Winds,* vols. 1–6 (Tokyo: Tokuma Shoten, 1987).

17. The quality of the different images varies greatly, and those pictures with the lowest resolution are quite clearly television screen captures (e.g., pp. 91, 172).

18. For example, many of the photos of the Ghibli Museum (pp. 220–33) were copied from the Chinese book *The Hot Air of Ghibli (Jibuli de refeng)* (Beijing: Feitian dianzhi yinxiang chubanshe, n.d.), which is also a pirated book.

19. Kanō Seiji, "*Kaze no tani no naushika* kara *Mononoke no hime* e–Miyazaki Hayao to Sutajio Jiburi no 13 nen" ("From *Nausicaä of the Valley of the Wind* to *Princess Mononoke* — 13 Years of Miyazaki Hayao and Studio Ghibli"). http://www.yk.rim.or.jp/~rst/rabo/miyazaki/ghibli13nen.html, accessed February 25, 2006.

20. Kazuto Tsukamoto, "Shanghai Surprise: Animation on the Rise," *Asahi Shimbun* (April 23, 200)5 (accessed through LexisNexis on March 2, 2006).

21. Kenji Kawase, "Hangzhou Aspires to Crown of Animation, 'Manga' Capital," *The Nikkei Weekly* (June 20, 2005) (accessed through LexisNexis on March 3, 2006).

22. Chan Siu-sin, "Animation Industry Lacks Talent and Chinese Brands, says Official," *South China Morning Post* (January 20, 2006).

23. Kazuto Tsukamoto, "Shanghai Surprise: Animation on the Rise."

24. For a historical overview of South Korea's animation industry, see Joon-Yang Kim, "Critique of the New Historical Landscape of South Korean Animation," *Animation* 1, no. 1 (2006): 61–81.

25. "Manga Course Attracts Lecturers," *The Daily Yomiuri* (June 9, 2004) (accessed through LexisNexis on March 3, 2006).

26. See Ae-Ri Yoon's work in this volume.

27. Paul Wells, *Understanding Animation* (London: Routledge, 1998), 190–6.

28. Ollie Johnston and Frank Thomas, *The Illusion of Life: Disney Animation* (New York: Disney Editions, 1981).

29. Thomas Lamarre, "Platonic Sex: Perversion and Shojo Anime (Part One)," *Animation* 1, no. 1 (2006): 45–59.

30. See, for example, Susan J. Napier, *Anime,* 172–7, 215–8.

31. Paul Wells, *Understanding Animation*, 34–67.
32. Lev Manovich, *The Language of New Media* (Cambridge, MA: MIT Press), 298–307. The current game culture has benefited much from the logic of cartoon culture.
33. For example, the 1928 *Steamboat Willie,* the first feature animation film of Walt Disney which made him and Mickey Mouse famous, was a spoof of a Buster Keaton film called *Steamboat Bill, Jr.*
34. See Toby Miller et al., *Global Hollywood* (London: BFI, 2001).
35. Salil Mehra, "Copyright and Comics in Japan: Does Law Explain Why All the Cartoons My Kid Watches are Japanese Imports?" *Rutgers Law Review,* 55 (Fall 2002). Available at SSRN: http://ssrn.com/abstract=347620 or DOI: 10.2139/ssrn.347620
36. Kōichi Iwabuchi, *Recentering Globalization: Popular Culture and Japanese Transnationalism* (Durham, NC: Duke University Press, 2002), 38. See also Sean Leonard, "Progress against the Law: Anime and Fandom, with the Key to the Globalization of Culture," *International Journal of Cultural Studies* 8, no. 3 (2005): 281–305.
37. Ian Rowley, Chester Dawson, Hiroko Tashiro, and Ihlwan Moon, "The Anime Biz: Still an Adolescent," *Business Week* no. 3939 (June 27, 2005): 50–2.
38. Editorial, "'Made in Japan' trademark to fight anime piracy," *Mainichi Shinbun* (July 3, 2004) (accessed through LexisNexis on March 8, 2006).
39. Japanese anime and manga are also popular in other places, as my chapter shows. But we must recognize that such popularities can by no means be compared to the national scene. See Anne Allison, "Can Popular Culture Go Global? How Japanese 'Scouts' and 'Rangers' Fare in the U.S.," in *A Century of Popular Culture in Japan,* ed. Douglas Slaymaker (Lewiston, ME: Edwin Mellen Press, 2000), 127–53; Anthony Fung, "Hong Kong as the Asian and Chinese Distributor of Pokemon," *International Journal of Comic Art* 7, no. 1 (2005): 432–48. Susan J. Napier, *Anime: From Akira to Princess Mononoke* (New York: Palgrave, 2001), 8.
40. See Amy Fung Kwan Li's "Slash, Fandoms, and Pleasures." M.Phil. thesis, Department of Cultural and Religious Studies, The Chinese University of Hong Kong, 2006. Amy has been both my source of inspiration and information for this paper. My sincere gratitude.
42. Lawrence Lessig, *Free Culture: How Big Media Uses Technology and the Law to Lock Down Culture and Control Creativity* (New York: Penguin, 2004), 25–8.
42. Iwabuchi, *Recentering Globalization* (2002), 23–35.
43. Iwabuchi (2002), 36.
44. Judith Butler, *Theories in Subjection: The Psychic Life of Power* (Stanford, CA: Stanford University Press, 1997), 28–30.

Chapter 8 The East Asian Brandscape: Distribution of Japanese Brands in the Age of Globalization

1. The fieldwork on which this essay is based was partly funded by a research grant from the Japan Foundation.
2. Naomi Klein, *No Logo: Taking Aim at the Brand Bullies* (New York: Picador, 2000).
3. Kōichi Iwabuchi, *Recentering Globalization: Popular Culture and Japanese Transnationalism* (Durham; London: Duke University Press, 2002), 48.
4. Arjun Appadurai, *Modernity at Large: Cultural Dimensions of Globalization* (Minneapolis: University of Minnesota Press, 1996).
5. There is an increasing number of works on inter-Asian cultural flow. See, for example, Larissa Hjorth, "Odours of Mobility: Mobile Phones and Japanese Cute Culture in the Asia-Pacific," *Journal of Intercultural Studies* 26, nos. 1–2 (2005): 39–55; Kōichi Iwabuchi, ed. *Feeling Asian Modernities: Transnational Consumption of Japanese TV Dramas* (Hong Kong: Hong Kong University Press, 2004); and Akio Igarashi ed., *Henyō suru Ajia to Nihon: Ajia Shakai ni shintō suru Nihon no popyurā karuchā* (Transformation of Asia and Japan: Japanese popular culture in East Asia) (Yokohama: Seori Shobō, 1998).
6. Douglas McGray, "Japan's Gross National Cool," *Foreign Policy* no. 130 (2002): 44–54.
7. "Daitōa Atsuzoko Kyōeiken" (The Greater East Asian Japanese Super Platform-Shoe Sphere), *Nikkei Business* (January 15, 2001): 21.
8. Leo Ching, "Globalizing the Regional, Regionalizing the Global: Mass Culture and Asianism in the Age of Late Capital," in *Globalization*, ed. Arjun Appadurai (Durham, NC: Duke University Press, 2001), 257.
9. Ching (2001), 281.
10. Herbert Schiller, "Not yet the Post-Imperial Era," in *Media and Cultural Studies: Keyworks*, eds. Meenakshi Gigi Durham and Douglas Kellner (Malden, MA: Blackwell Publishers, 2001), 318–33.
11. Kevin Robins, "What in the World Is Going On?" in *Production of Culture/ Cultures of Production*, ed. Paul Du Gay and Open University (London; Thousand Oaks, CA: Sage in association with the Open University, 1997), 11–66.
12. Stuart Hall, "The Local and the Global: Globalization and Ethnicity," in *Culture, Globalization, and the World-System: Contemporary Conditions for the Representation of Identity*, ed. Anthony D. King (Minneapolis: University of Minnesota, 1997), 41–69.
13. Roland Robertson, "Glocalization: Time-Space and Homogeneity-Heterogeneity," in *Global Modernities*, eds. Mike Featherstone, Scott Lash, and Roland Robertson. (Thousand Oaks, CA: Sage, 1995), 28.
14. James L. Watson, *Golden Arches East: McDonald's in East Asia* (Stanford, CA: Stanford University Press, 1997).

15. Takeshi Matsui, "Seiryō Inryō: Genchika to hyōjunka no hazamade" (Soft drink: Standardization and localization), in *Branding in China: Kyodai shijō Chūgoku o seisuru burando senryaku* (Branding in China: Brand strategy for the huge China market), ed. Yuko Yamashita (Tokyo: Tōyō Keizai Shinpō Sha, 2006), 75–108.

16. Celia Lury, *Brands: The Logos of the Global Economy* (London: Routledge, 2004), 6.

17. "The Beauty Top 100," *WWD Beauty Report International* (September 2007) 27. Here, the cosmetics market is made up of fragrance, makeup, skin care, sun care, hair care, deodorant, cellulite and shaving products. This paper does not discuss Procter & Gamble, Unilever, and Avon — ranked second (US$17.5 billion), third (US$12.8 $ billion), and fifth (US$6.0 billion) respectively — because of their relative weakness in luxury fragrance, makeup, and skin-care brands.

18. Data collected by the author between July 2006 and January 2007.

19. The largest Japanese toiletry company, Kao, acquired the struggling Kanebo cosmetic brand in 2006 as part of its bid to become serious contender in the lucrative cosmetics industry.

20. Mike Featherstone, *Undoing Culture: Globalization, Postmodernism and Identity* (London; Thousand Oaks, CA: Sage Publications, 1995), 8–9.

21. Iwabuchi (2002), 27–8.

22. Interviews with current and former brand marketers who handled most of the brands discussed in this essay were conducted in November and December 2006.

23. Liz Moor, "Branded Spaces: the Mediation of Commercial Forms" (Ph.D. Dissertation, Goldsmiths College, University of London, 2004), 11–5.

24. www.brandchannel.com/education_glossary.asp.

25. Lury (2004), 6.

26. Manuel De Landa, *A New Philosophy of Society: Assemblage Theory and Social Complexity* (London; New York: Continuum, 2006). This innovative book presents a social ontology that asserts the autonomy of social entities from the conceptions we have of them.

27. Adam Arvidsson, *Brands: Meaning and Value in Media Culture* (London; New York: Routledge, 2006).

28. John Murphy, "What Is Branding?" in *Brands: The New Wealth Creator*, eds. Susannah Hart and John Murphy (London: Macmillan, 1998) 3.

29. This definition is taken from the *Oxford American Dictionary* on Apple Mac OX 10.4.10. This is an anti-Kantian definition in disagreement with the structuralist insistence on the total linguisticality of experience. See Howard Caygill, *Walter Benjamin: The Colour of Experience* (London: Routledge, 1998) for the analysis of Benjamin's anti-Kantian idea of experience. See also Gregory J. Seigworth, "Cultural Studies and Gilles Deleuze," in *New Cultural Studies*, eds. Gary Hall and Clare Birchall (Edinburgh: Edinburgh

University Press, 2007), 107–27, for a Deleuzean attempt to resuscitate Raymond Williams's culturalist project on experience. Martin Jay in *Songs of Experience: Modern American and European Variations on a Universal Theme* (Berkeley: University of California Press, 2005) provides a comprehensive account of "experience" in Western philosophical thought.

30. http://www.lovemarks.com/index.php?pageID=20015&lovemarkid=910.
31. http://www.lovemarks.com/index.php?pageID=20015&start=10&order =commentdate&direction=DESC&lovemarkid=910&display=&move=1.
32. Shaun Smith, "Brand Experience," in *Brands and Branding*, ed. The Economist et al. (London: The Economist, 2003), 97–111; see also B. Joseph Pine II and James H. Gilmore, *The Experience Economy: Work Is Theatre & Every Business a Stage* (Boston, MA: Harvard Business School Press, 1999); and Martin Lindstrom, *Brandsense: How to Build Powerful Brands through Touch, Taste, Smell, Sight & Sound* (London: Kogan Page Limited, 2005).
33. Arvidsson (2006). In this sense, the value of brands depends on "immaterial labour," defined by Lazzarato "as the labour that produces the informational and cultural content of the commodity." Maurizio Lazzarato, "Immaterial Labour," in *Radical Thought in Italy: A Potential Politics*, eds. Paolo Virno and Michael Hardt (Minneapolis: University of Minnesota Press, 1996), 133–47.
34. Based on onsite observation of the M.A.C Cosmetics counter at London department stores Harvey Nichols and Selfridges in November 2007.
35. Based on interview. See also Emily Ross and Angus Holland, *100 Great Businesses and the Minds Behind Them* (Naperville, IL: Sourcebook, Inc., 2006) for the history of M.A.C. Cosmetics.
36. Smith (2003), 97–8.
37. See Brian Massumi, *Parables for the Virtual: Movement, Affect, Sensation, Post-Contemporary Interventions* (Durham, NC: Duke University Press, 2002) for an influential discussion of the Spinozean-Deleuzean notion of affect that has set the tone for the recent surge of interest in affect.
38. Here I use the term *virtual* not in the simple sense of being immaterial but in the Bergosonian/Deleuzean sense, in which the virtual is always compared with the actual as two ontologically distinct dimensions of reality. See Andrew Murphie, "Putting the Virtual Back into VR," in *A Shock to Thought: Expressions after Deleuze & Guattari*, ed. Brian Massumi (London: Routledge, 2002), 188–214; and Pierre Levy, *Becoming Virtual: Reality in the Digital Age* (Peseus Books, 1998).
39. Rosemary J. Coombe, *The Cultural Life of Intellectual Properties: Authorship, Appropriation and the Law* (Durham, NC: Duke University Press, 1998), 318–9.
40. Janet Fogg, "Brands as Intellectual Property," in *Brands: The New Wealth Creators*, eds. Susannah Hart and John Murphy (London: Macmillan, 1998), 72–81.

41. This information can be found in the IR sections of their corporate website. Shiseido annual report, http://www.shiseido.co.jp/ir/library/annual/index.htm (accessed November 1, 2007); L'Oréal annual report, http://www.loreal-finance.com/v9/us/contenu/rapport.asp (accessed November 1, 2007); Estée Lauder annual report, http://www.elcompanies.com/investor_relations/financial_reports/annual_reports.asp (accessed November 1, 2007).

42. Raymond Perrier, "Brand Licensing," in *Brands: The New Wealth Creators*, eds. Susannah Hart and John Murphy (London: Macmillan, 1998), 104–13.

43. David Aaker, *Brand Portfolio Strategy: Creative Relevance, Differentiation, Energy, Leverage and Clarity* (New York: Simon & Schuster, 2004).

44. Aaker (2004).

45. Appadurai (1996), 37.

46. Lawrence Grossberg, "Cultural Studies, Modern Logics, and Theories of Globalisation," in *Back to Reality? Social Experience and Cultural Studies*, ed. Angela McRobbie (Manchester: Manchester University Press, 1997), 25.

47. In 1995, imported Japanese women's fashion magazine *non-no* was the best-selling magazine ahead of any local or localized Western magazines in a large bookshop in Taiwan, according to Kenichi Ishii in *Higashi Ajia no Nihon taishū bunka* (Japanese popular culture in East Asia) (Tokyo: Sōsō-sha, 2001), 147. The publisher Shufunotomosha alone has twelve licensing deals in Asia, which it signed between 1995 and 2006. One of its magazines, *Ray*, a women's fashion magazine, has been licensed to Taiwan, Thailand, and mainland China. In China, its circulation is among the largest and significantly larger than the Japanese edition. Local licensees for Ray or other magazines translate and publish between 60 and 95 percent of the original Japanese content, including editorial and advertorial. (Interview with the company's international rights manager, November 2006.)

48. Geoffrey G. Jones, David Kiron, Vincent Dessain, and Anders Sjoman, "L'Oreal and the Globalization of American Beauty," *Harvard Business School Case* 805–086 (2005).

49. Appadurai (1996), 42.

50. Beng Huat Chua, "Conceptualizing an East Asian Popular Culture," *Inter-Asia Cultural Studies* 5, no. 2 (2004): 200–21.

51. Scott Lash and Celia Lury, *Global Culture Industry: Mediation of Things* (Oxford: Polity Press, 2007). See also Nicholas Thoburn, "Patterns of Production: Cultural Studies after Hegemony," *Theory, Culture & Society* 24, no. 3 (2007): 79–94.

52. Smith (2003).

53. Imre Szerman, "Cultural Studies and the Transnational," in *New Cultural Studies — Adventure in Theory*, eds. Gary Hall and Clare Birchall (Edinburgh: Edinburgh University Press, 2006), 213.

Chapter 9   Korean Pop Music in China: Nationalism, Authenticity, and Gender

1. This essay does not consider the consumption of North Korean culture in China. Hereafter, when I refer to Korea, this should be understood as South Korea (Republic of Korea).

2. McCune-Reischauer romanization is used for Korean terms, except personal names, where I retain preferred spellings where known, giving on the first appearance McCune-Reischauer equivalents in square brackets. Pinyin romanization is used for Chinese terms, except for Hong Kong names, where I retain preferred spelling.

3. The word pronounced *Han* means cold or Korea, depending how it is written. As far as I know, it has no connotations of "cool" (as in fashionable), which is generally transliterated as *ku* in Chinese. Cho Hae-Joang traces the word *Hanliu* to 1999 and suggests that there is a cynical edge to this play on words (Hae-Joang Cho, "Reading the 'Korean Wave' as a Sign of Global Shift," *Korea Journal* 45, no. 4 [2005]: 172), perhaps because the word *han* (cold) has connotations of fear, suggesting that Chinese may fear excessive cultural influence from Korea. However, I have not detected a pejorative edge to the use of the term.

4. Generally focussed on consumption of TV drama and film, English language studies of *Hanliu* include: Sora Park, "China's Consumption of Korean Television Dramas: An Empirical Test of the 'Cultural Discount' Concept," *Korea Journal* 44, no. 4 (2004): 265–90; a special issue of *Korea Journal* 45, no. 4 (2005) including essays by Kelly Fu Su Yin and Kai Khiun Liew ("*Hallyu* in Singapore: Korean Cosmopolitanism or the Consumption of Chineseness?" 206–32), Doobo Shim ("Globalization and Cinema Regionalization in East Asia," 233–60) and Hyun Mee Kim ("Korean TV Dramas in Taiwan: With an Emphasis on the Localization Process," 183–205). Studies focussing on music include Rowan Pease, "Internet, Fandom and K-wave in China," in *Korean Pop Music: Riding the Wave*, ed. Keith Howard (Folkestone: Global Oriental 2006), 176–89; and Sang-Yeon Sung, "The *Hanliu* Phenomenon in Taiwan: TV Dramas and Teenage Pop," in *Korean Pop Music: Riding the Wave*, ed. Keith Howard (Folkestone: Global Oriental 2006), 168–75.

5. Musically, in China H.O.T. were most readily compared with the Backstreet Boys, for instance, although they incorporated rock elements that were not part of the American band's style. In China, the ability of musicians to present competence in a range of styles is valued as proof of their musicianship and broad appeal; in the West, it might be read as "inauthentic," or threaten their niche in a more segmented market. There is a great diversity of Korean pop music genres besides R&B and hip-hop. These are explored in *Korean Pop Music: Riding the Wave* (Folkestone: Global Oriental 2006), ed. Keith Howard.

6. Kōichi Iwabuchi, "Becoming 'Culturally Proximate': The A/scent of Japanese Idol Dramas in Taiwan," in *Asian Media Productions*, ed. Brian Moeran (Richmond: Curzon, 2001), 54–74.

7. An onomatopoeic term that evokes the rhythmic accompaniment to the songs, which are also known as "trot" (*t'ŭrot'ŭ*, after foxtrot). These ballads are sometimes compared to Japanese *enka*, and the origins of both genres are fiercely debated in Korea. On this, see Gloria Lee Pak, "On the Mimetic Faculty: A Critical Study of the 1984 *Ppongtchak* Debate and Post-colonial Mimesis," in *Korean Pop Music: Riding the Wave*, ed. Keith Howard (Folkestone: Global Oriental 2006), 62–71.

8. The origin of this term is a pun on sun-sickness, used in the Taiwanese phrase *haRizu*, for fans of Japanese culture. See Hélène Le Bail, "Japanese Culture in Asia: Infatuation, Identification and the Construction of Identity: The Example of Taiwan," *China Perspectives*, 43 (2002): 52–62. The *haHanzu* are just one of many lifestyle "tribes" in China, on which see Jing Wang, "Bourgeois Bohemians in China? Neo-tribes and the Urban Imaginary," *The China Quarterly* no. 183 (2005): 543–7.

9. Pease (2006), 177, 180.

10. The main companies of concern to this article are SM Entertainment, JYP Entertainment, and YG Entertainment (Yedang Media).

11. John Fiske, "The Cultural Economy of Fandom," in *The Adoring Audience: Fan Culture and Popular Media*, ed. Lisa Lewis (London and New York: Routledge, 1992), 30.

12. Cho (2005).

13. Kōichi Iwabuchi, "Time and the Neighbour: Japanese Media Consumption of Asia," in *Rogue Flows: Trans-Asian Cultural Traffic*, eds. Kōichi Iwabuchi, Stephen Muecke, and Mandy Thomas (Hong Kong: Hong Kong University Press, 2004), 151–74.

14. According to Chinese newspaper reports, his concert at the Olympic Stadium in Beijing in 1999 earned him US$100,000 performing to 17,000 fans (*Hanju gongli shenhou, daihuo Hanliu jingji* [South Korean Drama's Profound Success, Fires the Korea Wave Economy]), World Media Lab. http://media.icxo.com/htmlnews/2005/08/24/653373.htm (accessed December 5, 2006).

15. Record sales in Korea have fallen drastically: in the late 1990s the best-selling records could top 2 million domestically. In 2006, very few could exceed 200,000. In 2001, the top ten best-selling albums made a combined total of over 10 million sales; in 2006 it was just 2 million. Undoubtedly the high number of illegal download sites contributed to the downturn, but the closure of such sites has done little to reverse the trend (annual sales figures available on the Music Industry Association of Korea website, http://miak.or.kr).

16. H.O.T., for example, sold over 400,000 albums in China in 2000 (Kim Youn-jun, "Korean Pop Culture Craze Hallyu Sweeps Through Asia,"

Koreana 16, no. 1 (2002): 46), while their album sales in Korea in the same year were just double that at 900,000 (Music Industry Association of Korea, "2002 *nyŏn kayo ŭmban palmae ryang chipkye*" [2002 Korean song album sales chart], Music Industry Association of Korea. http://miak.or.kr/navigator.php?contents=html&usemode=list&DB=117 (accessed May 14, 2007).

17. International Federation of Phonographic Industries, "IFPI Music Piracy Report 2002," International Federation of Phonographic Industries, http://www.ifpi.org/site-content/antipiracy/piracy2002.html (accessed 14 February 2003); Thomas Crampton, "Pop Stars Learn to Live with Pirates," *International Herald Tribune* (February 21, 2003). http://www.iht.comcgi-bin/generec.cgi?template+articleprint.tmplh&AR (accessed April 29, 2003).

18. Anthony Fung, "Marketing Popular Culture in China: Andy Lau as a Pan-Chinese Icon," in *Chinese Media: Global Contexts*, ed. Chin-Chuan Lee (New York; London, Routledge, 2003), 257–69. Anthony Fung, "Western Style, Chinese Pop: Jay Chou's Rap and Hip-Hop in China," *Asian Music* 39, no. 1 (2008): 69–80.

19. The sale and manufacture of records has for some time been of less importance to the global music industry than the creation of rights. See Simon Frith, "Copyright and the Music Business," *Popular Music* 7, no. 1 (1988): 57.

20. Executive Producer Hao Fang at Starry Sky TV, interview by author, August 11, 2003, Beijing.

21. Laikwan Pang, *Cultural Control and Globalization in Asia: Copyright, Piracy and Cinema* (London; New York: Routledge, 2006), 109, 103. See also her essay in this volume.

22. During July–August 2003, I interviewed record company and media workers including Ji Lingli (public relations, Baidie Record Company, Beijing), Gu Hong (Star River Audio-visual, Shanghai), Wu Qi (chief editor, Joy Entertainment Channel online, Shanghai), Hao Fang (executive producer, Starry Sky TV, Beijing), Robin Pak (programme presenter, Radio Television Hong Kong), Kelly Cha (presenter, Beijing Music Station), Ben Xu (production manager, MTV China, Shanghai), Zhang Ming (presenter, Shanghai East Radio). Hereafter, in order to protect their professional relationships, I will not attribute comments to specific individuals.

23. The number of votes cast was 35,314. For the full poll results, see *Sina Yingyin yule*, "*Diaocha: Ni renwei zai Zhongguo zui you renqi de Hanguo geshou she shei?*" (Survey: Whom do consider to be the most popular Korean singer in China?), *Sina Yingyin yule*. http://ent.sina.com.cn/y/2006-02-10/2009982389.html (accessed March 13, 2006).

24. Deborah Sontag, "A Strong Forecast for Korean Pop's Rain," *New York Times* (January 27, 2006). http://www.iht.com/articles/2006/01/27/news/rain.php (accessed December 13, 2007).

25. KR Jeami, "Interview with Lee Soo Man" *BoAjjang.com* (September 1, 2005).

http://forums.boajjang.com/index.php?act=ST&f=1&t=34315 (accessed June 6, 2008).

26. News of H.O.T. revival concerts were a common feature in *Hanliu* magazines and websites, but these never materialized. For example "*H.O.T. chongzu kenengxing zengjia*" (The possibility of re-forming H.O.T. is increasing), *Yule wuxian* (Entertainment Unlimited), no. 152 (July 2003).

27. SM Entertainment 2001, Video segment entitled "SM Entertainment, China Auditions." http://www.smtown.com/smtown/audition/china2001/china_audition_ch3.html (accessed May 7, 2005).

28. Seoul Broadcasting System (SBS), *Ashia shyobijŭ: samgukji, Yi Suman ŭi CT ron kwa Hallyu ŭi mirae* (Asia Showbiz: The History of Three Kingdoms, Lee Soo Man's CT theory and the future of Korea wave) SBS special, March 12, 2006.

29. SBS (2006).

30. "TVXQ" *Wikipedia*. http://en.wikipedia.org/wiki/TVXQ (accessed September 15, 2006).

31. World Media Lab, *Hanju gongli shenhou, daihuo Hanliu jingji* (South Korean drama's profound success, fires the Korea Wave economy), World Media Lab. http://media.icxo.com/htmlnews/2005/08/24/653373.htm (accessed December 5, 2006).

32. Cho (2005), 169.

33. World Media Lab, *Hanju gongli shenhou, daihuo hanliu jingji.*

34. Figures derived from Robert Ash, "Quarterly Chronicle," *The China Quarterly* 190 (2006): 533.

35. Korea Culture and Contents Agency, "About KOCCA: Mission," *KoreanContent.org* (2003). http://www.koreacontent.org/weben/etc/kocca3.jsp (accessed December 5, 2006).

36. Korean National Tourism Office, "*Survey* Report on Actual Conditions of *Hallyu* (Korean Fever) Tourism, 2004." http://www.knto.or.kr/eng/hallyu/hallyusurvey.html#top (accessed April 2, 2005).

37. Korean National Tourism Office 2004; Joseph. D. Straubhaar, "Beyond Media Imperialism: Asymmetrical Inter-dependence and Cultural Proximity," *Critical Studies in Mass Communication* 8 (1991): 39–59.

38. Keith Howard, "Coming of Age: Korean Pop in the 1990s," in *Korean Pop Music: Riding the Wave*, ed. Keith Howard (Folkestone: Global Oriental 2006), 82.

39. Paik Won Dam, cited in Cho (2005), 163.

40. Cho (2005).

41. "S Korean Soap Opera Sparks Boom in China," *China Daily* (September 30, 2003). http://news3.xinhuanet.com/english/2005-09/30/content_3567436.htm (accessed March 14, 2006).

42. Executive Producer at Starry Sky TV Hao Fang, interview by author, August 11, 2003, Beijing.

43. Fang (2003).
44. Program Presenter Robin Pak of Radio Television Hong Kong, interview by author, July 2003, Hong Kong.
45. Jin Chenguang, student, interview by author, August 3, 2003, Changchun.
46. Public Relations Officer Ji Lingli of Baidie Record Company, interview by author, August 2003, Beijing.
47. Gu Hong of Star River Audio-visual, interview by author, July 2003, Shanghai.
48. Robin Pak (2003).
49. Henry Jenkins, *Textual Poachers: Television Fans and Participatory Culture* (London: Routledge, 1991), 175.
50. Barbara Ehrenreich, Elizabeth Hess, and Gloria Jacobs, "Beatlemania: Girls Just Want to Have Fun," in *The Adoring Audience*, ed. Lisa A. Lewis (London: Routledge, 1992) 84–106; and Jennifer Robertson, *Takarazuka: Sexual Politics and Popular Culture in Modern Japan* (Berkeley; London: University of California Press, 1998), 140–3.
51. Qiao Fei, "Korean Culture According to Foreigners 2," *KoreanContent.org*, 2004. http://www.koreacontent.org/weben/inmarket/Ns_knews_view.jsp?news_seq=11298 (accessed December 5, 2006).
52. Robin Pak (2003).
53. As Ehrenreich, Hess, and Jacobs note, this is partly an expression of the fans' power: "knowing, subconsciously, that the Beatles were who they were because girls like oneself had made them that" (Ehrenreich, Hess, Jacobs 1992, 103).
54. From April to September 2003, I sent out about 600 email questionnaires on Korean music consumption to participants on bulletin boards, websites, QQ messaging system users, and fans who had written to magazines. I received 107 replies, which I then followed up with further questionnaires and correspondence. Survey responses are referred to in the following format: (nickname, date, response number).
55. Such petitions are characteristic of grassroots protests on the Internet, as outlined by Shih-ding Liu, "China's Popular Nationalism on the Internet: Report on the 2005 Anti-Japanese Network Struggles," *Inter-Asia Cultural Studies* 7, no. 1 (2006): 144–55.
56. hyun&hyuk, "Di yi ge, ai wo de ren" (The first person who loves me), LKPM forums. http://lkpm.w103.leoboard.com/novel/novel/02.htm (accessed September 10, 2003).
57 Eun-Young Jung, "Articulating Korean Youth Culture through Global Popular Music Styles: Seo Taiji's Use of Rap and Metal," in *Korean Pop Music: Riding the Wave*, ed. Keith Howard (Folkestone: Global Oriental 2006), 113–7. Similar sentiments are expressed in the songs of Taiwanese pop star Jay Chou since 2003 (Fung 2008).
58. Yoo Young Jin, "We Are the Future," *H.O.T. II: Wolf and Sheep*, 1997, S.M. Entertainment, SSM-20 (1997).

59. Nimrod Baranovitch, *China's New Voices: Popular Music, Ethnicity, Gender and Politics, 1978–1997* (Berkeley: University of California Press 2003), 108–89.
60. Baranovitch (2003), 155.
61. Baranovitch (2003), 144.
62. Baranovitch (2003), 153.
63. Jing Wang, *Brand New China Advertising, Media, and Commercial Culture* (Cambridge, MA: Harvard University Press, 2008), 77.
64. Laikwan Pang (2006) forcefully argues the creative nature of film piracy in China, and her ideas can be applied to music piracy.
65. Pease (2006), 185–6.
66. In this regard, compare this reaction of Japanese fans to Hong Kong stars "with a sensitivity so delicate as to appeal to the maternal instinct" (Iwabuchi 2004, 160).
67. TVXQ 2006, *TVXQ! Third Album: The another story of balloon* (Seoul: SM Entertainment SMCD137).
68. Wim Lunsing, "*Yaoi Ronsō*: Discussing Depictions of Male Homosexuality in Japanese Girls' Comics, Gay Comics and Gay Pornography," *Intersections: Gender, History and Culture in the Asian Context* 12 (2006). http://wwwsshe.murdoch.edu.au/intersections/issue12/lunsing.html 2006 (accessed January 5, 2007).
69. Literally *feiyi suosi*, which my dictionary translates as "unimaginably queer."
70. Iwabuchi (2004), 169.
71. Iwabuchi (2004), 153–5.
72. Kōichi Iwabuchi, "Embracing Korean Wave: Japan and East Asian Media Flows." Unpublished paper presented at the symposium "*Hallyuwood:* Korean Screen Culture goes Global," School of Advanced Study, University of London (May 20, 2005).
73. Iwabuchi (2004), 162.
74. Cuncun Wu, "'Beautiful Boys Made up as Beautiful Girls:' Anti-masculine Taste in Qing China," in *Asian Masculinities: The Meaning and Practice of Manhood in China and Japan*, eds. Kam Louie and Morris Low (London; New York: RoutledgeCurzon, 2003), 28.
75. Wu (2003), 29.
76. See also Baranovitch (2003), 132–44, on "neo-traditional" male pop stars in China.
77. Wu (2003), 29.
78. Louie (2003), 6.
79. Hui Xiao, "Narrating a Happy China through a Crying Game: A Case-study of post-Mao Reality Shows," *China Media Research* 2, no. 3 (2006): 62.
80. Robertson (1998), 144.
81. Heather Willoughby, "Image is Everything: The Marketing of Femininity in South Korean Popular Music," in *Korean Pop Music: Riding the Wave*, ed. Keith Howard (Folkestone: Global Oriental, 2006), 107.

82. Ehrenreich, Hess, Jacobs (1992), 102.
83. Robertson, (1998), 42–3.
84. Cited in Ehrenreich, Hess, Jacobs (1992), 102.
85. Ehrenreich, Hess, Jacobs (1992), 85.
86. Described in Pease (2006), 186–7.
87. *Rain Zhongwen wang* (Rain Chinese Net), "*Zui xiang he Rain zuo de guanxi*" (The relationship you would most like to have with Rain), *Rain Zhongwen wan*. http://bbs.raincn.com/thread-32595-1-1.html (accessed January 3, 2007).
88. Ehrenreich, Hess, Jacobs (1992), 103.

Chapter 10 Surfing the Neo-Nationalist Wave: A Case Study of *Manga Kenkanryū*

1. Takeshima is the Japanese name for the Liancourt Rocks, called Dokdo in Korea. Both countries claim the tiny rocky islands as sovereign territory. The "Takeshima Day" event was meant to reinforce the Japanese historical claim to the islands.
2. Cited in James Card, "A Chronicle of Korea-Japan 'Friendship,'" *Japan Focus* (January 4, 2006). http://japanfocus.org/products/topdf/1778 (accessed December 17, 2007).
3. The term "Korean Wave" (*Kanryū* or *Hanryū*) was coined to describe the remarkable influx and popularity of South Korean TV drama in Japan from the late 1990s. For a detailed analysis of the "Korean Wave" phenomenon in Japan, see Yoshitaka Mōri ed., *Nisshiki hanryū: "Fuyu no sonata" to nikkan taishū bunka no genzai* (Korean Wave Japanese style: The TV drama "Winter Sonata" and the present state of Japanese-Korean popular culture) (Tokyo: Serika Shobō, 2004).
4. Japanese-Korean co-productions of film, anime, manga, or music should, of course, also be mentioned on the "positive" side. See essay by Yoshitaka Mōri in this volume.
5. See, for instance, the study by Iwabuchi Kōichi, *Recentering Globalization: Popular Culture and Japanese Transnationalism* (Durham, NC: Duke University Press, 2002) and the essays by Mōri, Pease, and Oyama in this volume.
6. Sharin Yamano, *Manga Kenkanryū* (Tokyo: Shinyūsha, 2005).
7. The Japanese title is ambiguous and can also be translated as "Anti-Korean Wave," "The Hate Korea Wave," "Hating the Korean Wave," "Disliking the Korean Wave." I have opted here for the relatively "neutral" "The Anti-Korean Wave," even though the first character of *kenkanryū* (*ken*) suggests "hate" or "dislike."
8. Heading on the inside cover of *Manga Kenkanryū 2*. Sharin Yamano, *Manga Kenkanryū 2* (Tokyo: Shinyūsha, 2006a).
9. Headings on the front cover of *Manga Kenkanryū 2* (Yamano 2006a).

10. Sharin Yamano, *Manga Kenkanryū — Kōshiki gaidobukku* (*Manga* Kenkanryū — Official Guidebook) (Tokyo: Shinyūsha, 2006b).

11. Rumi Sakamoto and Matt Allen, "Hating the 'Korean Wave'" Comic Books: A Sign of New Nationalism in Japan?" *Japan Focus* (October 4, 2007). http://www.japanfocus.org/products/details/2535 (accessed December 17, 2007).

12. This term is borrowed from Kenta Tanimichi's article "The Youthful Face of Japanese Nationalism," *Far Eastern Economic Review* 168 (November 2005): 45–7.

13. Benjamin Lee and Edward LiPuma, "Cultures of Circulation: The Imaginations of Modernity," *Public Culture* 14, no. 1 (2002): 191–213.

14. Henry A. Giroux, *Beyond the Spectacle of Terrorism: Global Uncertainty and the Challenge of the New Media* (Boulder; London: Paradigm Publishers, 2006), 74.

15. Volume 2 of the manga was published in February 2006 to coincide with Shimane Prefecture's celebration of "Takeshima Day." The publication of volume 3 in August 2007 coincided with Japanese commemorations of the end of WWII and debates about prime-ministerial visits to Yasukuni Shrine.

16. Figures on publisher homepage. Shinyūsha, *"Kenkanryū* site," Shinyūsha, www.shinyusha.co.jp/~kenkanryu/ (accessed March 7, 2007).

17. During the visit of Japanese Prime Minister Koizumi to North Korea in September 2002, the North Korean President Kim Jong-il admitted publicly and for the first time that North Korean agents had abducted a number of Japanese citizens. This revelation sparked major political tensions between the two countries (when it was meant to achieve the opposite, i.e., normalization of ties) and fierce reactions from some Japanese groups against North Korea and Resident Koreans affiliated with North Korea.

18. Giroux (2006), 73.

19. On the aspect of pleasure in the consumption of revisionist narratives, see Aaron Gerow, "Consuming Asia, Consuming Japan: The New Neonationalist Revisionist in Japan," in *Censoring History: Citizenship and Memory in Japan, Germany, and the United States*, eds. Laura Hein and Mark Selden (Armonk, NY: M. E. Sharpe, 2000), 74–8.

20. See, for instance, the various reviews in Yamano (2006b) or the *Manga Kenkanryū* page on the Amazon Japan website at Amazon.co.jp, http://www.amazon.co.jp/review/product/488380478X/ref=cm_cr_dp_all_summary?%5Fencoding=UTF8&showViewpoints=1&sortBy=bySubmissionDateDescending (last accessed January 8, 2008). I also encountered similar comments when I spoke with a Japanese MA student.

21. Giroux (2006), 12.

22. Giroux (2006), 70.

23. Giroux (2006), 75.

24. On the concept of "public technologies," see Dilip Parameshwar Gaonkar

and Elizabeth A. Povinelli, "Technologies of Public Forms: Circulation, Transfiguration, Recognition," *Public Culture* 15, no. 3 (2003): 385–97.

25. Blurb on back cover of *Manga Kenkanryū*. Sharin Yamano, *Manga Kenkanryū* (Tokyo: Shinyūsha 2005).
26. Yamano (2006b), 52.
27. Yamano (2006b), 58.
28. Yamano (2006b), 61.
29. Yamano (2006b), 63.
30. Scott McCloud, *Understanding Comics — The Invisible Art* (New York: HarperPerennial, 1994), 44.
31. McCloud (1994), 44–5.
32. Nishio Kanji is one of the leading figures of the neo-conservative Society for History Textbook Reform (*Atarashii Rekishi o Tsukuru-kai*, usually abbreviated to *Tsukuru-kai*).
33. Yamano (2005), 3.
34. Yamano (2005), 4.
35. Yamano (2006), 2.
36. Blurb on back cover of Volume 1 of *Manga Kenkanryū*, Yamano (2005).
37. Yamano (2006a), 137.
38. Yamano (2006a), 136.
39. Yamano (2006a), 139.
40. Yamano (2006a), 160.
41. *Utsukushii kuni e* (Towards a beautiful nation) is the title of former Prime Minister Abe Shinzō's book, published by Bungei Shunjū in 2006, which proposes the formation of a "true nationalism" and the renewal of a strong, proud, hence beautiful Japan.
42. Yamano (2005), 240.
43. Yamano (2005), 213.
44. Yamano (2005), 216.
45. Yamano (2005), 217.
46. Yamano (2005), 221.
47. See episode 3 (Yamano 2005), 84–5.
48. Yamano (2005), 84–5.
49. I am grateful to Susanne Koppensteiner for this insight.
50. Yamano (2006b), 31.
51. Yamano (2005), 230.
52. *Freeter* refers to young people who are working freelance, are un- or underemployed. *Neets* refer to young people not in education, employment, or training.
53. On this aspect of self-esteem, see also Naoki Sakai, "Two Negations: The Fear of Being Excluded and the Logic of Self-Esteem," in *Contemporary Japanese Thought*, ed. Richard F. Calichman (New York: Columbia University Press, 2005), 159–92.

54. Kōichi Iwabuchi calls this the "'trichotomy' of 'Japan', 'the West' and 'the rest'" that does not change "the binary logic." "Complicit Exoticism: Japan and Its Other — Who Imagines 'Japaneseness'?: Orientalism, Occidentalism and Self-Orientalism," *The Australian Journal of Media & Culture* 8, no. 2 (1994), 49–82.
55. Yamano (2005), 116.
56. Yamano (2006b), 18, 27.
57. Yamano (2005), 118.
58. Yamano (2006b), 60.
59. Thus, when Yasuhiro is in the running for president of the committee he decides to leave the group and establish his own network for the re-education of *Zainichi* Koreans. The committee remains under ethnic-Japanese leadership.
60. Yamano (2006a), 194.
61. Homi Bhabha, *The Location of Culture* (New York: Routledge, 1994), 36–9.
62. Morita Akiō and Shintarō Ishihara, *Nō to ieru nihon: shin nichi-bei kankei no hōsaku* (The Japan that can say no: Why Japan will be first among equals) (Tokyo: Kōbunsha, 1989).
63. See Sharin. Yamano, "Sharin *purofiiru*" (Sharin profile), Yamano Sharin web page. http://propellant.fc2web.com/contents/sharin/sharin.html (accessed March 7, 2007).
64. On these surveys, see Hironori Sasada, "Youth and Nationalism in Japan," *SAIS Review* XXVI, no. 2 (2006): 111–6.
65. Article 9 is the famous "No War" clause of the Japanese postwar constitution and states: "Aspiring sincerely to an international peace based on justice and order, the Japanese people forever renounce war as a sovereign right of the nation and the threat or use of force as means of settling international disputes. In order to accomplish the aim of the preceding paragraph, land, sea and air forces, as well as other war potential, will never be maintained. The right of belligerency of the state will not be recognized." http://www.constitution.org/cons/japan.txt (accessed December 17, 2007).
66. Giroux (2006), 1.
67. Giroux (2006), 3.
68. From the discussion of Guy Debord's *Comments on the Society of the Spectacle* (1988) in *Afflicted Power: Capital and Spectacle in a New Age of War*, ed. Retort (London: Verso, 2005), 22–3.
69. According to a study by a group of Japanese sociologists, 2channel has around 3 million "unique users" and the number of visitors/accesses exceeds 8 million per day. Matsumura, Miura, et al., "The Dynamism of 2channel," *AI & Society* 19:1 (January 2005), 84–92. http://www.rhul.ac.uk/Management/News-and-Events/conferences/SID2003/Tracks-Presentations/12%20-%20Matsumura%20et%20al.pdf (accessed December 17, 2007).
70. Nevin Thompson, "Inside the Japanese Blogosphere — The Anti-Korea Wave," Global Voices Online, report posted on July 29, 2005. http://

www.globalvoicesonline.org/2005/07/29/inside-the-japanese-blogosphere-the-anti-korea-wave/ (accessed January 23, 2007).

71. This category of the Japanese *Ninki burogu rankingu* (Popular blog ranking) can be accessed at http://blog.with2.net/rank1500-0.html.

72. For an insightful discussion of these mechanisms of fragmentation and reductionism, see Tessa Morris-Suzuki's study, *The Past Within Us: Media, Memory, History* (London: Verso, 2005), especially Chapter 6.

73. See, for example, letter by 36-year old "salaryman" reader from Tokyo in Yamano (2006b), 17.

74. Yamano (2005), 232–3.

75. Norimitsu Onishi, "Ugly Images of Asian Rivals Become Best Sellers in Japan," *New York Times*, November 19, 2005. http://www.nytimes.com/2005/11/19/international/asia/19comics.html (last access December 17, 2007).

76. Leo Lewis, "Neighbour fails to see funny side of comic," *The Times* (November 1, 2005). http://www.timesonline.co.uk/tol/news/world/article585019.ece (last access December 17, 2007).

77. Julian Ryall, "Comic Twist to Japanese Nationalism," *Aljazeera.net* (January 30, 2006). http://english.aljazeera.net/English/Archive/Archive?ArchiveID=21164 (last access December 17, 2007).

78. "Kenkanryu in the New York Times," Occidentalism.org, comment posted on November 21, 2005. http://www.occidentalism.org/?p=104 (accessed December 17, 2007).

79. Onishi (2005). See note 75.

80. Posting on same page of Occidentalism.org under "Wiesunja said: …" "Kenkanryu in the New York Times," Occidentalism.org, comment posted on November 21, 2005. http://www.occidentalism.org/?p=104 (accessed December 17, 2007).

81. On this lack of alternative Internet sites, see also Sakamoto and Allen (2007).

82. Giroux (2006), 68.

Chapter 11 Melodrama, Exorcism, Mimicry: Japan and the Colonial Past in the New Korean Cinema

1. Mark Shiel, *Italian Neorealism: Rebuilding the Cinematic City* (London; New York: Wallflower, 2006), 6–7. (Citing Marcia Landy, *Italian Film* [Cambridge: Cambridge University Press, 2000], xiv.)

2. "The postcolonial does not privilege the colonial. It is concerned with colonial history only to the extent that that history has determined the configurations and power structures of the present, to the extent that much of the world lives in the violent disruptions of its wake." Robert C. Young, *Postcolonialism* (Oxford: Blackwell, 2001), 4. See note 16 for qualifications

about the situation of contemporary South Korea and conceptual notions concerning the postcolonial.

3. See, for instance, Darcy Paquet, "Japanese Films in Korea," *Koreanfilm.org* (2004), http://koreanfilm.org/japanfilm.html; Chaibong Hahm and Kim Seog-gun, "Remembering Japan and North Korea: The Politics of Memory in South Korea,' in *Memory and History in East and Southeast Asia*, ed. Gerrit W. Gong (Washington, DC: CSIS Press, 2001), XX; Kim Hyun-mee, "Kankoku ni okeru Nihon taishū bunka no jūyō to 'Fuan ishiki no keisei" (The significance of Japanese popular culture in Korea and the formation of a consciousness of anxiety), in *Nisshiki Hanryū: "Fuyu no sonata" to nikkan taishū bunka no genzai* (Korean Wave Japanese Style: The TV-Drama "Winter Sonata" and the Present State of Japanese-Korean Popular Culture), ed. Mōri Yoshitaka (Tokyo: Serika Shobō, 2004).

4. Korean has one of the most efficient systems of writing on the planet, but it is transcribed by several different styles of romanization. In this chapter I generally transcribe Korean film titles, words, or names via the clumsy McCune-Reischauer system but leave alone titles or names in direct quotations, names of Korean authors writing in English, and well-known names such as Korean presidents and their families.

5. See, for example, Darcy Paquet, "The Korean Film Industry: 1992 to the Present," in *New Korean Cinema*, eds. Chi-Yun Shin and Julian Stringer (Edinburgh: University of Edinburgh Press, 2005), 32–50.

6. Korean Film Council, "Statistics," *Korean Cinema 2006*, 494–6. http://www.kofic. or.kr/english (accessed November 20, 2007).

7. As Darcy Paquet reported in 2005, "Korea's TV, cable and video/DVD markets remain miniscule. Online piracy and high prices have stunted the DVD sector, which is dominated by rentals rather than sell-through. Surveys indicate that only 29% of the two million households that own a DVD player have ever bought a DVD. Whereas US or European releases can double their revenues on DVD sales alone, Korea more resembles the US in the 1970s, when films had to earn two and a half times their budget in theaters just in order to break even." "Essays from the Far East Film Festival: Korea Main Essay, 2005." http://koreanfilm.org/feff.html#2005 (accessed November 20, 2007).

   Without the use of subscription websites, it is not easy to locate reliable figures on DVD sales of Korean film within the East and Southeast Asian region. In general, Chinese subtitled VCDs and DVDs sell well throughout the region but are subject to all the usual hazards of piracy; English subtitling of VCDs and DVDs (with or without Chinese) is fairly common and usually bumps up the price; at the top of the price scale are Japanese subtitled DVDs. Regional flows of DVDs (direct sales or licensing) therefore flow rather uphill as regards the Japanese market, and rather outside the corporate channels for Chinese-subtitled VCDs and DVDs.

8. Korean Film Council, "Statistics," *Korean Cinema 2006*, 494–500. The "Foreword" to this official publication does, however, note that, as regards the Japanese market, the "Korean Wave may be retreating to a more realistic level."

9. Youna Kim, "The Rising East Asian 'Wave': Korean Media Go Global," in *Media on the Move: Global Flow and Contra-flow*, ed. Dayan Kishan Thussu (London; New York: Routledge, 2007), 135–52.

10. Chris Berry, "From National Cinema to Cinema of the National: Chinese-language Cinema and Hou Hsiao-hsien's 'Taiwan Triology'," in *Theorising National Cinema*, eds. Valentina Vitali and Paul Willemen (London: BFI Publishing, 2006), 148.

11. See, for just one of many recent rebuttals, Alexis Dudden and Kozo Mizoguchi, "Abe's Violent Denial: Japan's Prime Minister and the 'Comfort Women'," *Japan Focus: An Asia-Pacific E-Journal* (2007). http://japanfocus.org/products/details/2368 (accessed November 20, 2007).

12. Hahm Chaibong and Kim Seog-gun, "Remembering Japan and North Korea: The Politics of Memory in South Korea," in *Memory and History in East and Southeast Asia*, ed. Gerrit W. Gong (Washington DC: CSIS Press, 2001), 101.

13. Gi-Wook Shin and Michael Robinson, *Colonial Modernity in Korea* (Cambridge, MA; London: Harvard University Asia Center, 1999), 12.

14. John Lie, *Han Unbound: The Political Economy of South Korea* (Stanford, CA: Stanford University Press, 1998), 181.

15. Kang Nae-hui, "Mimicry and Difference: A Spectraology of the Neo-Colonial Intellectual," in *Specters of the West and the Politics of Translation: Traces 1*, eds. Naoki Sakai and Yukiko Hanama, 123–58 (Hong Kong: Hong Kong University Press, 2000), 133.

16. Kang refers to an important article by Anne McClintock, in which she noted that "the term 'post-colonialism' is, in many cases, prematurely celebratory. Ireland may, at a pinch, be 'post-colonial,' but for the inhabitants of British-occupied Northern Ireland, not to mention the Palestinian inhabitants of the Israeli Occupied Territories and the West Bank may be nothing 'post' about colonialism at all": see "The Angel of Progress: The Pitfalls of the Term 'Postcolonialism'," in *Colonial discourse/postcolonial theory*, eds. Francis Baker, Peter Hulme, and Margaret Iversen (Manchester; New York: University of Manchester Press, 1994), 256. In Kang's eyes, the continued division of the Korean peninsula and the massive presence of the US military in South Korea mean that any actually existing postcoloniality may still lie on some optimistic horizon.

17. Kang (2000), 133.

18. Kang (2000), 135.

19. "The discourse of mimicry is constructed around an ambivalence; in order to be effective, mimicry must continually produce its slippage, its excess, its difference. The authority of that mode of colonial discourse that I have

called mimicry is therefore stricken by an indeterminacy: mimicry emerges as the representation of a difference that is itself a process of disavowal. Mimicry is thus the sign of a double articulation; a complex strategy of reform, regulation and discipline, which 'appropriates' the Other as it visualizes power:" Homi Bhabha, "Of Mimicry and Man: The Ambivalence of Colonial Discourse," in *The Location of Culture* (London: Routledge, 1994), 85.
20. Kang (2000), 151.
21. See Yoshikuni Igarashi, *Bodies of Memory: Narratives of War in Postwar Japanese Culture, 1945–1970* (Princeton, NJ; Oxford: Princeton University Press, 2000), 122–9; John Lie, *Multiethnic Japan* (Cambridge, MA; London: Harvard University Press, 2001), 61–63.
22. KBS Global, "'Rikidozan' to Hit Japanese Theaters in March," KBS Global website (August 22, 2005). http://english.kbs.co.kr/ (accessed August 24, 2005).
23. Bhabha (1994), 85.
24. Susan Hayward, *Cinema Studies: The Key Concepts* (3rd ed.) (London; New York: Routledge, 2006), 239.
25. Darcy Paquet, "Essays from the Far East Film Festival: Korea Main Essay 2006," *Koreanfilm.org* (2006). http://koreanfilm.org/feff.html#2006 (accessed November 20, 2007).
26. Kathleen McHugh and Nancy Abelmann, *South Korean Golden Age Melodrama: Gender, Genre, and National Cinema* (Detroit, MI: Wayne State University Press, 2005).
27. "The share of Hollywood films in the Korean market remained higher than in Japan proper, reaching heights of 40 percent of the length [footage] of film actually screened in Korea." Brian Yecies, "Systematization of Film Censorship in Colonial Korea: Profiteering from Hollywood's First Golden Age," *Journal of Korean Studies* 1, no. 10 (2005): 65. In his pioneering research, Yecies has been able to demonstrate that the censorship fees paid by Hollywood distributors provided a flow of income which substantially funded the Government General's film censorship apparatus.
28. Min Eungjun, Jinsook Joo, and Kwak Han Ju, *Korean Film: History, Resistance, and Democratic Imagination* (Westport, CT; London: Praeger, 2003), 33.
29. Min, Joo, and Han (2003), 35.
30. Thomas Elsaesser, "Tales of Sound and Fury," in *Film Genre Reader III*, ed. Barry Keith Grant (Austin: University of Texas Press, 2003), 370–1.
31. For more about *Hanbando*, see my "The Political Economics of Patriotism: The Case of *Hanbando*," in *Korea Yearbook 2007: Politics, Economics, Society*, eds. Ruediger Frank, James E. Hoare, Patrick Koellner and Susan Pares (Leiden and Boston: Brill, 2008), pp. 171–98. See also the comments and debate in websites such as *koreanfilm.org*; *The Korea Times*, http://times.hankooki.com/; and the website of the Korean Film Council, http://www.koreanfilm.or.kr/.

32. Tae-jong Kim, "Nationalistic 'Hanbando' Lacks Healthy Perspective," *Korea Times* (July 13, 2006).

33. Tae-jong Kim, "Local Movies Thrive on Nationalism," *Korea Times* (July 19, 2006).

34. Tae-jong Kim (2006).

35. For the official International Olympic Committee profile on Son, see International Olympic Committee, "Kitei Son." http://www.olympic.org/ uk/athletes/profiles/bio_uk.asp?par_i_id=88103 (accessed November 29, 2007).

36. For a brief sketch of Im and his films up to 2005, see Davide Cazzaro and Giovanni Spagnoletti, *Il cinema sudcoreano comtemporaneo e l'opera di Jang Sun-woo* (Contemporary South Korean Cinema and the Work of Jang Sun-Woo) (Venezia: Marsilio, 2005), 224–6.

37. For *Time Magazine*'s November 5, 1979 account of the assassination, see "Assassination in Seoul," *Time* (November 5, 1979). http://www.time.com/ time/magazine/article/0,9171,912509,00.html (accessed November 20, 2007).

38. Miyako Harumi's Korean father had come to Kyoto in 1940 and proved successful in that city's famous silk business. Harumi claimed to have been unaware of his foreign origins until her late twenties. See any of the many Japanese sites devoted to the singer, or the entry in the Japanese Wikipedia, *Uikipedeia*, "Miyako Harumi," *Uikepedeia* (Wikipedia). http://ja.wikipedia.org/ wiki/%E9%83%BD%E3%81%AF%E3%82%8B%E3%81%BF (accessed November 20, 2007).

39. Seungsook Moon, "Begetting the Nation: The Androcentrric Discourse of National History and Development in South Korea," in *Dangerous Women: Gender & Korean Nationalism,* ed. Elaine H Kim and Chungmoo Choi (New York; London: Routledge, 1997).

40. Im Sangsu has been quite open about his tactical use of language. See Paolo Bertolin, "An Interview with Im Sang-soo," *Koreanfilm.org*, 2005. http:// koreanfilm.org/imss.html (accessed November 20, 2007).

41. Paquet Review (2005).

42. Sheila Miyoshi Jager, "Korean Collaborators: South Korea's Truth Committees and the Forging on a New Pan-Korean Nationalism," *Japan Focus: An Asia-Pacific E-Journal* (2004). http://www.japanfocus.org/products/details/2170 (accessed November 20, 2007).

43. The shot also incorporates an oblique homage to a similar scene: Martin Scorsese's camera on its overhead path through the mayhem wrought by Travis Bickle (Robert De Niro) near the end of *Taxi Driver* (1976).

Chapter 12 Reconsidering Cultural Hybridities: Transnational Exchanges of Popular Music in between Korea and Japan

1. See Tatsurō Hanada, Colin Sparks, and Shunya Yoshimi, eds., *Karuchuraru sutadeiizu tono taiwa* (Dialogues with cultural studies) (Tokyo: Shinyō-sha, 1999).

2. Minoru Iwasaki and Hiroaki Ozawa, eds. *Gekishin! Kokuritsu daigaku* (The National university great shake-up!) (Tokyo: Miraisha, 1999). This collected volume offers a good critical review of the neoliberalist university.

3. The teaching of popular culture in higher education has recently become popular. For example, Kyoto Seika University established the Faculty of Manga in 2006, and Tokyo National University of Fine Arts and Music is planning to launch an MA program in animation.

4. Consider, for example, Azuma Hiroki, who started his career as a Derridian and who then shifted his attention to become a critic of popular — and *otaku* (individuals defined as "geeks" and who are often associated with underground or subcultural forms of animation, manga cartoons, niche music, and so on) — culture. Although he does not see himself as a Cultural Studies scholar, he is a good example of how postmodern/Cultural Studies theory survives in market-oriented academia in Japan.

5. The former minister of Foreign Affairs, Asō Tarō, officially stated that manga is an important cultural product in Japan and proposed to establish the International Manga Award "as a Nobel-like prize of manga" in 2007 (*Sankei Shinbun*, June 29, 2006).

6. The "Korean Wave" represents a boom of Korean popular culture across East and Southeast Asia in the early 2000s that was focused, in particular, on TV dramas, for example, *A Jewel in the Palace* (*Tae Changgŭm*, 2003) and *Winter Sonata* (*Kyŏul yŏn'ga*, 2002), which were the most successful. It started in mainland China in 1999 and expanded to Japan, Taiwan, Thailand, and Singapore. See Mōri Yoshitaka, ed. *Nisshiki-Hanryū: "Fuyu no sonata" to nikkan taishū bunka no genzai* (Korean Wave Japanese Style: The TV-Drama "Winter Sonata" and the Present State of Japanese-Korean Popular Culture) (Tokyo: Serika Shobō, 2004).

7. *Zainichi* is a term that represents those who have North or South Korean nationality but who reside in Japan. Historically, most *Zainichi* moved (or were forced to move) to Japan in the colonial period (1910–45) and remained there after the war. The number of *Zainichi* at the end of the war was 2,100,000 but due in part to the return of many to the Korean Peninsula and the Japanese naturalization of others, this figure now stands at about 600,000. Although there are not many available texts concerning *Zainichi* in English, the following offer good introductions: Chapter 5 especially of Yoshio Sugimoto, *An Introduction to Japanese Society* (Cambridge: Cambridge

University Press, 2003); and John C. Maher, Yumiko Kawanishi, and Yong-
Yo Yi, "Maintaining Culture and Language: Koreans in Osaka with Ikuno-
ku, Osaka: Centre of Hope and Struggle," in *Diversity in Japanese Culture
and Language*, eds. John Christopher Maher and Gaynor Macdonald (London:
Kegan Paul International Ltd, 1995), 160–77.

8. Stuart Hall, "New Ethnicities," in *"Race," Culture and Difference*, eds. Ali
    Rattansi and James Donald (London: Sage Publications in association with
    The Open University, 1992), 252–9; Paul Gilroy, *The Black Atlantic: Modernity
    and Double Consciousness* (London: Verso, 1993); Kobena Mercer, *Welcome
    to the Jungle: New Positions in Black Cultural Studies* (London: Routledge,
    1994); Homi K. Bhabha, *The Location of Culture* (London: Routledge, 1994).

9. See, for example, Phil Cohen, ed., *New Ethnicities, Old Racisms* (London:
    Zed Books, 1999), especially Cohen's introductory chapter ("Introduction:
    Through a Glass Darkly: Intellectuals on Race") and Jayne O. Ifekwunigwe's
    chapter in the same volume, "Old Whine, New Vassals: Are Diaspora and
    Hybridity Postmodern Interventions?" See also Pnina Werbner and Tariq
    Modood, eds. *Debating Cultural Hybridity: Multi-Cultural Identities and the
    Politics of Anti-Racism* (London: Zed Books, 1997), 180–204; and Avtar
    Brah and Annie E. Coombes, eds. *Hybridity and Its Discontents: Politics,
    Science, Culture* (London: Routledge, 2000).

10. Jonathan Friedman, "Global Crises, the Struggle for Cultural Identity and
    Intellectual Porkbarrelling: Cosmopolitans versus Locals, Ethnics and Nationals
    in an Era of De-hegemonisation," in *Debating Cultural Hybridity: Multi-
    Cultural Identities and the Politics of Anti-Racism*, eds. Pnina Werbner and
    Tariq Modood (London: Zed Books, 1997), 73.

11. Friedman (1997), 72–82.

12. Nakasone also faced domestic criticism. For example, Hokkaido Utari Kyōkai,
    one of the human rights organizations of the Ainu, a major ethnic minority
    in Japan, delivered a strong protest to the prime minister just after the
    apology (*Asahi Shinbun*, August 5, 2001).

13. During the Koizumi-Abe administration, government ministers repeated the
    gaffe of describing Japan as "a racially homogenous nation." For example, in
    2005, the Minister of International Affairs and Communications, Asō Tarō,
    said in a public speech that Japan is a unique country because it is one state
    and one civilization, has one language, one culture and one race. There is no
    other country like Japan in the world (*Asahi Shinbun*, October 15, 2005). Despite
    severe public criticism, the government has never issued an apology.

14. From a sociological perspective, *Zainichi* may be categorized as an ethnic
    group rather than a racial one, because *Zainichi* cannot be distinguished
    from *nihonjin* (Japanese people) according to racial/biological features such
    as skin color or face. Second- and third-generation *Zainichi* are often much
    more enculturated into Japanese culture, language, and moral values. The
    problem arises in relation with the Japanese language's unique definition of

nihonjin, which is not a territorial category but an ethnic one. In ethnicity, the term *nihonjin* is always a heavily racialized one in Japanese public discourse since it makes particular references to (mythic) Japanese blood. See, for example, Kōsaku Yoshino, *Cultural Nationalism in Contemporary Japan* (London: Routledge, 1992). The category of *nihonjin* also functions as an official status of nationality as legitimized by the Japanese passport. As a result of this racial-ethnic-political slippage, racism is viewed only as a "Black" or "Jewish" problem in the United States and Europe, while *nihonjin* believe themselves to be "innocent" to race. Japan, after all, is supposed to be a "mono-racial" nation. *Minzoku* is a powerfully confusing word that blurs the distinction between nation, race, and ethnicity, as it is used as an equivalent term in translation to all the three English terms.

15. In 2003, the Tokyo Metropolitan Government sued Edagawa Chōsen gakkō, one of Japan's oldest ethnic primary schools established in 1946. In so doing, the long-term consensus existing between the local authority and the school was broken. The case was eventually settled out of court and the school agreed to pay 170 million yen in 2007. This incident is a recent example of the regional and national governments trying to repress ethnic schools. See Kinohanasha Publishing Ltd. Homepage, "*Edagawa chōsen gakkō shien pēji*" [Edagawa Korean School Support Page], Kinohanasha Publishing Co. Ltd. http://kinohana.la.coocan.jp/court.html (accessed December 18, 2007).

16. See Ken'ichi Ueda, *Shanhai Bugiugu 1945: Hattori Ryōichi no Bōken* (Shanghai boogie woogie 1945: The adventures of Hattori Ryōichi) (Tokyo: Nihon Bungeisha 2003).

17. Makoto Sataka, *Hika: Koga Masao no jinsei to merodī* (A sad song: The life and melodies of Koga Masao) (Tokyo: Mainichi Shinbunsha, 2005), 57–68.

18. Nobuko Kyō, *Nikkan ongaku nōto: "Ekkyō" suru tabibito no uta o otte* (Notes on music in Japan and Korea: Following the songs of travellers who "cross national borders") (Tokyo: Iwanami Shoten, 1998), 97–8.

19. Sataka criticized Koga's problematic political comments. For instance, in a symposium in the journal *Shintaishū* (*The New Masses*) in 1940, Koga is recorded as having said, "they should kick out all sentimental songs. Popular and vulgar sentimentalism that only appeal to the people is inappropriate. The government should censor all the music. I can appreciate such an action. Censorship gives me a guideline as to which way we should go." Sataka suggested that this was unbearably offensive. Sataka (2005), 64.

20. Roland Barthes, *Image-Text-Music* (New York: Fontana Press, 1993), 142–9.

21. Hall (1980).

22. Masao Koga, *Jiden: waga kokoro no uta* (My story: Songs in my mind) (Tokyo: Tenbōsha, 2001), 205. In spite of Koga's nationalist leanings in the postwar period, rumors have circulated in Japan that he is *Zainichi*. In fact, Koga would not be exceptional were this the case. Many popular music singers

are often rumored to be *Zainichi* since they actually are, even though most do not come out for fear of social discrimination.

23. "Japanese Bring Latest in Music: Composer Plans to Introduce New Songs on Good-Will Mission," *The Los Angeles Times*, December 6, 1938.

24. See Yoshitaka Mōri, "Winter Sonata and Cultural Practices of Active Fans in Japan: Considering Middle-Aged Women as Cultural Agents," in *Approaches to East Asian Pop Culture: Examining Korean TV Dramas*, eds. Beng Huat Chua and Iwabuchi Kōichi (Hong Kong: Hong Kong University Press, 2008).

25. Christine Yano's analysis of Kim Yŏnja, a Korean *enka* singer, is one of the few introductions available in English. Christine R. Yano, "Raising the Ante of Desire: Foreign Female Singers in a Japanese Pop Music World," in *Refashioning Pop Music in Asia: Cosmopolitan Flows, Political Tempos and Aesthetic Industries*, eds. Allen Chun, Ned Rossiter, and Brian Shoesmith (London: Routledge, 2004), 159–211. It is rather a pity that even though Yano was very aware of *enka*'s hybrid nature in her early work, her research concerns are more about Japaneseness and the Japanese heart/soul of *enka*. Christine R. Yano, *Tears of Longing: Nostalgia and the Nation in Japanese Popular Song* (Cambridge: Harvard University Press, 2002), 30.

26. Gilroy (2006).

27. Transnationalism and "hybridity-as-origin" similarly helps us to understand other cultural phenomena. Consider, for example, the "Korean Wave" today, which has to be understood not as something made in Korea but as a hybrid product influenced by American film technology, Japanese drama and animation stories, and by a transnational marketing strategy in the media industry. It would be more culturally and politically fruitful to see the "Korean Wave" as a transnational project than as a Korean nationalistic one; in other words, we can see emerging forms of hybridity in Korean culture in the "Korean Wave" through the development of transnational cultural flows and exchanges.

28. Kangnam is an area located in the southern part of Seoul City that has recently become popular with wealthy young people for its fashion boutiques, clubs, bars, and restaurants.

29. Hiromichi Ugaya, *J-pop towa nanika* (What is J-pop?) (Tokyo: Iwanami-shoten, 2005), 17–21.

30. In an interview on February 20, 2005, Yi Ilwhan explained to me that he introduced J-pop to Korean listeners in his radio program between 2004 and 2005 while working at a production company, Satio. I would like to thank Professor Hyunjoon Shin for organizing the interview.

31. *Visual kei* (literally, visual style) is a kind of hard rock or gothic-styled rock music that is famous for its visual elements, for example, its flamboyant makeup and costumes.

32. One of the most successful examples is *Rollercoaster Come Closer* (Sony 2001, ARCJ-2003) mixed by Konishi Yasuharu, a member of Pizzicato five.

33. Musicians and DJs include Towa Tei, Fantastic Plastic Machine, Konishi Yasuharu, Jazztronik and Free Tempo.

34. VERBAL, *Verbal: Alien Alter Egos — Kami no pazuru sore wa boku jishin* (Puzzles of the gods, it is myself) (Tokyo: Kyūsokuteki jikan, 2002), 24–5.

35. m-flo, "m-flo loves WADA Akiko 'Hey!'" on *m-flo loves Emyli & Yoshika / WADA Akiko* (Rhythm Zone, 2005, ASIN: B0009N2XXK).

36. Ryūtarō Nakamura, " '*Chi to hone' no burūsu*" ("Blues of 'Blood and Bones'"), *Shūkan Bunshun* (August 11/18, 2005).

37. Yasuharu Konishi, "*Furii sōru: Wada Akiko*" ("Free Soul: Wada Akiko") (Teichiku, 2004, ASIN: B000657REQ).

38. Nina Cornyetz, "Fetishized Blackness, Hip Hop and Racial Desire in Contemporary Japan," *Social Text* 41 (1994): 113–39.

39. See Ian Condry, *Hip Hop Japan: Rap and the Paths of Cultural Globalization* (Durham, NC: Duke University Press, 2006).

40. Yoshitaka Mōri, "Culture=Politics: The Emergence of New Cultural Forms of Protest in the age of Freeter," *Inter-Asia Cultural Studies* 6, no.1 (2005): 17–29.

General Bibliography

"356 Yi wenren gong kai xin yu Bian 'zi ai yin tui' " [356 Artists' Open Letter Appeals to A-Bian to 'Show Self-Respect and Resign']. *Lianhe Bao* [United Daily News], August 25, 2006.

Aaker, David A. *Brand Portfolio Strategy: Creative Relevance, Differentiation, Energy, Leverage and Clarity.* New York: Simon and Schuster, 2004.

Abbas, Ackbar. *Hong Kong: Culture and the Politics of Disappearance.* Hong Kong: Hong Kong University Press, 1997.

Abbas, Ackbar and John Nguyet Erni (eds.). *Internationalizing Cultural Studies: An Anthology.* Oxford: Blackwell, 2005.

Agency for Cultural Affairs, Japan. "Building a Society that Values Culture." Agency for Cultural Affairs, http://www.bunka.go.jp/english/pdf/chapter_01.pdf (accessed October 30, 2007).

Ahn, Jiwon. "Animated Subjects: On the Circulation of Japanese Animation as Global Cultural Products." Paper presented at The Globalization and Popular Culture: Production, Consumption and Identity Workshop, University of Manitoba, 2001, http://www.umanitoba.ca/faculties/arts/english/media/workshop/papers/ahn/ahn_paper.pdf (accessed April 30, 2002).

Alasuutari, Pertti. *Researching Culture: Qualitative Method and Cultural Studies.* London: Sage, 1995.

Allison, Anne. "Can Popular Culture Go Global? How Japanese 'Scouts' and 'Rangers' Fare in the U.S." In *A Century of Popular Culture in Japan*, ed. Douglas Slaymaker, 127–53. Lewiston: Edwin Mellen Press, 2000.

Amano, Mad. "Shogun boom no nazo o toku: hainichi ka hainichi ka" [To Resolve the Mystery of the *Shogun* Boom: Bashing Japan]. *Ushio* (January 1981): 104–13.

Amazon.co.jp. *"Manga Kenkanryū Mukku"* [*Manga* The Anti-Korean Wave]. Amazon.co.jp, http://www.amazon.co.jp/%E3%83%9E%E3%83%B3%E3% 82%AC%E5%AB%8C%E9%9F%93%E6%B5%81-%E5%B1%B1%E9%87%8 E-%E8%BB%8A%E8%BC%AA/dp/488380478X/ ref=pd_bbs_sr_2?ie =UTF8&s=books&qid=1199783258&sr=8-2 (accessed January 8, 2008).

Anderson, Joseph L. and Donald Richie. *The Japanese Film: Art and Industry*. Expanded ed. Princeton, NJ: Princeton University Press, 1982.

Ang, Ien. "Who Needs Cultural Research?" In *Cultural Studies and Practical Politics: Theory, Coalition Building, and Social Activism*, ed. Pepi Leystina, 477–83. New York: Blackwell, 2004.

Anonymous. *Jibuli de refeng* [The Hot Air of Ghibli]. Beijing: Feitian dianzi yinxiang chubanshe, n.d.

Anonymous. *"Kaikyo! Nihon anime-shijō hatsu no Chūgoku kōkai kettei!! Gin'iro no kami no agito"* [What a Feat! The First Chinese Release in the History of Japanese Anime: *Silver-haired Agito*!!]. http://www.gin-iro.jp/ web/news_html/news_bn.php?REC=18 (accessed February 20, 2006).

Anonymous. "The Rising Sun of the Problematic Chinese Manga and Anime" [Zhongguo Dongman Chongman Wenti de 'Chaoyang']. Chinanim.com, October 16, 2005, http://www.chinanim.com/dh1/newsxx.asp?newsid=9856 (assessed March 3, 2006).

Appadurai, Arjun. *Modernity at Large: Cultural Dimensions of Globalization, Public Worlds; V. 1*. Minneapolis: University of Minnesota Press, 1996.

Arvidsson, Adam. *Brands: Meaning and Value in Media Culture*. London and New York: Routledge, 2006.

ASEAN Homepage. "Declaration of ASEAN Concord II (Bali Concord II)," ASEAN, http://www.aseansec.org/15159.htm (accessed October 30, 2007).

Ash, Robert. "Quarterly Chronicle." *The China Quarterly* 190 (2006): 509–51.

Baldwin, Richard. "Prospects and Problems for East Asian Regionalism: A Comparison with Europe." Paper presented at the Research Institute of Economy, Trade and Industry, January 31, 2003, http://www.rieti.go.jp/ en/events/bbl/03013101.html (accessed October 30, 2007).

Baranovitch, Nimrod. *China's New Voices: Popular Music, Ethnicity, Gender and Politics, 1978–1997*. Berkeley: University of California Press, 2003.

Barlow, Tani E. "Colonialism's Career in Postwar China Studies." In *Formations of Colonial Modernity in East Asia*, ed. Tani E. Barlow, 373–412. Durham, NC: Duke University Press, 1997.

Barthes, Roland. *Image-Text-Music*. New York: Fontana Press, 1993.

Bataille, Georges. "The Psychological Structure of Fascism." *New German Critique*, no. 16, (1979): 64–87.

Bauman, Zygmunt. *Globalization: The Human Consequences*. Cambridge: Polity, 1998.

Beals, Gregory and Kevin Platt. "The Birth of Asiawood." *Newsweek* (May 21, 2001).

Beck, Ulrich. "Cosmopolitan Society and Its Enemies." *Theory, Culture and Society* 19, nos. 1–2 (2002): 17–44.

———. *The Cosmopolitan Vision.* Cambridge: Polity, 2006.

Berger, Mark. *The Battle for Asia: From Decolonization to Globalization.* London: RoutledgeCurzon, 2004.

Berry, Chris. "From National Cinema to Cinema of the National: Chinese-language Cinema and Hou Hsiao-hsien's 'Taiwan Trilogy'." In *Theorising National Cinema*, eds. Valentina Vitali and Paul Willemen, 148–57. London: BFI Publishing, 2006.

———. "'What's Big about the Big Film?': 'De-Westernizing' the Blockbuster in Korea and China." In *Movie Blockbusters,* ed. Julian Stringer, 217–29. London: Routledge, 2003.

Bertolin, Paolo. "An Interview with Im Sang-soo." *Koreanfilm.org*, 2005, http://www.koreanfilm.org/imss.html (accessed November 20, 2007).

Bezlova, Antoaneta. "From Cultural Revolution to Culture Exports." *Global Policy Forum* (July 28, 2006), http://www.globalpolicy.org/globaliz/cultural/2006/0728china.htm (accessed October 30, 2007).

Bhabha, Homi K. *The Location of Culture.* London: Routledge, 1994.

———. "DissemiNation: Time, Narrative, and the Margins of the Modern Nation." In *Nation and Narration*, ed. Homi K. Bhabha, 291–322. London: Routledge, 1990.

Bloomberg News, Reuters. "File-sharers in Europe Face a Wave of Lawsuits?" *The International Herald Tribune,* April 5, 2006.

Brah, Avtar and Annie E. Coombes, eds. *Hybridity and Its Discontents: Politics, Science, Culture.* London: Routledge, 2000.

Brown, Jonathan. "Illegal File-sharers Fined for First Time in Britain." *The Independent* (London), January 28, 2006.

Burgess, Chris. "The Asian Studies 'Crisis': Putting Cultural Studies into Asian Studies, and Asia into Cultural Studies." *The International Journal of Asian Studies* 1, no. 1 (2004): 121–36.

Burris, Val. "Review: The Transnational Capitalist Class." Contemporary Sociology 31, no. 4 (2002): 416–7.

Butler, Judith. *Theories in Subjection: The Psychic Life of Power.* Stanford, CA: Stanford University Press, 1997.

———. *Gender Trouble.* London: Routledge, 1990.

Card, James. "A Chronicle of Korea-Japan 'Friendship'." *Japan Focus* (January 2006), http://www.japanfocus.org/products/topdf/1778 (accessed December 17, 2007).

Castells, Manuel. *The Power of Identity*, 2nd ed. Malden; Oxford: Blackwell, 2004.

Caygill, Howard. *Walter Benjamin: The Colour of Experience.* London: Routledge, 1998.

Cazzaro, Davide and Giovanni Spagnoletti. *Il cinema sudcoreano comtemporaneo e l'opera di Jang Sun-woo* [Contemporary South Korean Cinema and the Work of Jang Sun-Woo]. Venezia: Marsilio, 2005.

Chan, Ho Hyun. *Waga shinema no tabi: Kankoku eiga o furikaeru* [My Cinema Journey — A Look Back through Korean Film]. Trans. Nemoto Rie. Tokyo: Gaifūsha, 2001.

Chan Siu-sin. "Animation Industry Lacks Talent and Chinese Brands, Says Official." *South China Morning Post,* January 20, 2006.

Chan, Stephen C. K. "Building Cultural Studies for Postcolonial Hong Kong: Aspects of the Postmodern Ruins in between Disciplines." *Critical Studies* 20 (2002): 217–31.

Chang, Mao-kuei. "Taidu shi wei toushen guoji de 'zhengming' yundong" [Taiwanese Independence Means Joining in the International Movement for the 'Rectification of Names']. *Zili Wanbao* [Independent Evening Post], April 1, 1992.

Chang, Sung-sheng Yvonne. *Modernism and the Nativist: Resistance Contemporary Chinese Fiction from Taiwan.* Durham, NC: Duke University Press, 1993.

Cheah, Pheng. "Cosmopolitical — Today." In *Cosmopolitics: Thinking and Feeling Beyond the Nation,* eds. Pheng Cheah and Bruce Robbins, 20–41. Minneapolis: University of Minnesota Press, 1998.

———. "Cosmopolitanism." *Theory, Culture and Society* 23, nos. 2–3 (2006): 486–96.

Chen Kuan-Hsing. "Why Is 'Great Reconciliation' Impossible? De-Cold War, Decolonization, or Modernity and Its Tears," Parts I and II. *Inter-Asia Cultural Studies* 3, nos. 1 and 2 (2002): 77–99, 235–51.

———. "The Decolonization Question." In *Trajectories: Inter-Asian Cultural Studies,* ed. Chen Kuan-hsing, 1–49. London: Routledge, 1998.

——— (ed.). *Trajectories: Inter-Asia Cultural Studies.* New York: Routledge, 1998.

Chen Yi-shen. "Zhongzheng miao de zhuangxing shunxu" [Taking Steps to Remake the Chiang Kai-shek Memorial]. *Ziyou Shibao* [Liberty Times], March 16, 2007.

Chen Yongxing. "Zou chu lishi yinying jianli hu ai shehui" [Stepping out of History's Shadow to Build a Society of Mutual Love]. *Zili Wanbao* [Independent Evening Post], February 28, 1988.

China Cultural Industries. "China Cultural Industries," China Cultural Industries, http://e.cnci.gov.cn/ (accessed October 30, 2007).

ChinaDaily.com. "Lovin' It: The Chinese Creativity Industry." *China Today* (March 3, 2004), http://www.chinadaily.com.cn/english/doc/2004-03/03/content_311221.htm (accessed October 30, 2007).

Ching, Leo. "Globalizing the Regional, Regionalizing the Global: Mass Culture and Asianism in the Age of Late Capital." In *Globalization,* ed. Arjun Appadurai, 233–58. Durham, NC: Duke University Press, 2001.

Chino, Keiko. "*Shogun* to karucha shokku" [*Shogun* and Culture Shock], *Kinema Junpō,* no. 797 (1980): 90.

Chiu, Kui-fen. "'Houzhimin' de Taiwan yanyi'" [The 'Post-Colonial' Logic of Taiwan]. In *Wenhua yanjiu zai Taiwan* [Cultural Studies in Taiwan], ed. Chen Kuan-hsing, 285–318. Taipei: Juliu Tushu, 2000.

Cho Hae-Joang. "Reading the 'Korean Wave' as a Sign of Global Shift." *Korea Journal* 45, no. 4 (2005): 147–82.

———. "Constructing and Deconstructing 'Koreanness'." In *Making Majorities: Constituting the Nation in Japan, Korea, China, Malaysia, Fiji, Turkey and United States*, ed. Dru. C. Gladney, 72–91. Stanford, CA: Stanford University Press, 1998.

Chow, Vivienne. "Internet Piracy Nightmare for Anime Director." *South China Morning Post*, January 9, 2006.

Chua, Beng Huat. "Conceptualizing an East Asian Popular Culture." *Inter-Asia Cultural Studies* 5, no. 2 (2004): 200–21.

Clavell, James. *James Clavell Interviews by Don Swain*, http://wiredforbook.org/jamesclavell/, 1986 (accessed November 5, 2007).

———. *King Rat*. London: Hodder and Stoughton, 1962.

———. *Tai-Pan*. London: Sphere Books, 1967.

Cohen, Phil (ed.). *New Ethnicities, Old Racisms*. London: Zed Books, 1999.

———. "Introduction: Through A Glass Darkly: Intellectuals on Race." In *New Ethnicities, Old Racism*, ed. Phil Cohen, 1–17. London: Zed Books, 1999.

Condry, Ian. *Hip-Hop Japan: Rap and the Paths of Cultural Globalization*. Stanford, CA: Duke University Press, 2006.

Constitution of Japan, The. http://www.constitution.org/cons/japan.txt (accessed December 17, 2007).

Coombe, Rosemary J. *The Cultural Life of Intellectual Properties: Authorship, Appropriation and the Law, Post-Contemporary Interventions*. Durham, NC: Duke University Press, 1998.

Cornyetz, Nina. "Fetishized Blackness, Hip-Hop and Racial Desire in Contemporary Japan." *Social Text* 41 (1994): 113–39.

Crampton, Thomas. "Pop Stars Learn to Live with Pirates." *International Herald Tribune*, February 21, 2003, http://www.iht.comcgi-bin/generec.cgi?template+articleprint.tmplh&AR (accessed April 29, 2003).

Cremin, Stephen. "Pucheon Set to Fill Regional Niche." *Hankyureh 21* (August 2, 2006), http://english.hani.co.kr/arti/english_edition/e_entertainment/146041.html (accessed December 13, 2007).

Crossley, Nick. *The Social Body: Habit, Identity and Desire*. London; Thousand Oaks, CA; New Delhi: Sage, 2001.

Czach, Liz. "Film Festivals, Programming, and the Building of a National Cinema." *The Moving Image* 4, no. 1 (2004): 76–88.

"Daitōa Atsuzoko Kyōeiken" (The Greater East Asian Japanese Super Platform-Shoe Sphere), *Nikkei Business* (January 15, 2001): 21.

Debord, Guy. *Comments on the Society of the Spectacle*. Trans. Malcolm Imrie. London: Verso, 1990.

De Landa, Manuel. *A New Philosophy of Society: Assemblage Theory and Social Complexity*. London; New York: Continuum, 2006.

Democratic Progressive Party. "Zuqun duoyuan guojia yi ti jueyiwen" [Resolution on Ethnic Pluralism and National Unity]. http://www.dpp.org.tw/history/pub/LIT_6.asp?ctyp=LITERATURE&catid=1742 (accessed September 10, 2006).

Department for Culture, Media and Sport, United Kingdom. *Staying Ahead: The Economic Performance of the UK's Creative Industries 2007*: 16, http://www.culture.gov.uk/NR/rdonlyres/6EF81987-5187-4B59-BE49-0DC140B99AB0/0/stayingahead_epukci_chp1.pdf (accessed October 30, 2007).

Dent, Christopher M. "Introduction: Northeast Asia — A Region in Search of Regionalism?" In *Northeast Asian Regionalism: Learning from the European Experience*, eds. Christopher M. Dent and David W. F. Huang, 1–15. London: RoutledgeCurzon, 2002.

Dent, Christopher M. and David W. F. Huang. *Northeast Asian Regionalism: Learning from the European Experience*. London: RoutledgeCurzon, 2002.

Dower, John. *Haiboku o dakishimete* [Embracing Defeat: Japan in the Wake of World War 2]. Trans. Yoichi Miura et al. 2 vols. Tokyo: Iwanami Shoten, 2001.

Dudden, Alexis and Kozo Mizoguchi. "Abe's Violent Denial: Japan's Prime Minister and the 'Comfort Women'." *Japan Focus: An Asia-Pacific E-Journal*, 2007, http://japanfocus.org/products/details/2368 (accessed November 20, 2007).

During, Simon. *Cultural Studies: A Critical Introduction*. New York: Routledge, 2004.

Dutton, Michael. "The Trick of Words: Asian Studies, Translation, and the Problems of Knowledge." In *Politics of Method in the Human Sciences: Positivism and Its Epistemological Others,* ed. George Steinmetz, 89–125. Durham, NC: Duke University Press, 2005.

———. "Lead Us Not Into Translation: Notes Toward a Theoretical Foundation for Asian Studies." *Nepantla: Views for South* 3, no. 3 (2002): 495–537.

Editorial. "'Anime' Subculture Exchange May Bridge Japan-China Gap." Jiji Press Ticker Service, October 29, 2005 (accessed through LexisNexis on March 2, 2006).

Editorial. "'Made in Japan' Trademark to Fight Anime Piracy." *Mainichi Daily News,* July 3, 2004 (accessed through LexisNexis on March 3, 2006).

Editorial. "Manga Course Attracts Lecturers." *The Daily Yomiuri,* June 9, 2004 (accessed through LexisNexis on March 3, 2006).

Editorial. "Zhongguo dongman chongman wenti de 'zhaoyang'" [The Problematic Rising Sun of the Chinese Manga and Anime]. *New Beijing Daily*, October 16, 2005, http://www.chinanim.com/dh1/newsxx.asp?newsid=9856 (accessed March 3, 2006).

Ehrenreich, Barbara, Elizabeth Hess, and Gloria Jacobs. "Beatlemania: Girls Just Want to Have Fun." In *The Adoring Audience*, ed. Lisa A. Lewis, 84–106. London: Routledge, 1992.

Elley, Derek. "Savvy Moves Boost Pusan Fest Fortunes." *Variety*, October 8, 2006.

———. "Pusan Pumps Korean Pic Profile." *Variety* (November 1–7): 1999.

Elsaesser, Thomas. *European Cinema: Face to Face with Hollywood*. Amsterdam: Amsterdam University Press, 2005.

———. "Tales of Sound and Fury." In *Film Genre Reader III*, ed. Barry Keith Grant, 366–95. Austin: University of Texas Press, 2003.

Featherstone, Mike. *Undoing Culture: Globalization, Postmodernism and Identity*. London; Thousand Oaks, CA: Sage Publications, 1995.

Fei Yuxiao. *Chuangzao mengxiang yu feixiang de laoren: Gong Qijun* [The World of Miyazaki Hayao]. Beijing: Dongfang yinxiang dianzi chubanshe and Kuilü wenhua, n.d.

Ferguson, Marjorie. "The Mythology about Globalization." *European Journal of Communication* 7 (1992): 69–93.

Feuchtwang, Stephan. "The Chinese Race-nation." *Anthropology Today* 9, no. 1 (February 1993): 14–5.

Fisher, K. Jerry. "*Shogun* ga beikoku ni uetsuketa 'nihonjin wa chujitsu' 'nihonjin wa kageki' no imēji" [*Shogun* Implanted the Image that 'Japanese Are Loyal' and 'Japanese Are Extremists' in American Minds]. *Asahi Journal* 22, no. 46 (November 14, 1980): 22–6.

Fiske, John. "The Cultural Economy of Fandom." In *The Adoring Audience*, ed. Lisa A. Lewis, 208–36. London: Routledge, 1992.

Fogg, Janet. "Brands as Intellectual Property." In *Brands: The New Wealth Creators*, eds. Susannah Hart and John Murphy, 72–81. London: Macmillan Press Ltd., 1998.

Foucault, Michel. *Discipline and Punish: The Birth of the Prison*. Harmondsworth: Penguin, 1979.

Fouche, Gwladys. "Pirates Pursue a Political Point: A New Swedish Party Aims to Abolish the Copyright Laws that Criminalise File Sharers." *The Guardian* (London), February 9, 2006.

Friedman, Jonathan. "Global Crises, the Struggle for Cultural Identity and Intellectual Porkbarrelling: Cosmopolitans versus Locals, Ethnics and Nationals in an Era of De-hegemonisation." In *Debating Cultural Hybridity: Multi-Cultural Identities and the Politics of Anti-Racism*, eds. Pnina Werbner and Tariq Modood, 70–89. London: Zed Books, 1997.

———. *Cultural Identity and Global Process*. London; Thousand Oaks, CA: Sage Publications, 1994.

Frith, Simon. "Copyright and the Music Business." *Popular Music* 7, no. 1 (1988): 57–75.

Fung, Anthony. "Western Style, Chinese Pop: Jay Chou's Rap and Hip-Hop in China." *Asian Music* 39, no. 1 (2008): 69–80.

————. "Hong Kong as the Asian and Chinese Distributor of Pokemon." *International Journal of Comic Art* 7, no. 1 (2005): 432–48.

————. "Marketing Popular Culture in China: Andy Lau as a Pan-Chinese Icon." In *Chinese Media: Global Contexts*, ed. Chin-Chuan Lee, 257–69. New York and London, Routledge, 2003.

Gamble, Andrew and Anthony Payne. "Conclusion: The New Regionalism." In *Regionalism and World Order*, eds. Andrew Gamble and Anthony Payne, 247–64. Basingstoke: MacMillan Press, 1996.

Gaonkar, Dilip Parameshwar and Elizabeth A. Povinelli. "Technologies of Public Forms: Circulation, Transfiguration, Recognition." *Public Culture* 15, no. 3 (2003): 385–97.

Garfield, Simon L. "Radio Research, McCathyism and Paul F. Lazarsfeld." Ph.D. thesis, MIT Political Science, 1987.

Gerow, Aaron. "Consuming Asia, Consuming Japan: The New Neonationalist Revisionist in Japan." In *Censoring History: Citizenship and Memory in Japan, Germany, and the United States*, eds. Laura Hein and Mark Selden, 74–95. Armonk, NY: M.E. Sharpe, 2000.

Gigi. "Maichu chanye diyibu? Ajide nian'nei shangying" [The First Step to the Industry: *Agito* Will be Screened in This Year]. March 17, 2006, http://news.myuni.com.cn/content/news/2107223556200631710354359444484_1.shtml (accessed January 30, 2007).

Gildenhard, Bettina. "History as Faction: Historiography within Japanese Comics as seen through Tezuka Osamu's Manga *Adolf*." In *Reading Manga: Local and Global Perceptions of Japanese Comics*, eds. Jaqueline Berndt and Steffi Richter, 95–106. Leipzig: Leipziger Universitätsverlag, 2006.

Gilroy, Paul. *Postcolonial Melancholia*. New York: Columbia University Press, 2006.

————. *The Black Atlantic: Modernity and Double Consciousness*. London: Verso, 1993.

Giroux, Henry A. *Beyond the Spectacle of Terrorism: Global Uncertainty and the Challenge of the New Media*. Boulder, CO; London: Paradigm Publishers, 2006.

Gold, Thomas B. "Taiwan Society at the Fin de Siècle." *China Quarterly*, 148 Special Issue: Contemporary Taiwan (December 1996): 1104.

Goldsmith, Ben and Tom O'Regan. *The Film Studio: Film Production in the Global Economy*. Lanham, MD; Oxford: Rowman and Littlefield, 2005.

Government Information Office, Republic of Taiwan. "Challenge 2008: The Six-Year National Development Plan (May 21, 2002)." Government Information Office, Republic of Taiwan, http://www.gio.gov.tw/taiwan-website/4-oa/20020521/2002052101.html (accessed October 30, 2007).

Grossberg, Larry. "Does Cultural Studies Have Futures? Should It? (Or What's the Matter with New York?)" *Cultural Studies* 20, no. 1 (2006): 1–32.

Grossberg, Lawrence. "Cultural Studies, Modern Logics, and Theories of

Globalisation." In *Back to Reality? Social Experience and Cultural Studies*, ed. Angela McRobbie, 7–35. Manchester: Manchester University Press, 1997.

Guo Hong. "Beijing, Shanghai qingshaonian donghua tiaocha" [Survey of the Reception of Animation among Beijing and Shanghai Youths]. July 2, 2004, http://www.chinanim.com/dh1/newsxx.asp?newsid=4709 (accessed March 13, 2006).

Hahm, Chaibong and Kim Seog-gun. "Remembering Japan and North Korea: The Politics of Memory in South Korea." In *Memory and History in East and Southeast Asia*, ed. Gerrit W. Gong, 101–12. Washington DC: CSIS Press, 2001.

Hall, Robert. *Area Studies: With Special Reference to Their Implications for Research in the Social Sciences*. New York: Committee on World Area Research Program, Social Science Research Council, 1948.

Hall, Stuart. "The Local and the Global: Globalization and Ethnicity." In *Culture, Globalization, and the World-System: Contemporary Conditions for the Representation of Identity*, ed. Anthony D. King, 41–69. Minneapolis: University of Minnesota Press, 1997.

———. "Cultural Studies and its Theoretical Legacies." In *Cultural Studies*, eds. Lawrence Grossberg, Cary Nelson, and Paula Treichler, 277–94. New York: Routledge, 1992.

———. "New Ethnicities." In *"Race," Culture and Difference*, eds. Ali Rattansi and James Donald, 252–9. London: Sage Publications in association with The Open University, 1992.

———. "The Local and the Global: Globalization and Ethnicity." In *Culture, Globalization, and the World-System: Contemporary Conditions for the Representation of Identity*, ed. Anthony King, 19–39. London: Macmillan, 1991.

———. "Encoding/Decoding in Television Discourse." In *Culture, Media, Language: Working Papers in Cultural Studies, 1972–79*, eds. Stuart Hall, Dorothy Hobson, Andrew Love, and Paul Willis , 128–38, 294–5. London: Hutchinson in association with the Centre for Contemporary Cultural Studies, University of Birmingham, 1980.

Han, Pao-Teh. "Developing the Creative Industry." *Taipei Times,* March 3, 2003. Trans. Jackie Lin, http://www.taipeitimes.com/News/editorials/archives/2003/03/03/196616 (accessed October 30, 2007).

Hanada, Tatsurō, Colin Sparks, and Yoshimi, Shunya, eds. *Karuchuraru sutadeiizu tono taiwa* [Dialogues with Cultural Studies]. Tokyo: Shinyō-sha, 1999.

Hannerz, Ulf. *Transnational Connections: Culture, People, Places.* London: Routledge, 1996.

Harrison, Mark. *Legitimacy, Meaning and Knowledge in the Making of Taiwanese Identity*. London: Palgrave MacMillan, 2006.

Harvey, David. *The Condition of Postmodernity: An Enquiry into the Origins of Cultural Change*. Oxford: Basil Blackwell, 1989.

Hayward, Susan. *Cinema Studies: The Key Concepts,* 3rd ed. London and New York: Routledge, 2006.

Hein, Laura and Mark Selden (eds.). *Censoring History: Citizenship and Memory in Japan, Germany, and the United States.* Armonk, NY: M.E. Sharpe, 2000.

Held, David and Anthony McGrew. "The Great Globalization Debate: An Introduction." In *The Global Transformations Reader: An Introduction to the Globalization Debate,* 2nd ed., eds. David Held and Anthony McGrew, 1–50. Cambridge: Polity Press, 2003.

Higashi, Chikara and G. Peter Lauter. *The Internationalization of the Japanese Economy,* 2nd ed. Dordrecht: Kluwer Academic Publishers, 1990.

Hirschberg, Lynn. "The Coppola Smart Mob." *New York Times,* August 31, 2003.

Hirst, Paul and Grahame Thompson. *Globalization in Question: The International Economy and the Possibilities of Governance,* Cambridge: Polity Press, 1996.

Hjorth, Larissa. "Odours of Mobility: Mobile Phones and Japanese Cute Culture in the Asia-Pacific." *Journal of Intercultural Studies* 26, nos. 1–2 (2005): 39–55.

Hong Kong Critics Society (ed.). *A Century of Chinese Cinema: Look Back in Glory: The 25th Hong Kong International Film Festival.* Hong Kong: Hong Kong Film Archive and Leisure and Cultural Services Department, 2001.

Hong, David and Darson Chiu. "Promoting the Cultural Industries." *Taipei Times,* June 18, 2006, http://www.tier.org.tw/03forum/pre_20060620.doc (accessed October 30, 2007).

Hong Kong International Film Festival Coordinator. Foreword to *The 10th Hong Kong International Film Festival Programme.* Hong Kong: The Urban Council, 1986.

Hong Kong Trade Development Council. "Creative Industries in Hong Kong" (September 5, 2002), Hong Kong Trade Development Council, http://www.tdctrade.com/econforum/tdc/tdc020902.htm (accessed October 30, 2007).

———. "Hong Kong's Creative Industries—Partner and Trendsetter for the Chinese Mainland (June 29, 2007)," http://www.tdctrade.com/econforum/tdc/tdc070605.htm?w_sid=194&w_pid=703&w_nid=&w_cid=&w_idt=1900-01-01&w_oid=181&w_jid= (accessed October 30, 2007).

Hook, Glenn. "Japan and the Construction of Asia-Pacific." In *Regionalism and World Order,* eds. Andrew Gamble and Anthony Payne, 169–206. Basingstoke: MacMillan Press, 1996.

Horkheimer, Max and Theodor W. Adorno. *Dialectic of Enlightenment.* Trans. John Cumming. London: Continuum, 1976.

"H.O.T. chongzu kenengxing zengjia" [The possibility of re-forming H.O.T. is increasing]. *Yule wuxian* [Entertainment Unlimited], no. 152, July 2003.

Howard, Keith. "Coming of Age: Korean Pop in the 1990s." In *Korean Pop*

Music: Riding the Wave, ed. Keith Howard, 82–98. Folkestone: Global Oriental, 2006.

"Huanying Guomindang xinsheng dai zai di hua" [Welcoming the Rebirth of the Sense of Place of the KMT]. *Ziyou Shibao* [Liberty Times], May 4, 2004.

Hur, Moon-yung. "Opening Film." In The 7th Pusan International Film Festival, Programme Booklet, 2002.

Hyde, Georgie D.M. *South Korea: Education, Culture and Economy*. New York: St. Martin's Press, 1988.

hyun&hyuk. "Di yi ge, ai wo de ren" [The First Person who Loves Me]. LKPM Bulletin boards, http://lkpm.w103.leoboard.com/novel/novel/02.htm (accessed September 10, 2003).

Ifekwunigwe, Jayne O. "Old Whine, New Vassals: Are Diaspora and Hybridity Postmodern Interventions?" In *New Ethnicities, Old Racisms*, ed. Phil Cohen, 180–204. London: Zed Books, 1999.

Igarashi, Akio (ed.). *Henyō suru Ajia to Nihon: Ajia Shakai ni shintō suru Nihon no popyurā karuchā* [Transformation of Asia and Japan: Japanese Popular Culture in East Asia]. Yokohama: Seori Shobō, 1998.

Igarashi, Yoshikuni. *Bodies of Memory: Narratives of War in Postwar Japanese Culture, 1945–1970*. Princeton and Oxford: Princeton University Press, 2000.

Im, Cheongsan. "Studies on Cartoons/Animation Courses," Curricula Development and Management. *Cartoon and Animation Studies* 3 (1999): 132–93.

International Federation of Phonographic Industries. "IFPI Music Piracy Report 2002." International Federation of Phonographic Industries, http://www.ifpi.org/site-content/antipiracy/piracy2002.html (accessed February 14, 2003).

International Olympic Committee. "Kitei Son." www.Olympic.Org., http://www.olympic.org/uk/athletes/profiles/bio_uk.asp?par_i_id=88103 (accessed November 20, 2007.)

Iordanova, Dina. *Cinema of the Other Europe: The Industry and Artistry of East Central European Film*. London: Wallflower Press, 2003.

Ishii, Kenichi. *Higashi Ajia no Nihon Taishū Bunka* [Japanese Popular Culture in East Asia]. Tokyo: Sōsō-sha, 2001.

Iwabuchi, Kōichi. "When Korean Wave Meets Resident Koreans in Japan." In *East Asian Pop Culture: Approaching the Korean Wave*, eds. Chua Beng-Huat and Koichi Iwabuchi. Hong Kong: Hong Kong University Press, 2008.

———. "Embracing Korean Wave: Japan and East Asian Media Flows." Unpublished paper presented at the symposium "*Hallyuwood:* Korean Screen Culture goes Global," School of Advanced Study, University of London, May 20, 2005.

———, (ed.). *Feeling Asian Modernities: Transnational Consumption of Japanese TV Dramas*. Hong Kong: Hong Kong University Press, 2004.

———. "Time and the Neighbour: Japanese Media Consumption of Asia." In

Rogue Flows: Trans-Asian Cultural Traffic, eds. Kōichi Iwabuchi, Stephen Muecke, and Mandy Thomas, 151–74. Hong Kong: Hong Kong University Press, 2004.

———. *Recentering Globalization: Popular Culture and Japanese Transnationalism.* Durham, NC: Duke University Press, 2002.

———. "Becoming 'Culturally Proximate:' The A/scent of Japanese Idol Dramas in Taiwan." In *Asian Media Productions,* ed. Brian Moeran, 54–74. Richmond: Curzon, 2001.

———. "Complicit Exoticism: Japan and Its Other — Who Imagines 'Japaneseness'?: Orientalism, Occidentalism and Self-Orientalism." *The Australian Journal of Media and Culture* 8, no. 2 (1994): 49–82.

Iwabuchi, Kōichi, Stephen Muecke, and Mandy Thomas (eds.). *Rogue Flows: Trans-Asian Cultural Traffic.* Hong Kong: Hong Kong University Press, 2004.

Iwasaki, Minoru and Hiroaki Ozawa (eds.). *Gekishin! Kokuritsu daigaku* [The National University Great Shake-up!]. Tokyo: Miraisha, 1999.

"Japan Looks to Play Leading Role in Regional Trade." *Daily Yomiuri,* September 15, 2006.

"Japanese Bring Latest in Music: Composer Plans to Introduce New Songs on Good-Will Mission." *The Los Angeles Times,* December 6, 1938.

Jay, Martin. *Songs of Experience: Modern American and European Variations on a Universal Theme.* Berkeley: University of California Press, 2005.

Jenkins, Henry. *Textual Poachers: Television Fans and Participatory Culture.* New York: Routledge, 1992.

Jerabek, Hynek. "Paul Lazarsfeld — The Founder of Modern Empirical Sociology: A Research Biography." *International Journal of Public Opinion Research* 13, no. 3 (2001): 229–44.

JETRO. "Japan Regains its Position as Global Cultural and Trend Leader." *Focus: Gross National Cool,* February 14, 2004, www.kwrintl.com/library/2004/focus32.html (accessed October 30, 2007).

Jin, Yoo Young. "We Are the Future." *H.O.T. II: Wolf and Sheep.* Seoul: S.M. Entertainment, SSM-20, 1997.

Jo, Joe. "Overseas Marketing Suggestions for the Korean Animation Industry." *Animation World Magazine* 4, no. 12 (2000) 1–3.

Johnston, Ollie, and Frank Thomas. *The Illusion of Life: Disney Animation.* New York: Disney Editions, 1981.

Jones, Geoffrey G., David Kiron, Vincent Dessain, and Anders Sjoman. "L'Oréal and the Globalization of American Beauty." *Harvard Business School Case* 805–086 (2005).

Jung, Eun-Young. "Articulating Korean Youth Culture through Global Popular Music Styles: Seo Taiji's Use of Rap and Metal." In *Korean Pop Music: Riding the Wave,* ed. Keith Howard, 109–22. Folkestone: Global Oriental, 2006.

Jung, Hye-jin. "*The Last Witness* Fails to Deliver." *Korea Times,* November 17, 2001.

Kakii, Michihiro. *Hariuddo no nihonjin: eiga ni arawareta Nichibei bunka masatsu* [Japanese in Hollywood: Representations of Japanese-American Cultural Conflicts in Film]. Tokyo: Bungeishunjū, 1992.

Kang, Nae-hui. "Mimicry and Difference: A Spectraology of the Neo-Colonial Intellectual." In *Specters of the West and the Politics of Translation: Traces 1*, eds. Naoki Sakai and Yukiko Hanama, 123–58. Hong Kong: University of Hong Kong Press, 2000.

Kanō Seiji. *"Kaze no tani no naushika kara Mononoke no hime e* — Miyazaki Hayao to Sutajio Jiburi no 13 nen" [From *Nausicaä of the Valley of the Wind* to *Princess Mononoke* — 13 Years of Miyazaki Hayao and Studio Ghibli]. http://www.yk.rim.or.jp/~rst/rabo/miyazaki/ghibli13nen.html (accessed February 25, 2006).

Katz, Ross, and Sofia Coppola. "Let's Get Lost: Translation Talk with Sofia Coppola and Ross Katz." DVD booklet for *Lost in Translation*, directed by Sofia Coppola. Momentum Pictures, 2003.

Kawase, Kenji. "Hangzhou Aspires to Crown of Animation, 'Manga' Capital." *The Nikkei Weekly*, June 20, 2005 (accessed through LexisNexis March 3, 2006).

KBS Global, "'Rikidozan' to Hit Japanese Theaters in March." KBS Global website, August 22, 2005, http://english.kbs.co.kr/ (accessed August 24, 2005).

Keane, Michael A. "Creative Industries: An Internationalizing Dynamic?" In *Proceedings Media Technology, Creative Industry, and Cultural Significance Conference*, Communications Arts Research Institute, Taipei, Taiwan, 2004, http://eprints.qut.edu.au/archive/00000610/01/Communications_Art_Research_Institute_Taiwan_Sept_2004.pdf (accessed 30 October 30, 2007).

Kelts, Roland. *Japanamerica: How Japanese Pop Culture Has Invaded the U.S.* New York: Palgrave MacMillan, 2006.

Kim, Hyun Mee. "Korean TV Dramas in Taiwan: With an Emphasis on the Localization Process." *Korea Journal* 45, no. 4 (2005): 183–205.

———. "Kankoku ni okeru Nihon taishū bunka no jūyō to 'Fuan ishiki no keisei" [The Significance of Japanese Popular Culture in Korea and the Formation of a 'Consciousness of Anxiety']. In *Nisshiki Hanryū: "Fuyu no sonata" to nikkan taishū bunka no genzai* [Korean Wave Japanese Style: The TV-Drama "Winter Sonata" and the Present State of Japanese-Korean Popular Culture], ed. Mōri Yoshitaka, 162–202. Tokyo: Serika Shobō, 2004.

Kim, Joon-Yang. "Critique of the New Historical Landscape of South Korean Animation." *Animation* 1, no. 1 (2006): 61–81.

Kim, Kwang-tae. "Korean Youth Culture Sweeping Across Asia." *Korea Times*, 2001, http://www.hankooki.com/kt_special/200108/t20010823 16230349110.htm (accessed November 21, 2002).

Kim, Kyung Hyun. "Male Crisis in New Korean Cinema: Reading the Early Films of Park Kwang-su." *positions* 9, no. 2 (2001): 371–99.

Kim, Seong Wook. *Hanguk aenimeisyeoneun eopda* [There Is No Korean Animation]. Seoul: YeSol, 1998.

Kim, Soo-kyung. "Hae-an-seon" [The Coast Guard]. *Dong-A Ilbo,* November 21, 2002, http://www.donga.com/fbin/output?code=Q__&n= 200211210301 (accessed December 13, 2007).

Kim, Soyoung. "Cine-mania or Cinephilia: Film Festivals and the Identity Question." *UTS Review* [Cultural Studies Review] 4, no. 2 (1998): 174–87.

Kim, Su-yun. "British Film Critic Pleased with Improved Facilities at PIFF." *Korea Times,* October 22, 1999.

Kim Tae-jong. "Local Movies Thrive on Nationalism." *Korea Times,* July 19, 2006.

———. "Nationalistic 'Hanbando' Lacks Healthy Perspective." *Korea Times,* July 13, 2006.

Kim, Youn-jun. "Korean Pop Culture Craze Hallyu Sweeps through Asia." *Koreana* 16, no. 1 (2002): 46–51.

Kim, Youna. "The Rising East Asian 'Wave': Korean Media Go Global." In *Media on the Move: Global Flow and Contra-Flow,* ed. Dayan Kishan Thussu, 135–52. London and New York: Routledge, 2006.

———. "Experiencing Globalization: Global TV, Reflexivity and the Lives of Young Korean Women." *International Journal of Cultural Studies* 8, no. 4 (2005): 445–63.

———. *Women, Television and Everyday Life in Korea: Journeys of Hope.* London and New York: Routledge, 2005.

Kinohanasha Publishing Ltd. Hompage. "Edagawa chōsen gakkō shien pēji" [Edagawa Korean School Support Page]. Kinohanasha Publishing Co. Ltd., http://kinohana.la.coocan.jp/court.html (accessed December 18, 2007).

Klein, Naomi. *No Logo: Taking Aim at the Brand Bullies,* 1st ed. Toronto: Knopf Canada, 2000.

Ko Kiansing, "On the Definition of the Formosan." *Independent Formosa* 4, no. 4 (August 1965): 10–4.

Koga, Masao. *Jiden: waga kokoro no uta* [My Story: Songs in My Mind]. Tokyo: Tenbōsha, 2001.

Konishi Yasuharu. "Furii sōru: Wada Akiko" [Free Soul: Wada Akiko]. Teichiku, 2004, ASIN B000657REQ.

———. "Roller Coaster Come Closer." Sony, 2001, ARCJ-2003.

Korea Culture and Contents Agency. "About KOCCA: Mission." *KoreanContent. org,* 2003, http://www.koreacontent.org/weben/etc/kocca3.jsp (accessed December 5, 2006).

Korean Film Council. "Statistics." *Korean Cinema 2006.* Korean Film Council. www.kofic.or.kr/english.

Korean Film Database Book from 2000 to 2006. Seoul: Korean Film Council, 2006.

Korean National Tourism Office. "Survey Report on Actual Conditions of *Hallyu* (Korean Fever) Tourism, 2004." Korean National Tourism Office, http://www.knto.or.kr/eng/hallyu/hallyusurvey.html#top (accessed April 2, 2005).

KRJeami. "Interview with Lee Soo Man." *BoAjjang.com*, September 1, 2005, http://forums.boajjang.com/index.php?act=ST&f=1&t=34315 (accessed June 6, 2008).

Kyō, Nobuko. *Nikkan ongaku nōto: "Ekkyō" suru tabibito no uta o otte* [Notes on Music in Japan and Korea: Following the Songs of Travellers who "Cross National Borders"]. Tokyo: Iwanami Shoten, 1998.

Kracauer, Siegfried. *The Mass Ornament: Weimar Essays*. Trans. and ed. Thomas Y. Levin. Cambridge, MA: Harvard University Press, 1995.

Lamarre, Thomas. "Platonic Sex: Perversion and Shojo Anime (Part One)." *Animation* 1, no. 1 (2006): 45–59.

Lash, Scott and Celia Lury. *Global Culture Industry: Mediation of Things*. Oxford: Polity Press, 2007.

Lazarsfeld, Paul. *Radio and the Printed Page*. New York: Duall, Sloane and Pierce, 1940.

Lazzarato, Maurizio. "Immaterial Labour." In *Radical Thought in Italy: A Potential Politics*, ed. Paolo Virno and Michael Hardt, 133–47. Minneapolis: University of Minnesota Press, 1996.

Le Bail, Hélène. "Japanese Culture in Asia: Infatuation, Identification and the Construction of Identity: the Example of Taiwan." *China Perspectives* 43 (2002): 52–62.

Lee, Benjamin and Edward Li Puma. "Cultures of Circulation: The Imaginations of Modernity." *Public Culture* 14 (2002): 191–213.

Lee, Dong-jin. "Sunsuhaettŏn kkum cha'cha 'twiro tora'" [To Get the Innocent Dream Back 'About-turn']. *Chosun Ilbo*, October 15, 1999.

Lee, Helen. *Gandong 228* [Touching 228]. DVD. Taiwan National Alliance, 2004.

Lee, Jin-woo. "Pusankukje yŏnghwajë kuwŏl kaech'oe" [PIFF Opens in September]. *Kukje Shimmun*, February 2, 1996.

―――. "Opening Film." In the 4th Pusan International Film Festival, Programme Booklet, 1999, 21.

Lee, Sang-Dawn. *Big Brother, Little Brother: The American Influence on Korean Culture in the Lyndon B. Johnson Years*. Lanham, MD: Lexington Books, 2002.

Lee, Young-il and Choe Young-chol. *The History of Korean Cinema*. Seoul: Jimoondang Publishing Company, 1988.

Lent, John A. "Animation in Asia: Appropriation, Reinterpretation, and Adoption or Adaptation." *Screening the Past* no. 11 (2000) http://www.latrobe.edu.au/screeningthepast (accessed February 16, 2007).

Leonard, Sean. "Progress against the Law: Anime and Fandom, with the Key to the Globalization of Culture." *International Journal of Cultural Studies* 8, no. 3 (2005): 281–305.

Leslie, Esther. "Space and West End Girls: Walter Benjamin versus Cultural Studies." *New Formations*, no. 38 (1999): 110–24.

Lessig, Lawrence. *Free Culture: How Big Media Uses Technology and the Law to Lock Down Culture and Control Creativity.* New York: Penguin, 2004.

Levy, Pierre. *Becoming Virtual: Reality in the Digital Age.* Perseus Books, 1998.

Lewis, Leo. "Neighbour fails to see funny side of comic." *The Times,* November 1, 2005, http://www.timesonline.co.uk/tol/news/world/article585019.ece (accessed December 17, 2007).

Lewis, Lisa, ed. *The Adoring Audience: Fan Culture and Popular Media.* London and New York: Routledge, 1992.

Li, Amy Fung Kwan. "Slash, Fandoms, and Pleasures." M. Phil. thesis, Department of Cultural and Religious Studies, The Chinese University of Hong Kong, 2006.

Li Chiao. "Taiwan guo gong he shenme?" [What Does a Taiwanese Nation Bring Together?]. *Zili Wanbao* [Independent Evening Post], December 12, 1991.

Li Jianping. "Tashan zhi shi — Riben donghuapian daigei women de sikao" [How We Could Learn from Japanese Animation]. *Dianshi Yanjiu* [Television Studies], no. 9 (2000): 69.

Li, Xiaofeng. *Taiwan, wode xuanze!* [Taiwan, My Choice!]. Taipei: Yushanshe chuban, 1995.

Liao, Joshua. *Formosa Speaks.* Hong Kong: Graphic Press, 1950.

Liao, Ping-hui. *Ling lei xiandai qing* [Alternative Modernities]. Taipei: Yunchen wenhua, 2001.

———. "The Case of Emergent Cultural Criticism in Taiwan's Newspaper Literary Supplements: Global/Local Dialectics in Contemporary Taiwanese Public Culture." In *Global/Local: Cultural Production and the Transnational Imaginary,* eds. Rob Wilson and Wimal Dissanayake, 337–46. Durham, NC: Duke University Press, 1996.

Liao, Thomas. *Inside Formosa: Formosans vs. Chinese since 1945.* Tokyo: Publisher unknown, 1956.

Liau, Kianliong. "Why Formosa Wants Independence." *Formosa Quarterly* 1, no. 1 (July 1962): 4–8.

Lie, John. *Multiethnic Japan.* Cambridge, MA; London: Harvard University Press, 2001.

———. *Han Unbound: The Political Economy of South Korea.* Stanford, CA: Stanford University Press, 1998.

Lim, Song Hwee. "Is the Trans in Trasnational the Trans in Transgender?" *New Cinemas* 5, no. 1 (2007): 39–52

Lin Yi-hsiung. *Xiwang you yi tian* [I Hope There Comes a Day]. Taipei: Yuwangshe, 1995.

Lin, Christine Louise. *The Presbyterian Church in Taiwan and the Advocacy of Local Autonomy.* Sino-Platonic papers, no. 92. Philadelphia: Dept. of Asian and Middle Eastern Studies, University of Pennsylvania, 1999.

Lindstrom, Martin. *Brandsense: How to Build Powerful Brands through Touch, Taste, Smell, Sight and Sound.* London: Kogan Page Limited, 2005.

Liu, Fu-Kuo. "A Critical Review of East and Northeast Asian Regionalism." In *Northeast Asian Regionalism: Learning from the European Experience*, eds. Christopher M. Dent and David W. F. Huang, 16–33. London: RoutledgeCurzon, 2002.

Liu, Shih-ding. "China's Popular Nationalism on the Internet: Report on the 2005 Anti-Japanese Network Struggles." *Inter-Asia Cultural Studies* 7, no. 1 (2006): 144–55.

Livingstone, Sonia, ed. *Audiences and Publics: When Cultural Engagement Matters for the Public Sphere*. Bristol: Intellect, 2005.

Lo, Ming-cheng. *Doctors Within Borders: Profession, Ethnicity, and Modernity in Colonial Taiwan*. Berkeley: University of California Press, 2002.

Louie, Kam. "Chinese, Japanese and Global Masculine Identities." In *Asian Masculinities: The Meaning and Practice of Manhood in China and Japan*, eds. Kam Louie and Morris Low, 1–16. London; New York: RoutledgeCurzon, 2003.

Lu, Myra. "President adds Weight to Chip Foundry Debate." *Taipei Journal* 19, no. 11 (March 22, 2002): 15.

Lunsing, Wim 2006. "*Yaoi Ronsō*: Discussing Depictions of Male Homosexuality in Japanese Girls' Comics, Gay Comics and Gay Pornography." *Intersections: Gender, History and Culture in the Asian Context* 12 (2006), http://wwwsshe. murdoch.edu.au/intersections/issue12/lunsing.html (accessed December 13, 2007).

Lury, Celia. *Brands: The Logos of the Global Economy, International Library of Sociology*. London: Routledge, 2004.

Maher, John C., Yumiko Kawanishi, and Yong-Yo Yi. "Maintaining Culture and Language: Koreans in Osaka with Ikuno-ku, Osaka: Centre of Hope and Struggle." In *Diversity in Japanese Culture and Language*, eds. John Christopher Maher and Gaynor Macdonald, 160–77. London: Kegan Paul International Ltd, 1995.

"The Making of *Shogun*," Disk 5 bonus feature. James Clavell's *Shogun*, directed by Jerry London, DVD box set. Paramount Pictures, 2004.

Manovich, Lev. *The Language of New Media*. Cambridge, MA: MIT Press, 2001.

Martin-Jones, David. *Deleuze, Cinema and National Identity*. Edinburgh: Edinburgh University Press, 2006.

Massumi, Brian. *Parables for the Virtual: Movement, Affect, Sensation, Post-Contemporary Interventions*. Durham, NC: Duke University Press, 2002.

Masuda, Sachiko. *Amerika eiga ni arawareta 'Nihon' imēji no hensen* [Changes in the Image of 'Japan' Represented in American Cinema]. Osaka: Osaka University Press, 2004.

Matsui, Takeshi. "Seiryō Inryō: Genchika to hyōjunka no hazamade" [Soft drink: Standardization and Localization]. In *Branding in China: Kyodai shijō Chūgoku o seisuru burando senryaku* [Branding in China: Brand Strategy for the Huge China Market], ed. Yuko Yamashita, 75–108. Tokyo: Tōyō Keizai Shinpō Sha, 2006.

Matsumura Naohiro, Miura Asako, Shibanai Yasufumi, Ohsawa Yukio and Nishida Toyoaki. "The Dynamism of 2channel." *AI and Society* 19:1 (January 2005), 84–92. http://www.rhul.ac.uk/Management/News-and-Events/conferences/SID2003/Tracks-Presentations/12%20-%20Matsumura%20et%20al.pdf (accessed December 17, 2007).

Mazdon, Lucy. *Encore Hollywood: Remaking French Cinema.* London: BFI, 2000.

McClintock, Anne. "The Angel of Progress: The Pitfalls of the Term 'Postcolonialism'." In *Colonial Discourse/Postcolonial Theory,* eds. Francis Baker, Peter Hulme, and Margaret Iversen. Manchester; New York: University of Manchester Press, 1994, 256.

McCloud, Scott. *Understanding Comics — The Invisible Art.* New York: HarperPerennial, 1994.

McGray, Douglas. "Japan's Gross National Cool." *Foreign Policy,* no. 130 (2002): 44–54.

McGuigan, Jim. *Rethinking Cultural Policy.* Open University Press, 2004.

McHugh, Kathleen and Nancy Abelmann. *South Korean Golden Age Melodrama: Gender, Genre, and National Cinema.* Detroit, MI: Wayne State University Press, 2005.

McLuhan, Marshall and Quentin Fiore. 1967. *The Medium Is the Message.* London: Penguin.

Mehra, Salil. "Copyright and Comics in Japan: Does Law Explain Why All the Cartoons My Kid Watches Are Japanese Imports?" *Rutgers Law Review* 55 (Fall 2002): 155–204.

Mercer, Kobena. *Welcome to the Jungle: New Positions in Black Cultural Studies.* London: Routledge, 1994.

Meyrowitz, Joshua. *No Sense of Place: The Impact of Electronic Media on Social Behaviour.* Oxford: Oxford University Press, 1985.

m-flo. "m-flo loves WADA Akiko 'Hey!'" On *m-flo loves Emyli and Yoshika/WADA Akiko.* Rhythm Zone, 2005, ASIN: B0009N2XXK.

Miller, Toby. *Cultural Citizenship: Cosmopolitanism, Consumerism, and Television in a Neoliberal Age.* Philadelphia, PA: Temple University Press, 2007.

Miller, Toby, Nitin Govil, and John McMurria. *Global Hollywood.* London: British Film Institute, 2001.

Miller, Toby and Marie Claire Leger. "Runaway Production, Runaway Consumption, Runaway Citizenship: The New International Division of Cultural Labor." *Emergences* 11, no. 1 (2001): 89–115.

Min, Eungjun, Jinsook Joo, and Han Ju Kwak. *Korean Film: History, Resistance, and Democratic Imagination.* West Port, CT; London: Praeger, 2003.

Ministry of Culture and Tourism, Korea. "Cultural Policies Bureau." Ministry of Culture and Tourism, http://www.mct.go.kr/english/section/bureau/cultural.jsp (accessed October 30, 2007).

———. "Culture Industry Bureau," Ministry of Culture and Tourism, http://

www.mct.go.kr/english/section/bureau/industry.jsp (accessed October 30, 2007).

————. "Culture Media Bureau," Ministry of Culture and Tourism, http://www. mct.go.kr/english/section/bureau/culture_media.jsp (accessed October 30, 2007).

Ministry of Education, Culture, Sports, Science, and Technology (MEXT), Japan Homepage. "Culture: Toward the Realization of an Emotionally Enriched Society through Culture." MEXT, http://www.mext.go.jp/english/org/f_culture.htm (accessed October 30, 2007).

————. *"Bunka geijutsu shinkō kihonhō"* [Fundamental Law for the Promotion of Culture and Arts]. MEXT, http://www.mext.go.jp/a_menu/bunka/geijutsu/01.pdf (accessed October 30, 2007).

"Minzhu guan jie pai Bian chi jiu wei quan huohai" [President Chen Condemns the Damage of Authoritarianism at the Inauguration of the National Taiwan Democracy Memorial Hall]. *Ziyou Shibao* [Liberty Times], May 20, 2007.

Mitchell, Wendy. "Sofia Coppola Talks about 'Lost in Translation,' Her Love Story That Is Not Nerdy." In *IndieWire*, http://www.indiewire.com/people/people_030923coppola.html (accessed November 7, 2007).

Mittelman, James H. "Rethinking the New Regionalism in the Context of Globalization." *Global Governance* 2 (1996): 189–213.

Miyazaki, Hayao. *Kaze no tani no naushika* [Nausicaa of the Valley of the Winds], vols. 1–6. Tokyo: Tokuma Shoten, 1987.

Miyoshi Jager, Sheila. "Korean Collaborators: South Korea's Truth Committees and the Forging on a New Pan-Korean Nationalism." *Japan Focus: An Asia-Pacific E-Journal*, 2004, http://www.japanfocus.org/products/details/2170 (accessed November 20, 2007.)

Monma, Takashi. *Ajiaeiga ni mieru Nihon II: Kankoku, Kita Chōsen, Tōnan Ajia* [Japan as seen in Asian Film II: South Korea, North Korea, South-East Asia]. Tokyo: Shakai Hyōronsha, 1996.

————. *Ōbeieiga Ni Miru Nihon—Japan in American and European Films* [The Representation of Japan in American and European Films]. Tokyo: Shakaihyōronsha, 1995.

Moon, Seungsook. "Begetting the Nation: The Androcentrric Discourse of National History and Development in South Korea." In *Dangerous Women: Gender and Korean Nationalism,* eds. Elaine H. Kim and Chungmoo Choi. New York and London: Routledge, 1998.

Moor, Elizabeth. "Branded Spaces: The Mediation of Commercial Forms." Ph.D. thesis, Goldsmiths College, University of London, 2004.

Mōri, Yoshitaka. "Winter Sonata and Cultural Practices of Active Fans in Japan: Considering Middle-Aged Women as Cultural Agents." In *Approaches to East Asian Pop Culture: Examining Korean TV Dramas*, eds. Beng Huat Chua and Iwabuchi Kōichi. Hong Kong: Hong Kong University Press, forthcoming.

————. "Culture=Politics: The Emergence of New Cultural Forms of Protest in the Age of Freeter." *Inter-Asia Cultural Studies* 6, no. 1 (2005): 17–29.

————, (ed.). *Nisshiki Hanryū: "Fuyu no sonata" to nikkan taishū bunka no genzai* [Korean Wave Japanese Style: The TV-Drama "Winter Sonata" and the Present State of Japanese-Korean Popular Culture]. Tokyo: Serika Shobō, 2004.

Morita Akiō and Shintarō Ishihara. *The Japan that Can Say No: Why Japan Will Be First among Equals.* Tokyo: Kōbunsha, 1989.

Morris, Mark. "The Political Economics of Patriotism: The Case of *Hanbando.*" In *Korea Yearbook 2007: Politics, Economics, Society,* ed. Phillip Köllner, forthcoming.

Morris-Suzuki, Tessa. *The Past Within Us: Media, Memory, History.* London: Verso, 2005.

Müller-Doohm, Stefan. *Adorno: A Biography.* Trans. Rodney Livingstone. Cambridge: Polity Press, 2005.

Murphie, Andrew. "Putting the Virtual Back into VR." In *A Shock to Thought: Expressions after Deleuze and Guattari,* ed. Brian Massumi, 188–214. London: Routledge, 2002.

Murphy, John. "What Is Branding?" In *Brands: The New Wealth Creator,* eds. Susannah Hart and John Murphy. London: Macmillan, 1998.

Music Industry Association of Korea. "*2002 nyŏn kayo ŭmban palmae ryang chipkye*" [2002 Korean song album sales chart]. Music Industry Association of Korea, http://miak.or.kr/navigator.php?contents=html&usemode=list&DB=117 (accessed May 14, 2007).

Music Industry Association of Korea. http://miak.or.kr (accessed December 13, 2007).

Napier, Susan J. *Anime: From* Akira *to* Princess Mononoke. New York: Palgrave, 2001.

Nakamura, Ryūtarō. "'*Chi to hone*' *no burūsu*" [Blues of 'Blood and Bones']. *Shūkan Bunshun,* August 11/18, 2005.

Negus, Keith and Michael Pickering. *Creativity, Communication and Cultural Value.* London; Thousand Oaks, CA: Sage, 2004.

Neumann, Franz. *Behemoth: The Structure and Practice of National Socialism, 1933–1944.* New York: Oxford University Press, 1942.

Ninki burogu rankingu [Popular Blog ranking], http://blog.with2.net/rank1500-0.html (accessed December 17, 2007).

O'Brien, Robert and Marc Williams. *Global Political Economy: Evolution and Dynamics.* New York: Palgrave Macmillan, 2004.

Occidentalism.org, "Kenkanryu in the New York Times." Comment posted on November 21, 2005, http://www.occidentalism.org/?p=104 (accessed December 17, 2007).

Onishi, Norimitsu. "Ugly Images of Asian Rivals Become Best Sellers in Japan." *New York Times* (November 19, 2005).

Onodera, Itsunori. "Creative Industry: A Key to Solidify Bases for Regional Cooperation in Asia." Speech to Asia Cultural Cooperation Forum, Hong Kong, November 15, 2004, http://www.mofa.go.jp/region/asia-paci/speech0411.html (accessed October 30, 2007).

Pak, Gloria Lee. "On the Mimetic Faculty: A Critical Study of the 1984 *Pongtchak* Debate and Post-colonial Mimesis." In *Korean Pop Music: Riding the Wave*, ed. Keith Howard, 62–71. Folkestone: Global Oriental, 2006.

Pang, Laikwan. *Cultural Control and Globalization in Asia: Copyright, Piracy, and Cinema*. London: Routledge, 2006.

Park, Eun-ju. "Hŭksusŏn" [The Last Witness]. *Hankook Ilbo*. November, 13, 2001.

Park, Sora. "China's Consumption of Korean Television Dramas: An Empirical Test of the 'Cultural Discount' Concept." *Korea Journal* 44, no. 4 (2004): 265–90.

Paquet, Darcy. "The Korean Film Industry: From 1992 to the Present." In *New Korean Cinema*, eds. Chi-yun Shin and Julian Stringer, pp. 32–50. Edinburgh: Edinburgh University Press, 2005.

———. "Essays from the Far East Film Festival: Korea Main Essay 2006." *Koreanfilm.org*, 2006, http://koreanfilm.org/feff.html#2006 (accessed November 20, 2007).

———. "Essays from the Far East Film Festival: Korea Main Essay 2005." *Koreanfilm.org*, 2005, http://koreanfilm.org/feff.html#2005 (accessed November 20, 2007).

———. Review of *The President's Last Bang*, directed by Im Sang-soo. *Koreanfilm. org*, 2005, http://www.koreanfilm.org/kfilm05.html#lastbang.

———. "Japanese Films in Korea." *Koreanfilm.org*, 2004, http://www.koreanfilm. org/japanfilm.html.

Pease, Rowan. "Internet, Fandom and K-wave in China." In *Korean Pop Music: Riding the Wave*, ed. Keith Howard, 176–89. Folkestone: Global Oriental, 2006.

People's Daily Online. "Creative Industry: New Economic Engine in Beijing." Xinhua, December 15, 2006, http://english.people.com.cn/200612/15/eng20061215_332904.html (accessed October 30, 2007).

Perrier, Raymond. "Brand Licensing." In *Brands: The New Wealth Creators*, eds. Susannah Hart and John Murphy, 104–13. London: Macmillan Press Ltd, 1998.

Pine, B. Joseph and James H. Gilmore. *The Experience Economy: Work Is Theatre and Every Business a Stage*. Boston, MA: Harvard Business School Press, 1999.

Probyn, Elspeth. *Sexing the Self: Gendered Positions in Cultural Studies*. London; New York: Routledge, 1993.

Qiao, Fei. "Korean Culture According to Foreigners 2." *KoreanContent.org*, 2004, http://www.koreacontent.org/weben/inmarket/Ns_knews_view.jsp?news_seq=11298 (accessed November 30, 2006).

Rain Zhongwen wang [Rain Chinese Net]. 2006. "Zui xiang he Rain zuo de guanxi" [The relationship you would most like to have with Rain]. *Rain Zhongwen wang*, http://bbs.raincn.com/thread-32595-1-1.html (accessed January 3, 2007).

Rayns, Tony. "Sexual Terrorism: The Strange Case of Kim Ki-duk." *Film Comment* (November–December 2004): 50–2.

Retort. *Afflicted Power: Capital and Spectacle in a New Age of War.* London: Verso, 2005.

Robertson, Jennifer. *Takarazuka: Sexual Politics and Popular Culture in Modern Japan.* Berkeley; London: University of California Press, 1998.

————. *Globalization: Social Theory and Global Culture.* London: Sage, 1992.

Robertson, Roland. "Glocalization: Time-Space and Homogeneity-Heterogeneity." In *Global Modernities*, eds. Mike Featherstone, Scott Lash, and Roland Robertson, 25–44. Thousand Oaks, CA: Sage, 1995.

Robins, Kevin. "What in the World's Going On?" In *Production of Culture/Cultures of Production*, eds. Paul Du Gay and Open University, 11–66. London; Thousand Oaks, CA: Sage in association with the Open University, 1997.

Rose, Nikolas S. *Powers of Freedom: Reframing Political Thought.* Cambridge: Cambridge University Press, 1999.

Rowley, Ian, Chester Dawson, Hiroko Tashiro, and Ihlwan Moon. "The *Anime* Biz: Still an Adolescent." *Business Week* 3939 (June 27, 2005): 50–2.

Ross, Emily and Angus Holland. *100 Great Businesses and the Minds Behind Them.* Naperville, IL: Sourcebook, Inc., 2006.

Rozman, Gilbert. *Northeast Asia's Stunted Regionalism: Bilateral Distrust in the Shadows of Globalization.* Cambridge: Cambridge University Press, 2004.

Ryall, Julian. "Comic Twist to Japanese Nationalism." *Aljazeera.net*, January 30, 2006, http://english.aljazeera.net/English/Archive/Archive?ArchiveID=21164 (accessed December 17, 2007).

"S Korean Soap Opera Sparks Boom in China." *China Daily*, September 30, 2003, http://news3.xinhuanet.com/english/2005-09/30/content_3567436.htm (accessed March 14, 2006).

Said, Edward. *Representations of the Intellectual.* New York: Pantheon Books, 1994.

Sakai, Naoki. "Two Negations: The Fear of Being Excluded and the Logic of Self-Esteem." In *Contemporary Japanese Thought*, ed. Richard F. Calichman, 159–92. New York: Columbia University Press, 2005.

Sakamoto, Rumi and Matt Allen. "Hating the 'Korean Wave' Comic Books: A Sign of New Nationalism in Japan?" *Japan Focus* (October 4, 2007), http://www.japanfocus.org/products/details/2535 (accessed December 17, 2007).

Sasada, Hironori. "Youth and Nationalism in Japan." *SAIS Review* XXVI, no. 2 (2006): 109–22.

Sataka, Makoto. *Hika: Koga Masao no jinsei to merodī* [A Sad Song: The Life and Melodies of Koga Masao]. Tokyo: Mainichi Shinbunsha, 2005.

Sato, Tadao. *Nihon eigashi* 2 [History of Japanese Cinema 2]. Tokyo: Iwanami Shoten, 1995.

Scheuerman, William E. *Between the Norm and the Exception: The Frankfurt School and the Rule of Law*. Cambridge, MA: MIT Press, 1994.

Schiller, Herbert I. "Not yet the Post-Imperial Era." In *Media and Cultural Studies: Keyworks*, eds. Meenakshi Gigi Durham and Douglas Kellner, 318–33. Malden, MA: Blackwell Publishers, 2001.

Schwab, Raymond. *The Oriental Renaissance: Europe's Rediscovery of India and the East, 1680–1880*. Trans. Gene Patterson-Black and Victor Reinking. New York: Columbia University Press, 1986.

Scollay, Robert. "Regional Trade Liberalization in East Asia and the Asia-Pacific: The Role of China." Paper presented at 2004 Latin America/Caribbean and Asia/Pacific Economics and Business Association Annual Conference, Beijing, People's Republic of China, December 3–4, 2004, http://www.iadb.org/laeba/downloads/WP_35_2004.pdf (accessed October 30, 2007).

Secretariat of the Pacific Community. "Draft Regional Framework for the Economic Valuing of Expressions of Culture." Document presented to Thirteenth Regional Meeting of Heads of Statistics, September 15–19, 2003, http://www.spc.int/statsen/English/News_and_Events/Stats13/WP_15.doc (accessed October 30, 2007).

Segers, Frank. "Hae-an-seon" [*The Coast Guard*]. *Moving Pictures*, November 2002.

Seigworth, Gregory J. "Cultural Studies and Gilles Deleuze." In *New Cultural Studies*, eds. Gary Hall and Clare Birchall. Edinburgh: Edinburgh University Press, 2007.

Seoul Broadcasting System (SBS). *Ashia shyobijŭ: samgukji, Yi Suman ŭi CT ron kwa Hallyu ŭi mirae* [Asia Showbiz: The History of Three Kingdoms, Lee Soo Man's CT Theory and The Future of Korea Wave], March 12, 2006.

Seth, Michael J. *Education Fever*. Honolulu: University of Hawaii Press and Centre for Korean Studies, University of Hawaii, 2002.

Shan Te-hsing. "Duihua, jiaotong, fansi, Sayide tanlun saiyide" [Dialogue, Communication, Remembrance: Said on Said]. *Ziyou Shibao* [Liberty Times], February 16, 2005.

Shiel, Mark. *Italian Neorealism: Rebuilding the Cinematic City*. London; New York: Wallflower, 2006.

Shim, Doobo. "Globalization and Cinema Regionalization in East Asia." *Korea Journal* 45, no. 4 (2005): 233–60.

Shin, Chi-yun and Julian Stringer, eds. *New Korean Cinema*. Edinburgh: Edinburgh University Press, 2005.

Shin, Dong-Myeon. *Social and Economic Policies in Korea: Ideas, Networks, and Linkages*. London and New York: RoutledgeCurzon, 2003.

Shin, Gi-Wook and Michael Robinson. *Colonial Modernity in Korea*. Cambridge, MA; London: Harvard University Asia Center, 1999.

Shin, Jeeyoung. "Globalization and New Korean Cinema." In *New Korean Cinema*, eds. Chi-Yun Shin and Julian Stringer, 51–62. Edinburgh: Edinburgh University Press, 2005.

Sina Yingyin yule [Sina film and music entertainment]. "Diaocha: Ni renwei zai Zhongguo zui you renqi de Hanguo geshou she shei?" [Survey: Whom do you consider to be the most popular Korean singer in China?]. *Sina Yingyin yule*, http://ent.sina.com.cn/y/2006-02-10/2009982389.html (accessed March 13, 2006).

Sklair, Leslie. *The Transnational Capitalist Class*. London: Blackwell, 2002.

———. "The Transnational Capitalist Class and the Discourse of Globalization." *Cambridge Review of International Affairs* 14, no. 1 (2000): 67–85.

SM Entertainment, 2001. Video segment entitled "SM Entertainment, China Auditions," http://www.smtown.com/smtown/audition/china2001/china_audition_ch3.html (accessed May 7, 2005).

Smith, Shaun. "Brand Experience." In *Brands and Branding*, eds. *The Economist* et al., 97–111. London: The Economist, 2003.

Sontag, Deborah. "A Strong Forecast for Korean Pop's Rain." *New York Times*, January 27, 2006, http://www.iht.com/articles/2006/01/27/news/rain.php (accessed December 13, 2007).

Soper, Kate. "Despairing of Happiness: The Redeeming Dialectic of Critical Theory." *New Formations*, no. 38 (1999): 141–53.

Sreberny-Mohammadi, Annabelle. "The Global and the Local in International Communications." In *Mass Media and Society*, eds. James Curran and Michael Gurevitch, 118–38. London: Edward Arnold, 1991.

Standish , Isolde. "Korean Cinema and the New Realism: Text and Context." In *Colonialism and Nationalism in Asian Cinema*, ed. Wimal Dissanayake, 65–89. Bloomington: University of Indiana Press, 1994.

Straubhaar, Joseph. D. "Beyond Media Imperialism: Asymmetrical Inter-dependence and Cultural Proximity." *Critical Studies in Mass Communication* 8 (1991): 39–59.

Sugimoto, Yoshio. *An Introduction to Japanese Society*. Cambridge: Cambridge University Press, 2003.

Sugiura, Tsutomu. "From Capitalism to Culturalism." Speech presented at OECD Forum 2005, Fuelling the Future: Security, Stability, Development — Creative Societies, Dynamic Economies, May 2–3, 2005, http://www.oecd.org/dataoecd/42/61/34825496.pdf (accessed October 30, 2007).

Sum, Ngai-Ling. "The NICs and Competing Strategies of East Asian Regionalism." In *Regionalism and World Order*, eds. Andrew Gamble and Anthony Payne, 207–45. Basingstoke: MacMillan Press, 1996.

Szerman, Imre. "Cultural Studies and the Transnational." In *New Cultural Studies — Adventure in Theory*, eds. Gary Hall and Clare Birchall, 200–19. Edinburgh: Edinburgh University Press, 2006.

"'Taidu' zai Riben gaojifenzi Qiu Yonghan zuo fanzheng gui guo" [The Leading 'Taiwanese Independence' Activist in Japan Qiu Yonghan Repudiates His

Cause and Returns to the Nation]. *Lianhe Bao* [United Daily News], April 3, 1972.

Tanaka, Jun'ichirō. *Nihon eiga hattatsu-shi*, Vol. 4: *shijō saikō no eiga jidai* [The History of the Development of Japanese Cinema, Vol. 4: The Zenith of the Age of Cinema]. Tokyo: Chukō bunko, 1976.

———. *Nagata Masaichi*. Tokyo: JiJi tsūshinsha, 1962.

Tanimichi, Kenta. "The Youthful Face of Japanese Nationalism." *Far Eastern Economic Review* 168 (November 2005): 45–7.

Thoburn, Nicholas. "Patterns of Production: Cultural Studies after Hegemony." *Theory, Culture and Society* 24, no. 3 (2007): 79–94.

Thompson, John. B. *The Media and Modernity: A Social Theory of the Media.* Cambridge: Polity, 1995.

Thompson, Nevin. "Inside the Japanese Blogosphere — The Anti-Korea Wave." *Global Voices Online.* Report posted on July 29, 2005, http://www.globalvoicesonline.org/2005/07/29/inside-the-japanese-blogosphere-the-anti-korea-wave/ (accessed January 23, 2007).

Time Magazine. "Assassination in Seoul." *Time* (November 5, 1979), http://www.time.com/time/magazine/article/0,9171,912509,00.html (accessed November 20, 2007.)

Tomlinson, John. "Globalization and Cultural Identity." In *The Global Transformations Reader: An Introduction to the Globalization Debate*, 2nd ed., eds. David Held and Anthony McGrew, 269–77. Cambridge: Polity Press.

Tsai, Ing-wen. "Rentong yu zhengzi: zhong lilunxing zhi fansheng" [Identity and Politics: A Theoretical Reflection]. *Zhengzhi kexue luncong* [Political Science Review] 8 (June 1997): 51–84.

Tschang, Ted and Goldstein, Andrea. "Production and Political Economy in the Animation Industry: Why Insourcing and Outsourcing Occur." Paper presented at DRUID Summer Conference on Industrial Dynamics, Innovation and Development. Elsinore, Denmark, 2004. Date of conference?

Tsukamoto, Kazuto. "Shanghai Surprise: Animation on the Rise." *The Asahi Shinbun*, April 23, 2005 (accessed through LexisNexis on March 2, 2006).

"TVXQ." *Wikipedia.* http://en.wikipedia.org/wiki/TVXQ (accessed September 15, 2006).

Ueda, Ken'ichi. *Shanhai Bugiugu 1945: Hattori Ryōichi no Bōken* [Shanghai Boogie Woogie 1945: The Adventure of Hattori Ryōichi]. Tokyo: Nihon Bungeisha, 2003.

Ugaya Hiromichi. *J-pop towa nanika* [What is J-pop?]. Tokyo: Iwanami-shoten, 2005.

Uikipedeia. "Miyako Harumi." *Uikepedeia* [Wikipedia], http://ja.wikipedia.org/wiki/%E9%83%BD%E3%81%AF%E3%82%8B%E3%81%BF (accessed November 20, 2007.)

Ursell, Gillian. "Television Production: Issues of Exploitation, Commodification and Subjectivity in UK Television Labor Markets." *Media, Culture and Society* 22 (2000): 805–25.

Van Ness Organization, The. *The Making of James Clavell's Shogun*: London: Hodder and Stoughton, 1980.

VERBAL. Verbal: Alien Alter Egos — *Kami no pazuru sore wa boku jishin* [Puzzles of the Gods, It is Myself]. Tokyo: Kyūsokuteki Jikan, 2002.

Vogel, Ezra F. *The Four Little Dragons*. Cambridge, MA: Harvard University Press, 1991.

Wang, Jing. *Brand New China Advertising, Media, and Commercial Culture*. Cambridge MA: Harvard University Press, 2008.

————. "Bourgeois Bohemians in China? Neo-tribes and the Urban Imaginary." *The China Quarterly* 183 (2005): 532–48.

————. "Taiwan Hsiang t'u Literature: Perspectives in the Evolution of a Literary Movement." In *Chinese Fiction from Taiwan: Critical Perspectives*, ed. Jeannette L. Faurot, 43–70. Bloomington: Indiana University Press, 1980.

Wang Meishu. "Xie gei qian lü xuezhe pengyoumen" [A Note to Light Green Scholarly Friends]. *Ziyou Shibao* [Liberty Times], June 15, 2006.

Wang, Xiaoming. "A Manifesto for Cultural Studies." Trans. Robyn Visser. In *One China, Many Paths*, ed. Chaohua Wang. London: Verso, 2003, 274–91.

Ward, Annalee R. "*The Lion King*'s Mythic Narrative: Disney as Moral Educator." *Journal of Popular Film and Television* 23, no. 4 (1996) 47–66.

Waters, Malcolm. *Globalization*. London and New York: Routledge, 1995.

Watson, James L. *Golden Arches East: McDonald's in East Asia*. Stanford, CA: Stanford University Press, 1997.

Watts, Jonathan. "Japan-Korea Team at Pusan." *Hollywood Reporter*, September 17–19, 1999.

Wells, Paul. *Understanding Animation*. London: Routledge, 1998.

Werbner, Pnina and Modood, T., eds. *Debating Cultural Hybridity: Multi-Cultural Identities and the Politics of Anti-Racism*. London: Zed Books, 1997.

Wiggershaus, Rolf. *Theodor W. Adorno*. Munich: C. H. Beck, 1998.

Willoughby, Heather. "Image is Everything: The Marketing of Femininity in South Korean Popular Music." In *Korean Pop Music: Riding the Wave*, ed. Keith Howard, 99–108. Folkestone: Global Oriental, 2006.

Wilson, Donald and Roger Smith. "Bulls and Bears." *Film Comment* (March/April 2006): 54–7, 60–1.

Winch, Christopher. *Education, Work and Social Capital: Towards a New Conception of Vocational Education*. London and New York: Routledge, 2000.

World Economic Forum on East Asia, June 15–16, 2006. "The Creative Imperative in East Asia." World Economic Forum, http://www.weforum.org/pdf/ SummitReports/eastasia2006/creative.htm (accessed October 30, 2007).

World Media Lab. "Hanju gongli shenhou, daihuo hanliu jingji" [South Korean drama's profound success, fires the Korea wave economy]. World Media

Lab, http://media.icxo.com/htmlnews/2005/08/24/653373.htm (accessed August 24, 2005).

Wu, Cuncun. "'Beautiful Boys Made up as Beautiful Girls': Anti-Masculine Taste in Qing China." In *Asian Masculinities: The Meaning and Practice of Manhood in China and Japan*, eds. Kam Louie and Morris Low, 19–40. London; New York: RoutledgeCurzon, 2003.

Xiao, Hui. "Narrating a Happy China through a Crying Game: A Case-study of Post-Mao Reality Shows." *China Media Research* 2, no. 3 (2006): 59–67.

"Xinpian 'Renshi Taiwan' jiaokeshu yinqi de zhengyi" [The Controversy over the New 'Understanding Taiwan' Textbooks]. *Lianhe Bao* [United Daily News], June 13, 1997.

Yamano Sharin. *Manga Kenkanryū* [Manga The Anti-Korean Wave]. Tokyo: Shinyūsha, 2005.

———. *Manga Kenkanryū 2*. Tokyo: Shinyūsha, 2006a.

———. *Manga Kenkanryū—Kōshiki gaidobukku* [Manga Kenkanryū — Official Guidebook]. Tokyo: Shinyūsha, 2006b.

———. "Sharin *purofiiru*" [Sharin Profile]. Yamano Sharin web page, http://propellant.fc2web.com/contents/sharin/sharin.html. [Date of access]

Yan, Yuanshu. "Dangqian Zhongguo wenxue wenti" [The Problems of Contemporary Chinese Literature]. In *Xiangtu wenxue taolun ji* [Discussing Nativist Literature], ed. Tiancong Wei, 761–85. Taipei: Wei Tiancong, 1978.

Yang Qingchu. "Huanying Guomindang xinsheng dai zai di hua" [Welcoming the Rebirth of the Sense of Place of the KMT]. *Ziyou Shibao* [Liberty Times], May 4, 2004.

Yang, Yoon-mo. "Olhae pŭrokŭraeming" [This Year's Programming]. *Pusan Ilbo*, November 17, 2001.

Yano, Christine R. "Raising the Ante of Desire: Foreign Female Singers in a Japanese Pop Music World." In *Refashioning Pop Music in Asia: Cosmopolitan Flows, Political Tempos and Aesthetic Industries*, eds. Allen Chun, Ned Rossiter, and Brian Shoesmith, 159–211. London: Routledge, 2004.

———. *Tears of Longing: Nostalgia and the Nation in Japanese Popular Song*. Cambridge, MA: Harvard University Press, 2002.

Yecies, Brian. "Systematization of Film Censorship in Colonial Korea: Profiteering from Hollywood's First Golden Age." *Journal of Korean Studies* 1, no. 10 (Fall 2005): 59–83.

Yeo, Lay Hwee. "Realism and Reactive Regionalism: Where is East Asian Regionalism Heading?" *UNISCI Discussion Papers*, May 2005.

Yin, Kelly Fu Su and Kai Khiun Liew. "*Hallyu* in Singapore: Korean Cosmopolitanism or the Consumption of Chineseness?" *Korea Journal* 45, no. 4 (2005): 206–32.

Yin, Zhangyi. "*Taiwan yishi shifen*" [Analysing Taiwan Consciousness]. *Zhongguo Luntan* [China Tribune] 25, no. 1 (October 10, 1987): 95–114.

Yoon, Suh-kyung. "Swept up on a Wave." *Far Eastern Economic Review*, October

18, 2001, https://www.feer.com/cgi.bin/prog/printeasty?id=69557. 2098557935 (accessed Jan. 21, 2003).

Yoshimoto, Mitsuhiro. "National/International/Transnational: The Concept of Trans-Asian Cinema and Cultural Politics of Film Criticism." In *The First Jeonju International Film Festival Symposium*, ed. Kim Soyoung, 61–9. Jeonju: JIFF, 2000.

Yoshino, Kōsaku. *Cultural Nationalism in Contemporary Japan*. London: Routledge, 1992.

Young, Robert C. *Postcolonialism*. Oxford: Blackwell, 2001.

Yúdice, George. *The Expediency of Culture: Uses of Culture in the Global Era*. Durham, NC: Duke University Press, 2003.

Yue, Mingbao and Jon Goss, eds. "De-Americanizing the Global: Cultural Studies Interventions from Asia and the Pacific." *Comparative American Studies* 3, no. 3, Special Issue (2005).

Zhao Hua and Xu Yang, "'Sun Wukong' weihe doubuguo 'mi laoshu'?" [Why Can't the 'Monkey King' Overcome 'Mickey Mouse'?] Xinhuanet.com, August 12, 2004, http://big5.xinhuanet.com/gate/big5/www.ln.xinhuanet. com/wangtan/katong/images.htm (accessed March 8, 2006).

"Zongtong zhongshen fangong fuguo juexin" [The President Resolutely Reiterates the Determination to Fight Communism and Recover the Mainland]. *Zili Wanbao* [Independent Evening Post], January 1, 1979.

"Zongtong zui mian quan guo tongbao jizhi chenglie fu guo jiu min" [The President Resolutely Urges Compatriots of the Whole Nation to Continue Towards Recovering the Nation and Saving the People]. *Lianhe bao* [United Daily News], January 1, 1961.

Index